1961

To Bill
from Her
& Jean
& Marie

PETER FREUCHEN'S ADVENTURES IN THE ARCTIC

Hope you get as many
chuckles out of this as
we have! Remember,
we do not advocate
the methods of bathing
used by the Eskimo beauties.

Dagnan

Peter Freuchen's

ADVENTURES
IN THE ARCTIC

Edited by

DAGMAR FREUCHEN

Julian Messner, Inc.   New York

Published by Julian Messner, Inc.
8 West 40 Street, New York 18

Published simultaneously in Canada
by The Copp Clark Publishing Co. Limited

© Copyright, 1960, by Julian Messner, Inc.

Printed in the United States of America

Library of Congress Catalog Card No. 60-13801

OLBC

FOREWORD

My husband had planned for a long time a book that would contain in chronological sequence all of his experiences in the Arctic where he made his home for so many years. But death came suddenly for him in 1957, and the book was not completed. Knowing how much he wanted to see it published, I decided to finish it for him, and I hope he would have liked it.

Peter wrote many books. I was privileged to help with some of them, acting mostly as a sounding board, and I was always flattered when he took my suggestions. He felt that *Arctic Adventure,* now long out of print, was his best book, even though it was written before his Arctic experiences came to an end. Knowing this, I have included much from it here, together with parts of his later books, so that a more complete picture of this amazing man would emerge.

Here, then, in Peter's own words are his battles against snow and ice, bears, wolves, walrus, and narwhals in a land where he faced death many times. Here, too, are the sagas of his explorations across the uncharted Arctic wilderness—stories of incredible hardship, hunger, and danger and of the incredible loyalty and bravery of his Eskimo companions, told with the modesty and rather special sense of humor so characteristic of him.

I met Peter for the first time in New York at a dinner party on Christmas Eve, 1944. Neither of us had been in Denmark for years. Peter, of course, had been in the Arctic, and I had been living in the United States since 1936, doing fashion illustrations for magazines and, during the war, Danish translations for the Office of War Information. That dinner party was one I will never forget. It was given by the Danish cartoonist, Hans Bendix, and his wife, Karen, who always invited stray, single, lonesome Danes on holidays. Peter had been invited for 7:30 P.M., but he arrived in the morning with two geese which he insisted on cooking himself and which he carved with a pocket knife from Thule. It was love at first sight for us, and we were married in June of 1945.

I knew, of course, that the man I married had a great reputation, but it was not until 1948, when we made our first trip to Denmark together, that I realized the scope of his fame. He seemed to be as well known there as the king!

At the time I married Peter I knew practically nothing about the Arctic. You can imagine my shock when, one day shortly after our marriage, I was trying to open a can of soup with an opener that didn't work, and he said: "My first wife did that with her teeth!" Of course, his first wife had been an Eskimo. During our twelve years together, Peter told me a great deal about his life in the Arctic and elsewhere, but it was the countless stories about the Arctic that fascinated me most. Though I have never had a chance to go to Greenland and have never seen the beautiful Arctic landscape he talked so often about, I almost feel that I have been there, seeing it with his eyes and living it with him.

The task of assembling chronologically Peter's experiences in the Arctic has been, for me, formidable, yet one of the most satisfying things I have ever done. The knowledge that I was finishing something very close to his heart made the task easier. I want to thank all those who encouraged me in this work and especially Maria Pelikan, whose help was invaluable.

Dagmar Freuchen

New York
July 1960

PART I

1

ON THE NINETEENTH OF FEBRUARY IN THE YEAR 1886 MY FATHER
bought a large, yellow dog from the butcher in our small town.
I do not remember the incident, however, since I was born the
following day.

One of my early memories is of my mother offending my
budding sense of justice. She used to tell the maids at home:
"Run down in the garden and see what the children are doing
and tell them not to!" It seemed to me a deplorable lack of
confidence, and I felt strongly that we deserved to be met with
more good will. But otherwise my mother was a very wise lady
with a great deal of understanding. In fact, we had the most
wonderful mother. If one can possibly use such a term to describe
the treatment to which we were exposed, one would say that we
were given a liberal upbringing. Hardly anything was forbidden
in our place, and our garden was the meeting ground for all the
children of the neighborhood. The result was a kind of group
complex which has followed me through my life. I like best to
be one of a crowd.

My first years were spent the way I suppose most first years
are spent. My parents had more and more children. After five
years of marriage there were five of us and my oldest sister, Polly,
at a very tender age was given the task of looking after us all.
It has been her fate throughout her life. When the youngest of
the Freuchen children was ready to stand on his own feet, the
oldest was already married, and soon Polly had nieces and
nephews to look after. The next generation again turned to
Polly. She has always had an abundance of love and understanding, with a profound knowledge of people, and the family adores
her.

My nature is a different one. At a very early stage I showed my
scientific interest, but my research usually brought me more

trouble than knowledge. The reason, of course, was that in childhood one does not have the ways and means to carry out laboratory experiments; one has to use real life, which is what I did. Thus I remember a very interesting biographical experiment carried out by my brother Tom and myself in our scientific zeal to prove a theory. In school we had a teacher with the most impressive hairdo and the largest amount of hair we had ever seen. One day we found a picture of a boy with his hair standing up straight, and our nurse, Claudine, explained to us that a real shock can make one's hair rise. Our scientific curiosity led us to have this strange fact demonstrated, and our teacher was the best possible research object. We put a pincushion on her chair in the expectation that the shock of sitting on it would make her magnificent hair stand up straight.

Our experiment failed, we got a beating and were sent home from school for the day. My parents, naturally, became suspicious of my scientific curiosity, but I did not give up. After a short while I carried out another interesting experiment, this time dealing with the laws of friction and inertia. Again I had to make real life my laboratory. Down by the harbor, where much of our life was spent, I had seen freight cars rolling down the railroad tracks to a place of loading. I realized that they would go farther if the brakes were not applied, and my problem was to find out whether the power that made them roll was still there after the cars stopped.

For natural reasons Sunday was the best day for my experiment. I had a hard time releasing the heavy brakes, but the street was slanted slightly, and to my great satisfaction the freight cars began moving. And soon they were rolling toward the pier with increasing speed. My scientific observations kept me far too busy to try turning on the brakes again, and the cars rolled straight onto a pier and into an enormous pile of fishermen's barrels. I watched with fascination as they were splintered like matchwood and scattered all over the water. There was a buffer, which probably was strong enough to keep the cars from going into the bay, but I had proved my point and staying longer was too risky. I ran home and kept away from the place for more than a month.

My first formal education took place in Miss Boysen's school, which was then modestly housed in the dining room of her sister's house in New Street. Her son Svend was my neighbor at the dining table, and his friendship was then the most important thing in my life. He was an unusual boy with many talents. He could draw pictures, something I had never seen done before.

One day in school Svend boasted that his father had spent his summer vacation in Norway where he had climbed mountains that were higher than the clouds. This was a revelation to me, who had never been outside my native Denmark, where the highest hill reaches only a few hundred feet above the ground.

Somehow the deep impression of mountain climbing in Norway made me overcome my natural shyness, and I finally approached Svend's father directly one day at the public bath. Was it true, I asked the great man, that he had been above the clouds?

He answered modestly that a great many people had had the same experience.

"Did you see heaven?" I wanted to know.

"Oh, yes. You see, the clouds are like a fog; you go through them and the sun shines above. The sky is clear above the clouds."

"But could you see the Lord?"

"You are talking nonsense, my boy. The Lord cannot be seen. You are no closer to him on top of a mountain than you are down here."

My brother Tom and I used language that horrified the neighborhood ladies. Their complaints would have been a serious threat to our blissful existence, if it had not been for one of the few principles in my father's upbringing. It was a standing rule that we children must never tell on each other. He warned us against the sin of "squealing." The result was a highly developed sense of loyalty between the Freuchen children. And the complaints did not matter so much since we considered them actually nothing but "squealing" on the ladies' part. At the supper table my mother—perhaps not too wisely—would tell us about the complaints, imitating the indignant ladies, and we all got a good laugh.

Svend's mother called at our house one day and asked to see my mother alone. She looked very solemn, and for once my mother was worried, thinking something serious had happened. My father was asked to leave the ladies to themselves, the children were sent outside, and the conversation began.

It appeared that Tom, in the presence of Svend and his

mother, had used a word too terrible to be repeated. My mother was relieved, and she calmly asked what the word was.

"But, my dear Mrs. Freuchen, don't you understand? I cannot possibly repeat it!"

"But I cannot punish the boy if I don't know what he has said."

"I cannot, I positively cannot say such a word!"

"In that case you must forgive me, there is nothing I can do."

"Well, if you force me to it . . ." And she whispered the terrible word in my mother's ear. "Is that all!" my mother exclaimed, and burst out laughing.

The visitor realized there was no hope for children with such a parent and that was the end of our friendship with Svend.

We were never spoiled or coddled as children. We had complete freedom and spent endless, glorious days in the forests or on the sound in our little boat. We would go out in any weather, and our parents encouraged us to do so. If we asked for more clothes before we set out, my mother would tease us and call us sissies. She never worried about our health. There was only one rule she was strict about: If we fell into the water we had to go to bed. It is the only form of punishment I can remember. The result was that I did not go home if I fell into the water, and summer or winter I let the clothes dry on my body. The habit was useful to me later in life when I was forced to do the same thing.

Some of our friends would fall into the water once in a while, and I remember how miserable they were. They had to run home and were often severely punished. Sometimes their mothers would bawl us out for trying to kill their precious brats, but we had developed a salty tongue by then and usually came out best in the argument. Then one day one of our friends fell into the water and did not come up again. The tragedy led to much talk about a general ban against children going out in boats. The ban could never touch us, however, since our parents assured us we were not to blame if our friend could not swim.

The episode had a bad influence on me. The boy who drowned had had an older brother who had died from diphtheria, and a well-meaning old lady told me that the good Lord always takes the best children to heaven. Consequently I decided that being good was not for me, and I dedicated myself to a life of crime. Only in the last moment when I was dying would I repent.

I was going to be a lone wolf and stand outside society.

There were always a lot of children in our part of town, and the difference between boys and girls was no secret to us. We simply were not interested. I cannot remember any particular time when I became conscious of the sexual facts of life. Our knowledge developed slowly, without our noticing it. We were close to nature, knew all about the animals, and realized that people were not much different. We were not like boys in the "better families" who were not allowed to play with girls. Our sisters and their girl friends were our companions, and the natural, easygoing fellowship which resulted has followed me throughout my life.

All in all I believe we were peaceful and harmless children. We obeyed our parents because they denied us only harmful things. This liberal attitude had an effect that has lasted until today. I have never been able to enjoy smoking, and it is due to my father. At a certain age Tom and I decided to take up smoking, as "Elephant" cigarettes could be had for about two pennies a pack, fifteen cigarettes and a wooden holder to a pack. We asked our father for permission, and he said it was all right if we could get anything to smoke. We went at it the hard way, buying a pack of pipe tobacco which we carefully planted in our garden and watered faithfully with no result. Axel finally told us that tobacco plants took two years to develop. We were stubborn enough to wait until the next year, but when our "plantation" still brought forth no tobacco I gave up in disgust. Other boys offered me their pipes from time to time, but I was a better fighter than most of them, and I did not have to smoke to keep their respect. They would never dare to tease me on that account —with the result I never learned to smoke.

Later in life I have often regretted it. In freezing blizzards in the Arctic I have felt green with envy, watching my friends enjoy their pipes. On the other hand, seeing their anguish when they ran out of tobacco, I have also had cause to feel fortunate. Three times I have tried to smoke a cigarette, but it did not agree with me, and I am too lazy to go through all the necessary torture and sickness before tobacco becomes a pleasure. I am still a very satisfied nonsmoker.

Every vacation was spent on the farm of my Uncle Kristen. He was really the uncle of my mother, and she had grown up on his farm. This uncle was the tallest man I had ever seen; he was

very strong and extremely good-natured. The most fascinating
thing about him was his past. He had spent years prospecting for
gold in Australia. This strange experience and the fact that he
was the largest landowner in the county made him a man of
importance.

We never tired of listening to his stories of Australia. I was
thrilled by his account of highwaymen attacking the gold trans-
ports, sometimes killing the gold miners protecting their treasure.
My uncle had often seen the robbers, many of whom later settled
down in England and the United States to become highly respected citizens.

I was absent from school a great deal during those early years,
due to strange intermittent pains in my arms and legs. At first I
was accused of making them up. Then our doctor decided I was
hysterical and that the only cure was strict discipline. I suffered
a great deal and feared I had gout, which I had seen cripple older
people. Such a disease would ruin all my plans for a glorious and
active future. I was growing older and presumably more subdued,
but I still had a burning desire to get away from the monotonous
life of our town. I had learned, however, to keep my plans to
myself. Even to my old friend Axel I revealed nothing except that
I was going to run away someday. I never told him what my goal
was, naturally enough, since I did not know it myself. But I had
intense self-pity when I spent weeks in my bed with strange pains.

We had probably the most ignorant doctor in the country. The
fact that he did not kill us with his remedies proves what a strong
family we were. He finally decided my pains were nothing but
"growing sickness." He explained that my muscles grew faster
than my bones and that the matter would take care of itself in
due time.

I was a grown man before my worried family sent me to a
sanatorium for a checkup. I had then just returned from an Arctic expedition where I had suffered a great deal from hunger. I
had trouble gaining weight after my return, and the family was
afraid I might have tuberculosis. The doctor made all the
necessary tests, and the results showed that I had suffered from a
severe case of tuberculosis as a child. All the cavities had calcified,
however, and the doctor pronounced me healthy enough.

"But couldn't you live a more sensible life?" he asked me.
"That is the only way to gain weight and get back your strength."

"I don't see how I can," I answered him honestly. "I don't

smoke. I don't drink. I am a fairly decent man. I go early to bed and spend most of my time out of doors. What more do you want me to do?"

"You are too sensible," he told me. "We should all have some vice as a safety valve if something goes wrong."

The doctor was a wise man, but how does one go about "picking up" a vice?

We found out later that all my brothers and sisters had suffered from tuberculosis as children. We managed to survive, however, and to grow healthy and strong. My poor father was not so fortunate. For more than twenty-five years he suffered agonies from what doctors later called a stomach ulcer, but our family doctor shrugged it all off as "nerves." Just ignore it was his advice.

I was hardly aware of the passing of time until suddenly one day I was ready to enter the gymnasium, which was comparable to the senior high school of today.

As students in the gymnasium, we were automatically granted certain privileges. Most of the teachers dropped the familiar "thou" and addressed us more formally by our last names. In the beginning it had a strange effect, it marked a definite transition from childhood and made us realize our importance. We were through playing in the yard at intermission time. We kept aloof from the younger boys, talked together in a new, reasoning way, and carried on violent arguments. We began feeling awkwardly grown up. For the first time in my life I became socially conscious, realizing that there was such a thing as a human society into which I had to fit somehow or other, no matter how hard it might be. And, without knowing it, I suffered then, as I have ever since, from an inferiority complex.

I was going through a great change at that period. I was growing tremendously, either because I had reached the age of puberty or because I had recovered from my tuberculosis. There was a great increase in my outdoor activities, and I took long trips by foot or in the sailboat, neither of which went well with my homework. I could not keep up with my class, which bothered me a little at first, and I tried to work hard for a while. But as Peter Freuchen was considered a lazy and independent pupil, nothing I could do would change the impression. And I soon gave up trying to please my teachers, especially since I had made up my mind to go to sea.

I was growing up, adding inches to my height, and I was not

the only one to notice it. This was clearly demonstrated by an episode that took place during a few weeks I spent at a nearby castle (one of my classmates was a count) in the company of some local gentry. We had no movie theaters in those days and no cars to rush around in. Instead, we were expected to enjoy ourselves in the evening playing party games. The atmosphere in the beautiful drawing rooms was strangely remote from the world, a curious mixture of aristocratic aloofness and pleasant gaiety—excluding anything requiring serious brain activity.

One night we were to have a fancy-dress ball. One of the most distinguished guests, a noble lady in her forties, approached me—accidentally, as I thought—and told me to come and see her after the rest of the party had said good night. She wanted my help in preparing a secret surprise for the ball. Bedtime was at ten o'clock, when the watchman first called out his ritual, which was repeated every hour through the night. The baroness arose, indicating it was time to retire. We shook hands, wishing each other a calm night and expressing polite hopes for favorable meteorological conditions the following day. And as we left the drawing room the distinguished lady whispered to me that I should give her half an hour to prepare the lists she wanted to show me and then come to her room.

The corridors were dark and deserted when I knocked on her door. She opened it quickly, told me to enter quietly, and did something quite unexpected. She turned the key in the lock and stood laughing in my face. It was only then I noticed that she was much smaller than I and dressed in a gown of a kind I had never seen before.

I did not know what to say or do. The situation was quite startling, and I felt very uncomfortable. My instinct told me that something was up, something I had better have nothing to do with. I tried to pass her and get to the door, but in that moment she let her robe fall to the floor and stood before me—stark naked!

Later in life when I fell into the water off the Greenland coast, with ice all around me and the bitter Arctic cold penetrating my body, I experienced the same sensation I felt at that moment. I remember I had to clench my teeth together to keep from screaming.

The lady came close to me, put her arms around my neck, and pulled me down on a sofa while she talked eagerly to me. I have no idea what she said. I was paralyzed and could not understand a word. I kept telling her that I knew nothing about such things and that I would like to go back to my room. She kept on laughing. That was just what she had expected, she told me, but she would not let me go.

I had seen girls in the nude before, of course, but not like this —only innocently while bathing on the beach. A boy should be allowed to discover life in his own way, but I was given no chance. This was rape, and there was nothing distinguished about the lady any more. She literally tore off my clothes while she kept telling me I would always be grateful for what she was about to teach me. She knew the needs of young men, she said, and she adored their "clumsy, awkward love."

"I'll keep the lamp burning," she said, "until I have explained it all to you."

Instinctive abilities are quickly discovered, once they are put to use, however, and the lamp did not have to burn very long. In the darkness it was easy to forget the distance in rank and age between us. Her physical energy was in no way restrained by any aristocratic aloofness from the lusts of common people, and as dawn arrived, with the danger of being discovered by servants, I sneaked away.

Back in my own room, I was honestly amazed that I did not seem changed in any way. Sleep was out of the question. I had visions of elopement with the lady with the vengeful husband in hot pursuit.

I was in utter confusion when I turned up for breakfast. One by one the sleepy guests took their places at the breakfast table, and my "mistress," as I called her in my mind, was full of good cheer.

"Good morning, good morning, what a glorious day! The sun woke me up, shining straight in my face. Marvelous!"

A prosaic elderly count remarked dryly he had noticed that her windows faced west.

"Yes indeed, so they do," she answered, unperturbed. For me she had only a nod and a smile.

Young and normal as I was, all thoughts of shame or elopement quickly evaporated as another happy vacation day passed. During the afternoon the guests were taken for an excursion through the woods to look at the largest oak in the country. For a moment my "mistress" walked beside me on the path.

"I'll see you again tonight," she whispered.

"No! Never!" I answered desperately.

She smiled at me. "I wonder," she said as she joined the rest of the party.

I felt very relieved that I had thus given her notice of the end of our "affair." The word itself made me feel good. I had read about affairs. I knew it was a word used among sophisticated people. I had arrived!

By the time the dinner gong rang I had decided that I had to speak to her the following day and then leave, never to return. During the dinner I felt her eyes on me and, somehow or other, when the night watchman called out eleven o'clock, I was back by her door. I hated myself and I hated her, but I had to talk to her, and I sneaked into the room with an apology and a tragic face. She locked the door again and laughed at me.

"How I love you innocent boys! You are all the same. I knew you would come."

And that night she turned out the lamp right away. I felt like an expert, and after a while I told her I must leave her. To make her understand she was dealing with a man I said my work made it imperative for me to go away.

"Yes, of course. You have to go back to school," she answered with a smile. I felt deeply hurt, but there was nothing I could say, since it was true enough. I was reduced to a schoolboy again.

"But what if you're going to have a baby?" I asked her.

"Oh, no, my little friend," she laughed. "Those days are past. It's sweet of you to think of it, but don't you worry."

During the remainder of the vacation I spent every night with her. I did not feel sorry to leave her and I did not miss her, but I was different when I went back to school. I felt grown-up and superior.

2

MY EARLY SCHOOLING AND PROVINCIAL BACKGROUND WERE NOT A good preparation for the university. I was very immature and quite incapable of concentrating on the medical studies which for some long-forgotten reason I had decided upon. I had no burning desire to heal and comfort sick and suffering mankind, nor did I plan to penetrate the mysteries of medical science, but it was still my intention to become a doctor.

The very first stumbling block was the study of philosophy. At that time a degree in philosophy was required regardless of the subject one was to take up at the university. There were two professors teaching elementary philosophy and I attended their lectures for a while, until I discovered that it was a complete waste of time. I quickly caught on to the more practical system then in use. One paid a tutor to knock into one's head the answers to the limited number of questions ever asked at a philosophy examination.

During the winter I moved to quarters closer to the university. My object was to concentrate on my studies, but the move had the opposite effect. I deserted my philosophy in favor of a dramatic group that was staging a series of amateur comedies. One of the students wrote a hilarious play making fun of a prominent figure of the day—a man by the name of Mylius-Erichsen, who had just returned from an Arctic expedition. I had previously read a number of books on polar explorers, and I now studied all the reports on Erichsen's sensational trip to the Far North. I was shocked that a student, who knew nothing of the terrible struggles the expedition had gone through, should make fun of the whole thing. His satirical comedy was highly amusing and I laughed with the rest of them, but I was torn by doubt. Could it possibly be true that even the polar heroes had their weaknesses? I wondered, and I decided to find out. Going to the Arctic and sharing their adventures became my glorious goal.

I had not yet given up my medical studies, and that winter I began working at Frederick's Hospital under a professor then at the height of his fame. We had no direct contact with his august person, of course, but we followed in his wake when he went his rounds in the morning. We heard him lecture during operations, and we were impressed by his personality.

One day while I was working at the hospital an accident occurred at the docks and the victim was brought in. For several minutes he had been thought dead; then a bystander discovered that he was breathing. The poor man was bruised and broken beyond recognition, his skull fractured, his ribs crushed, and his ligaments ripped loose from their moorings. But undeniably his heart was beating feebly.

All the doctors said he would not live, he could not live. They said it then, and they continued to say it for months while he doggedly refused to fulfill their prophecies. Six months later his recovery was pronounced complete.

It was, everyone said, a miracle of modern medicine and surgery. A human being had been wrought from three buckets of blood and flesh and bone. Surgeons flocked to Copenhagen from all over the Continent to look at him. He was discussed, examined, and photographed and prodded. Finally the doctors reluctantly turned him out into the world again. We all watched him go. We all watched him stop at the corner, and then start hesitantly across the street. And we all watched him as an automobile—one of the first in Copenhagen—ran him down and killed him.

That made me burn with impotent fury. I decided I was not cut out to be a doctor.

I made up my mind, however, to get my philosophy degree before leaving the university. Afterward I wanted to go to sea. The examination was coming up early in spring, and my roommate and I settled down for some real cramming.

One evening we were out later than usual. It was a rainy night and pitch black. In a minute we were surprised by two thugs who were in a nasty mood, and we had a violent fist fight in the darkness until my friend escaped and ran home for his revolver. In the meantime I had fallen to the ground, and as I tried to rise one of the men kicked me in the head and shoulder. My head was not hurt much—probably made of bone all through, as some of my friends claim—but I could feel my shoulder crack. My roommate's arrival with the revolver decided the issue, however, and the thugs fled.

When we finally got home I was in considerable pain, and our efforts to take care of my injuries were not successful. The following morning I had to return to my old hospital, where my professor quickly discovered fractures in the arm and shoulder. They were put in a cast, and I returned to my cramming. The injuries, as it turned out, were a blessing in disguise. In due time I received the only degree I have ever been granted from any temple of learning. I became a *Candidatus Philosophiae,* passing my examination without any distinction and, to be quite honest, in rather an extraordinary way.

During the last few days of my studies my right arm was caged in its cast and, in trying to do everything with my left, I cut myself deeply in the hand and got a nasty infection in two fingers. The left hand had to be bandaged, so we decided to capitalize on my bad luck. When I turned up to face my professors in my first and last test, my right arm was in the cast, my left was in a sling, and for good measure my friends had put a white turban around my head. One student opened the door for me, another helped me to the chair from which I was going to reveal my philosophical wisdom, a third one gave the professor a whispered warning to treat the patient carefully. The students withdrew, but before the ordeal began I asked in a weak voice for a glass of water. Under the circumstances they damned well had to pass me.

No matter how I achieved it, the degree bolstered my morale, gave me more self-confidence, and I did not waste any time. At the earliest possible moment I went to see Mylius-Erichsen, the explorer whom my friends had ridiculed in their comedy. I was shivering in my boots as I stood before his door, expecting to meet a superman. He was planning another expedition to Greenland, and I wanted him to take me along. He treated me like an old friend and encouraged me to talk about myself. I told him that I was not stupid, but I just could not settle down to studies. I wanted to use my strength and my hands. At the moment, of course, my strength was not too impressive, since my right arm was still in a cast, but I guaranteed that in a few weeks I would be able to walk on my hands. The outcome was that Erichsen told me he might find some use for me and asked me for references.

I was in seventh heaven and felt my future was made. I wrote to my parents immediately to tell them that I would not keep on with my studies—at least not for the time being—and that I was going on an expedition to Greenland. My mother answered that she was not surprised. She said that my restlessness and spirit of adventure were inherited from her and her seafaring father, and she was sure that I was doing the right thing. In due time my references were found acceptable and I was all set to go north.

Erichsen asked me one day whether I could manage the job of stoker. I had never seen the inside of an engine room and never handled a larger fire than the one in our kitchen stove, but I felt sure that I could do the job. I was taken at face value

and Erichsen got me signed on the *Hans Egede,* the regular
steamer going up to Greenland that spring.

My work in the engine room was tough but an interesting
experience. At that time firemen and stokers were regarded as the
scum of humanity. They were a rough crowd, and we had hardly
a day without fist fights below deck—not because of any great
hostility between the men but because a fight was the simplest
way of settling things.

At that time the engine crew received their food in weekly
rations. Once a week we would line up for our allotments which
must last us for seven days. The weekly bread ration came in a
big wooden box, and we were allowed one pound of white flour
a week, the rest of the ration was rye bread. We had a choice of
white flour in the form of pancakes, "pudding," or white bread.
We always chose the bread because we thought it would last
longer, but the soot in our messroom made it as black as coal
after one day. To supplement our meager rations we all stole
from the ship's stores. It was not only a tradition, it was regarded
as a duty. But I don't think any of my friends in the engine room
would ever have stolen as much as a penny on shore. They were
honest men.

My work was much harder than I expected, but slowly I
learned to master it.

As soon as I had proved a reasonably efficient fireman the
officers decided to give me a turn at the engine to learn the duties
of an oiler. One dark night I was sitting between pistons and
connecting rods with my oil can when I heard a shattering noise.
The whole ship trembled, the floor of the engine room tilted to
a sickening angle, and I fell off my precarious seat on the cylinder
block. The next moment I heard the bell from the bridge signal
and a confusion of shouts and screams. The chief engineer came
running down, clad only in dirty shorts. Suddenly the engines
stopped and everything was ominously quiet.

In a moment the chief enlightened us on the duty of the
engine crew to remain by their posts and drown like rats if necessary—whereupon he climbed up on deck, to see what was wrong,
he said. The second engineer swore loudly at the cowardice of
superior officers who left their men to sink with the ship, and I
felt quite indignant that nobody noticed my heroic calm. With
my limited experience I had no idea that anything could be
seriously wrong, and fortunately I was right.

In the dark night we had run into some heavy pack ice. The ship had cut into a solid ice floe with such speed that the bow was lifted clear of the water. In due time the ice broke, we were once again afloat, and the ship was undamaged. The ice was much farther south than usual, and we turned far below Cape Farewell to avoid it. And after a few days I was told we were approaching Greenland and would soon be in Godthaab.

The first Eskimo came out to meet us in his kayak. Two lines were lowered and made fast to stem and stern of his little craft, which was hoisted up with him in it. It was a great honor to be the first to meet a ship and also a profitable experience. He served as pilot and was given a loaf of rye bread and two dollars.

I was off duty when he arrived, and I was deeply impressed by this first meeting with a native. But even more thrilling was the sight of the Greenland coast and the snow-covered Saddle. I felt I had never seen such beauty. As we approached the harbor of Godthaab several people came on board, and I felt a profound admiration for them all. They spent their lives in an unending series of dramatic adventures, it seemed to me. The Greenlanders, I thought, were all innocent primitives, equipped with highly developed senses and a profound knowledge of wind and weather and all the mysteries of the animal kingdom.

It was the end of April when we arrived. Godthaab was still covered by snow, but spring was coming to Greenland. I was lost in the beauty of the Arctic island, and I felt sick when I had to return to the messroom. The air was thick, the food repulsive, the language foul, as the crew members discussed the sex life of the natives. I was struck by the contrast between the natural beauty of this Arctic outpost and civilization as represented by our ship and my crew mates. But I did not let it bother me. I had arrived where I had always wanted to be. Everything else was of no importance. I was in Greenland!

3

AS SOON AS POSSIBLE I GOT MY SHORE LEAVE AND WITH A FEW OF my mates rowed down the bay to a large storehouse. There was no other building in sight, and I was told that it was quite a distance from the harbor to the small colony of Godthaab and that the way lay across large boulders and deep snow. But the more difficult it sounded, the happier I was, and off we started. After a few minutes we sank down to our hips in the snow and were wet through long before we reached the colony, where we were made welcome and invited to a dance that evening in the carpenter's shop.

It was a small wooden structure, and a large crowd of children sat on barrels along the walls, holding lighted candles in their hands, while a noisy harmonica provided the music.

When the dance was over a young Greenlander asked me to go to his house for coffee, and I felt deeply honored. I had imagined he would lead me to a small earth hut where we would sit around an open bonfire, sucking walrus bones and drinking coffee from cups made of whale barbs. During the short walk to his home I had to revise my impression. My host was a professional photographer and taxidermist, a very intelligent man whose wise answers to my foolish questions told me things about Greenland I had never heard. In return I told him about Mylius-Erichsen's forthcoming expedition. The native had many good things to say both about Erichsen and the great explorer Knud Rasmussen, who was to mean much to me in the years to come.

While I was having coffee my crew mates had left, and it was late when I finally said good-by to my new friend. He asked me if I knew my way back to the ship. I told him I would have no trouble, trying to give the impression of an experienced traveler. Unfortunately he believed me.

It was pitch dark and the deep snow impeded my progress. All the enormous boulders looked exactly alike, and I was lost until I came across some tracks. With renewed confidence in my gifts as a polar explorer I set out along the deep footprints. I discovered finally faint lights in the distance, and after a long time an enormous house loomed in front of me. It did not look like the storehouse by the harbor and turned out to be an empty assembly hall or church. Right next to it was a cluster of miserable Eskimo huts, the kind I had expected to find in Greenland. A small child peeked out from one of the dwellings, took one look at me, and quickly disappeared.

After a while an ancient woman appeared. She was making weird and rapid sounds, and I could not understand a word she was saying, so I shouted *"Hans Egede"* and "ship" and pointed in various directions. She seemed to follow my gesticulation, and I pulled out some coins to give her. But she only gurgled and laughed, grabbed my money and disappeared. I waited patiently for her to come back, but I never saw her again. Instead, a young boy came out of the hut. He didn't look at me, just ran across to the other houses and shouted something through the window of each one.

In a moment I felt as if I were in the center of a circus ring. An incredible number of people poured out from the huts, young and old, men, women and children. They surrounded me, laughing and singing and pointing their fingers at me. My first thought was that they were competing for the honor of being my guide, but I was soon disillusioned. They pointed at my pockets, and their sign language made it clear they were interested only in my coins. I did not have much money, but I gave them what I had. In a few seconds the whole circus was gone and once more I was left alone in the night.

I was about to set out by myself again when two Eskimo girls came to my rescue. I tried to make them understand that I would like them to accompany me on my journey. And for a while the three of us walked together, laughing with each other to make up for our lack of common language. Suddenly one of them shouted and pointed ahead where I could see Godthaab in the first shimmer of dawn.

The sight of the colony did not enchant me as it had done twelve hours before. I realized I had to begin all over again, and yet I was exhausted from my night's exertions. But I had no choice, and after the Eskimo girls had left me I set off again in what I hoped was the right direction.

Suddenly I felt delirious, and in my utter exhaustion I had the delusion that I was the only human being left in the world. Then I stumbled into a group of men! They were the local stevedores making their way down to the *Hans Egede*. One of them asked me if I was going on board.

"I might just as well," I managed to answer in a casual way.

"But why have you been going in the opposite direction?" they asked me. I told them I was trying to familiarize myself with the region.

"You have been walking around all night long. You have been seen all over the place," they told me. "Are you a botanist perhaps?"

"Yes," I said, "I have been out studying the vegetation." As we approached the *Hans Egede* I realized I had been going around in circles in my frantic march. Several times I had been not far from the ship.

When I finally went on board the chief engineer received me warmly.

"What the hell have you been doing and who gave you permission to spend the night on shore?" he roared.

I had to stick to the explanation I had given the stevedores, but the chief was not taken in so easily.

"That's a damn lie! Just look as you! All worn out, no juice left in you! Don't tell me where you've spent the night—it's written all over you. You leave the girls alone, you old goat!"

The last word made me angry and I talked back. I swore that I had not broken the rule about having nothing to do with the Eskimo women, that I had been alone all night and that I was quite pure and innocent.

"In that case you are an imbecile, which is worse," he answered. "All right, go down in the engine room and clean out the boiler. That's a good cure for such nonsense!"

I tried to follow his orders, but my first night in Greenland proved my undoing. After a few minutes at the boiler I fainted and had to be carried back to my bunk, where I slept for forty-eight hours. By the time I was able to go on duty again we were leaving Godthaab.

After a day and a night we arrived in Sukkertoppen, where I was invited twice for dinner at the post manager's house. These visits were noticed by the local population and gave me quite a reputation. The Eskimos considered me a big shot, and this fame brought me a friendship which I still treasure.

I met Arnarak, a great beauty, my first evening in Sukkertoppen. She has been painted by a great Danish artist, and her portrait now decorates a museum wall in Germany. The famous explorer Knud Rasmussen was her admirer, and she has been praised in many a song. She was most alluring and she knew it.

She invited me to her house, served me coffee, and sold me a great many leather objects at double or triple the normal rate, which I thought a good bargain. In the evening we went to the dance together, and I was miserable when I was invited to join the post manager and his wife for coffee. My misery changed to despair when the captain, immediately after the coffee, decided to return to the ship—with me. I had no choice, and in my mind I saw Arnarak in the company of the third engineer.

I made up for lost time the following day. I visited the house of Arnarak's parents, I went for a walk with her, and when the time for the dance was approaching I walked home with her to wait while she got ready. It was clearly a case of love at first sight, since we could not speak one word intelligible to the other. Quite unabashed, she took me inside her hut while she prepared herself for the great evening. She removed her *anorak* to put on a more colorful costume, and I admired her shiny white underwear, revising my ideas of cleanliness among Greenlanders.

Suddenly her fingers went to her hair and removed the red silk ribbons which kept it in place. The hair fell down around her shoulders, and in sign language she told me she wanted to do a special job on it when she went dancing with a man like me. She bent forward and let her marvelous black hair fall to the floor. I felt weak from love and my sailor's heart was bursting with pride—all this beauty was for me and not for any second or third engineer.

The success would have been assured if the girl had not been determined to make a still deeper impression on me. To prove her exceptional cleanliness, she now followed an old Greenland ritual which I witnessed for the first time. From below her bed she pulled out an enormous pail, filled to the rim with human urine, which the Eskimos use both for tanning hides and for cleansing purposes. Carefully she let her black hair down into the pail, gave it a good shampoo, and then wrung it out, with my love ebbing faster than the tide in the English Channel. All that was left, as we set off for the dance, was my self-control, my good manners, and the odors from her proud coiffure. When we arrived at the carpenter's shop I no longer had my arm around her. My gallant spirit had strangely evaporated.

Arnarak's hair was the envy of the other girls. She wore it in a proud upsweep with its top perched precariously on the crown of her head. While she was dancing her tower of hair swayed back and forth. Fortunately I am very tall, but the roof in the shop was very low, and I was forced to bend my head over my partner. As we turned in the dance, her hair, waving in front of my nose, produced a strange, anesthetic effect. In the end the ammonia proved stronger than love. And when the third engineer turned up I was quite content to leave her in his arms and to find other partners less ammoniated.

I had to say good-by to her the following day, as we were to continue up the coast to Holsteinsborg, but in spite of this initial disillusion she has remained my friend for life.

In Holsteinsborg I got a welcome respite from my duties on shipboard. We had the new doctor as a passenger, but he was so sick when we arrived he had to be carried on shore. The Greenlanders screamed with laughter when they saw him. He was their first doctor and he himself was unable to resist the diseases from which he was going to save them, and they laughed and laughed.

The doctor was put to bed, and I was called upon to unpack his supplies and to dispense the medicines he was in need of himself. I took my job seriously, but fortunately there were no other patients to be cared for, as the hospital had only two small rooms, and it was the Eskimo custom for the entire family of the patient to accompany him to the hospital and go to bed with him. Changing this custom proved to be one of the many Danish reforms that caused native resentment.

As a result of my new dignity I had to take my meals on shore, and again I was invited to the home of the local post manager. He had two young assistants, whom I have followed through the years and seen assume high and responsible positions, but at that time they were not burdened by too much responsibility—which I was soon to discover. When I was first invited for dinner they were present, as was the local minister. I had been told that the manager probably had the best kitchen in all of Greenland, and I had a vast appetite when we sat down at his table. The great meal was served by the native cook, Exekias, immaculately dressed in a white mess jacket and white slacks.

As the guest of honor I was served first, and, trying to be polite, I took a very small helping of the first course.

"Ai ai! Leave some for the others," said Exekias in a booming voice. My cheeks burned and I felt miserable, but the rest of the party pretended not to notice, and, when the food was passed a second time, I firmly declined another helping. The next course was brought in, and it looked mouth-watering. With admirable self-control I helped myself to a minute portion.

"Ai ai! Leave some for the rest," came the same booming voice. I looked at Exekias and his face was quite serious. Again nobody seemed to notice and I sat there with less than a third of what I

wanted to eat. The other plates around the table were generously filled, and they all ate with a hearty appetite.

The dessert was served with the same warning, so I began to
suspect that the cook's intention was to insure himself a plentiful
meal.

The conversation was very serious, but in the middle of it I
happened to glance at one of the manager's assistants and the
spoon fell out of my hand. His face looked like a sea in a storm,
it was so contorted.

In another moment the meal was over and we retired to the
living room for coffee. The manager lit his pipe and stretched
out on the couch, while the rest of us settled down in comfortable chairs. I finally risked another glimpse at the assistant.
He stood in the middle of the floor, moving with most terrible,
epileptic gestures, and suddenly fell to the floor with a crash.

I jumped up, shouting to the manager: "Your assistant has
collapsed!"

The old man calmly removed his pipe. "Yes, it does look that
way," he murmured sleepily, and settled down once more.

I could hardly believe my ears. Nobody lifted a finger to aid
the poor man.

"What shall I do? What is wrong with him?" I asked. "Shall
I give him some water?"

"Might be an interesting experiment," agreed the manager.
"It would probably be a new experience for him."

I tried to loosen his tie and undo his belt, and I called to
Exekias for water.

"What do you say, my precious lamb?" answered the cook,
and showed no desire to help me.

The sick man was still rattling, but during my efforts to open
his shirt I must have tickled him. He let out a scream of laughter,
and the whole thing proved to be a carefully rehearsed comedy
for my benefit. Every new guest in the house had to go through
a similar experience. The cook had been taught to say the only
two sentences he knew in Danish: "Leave some for the others"
and "What do you say, my precious lamb?" He had no idea
what the words meant. The manager and his assistants became
my good friends, however, in spite of this harrowing first meeting.

Jorgen Bronlund, the Greenlander who had come on the trip
as a passenger, now had to set about the task of buying fur and
dogs for our future expedition. The dogs in the Holsteinsborg

district were not the best, as they had mixed with the New-foundland breed, but they would still serve our purpose. Jorgen had to go in to Sarfanguaq at the bottom of a deep fjord for the dogs, and he asked me to go with him.

This was my first experience with an Eskimo "woman boat," which I had often read about. Such a trip seemed to me the height of adventure, and I was not disappointed. Eight strong women met us early in the morning. They were given the oars and were to do all the rowing. We were accompanied by two men in kayaks, who would be called upon only if the going got rough.

Two passengers and a crew of ten! It was a most unusual experience, and I did not at all enjoy sitting idle while the women rowed. After a while I offered to take one of the oars and was met with scornful laughter. Jorgen explained that no man with self-respect would ever touch an oar in such a boat. He had to maintain calm and dignity while the women did the work.

A woman boat is made of sealskin and floats on top of the water like a gigantic sea gull. It never takes any water except when the wind blows in spray from the crest of a wave. If it gets very windy the two kayak men paddle up to take care of the wind and water. Covered by fur from bottom to top as they were, they could laugh at the waves.

Most of the time we followed the coast very carefully, going into every bay and inlet except when we had to cross the mouth of a fjord. The kayaks moved like graceful cruisers, the woman boat went along like a powerful battleship. The men could travel fast and amused themselves by shooting eiders and gulls with bows and arrows, or harpooning a seal, which happened only once during the trip.

When the seal was killed there was great excitement in our boat. One of the girls, Magdalerak, was in a frenzy. She jumped up, and, in trying to get into the bow to see better, she stumbled against one of the other girls and stuck one foot right through the skin. Instinctively she pulled her foot back. The water came pouring in and in a moment the boat was half filled. The leader of our party took charge. "Foot in the hole!" he roared furiously, and the poor girl had to do as she was ordered. We went straight to shore to repair the damage and were soon on our way again.

During the afternoon I once more asked to relieve one of the girls. They all laughed, but I insisted and grabbed one of the oars. A couple of hours was more than enough for me. The rowers were remarkable—every time they pulled on their oars they had to stand up. They kept it up for hours, and while they rowed they sang. As a rule their songs are improvised. They make up their own words to some Danish folk tune, which they change to suit their mood. They giggle and laugh, telling stories which usually concern the passengers in an unflattering way.

Several of the women in our boat were quite old, one was middle-aged. Her fourteen-year-old son followed us in his own kayak. Every time we made a short stop he would paddle over to us, and his mother would pull up her *anorak* and offer him her breast. I learned this was a custom of Eskimo women. They continue nursing their boys for years and years. Knud Rasmussen once told about a man who was nursed by his mother until he married. The mothers insist on this practice because it proves they are still young and vigorous. The moment a woman can no longer nurse her boy she is considered old.

The trip lasted for thirteen hours, and I felt sorry for the poor women when we reached our destination. I was sure they were exhausted, but when they were told there was going to be a dance that evening, they shrieked with delight and rushed off to get ready for the party.

Magdalerak, the one who had put her foot through the boat, was my girl at the dance. She was small and strong, with a wonderful *joie de vivre,* which would have taken her far on the stage. As it was she put all her energy into dancing and having a good time. During the evening I was asked "to give coffee." I gladly paid the price and ordered the beverage for the whole population.

Magdalerak had a special purpose with her suggestion. She had an aunt living in Sarfanguaq who felt duty bound to look after the girl. The family had decided to marry Magdalerak off to a man who did not appeal to her. And the aunt, who was promoting the interests of the young man, consequently tried to keep me at a safe distance. Magdalerak was sly enough to make her aunt the "coffee dispenser," which meant that the old woman would get more coffee than the rest and could keep all the precious suds.

I provided the coffee—the kind universally used in Greenland —raw, green coffee. In hot frying pans it was roasted until it became dark brown and finally black as coal. Dried peas were added, the mixture was roasted again until all aroma disappeared, and then ground. This process obviously would keep the old lady too busy to look after her niece, who returned to the dance with me.

The dance was always given in the carpenter shop with its low roof. Fortunately I discovered a trap door going up to the attic. I quickly removed it, and for once I could dance with a straight back. My field of action was limited and my nose was tickled by the smell of the hides stored in the attic, but the rest of my body enjoyed the dance below.

Finally the players put away their instruments. It was their turn to indulge in my coffee, and my girl and I decided it was time to rest. She had been rowing for thirteen hours, we had been dancing for five, and we felt no need to take part in the coffee-drinking ceremony. I decided to make use of my discovery of the attic, and I pulled Magdalerak up and replaced the trap door.

The sun was shining brightly when we woke up. My friend Jorgen spent the morning bargaining about the dogs, and as soon as he had the number he wanted we set off on our journey back to Holsteinsborg. I never saw Magdalerak again, but always I have kept her in fond memory.

Sailing back to Holsteinsborg, we stopped on the way at a spot with nice grass, completely unloaded the boat, pulled it on shore, and turned it upside down to make a shelter to sleep under. Outside we cooked birds over a big fire. There were of course coffee and biscuits and also candy. Oh, it was lovely. This was the first of my many improvised living quarters in the Arctic.

After another day in Holsteinsborg we returned from this the first of my innumerable trips to Greenland. We retraced our course and arrived without incident in Copenhagen, where we were met on the pier by Mylius-Erichsen. I was touched by this thoughtfulness, but he was less interested in us than in the thirty-two dogs we brought with us.

I paid a short visit to my parents and my home town and brought home some things I had bought in Greenland, mostly leather things, tanned in urine, and my mother was not enthusiastic, as they smelled. Then I returned quickly to Copenhagen— more than ever eager to explore Greenland, the island of my dreams.

4

WHILE I HAD BEEN IN GREENLAND, MYLIUS-ERICHSEN, THE LEADER of our expedition, had purchased the vessel which was to take us north. *Magdalene* was an old Norwegian sealing vessel, strong as few ships and built of solid oak. She had been towed to Copenhagen, and when I reported for duty the ship was bustling with activity and we were rapidly approaching the long-awaited departure. *Magdalene* was renamed *Danmark* and due to increased publicity crowds of sight-seers came swarming over the ship. Some wanted to see us to find out what could possibly make a man foolish enough to go to the Arctic, from which we would probably never return alive. A polar expedition was quite a sensation in those days, and Mylius-Erichsen did nothing to make our undertaking appear less dangerous.

We were constantly pestered by crowds of people who blocked the decks and asked the most foolish questions. And we retaliated by telling them the most outrageous lies and sometimes by playing tricks on them. We would tempt the more inquisitive visitor to climb up the mast, and when he was up a seaman would come rushing with a line to tie up the sight-seer "for the sake of safety." And there we would keep him until he would promise us a quantity of beer.

One day shortly before our departure his majesty paid an official visit to the *Danmark,* accompanied by the crown prince. He gave his royal blessings to the expedition, and we were finally ready to sail. Hundreds of curious spectators lined the piers to see us off, with everything in chaos on board. Nothing was in order, the hatches were open, the deck was piled high with cargo and equipment. If it had not been for the royal blessing the harbor authorities undoubtedly would have delayed our sailing. But they closed their eyes and we moved slowly down the harbor.

That we moved at all was a minor miracle. The *Danmark* was probably the last ship in Scandinavia with a one-cylinder engine. The two engineers performed wonders to make the screw turn round, and as a fireman I played my small part in the miracle. As we moved slowly into the Kattegat we met a fresh breeze and could set sail. Fortunately we had two experienced seamen on board and the two naval officers who were supposed to be our navigators watched the maneuvers with interest, since they had no practical experience at sea. All went well until the third day, when the gaff broke. The rotten wood had to be replaced, and it was decided to go into the harbor of Frederikshavn at the northern tip of Denmark.

Some of us felt it slightly humiliating for the proud expedition to enter port after only three days at sea, but Mylius-Erichsen rose nobly to the occasion. He sent off dispatches to the Copenhagen newspapers, describing our first encounter with a terrible storm which the expedition had survived, due to the superb seamanship of the crew. His news brought immediate protests from other ships which had been in the Kattegat at the same time without seeing a trace of Erichsen's "towering waves."

We did not hear of this until we were settled in our winter headquarters in the north, and by that time such news was of minor interest. Repairing the damage, unloading the vessel in order to get rid of all superfluous cargo, including ten tons cf sand which someone had insisted on bringing along, and reloading in a safe and orderly manner took us the better part of a week; and we left before any drastic action was taken in Copenhagen.

Proudly we sailed up the Norwegian coast, and balmy weather gave our motley crew a chance to get used to the ship. Most of them were scientists of one sort or another who had signed on as seamen. They had never been to sea before, half of them got seasick, and none of them knew how to handle the ship. But they learned and without mishap we crossed to the Faroe Islands and went up north to Iceland, where we took on a great deal of additional cargo.

Our expedition was scheduled to last for three years, so we had to take along an enormous amount of supplies of every description. The most meticulous preparations are essential to make such an expedition safe and self-sufficient for three whole years. In Iceland it turned out, however, that nobody had any idea of the amount of cargo we could take. There was not a thing we had forgotten except that our cargo would fill at least two ships the size of the *Danmark,* and, consequently, we had to leave a great deal behind. The first victims were the six horses Erichsen had purchased in Iceland. We were supposed to use them for pack horses the first year and for food the next two years. We also had to sacrifice eight thousand bottles of beer which a brewery in Denmark had donated, and during our stay in Iceland we had to finish several cases of champagne which someone had given us for the express purpose of celebrating three Christmas Eves in the Arctic.

Some of our dogs had been lost on our way to Iceland. Nobody had arranged for any quarters for them, and they were left to shift for themselves on deck. The first day of heavy sea three of them were washed overboard. The dogs that lived were everywhere and the deck was soon covered with their discharges. They had very little food, and nobody had thought of bringing along water supplies for them. They had only enough to drink when it rained, but they managed remarkably well. I was deeply impressed by these Greenland dogs, for whose qualities I have a profound admiration.

After days of celebrations we finally set sail, and at last the expedition was really on its own.

I was promoted to be "scientific assistant" to Dr. Wegener, the meteorologist who was in need of a man to accompany him on his excursions to the mountains to help with his monthly twenty-four-hour observations and other work. I became increasingly interested as I slowly earned the ambitious title of scientific assistant.

Sometime after we left Iceland we had our first meeting with pack ice—always an awe-inspiring experience. The incredible formations, the myriads of changing colors, the mysterious grandeur of the Arctic ice is always a breath-taking sight. The ice is inscrutable, sometimes smiling and kind and graceful, at other times displaying a merciless force. Sometimes the ice is firm and compact, appearing to be an impenetrable barrier. With a sudden change of weather or current it may move and in a matter of moments completely surround the vessel, no matter how fast it tries to escape. As far as the eye can see the cruel glittering ice covers the ocean from north to south.

The *Danmark* was old but strong. With her solid oak hull she was not easy to maneuver. The sails might be blown to shreds in a storm without the *Danmark* showing the least strain. With a stern wind there had to be two men at the helm, which was placed on the poop, with the result that the helmsman had no visibility and had to steer according to instructions from the bridge or the mast.

While we were still in the ice Mylius-Erichsen one day decided to have a boat drill that proved to be a mixed blessing. The whistle blew and we all met promptly at our boat stations, launched the boats, and made our way to the nearest ice floe, according to instructions.

The leader of my boat decided to inspect the emergency supplies which had been stored in the boats. We were curious to see what we were supposed to eat, in case we were compelled to spend any length of time in a lifeboat, and one of the six metal boxes was opened. It contained sweet pickles, nothing but sweet pickles. Well, a little spice is always good, our leader remarked, and calmly proceeded to break open the next box and the next, until all six were opened. Every one contained nothing but pickles.

This discovery was soon forgotten, however, when we met a larger calamity after we were safely aboard again. The last man out of the messroom had forgotten to close the door, and our dogs had entered the galley and the pantry and devoured everything in sight—a barrel of butter, all our bread, a sack of flour, even leather articles. Whatever they left behind was covered with filth and dirt.

This was the occasion for Mylius-Erichsen's first fit of hysterical fury. We were to experience many of them later, but this was the first demonstration. He screamed and shouted, stamped on the deck, and nearly wept in his fury.

"I am in command here, I am the owner of the ship and everything in it! Whoever left that door open will get a punishment he will not forget! I'll put him in chains!" he shrieked.

While we were stuck in the pack ice we spent our days seal hunting with great enthusiasm, and I earned an entirely undeserved reputation for my marksmanship. One morning a very large seal appeared close by the ship, and in a moment the shots were coming fast from all parts of the vessel. The bullets were whistling all around the poor animal, which quickly submerged. The bold hunters began arguing about whose shot had come the closest, and while they quarreled the seal appeared once more, this time far away.

I wanted to make fun of the hunters by imitating their silly gestures. Quickly I grabbed a gun and let it off without taking aim. By an incredible chance the bullet happened to fall exactly where the poor animal was resting in the water.

Everybody was greatly amazed. I calmly put away the gun, spat on the deck, and said something about leaving guns alone if you don't know how to shoot. At the same time I promised myself not to touch a gun again unless I was forced to it.

After days of delay the ice split open before us and we knifed through it, reaching Greenland's east coast at a point farther north than white men had ever touched before. We established camp there for three years. The boat was to serve as living quarters for the majority, but a makeshift house was built on shore to accommodate four persons.

We did not know how to build snowhouses. Traveling during the winter, we lived in tents and all but froze to death because of our inadequate equipment. However, we were young and devoted to our task and eager for hardship. We thought we could stand anything. Most of our work, in retrospect, seems puerile. Now, with the aid of radio and modern scientific instruments, we have only to look at a chart to inform ourselves of the velocity of the wind and the weather conditions anywhere on the globe. But then we recorded every change in temperature, every vagary of the barometer to study it later at leisure and compare it with similar charts of other localities.

Dr. Wegener was one of the leading men of his day, and he specialized in the inversions of temperature which are now elementary knowledge to every airplane pilot. To ascertain the inversions we placed thermographs on the mountain peaks and I climbed up each day to get the readings. We also sent up kites and captive balloons carrying instruments. Science was then unconsciously paving the way for the aeronautics to come.

Our camp soon settled down to the routine of expedition life. We built an observatory for the large instrument for determination of the longitude—a main problem in those days when one could not through radio ascertain time and place in a moment. Lieutenant Koch was usually in charge of these observations, and with his assistants he soon began making detailed maps of the harbor and the surrounding area. As a general staff officer he strove for perfection in his map making and turned out works of art.

In those days it was customary, whenever an expedition returned from East Greenland, simply to state that "Greenland is an island," as maps were lacking for a large part of the coast—not to mention the interior. It was our task to complete the map making and we soon began using our sleds for excursions. In spring we were to take the long sled rides along the coast (on the ice), and late that first fall we set up depots along the projected routes.

The food problem was then far more complicated and costly than it is today. The greatest headache was always the dog food, and we had to organize hunting expeditions to get supplies. Erichsen took charge of this part of the work, as soon as we had made the camp—hunting being far more romantic than unloading ship, carrying supplies ashore, and building the villa.

Walrus made wonderful dog food, and later on bear hunts were popular. During the early part of the winter a polar bear or two would approach the camp nearly every day. On their way south, they were attracted by our smell, and, utterly unsuspicious as they were, they came down to investigate. The cook felled more bears than any other man those first winter days. He was strategically situated, for when working over his pots and pans he had a clear view north and he was usually the first to see the bears making their way south. Every time he shot one it caused a riot.

At first we had a special motor to pull down the weather balloons: our famous "automobile," undoubtedly the first to appear in Arctic regions. It was an extraordinary affair, put together by our engineers, who had a hard time keeping it in operation. Among other things it was used to pull down four thousand yards of balloon wire, until the whole contraption was iced down. One day the automobile got stuck in some screw ice and the drivers had to walk back to camp for the tools to get it out again. By the time they returned it was covered by large drifts of snow, and before they could dig their way down to it screw ice had claimed it for good. After that I had to operate Wegener's kites and balloons by hand.

My monthly twenty-four-hour observations were exhausting, but they also saved me once from being poisoned. After spending a whole day and night at the stations in the mountains or in the barrel at the top of the mast, I was pretty tired and usually slept for a solid twelve hours afterward. During one of those sleeping spells the rest of the camp enjoyed a great dinner of bear liver.

I was rudely awakened from my sleep by the doctor asking how I felt. Since I felt nothing but sleepiness I told him I was all right and he ordered me to get up at once and help him. As I got out of my bunk I noticed his green face, and the next moment he turned around and vomited. Every man in camp was sick from liver poisoning.

A hunting party had brought back a large amount of bear's liver, and the cook had turned it into a delicious ragout. We had never heard the old superstition that bear's liver is poisonous, but in our case the superstition certainly proved true.

I helped the doctor take care of the men, and I was deeply impressed by his resistance and his will power. He was as sick as any of them, but he carried on without interruption.

Everyone recovered eventually, but it took a surprisingly long time and the after effects were most unpleasant. Some had their eyesight affected, all ran a high temperature, suffered from diarrhea, and after a while their skin began peeling. I learned later that some people have eaten bear's liver without any ill effects, while others have shared our experience. So it seems likely that only some livers are dangerous. Years later when I became a professional bear hunter I discovered that the Eskimos never eat the liver. I also noticed that their dogs sometimes leave it alone and sometimes eat it with relish. Apparently their sense of smell or taste tells them which livers are poisonous.

Christmas came and went in the camp with a great celebration, including rum and champagne punch. As usual when there was anything to drink I was on watch. On such days I was at first angry with myself because I could never learn to enjoy tobacco or alcohol, but I soon realized the advantage it gave me. I have never been more popular than on Saturdays when punch was served. Everyone wanted to sit next to me, and the fact that it was less my person than my ration which was the attraction never bothered me. Since I did not smoke I was also well equipped with another article in demand—matches.

In Denmark we had been given an enormous amount of matchboxes designed and printed especially for the expedition. There are always people with the curious mania of collecting match books and boxes, and before we left we were beleaguered by these collectors. We had been very generous, and only when we arrived in Greenland did we discover we had far too few matches for ourselves. We were rationed to one box every other month—not much for smokers. Some of the men carefully split each match into four parts lengthwise and when they played poker they played for matches.

5

AS SOON AS SPRING ARRIVED WE BEGAN PUTTING INTO EFFECT OUR plan for the overland expeditions by dog sleds to the north. Four groups were sent out, each with three dog teams. Our ambition was to complete the maps of the east coast of Greenland all the way up to the northern tip. Dr. Wegener went north with one group, and during his absence I was in charge of the meteorological stations. At the same time I had to join some of the short excursions to the north, walking as far as we could to leave depots for the returning map makers.

Since I was tall and strong I was considered a good pack animal and had to carry a great many of Mylius-Erichsen's sled boxes. These were carefully planned by him before our departure from Denmark, but they did not prove very practical. They were hermetically sealed metal boxes supposed to contain sufficient stores for one man for thirty days. Among the contents was a box of ground pepper, the lid of which invariably fell off when the boxes were moved, generously sprinkling everything with the condiment.

That other plans of Erichsen were less than perfect became obvious on these sled trips. He had previously spent a winter at Cape York, but he had never learned to appreciate the advantages of snow huts or igloos. And we suffered quite unnecessary hardships because we did not make use of this practical shelter which gives comfort and warmth to the weary Arctic traveler. During the whole *Danmark* expedition we used our clumsy tents with the bottoms attached, which gradually froze into solid ice sheets. They never gave us any comfort at night.

Our sleds were equally bad. When we left Denmark Mylius-Erichsen had declared that the sleds would be made on the way to Greenland. Each man was supposed to make his own sled. He had never made one himself, and with all his experience he had never noticed there were no convenient trees in the Greenland ice from which sleds could be made. Fortunately the carpenter on board the ship had brought along some heavy boards—against the wishes of Erichsen—and he made some serviceable sleds.

The summer went by, and in Erichsen's absence Koch took charge of the expedition. I saw a great deal of him during that summer and learned both to like and admire him. At first I thought him a hard man. I remember once we had to pull a sled across the ice to a small island in the bay. The ice was full of crevices with deep water. My boots were full of holes, which I happened to mention. Koch asked me why on earth I bothered to wear boots. I told him I didn't think it was a good idea to walk barefoot on the ice.

"I don't see why not," he answered dryly, and I soon discovered it was infinitely more comfortable to walk barefoot on the melting ice.

By the end of the summer it was decided to set up a secondary meteorological observation post on the inland ice. I was selected to man this station.

In the fall of 1907 we went in to build the cabin. We had to wait until the water froze so that we could transport lumber for the shelter by dog sled. As the amount of lumber was limited the house was correspondingly small. When first completed it measured about nine by fifteen feet, but as the winter wore on and the cold increased, the interior of the house decreased in size, a layer of ice forming on the walls and ceiling as a result of respiration. Toward the last the room became so small two men could not pass each other without rubbing elbows.

After some time my company became so unbearable to everybody, I guess, that no one volunteered to join me in my isolation, and I was given the choice of returning to the boat or staying out the winter alone. If I stayed I would not see a human soul, as we were far north of the remotest Eskimo settlement. But I was just past twenty-one, full of a lust for novel adventures, and, like a fool, I offered to stay out the year alone.

My main object was to make daily observations—one at the base of the mountain close to the ice, another halfway up, and a third at the top, about three thousand feet above sea level. The cliffs were almost perpendicular and were hazardous to climb, and I realized that the only way to negotiate the trek during the dark winter months would be to learn every crevasse, every foothold, every ledge so well while daylight lasted that a mere matter of darkness should not deter me later. And it didn't.

My cabin, constructed of stone and lumber, was located in a narrow cleft which, at best, was gloomy. Then the sun dropped below the horizon in the middle of October and darkness shut down around me. For many days I could see the almost horizontal rays of the sun red upon the face of the cliffs, and for more than a week I climbed into the sunlight as I walked to the top of the mountain. When at last there was no more light even at noonday the Arctic night and the wolves were my sole companions.

No man should be left alone in the Arctic if it can possibly be avoided. So many situations may arise which, almost insurmountable to one man, are no trouble at all for two to overcome.

The small amount of coal I had brought in with me—the one factor that had kept the house from growing in upon me—was soon exhausted, and I had only a limited supply of spirits to burn for cooking. The coal stove merely cluttered up the room, and I finally heaved it out in disgust.

In the end the wolves, rather than the loneliness, bothered me most. They became an obsession with me. I have never been so frightened in my life. After my last dog was killed there was nothing to warn me of their approach, and often I wakened to hear them pawing on the roof of my cabin.

I caught three foxes and two wolves in a most unusual way. I set a trap on my roof, let a chain attached to it down through an air hole into the cabin, and tied a crossbar to the other end of the chain so that it could not slip out. Then when the wolves approached, attracted by the smell of my cooking, and fell for the bait in my trap, I heard a fearful noise as the stick rattled against the ceiling and the trapped animal scrambled across the roof fighting for freedom. Then all I had to do was to step out the door and shoot him.

But the first time I trapped a wolf I had neglected to make the chain short enough, and when I crawled outside the wolf charged me. His teeth were far too close for comfort. I knew that I could not get out of the cabin so long as that animal was on my roof, even if I carried my gun with me, for I could not crawl out the tunneled passage, whirl, and aim before he would be at my throat. I sat down and wiped the cold sweat off my face and for several moments could think of no solution. I was a fine trapper—caught in my own trap. Suddenly it occurred to me that all I had to do was to haul a few feet of the chain down through the hole and secure it, shortening the wolf's roving radius enough to keep him away from my door. The plan worked beautifully, and I killed him. But this was hardly sufficient revenge for my dead dogs.

It was a fine day for me when I first saw the faint purple outline of the horizon to the south, and I knew that before long the sun would be back. I shall never forget my joy at the return of color. The prismatic beauty of the northern lights was so heady that for long minutes I could stand there and forget even the stinging cold.

And then at last, after four months of darkness and six months of absolute isolation for me, a lucky sled ran the gauntlet of wolves and got through with food and fuel and, what was just as important to me, a companion for the short time before I went back to the base.

Unless a man has lived apart from human beings for a long period he does not know what he is saying when he cries that he wants to get away and be alone with his thoughts. Those thoughts can be extremely sterile and unattractive. It was heaven just to hear the new man complain about the weather or talk of the most commonplace events—anything was better than the silence or the sound of my babbling to myself or singing to the wolves. To know that if I should speak or ask a question it would evoke a reply made me tag him about like a lonesome hound.

6

YEARS LATER, I HEARD THE STORY OF A MAN WHOSE NERVES HAD snapped under the strain of arctic loneliness. He was a good trapper and a fine fellow who had spent winter after winter in Greenland. His name was Olav. He was an old-timer in Greenland. A simple man, perhaps, without much learning or imagination, but as good as they come and a first-rate trapper.

For many years he had always spent the long winter in Greenland with the same partner, a man by the name of Thomas Vold. The two of them went up north together and stayed alone miles and miles from the nearest human habitation until they were picked up in the spring to go south with their catch. But

one year Olav quarreled with his partner about the division of
the catch, with the inevitable result that the partnership split
up. Next year Olav did not go to Greenland with Thomas Vold.
He had got himself a new partner, Gustav Krakau, a stranger to
Greenland.

After the first few days with Krakau, Olav knew that he had
never met a better man for a companion. Gustav was clever, and
what he did not know he learned fast. He had never seen a
walrus before, but as soon as he was shown how to hit the animal right behind the ear he got the knack of it in no time. He
had no idea about skinning and flensing the animals, but he
stood watching Olav like a little boy. Then he asked for permission to do the next walrus himself in order to learn it. And he
worked all night long before he was satisfied.

He was a wizard in the kitchen. Olav had never tasted any
cooking like it. Besides the usual supplies, Gustav had brought
along all sorts of other things: curry and spicy sauces, things Olav
had never heard about. The way he prepared the food made Olav
feel like staying on at table long after a meal was finished just
to keep the good taste in his mouth.

After a while it was getting noticeably darker every day and
soon the sun would be gone for a good many months. It was
time to set the traps, and that was something new to Gustav. First
he worked at it at home by the blockhouse, and he got to be
pretty good at it before they set out. In no time he caught on to
the trick of setting the traps and covering them with a thin layer
of snow to hide them from the foxes. In a couple of days he was
as good as Olav, and they set out together. At first Olav went with
him, showing him where to put the traps and how to find them
again when he came back. After that the two men split up the
territory between them.

Everything to the north was Gustav's area while Olav kept to
the south. They made a regular routine of it. Every Monday
morning they set out with two dogs each. The dogs pulled the
small sleighs with the sleeping bags and food because they could
move much faster that way. Olav had had the same four dogs for
some time, and it was funny to see how they took to Gustav right
away. The old partner, Thomas Vold, always had a hard time
getting along with the dogs, but Gustav had a wonderful way
with the animals and they were his friends from the first day.

Gustav went north and Olav went south—and they kept walking away from each other all day Monday and Tuesday. At night they slept in small huts which Olav had built years before for that purpose. Half of Wednesday they kept on walking, checking the traps. In the afternoon they turned around. Wednesday they slept in the Tuesday huts and Thursday night they spent in the Monday huts. Friday night they were back at the blockhouse. If they met a snow storm they might have to spend another night in one of the small huts, and then they would not meet again until Saturday. Sometimes they did not reach the blockhouse until Sunday, and once in a long while they did not see each other again until the end of the next week. But Olav had stored plenty of food in all the huts for an emergency. They were both careful and Olav knew he did not have to worry about Gustav Krakau.

Soon Olav noticed that he was more and more looking forward to Friday. He began missing Gustav when he was alone with the dogs, and he was eager to sit listening to his strange partner. Life with Gustav was very different from all the winters he had spent with Thomas Vold. They had hardly ever spoken a word to each other, Olav and Thomas. What did they have to talk about? They knew the work and did it well enough, both of them. That was all. Gustav was just the opposite. He always had lots to tell when he met Olav again. During the week he had seen so many things he had to talk about—things that Olav and Thomas had always known but never bothered to mention because they did not seem worth wasting a word on.

What a talker Gustav was! When Olav was alone during the week he could not help thinking of all the things Gustav had said. In the end he got so used to all the talk that he even began saying things on his own. Gustav knew how to draw him out, get him into a discussion.

After a while it got to be with Gustav the way it was with the heat in the house: you can do without it, but it gets mighty cold. Olav missed him more and more during the week. Gustav made the winter quite different for him.

Shortly after New Year's Day, Gustav complained that he did not feel so well. His arms and legs were like lead when he walked any distance. Olav could see that he moved very slowly and went to bed early.

The next Monday they got ready as usual. Gustav still moved slowly, but he seemed all right as they parted on their separate rounds.

But when Olav returned to the house on Friday, he found Gustav lying in bed with his face to the wall.

"Gustav!" he called. There was no movement. It did not take him long to understand that Gustav Krakau was dead.

At first he would not let it be true. He made a fire in the stove and cut some ice for the pot. The whole water barrel outside was a solid block of ice, and it always was the chore of the first man home to thaw some ice. Without thinking about it Olav began scolding Gustav for neglecting his duty. He did not want to look at Gustav. As long as he didn't he could pretend that the man was asleep and that he would soon wake up. He fed the hungry dogs and told them Gustav was drunk: that was the reason why they never got their food. He knew it was a lie but he felt that he had to say something.

He kept up the pretense that Gustav was asleep. He knew how miserable he would be once he admitted that his partner was dead. Suddenly he felt utterly exhausted. He stumbled into his own bed and fell asleep.

When he got up the following morning Olav made hot cereal for both of them.

"Do you want some?" he called out to Gustav. There was no answer, of course, since the man was dead, but Olav did not want to let Gustav see that he knew it. That was Saturday morning, and Olav decided to keep Gustav where he was until Sunday night. He wanted some company over the week end at least; then he could bury the body Monday morning and set out on his usual round so he would not have to sit alone at home feeling miserable.

Gustav was lying hunched up in the bed with his legs pulled up. He looked just as if he were sitting in a chair. He was frozen stiff, of course, but the face looked as if Gustav were laughing at some last, private joke. Olav lifted him out of the bunk and put him down on a chair by the table, and then he sat down at his lonely breakfast.

Olav talked to the dead man as he ate his food.

In the evening he took Gustav outside. He put him on a sled and pulled him over to a small cliff near the house. First he put the body down in the snow, then he covered it with stones, lots of stones piled neatly on top of the body. He did not want wolves and bears to eat his good friend Gustav.

As he sat by himself in the blockhouse, Olav began thinking that it had been better, after all, when he had Gustav at the table with him, even though he was dead. Now Gustav was outside, freezing in the terrible cold.

In short, he took Gustav inside again. He regretted it immediately, but now that it was done he had to stick to it. When he had his friend propped up on the other side of the table things seemed a little brighter. Olav talked to him and went right on answering him. He knew Gustav pretty well by then, so it was a little like playing with dolls. And he was sure Gustav would never have objected to it.

They had quite a good time together, he felt. Olav prepared food for both of them and set a place for Gustav. He even served him and got angry when Gustav did not eat. "I know I am not such a fancy cook as you," he complained when he had to give the food to the puppies. He pretended to be angry because Gustav was finicky about his meals—that was part of the game.

When he went to bed that night he left Gustav sitting by the table. That was a great mistake! In the middle of the night he woke up and Gustav was moving! He could have sworn that the dead body was moving. He was wide awake in a second—and here is the strange part of it: he really wanted desperately to be afraid that the body was moving. He knew all the time that the body was only thawing, but he did not want to admit it. If he did he would have to give up the game of make-believe, of pretending that Gustav was still alive.

Finally, Olav took Gustav back to his grave, but every time he came back from visiting the traps he brought the dead man back into the house.

One day he noticed the first snow sparrow outside, and he knew that he had to do something. The bird was a sure sign that spring was coming. The fox trapping was over for the winter, the ice would soon break up, and the ship would return to take them back to Greenland.

He was afraid—he was really scared—when he returned to the house with the last traps. Frightened of himself, scared of Gustav, scared of his ghost, for he was really a ghost now. The only difference was that Gustav did not walk around by himself, for he had Olav to carry him. It was just the way it had been when he was alive. He could make Olav do things he would never had dreamed of doing of his own free will. He knew he had to get rid of him before the ship arrived, but he did not know how.

The idea came to him all of a sudden. He knew what he had to do—and he knew that it was the only right thing to do. He took Gustav inside once more and went on talking to him as if he had nothing at all up his sleeve. He smiled to himself when he told Gustav about all the things they would do the next day, just to reassure his friend. After a while he told Gustav that he had to go outside for a moment to get some more coal for the fire. He had his gun outside. He did not close the door all the way, he left it open just a little crack. It did not matter to Gustav, he could not call out to complain of the draft anyway, and Olav needed that little crack. And he knew that this time he was going to fool his friend.

He sneaked back to the house with the loaded gun in his hand. It took him a long time—a small eternity, it seemed—before he pushed the barrel of the gun through the crack and put it in just the right position without letting Gustav notice anything. He just sat where Olav had put him, his arm leaning on the table. He had his back to Olav, but he was turned a little sideways, enough to let Olav see his smile—a disgusting grin which was not really like Gustav at all.

This time he was alive! Olav was sure of it, but he finally had enough of him. And he cocked the gun. Taking good aim was a difficult business, since he was so excited that his hands were trembling. Even if the man was dead, it was, after all, a friend that Olav was going to shoot. Just as he was ready to pull the trigger, Gustav moved. The arm on which he was leaning had softened. It was hard to shoot him while he was moving, but Olav had to rid himself of Gustav. Suddenly he was furious with the man for trying to scare him right up to the last moment. And then he shot his friend.

He buried his friend properly this time. From one of the wooden boxes he made a plain cross for the grave. It felt good to be alone, nobody to pay any attention to. He did not miss Gustav. He was only relieved to be rid of him and his crazy obsession. His friend was really dead now, true enough, and it was a great pity, but there was nothing he could do about it.

Quietly and peacefully Olav prepared for the trip home. The ship would come any day now.

During the trip home Olav wanted to throw himself overboard. The only thing that kept him from it was the feeling that people would only think the worse of him if he did.

"I knew what they thought of me and I knew what would happen," Olav concluded. "And I was right. This morning the whole police force came to get me. Yesterday we arrived in port and I was allowed to walk alone to my house, but today you needed four policemen to bring me down here.

"I am no murderer, Sheriff! I only used my gun to make Gustav leave me in peace, once he was dead. I only killed a dead man. You've got to believe me. There is no law against that! Or is there? You tell me!"

Olav was taken back to his cell that night, and in prison they must have called him a murderer and told him that he had taken his best friend's life. That proved too much for him. Olav had always been a strong man, a good and honest man, but this was more than he could take. All winter he must have been on the border line—and that night in prison he finally lost his mind.

An autopsy of Gustav's body quickly confirmed Olav's story. The medical examination showed clearly that the body had been dead for some time and frozen stiff when it was shot in the head. Olav's name was cleared, there could be no question of murder, and the sheriff announced that no charge would be made against him.

But it was too late. Olav was incurably insane by then.

7

WHEN I FINALLY RETURNED TO THE SHIP AFTER MY LONG SOLITARY stint I learned that three of my companions were dead—Mylius-Erichsen, the leader, Lieutenant Hagen, and an Eskimo, Joergen Broenlund.

In the early spring of 1907 these three men had gone off to the north on a long mapping expedition, and they had not returned by the time the ice broke up. Sleds were sent north to leave supplies at points agreed upon beforehand, and in this way their journey back to the base at least would be provided for. But it was not until the winter of 1907–8 that any trace of the three was discovered.

The diary found on the body of Broenlund told the grim story: The men had run into an unexpected fjord. It took them so long to traverse it that they were delayed in accomplishing their ultimate objective, which was to verify the existence of what was then believed to be the Peary Channel between Greenland and Pearyland. But Mylius-Erichsen wanted to complete his task and went on, hoping the ice would stay in just a week longer than it had the year before. The ice went out, and with it all hope of the party's return until fall.

They had to depend upon hunting for their own and their dogs' food, and game was scarce. Their suffering must have been excruciating before they died, for they fought all summer long against the weather and ultimate starvation. Perhaps their worst piece of luck was the loss of their sewing kit, which made it impossible for them to repair their clothing. Broenlund had repaired his own boots with a nail, and his diary told how the other two had descended the glacier in their stocking feet in an effort to reach the coast.

Hagen had died November 15, and Mylius-Erichsen ten days later. Broenlund, who must have been near death at the time, managed to struggle on to the food depot ten miles distant. Poor man, he was too weak to open the cache, and he died beside plenty of food and fuel.

Broenlund became a hero in Greenland. Monuments have been erected to his memory in Godthaab and in Copenhagen. His bravery was admirable, and though he had no reason to risk his life for science, his last trip to the depot, where he knew his body would eventually be found, was accomplished only to save the maps and tell what his companions had done.

The realization of the sacrifice these men had made impressed me greatly. Three men I knew well and admired suddenly were no more.

We had all grown very fond of Erichsen. We knew his faults, but his shortcomings had not hurt his great popularity. If he had had the sense of order and organization of his second in command, Koch, he would have survived. But Erichsen was of another caliber. He paid with his life for the honor of having carried through the *Danmark* Expedition, and his name will always live in the history of the exploration of Greenland.

It was on this first expedition that I came to love the Eskimos. There were three of them with us: Joergen Broenlund, who died, and two other boys, Henrik and Tobias. From them I learned how gentle and fine primitive people can be. None of these boys had ever been away from home before, and life with members of the expedition was a drastic change from anything they had known. Their knowledge was limited, but they were to a great degree responsible for the success of the expedition. They acted as dog drivers and hunters, and on our trips we were given many opportunities to marvel at their skill.

Henrik was a little fellow who had not amounted to much at home. With us he got his first opportunity to prove his worth. He became an excellent bear hunter and walrus killer, and when later on he received the Order of Merit from the King of Denmark he reached his full stature, at least in the eyes of his own people.

What he lacked in size he made up in courage. The first time he ever killed a bear he was alone in his tent. He wakened suddenly and to his great surprise saw an enormous bear standing with his immense head inside the flap of the tent. Henrik's rifle lay alongside his sleeping bag, but he was so frightened, he told us later, that for a moment he did not know what to do. Surely any move he made to pick up the long weapon would attract the attention of the bear. But this was no time for indecision. Henrik grabbed for the gun and fired without sighting. The bear fell dead, but the skin of the head was ruined, as the exploding powder had scorched it.

Tobias had enjoyed great fame as a hunter at home, but when he got the chance to come with us and see more land than he could have reached with his kayak, he left his wife and son and skipped out. He never once fell short of what was expected of him. His greatest concern was that he was unable to read. He and I became fast friends, but I have always felt I tricked him, unintentionally, into the admiration he felt for me.

The two of us were camped one night on a bank close to the sea, and in the morning, half asleep, I peered out to have a look at the weather. Just over the bank stood a polar bear, sniffing uncertainly in our direction. Wide awake at once, I jumped back and whispered.

"There's a big bear standing right outside on the ice!"

Tobias leapt to his feet and seized his gun as I did. We needed bear meat badly, for we were a long way from the ship and short of provisions. Both of us aimed and fired simultaneously. The bear struggled for a few moments, and then lay down and died, realizing he hadn't a chance against two hunters.

I went back into the tent to dress, and Tobias ran down to the bear. In a moment he called:

"Come down and look at the wounds!"

There were two small holes not two inches apart.

"Which one is yours?" asked Tobias.

How could I know? It was enough for me that I had hit the animal at all, so I pointed my finger at the nearest hole and answered, without knowing how much hung upon my guess:

"That's the spot I aimed at."

"Yes, that must be yours," Tobias agreed. "I was too high. I knew it. You are a fine shot."

Later on when we cut the bear up we found the lead from the lower hole in the heart. There isn't a doubt in my mind that it was Tobias' bullet, but I had already taken the credit for it. He assured me of his lifelong friendship, and he has never failed me. For my part, I always feel that I did him an injustice.

During our last six months in the Arctic we lived on little but tomato soup and fishballs. Both those dishes are excellent, but one can easily get too much of them. We had, however, been careless with our supplies, and we now had to pay for it.

With Erichsen's death we gave up our plans to cross the inland ice with sleds to the west coast. I had looked forward to it as the high light of the whole expedition. Instead, some of us made shorter excursions inland. And my first trip across the huge glaciers might have put an early end to my career. As we walked across the ice we met occasional crevasses. Suddenly the surface below me gave way and I started falling through the air.

After some eternal seconds I stopped falling. My right leg was against one wall of the crevasse, my back was against the other. I did not dare make the slightest move, for fear I would fall into the bottomless pit below. At last I heard my companions calling me, and I peered up at them. Far above I could see the small hole I had made in the ice as I crashed through. My friends were cutting through the ice around the hole to find the actual edge of the crevasse. When at last they caught sight of me, they called out something unintelligible and disappeared. Had they given me up, had they left me to die in the ice? I was in a panic.

At last they reappeared with a long rope which they slowly let down the ice wall. But when it finally reached me I feared to make a move. Then with infinite care I caught the rope, pulled it twice around my body and made it secure. In a moment I was suspended in air and carefully hauled to safety.

I had to lie down for a moment when I was on top again— just to look at the beauty of the sun and sky. In the most casual way Koch asked if I was hurt and then if I had noticed any blue veins in the ice down there.

The following days I stepped through the ice several times without mishap, and it did not worry me. But in later years I have had nightmares of falling down such crevasses, and I never lost the conviction that my grave would be in the inland ice.

There had been considerable fear for our safety in Denmark. Ice was very bad in the summer of 1907, and it had been impossible even to make contact with a colony farther south along the east coast of Greenland. Seal hunters had reported vast quantities of ice in polar waters, and as a result the Danish government had sent out a ship to look for us, but it had failed to get through.

In 1908 the government promised a reward to any seal hunters who could make contact with us. One day three boats, so small that only Norwegian hunters would dare take them into the ice pack, appeared outside our harbor. While our ship was in the harbor and would not be free of the ice for months, nearly everyone on the expedition—I was away from the ship at the time— hurried out to visit the foreigners. And a little disappointed our men were, too, when they were fed fishballs and tomato soup on all three boats. The seal hunters considered it "Sunday food."

The captains of the sealers were told that three of our party were lost. By the time they reached the mainland they had forgotten the names of the three lost men, and my mother was informed that I was one of the ill-fated number. So widespread was the story that some of my countrymen began to speak well of me.

8

AT LAST OUR EXPEDITION WAS OVER. FOR ME IT HAD BEEN AN INITIA-tion into my future life, and it added to science more specimens and information of the Arctic than any other had secured. The price had been the lives of three of our comrades.

We left our harbor after building a large cairn to the memory of Mylius-Erichsen, Lieutenant Hagen, and Joergen Broenlund, who had given their lives.

In the late summer of 1908 we returned to civilization, and our appearance caused a sensation although it was rather inglorious to our mind. Our boiler was cracked and rusty, and we had to be towed by a tug into the harbor of Bergen in western Norway. The first day on shore we went wild and behaved like savages. The following days a constant stream of Norwegians came on board to have a look at the crazy Arctic explorers. One of the first visitors was a great Norwegian, Roald Amundsen, who was then preparing his expedition to the South Pole. Our meeting was the beginning of a friendship which lasted until his tragic death, during his efforts to rescue the lost Nobile Expedition.

After a few days of celebration we received a cable from Copenhagen. A hero's welcome was being prepared for each of us, and a tugboat was sent up from Denmark to tow us down the last leg of our trip. We had to man the pumps day and night during the last few days until we arrived safely, and for the first time in my life I heard deafening cheers of greeting for me and my friends. After the reception in the harbor we were taken straight to the university where we were feted with a banquet and laudatory speeches.

The next day we were received by King Frederick VIII. He had quite forgotten he had visited our ship before our departure. He told us that his father, who had died during our absence, had asked many times what had happened to the heroic men who had gone north on that hazardous undertaking. He ended by decorating each of us with the Order of Merit and shaking hands.

After this official blessing from the king, we celebrated our return for days, but one cannot live forever on the glories of a past expedition. And with the best of intentions I tried to resume my studies and went to live with my good friend, Koch, whose incredible energy and sense of duty were a good example to me.

But my university career proved a failure once more. I was not lazy, nor was I stupid—as far as I know. During the long months in the ice I had been longing for the quiet life of the student, for the opportunity to add to my scanty knowledge. But it was hard for me to settle down to the university atmosphere.

During those restless days I met and became closely attached to the one man who came to mean more to me than any other man in my whole life—Knud Rasmussen. I had heard a great deal about him, for he was already regarded as quite a hero. He had accompanied Mylius-Erichsen on the so-called Literary Expedition to Greenland, and while I was gone on the *Danmark* Expedition he had been to Lapland and Greenland. I had met him briefly in Bergen when we came back from our expedition, and I had promised myself to see more of him.

Knud Rasmussen was born in Greenland. His father had been a missionary there for twenty-eight years, and his mother was part Eskimo. My Eskimo friends, Henrik and Tobias, paid a visit to Knud's father on their return to Denmark and sang my praises. Their affection and admiration for me were quite undeserved, but they aroused Knud's respect even before he knew me. He was at heart an Eskimo, and the fact that I had been friendly to two of his people, and had learned a little of their language and special skills, convinced him that I was the right man for him. And we spent a great deal of time together those first few months after my return to Copenhagen.

One evening in the fall of 1909, while I was still living with Koch, I received a letter from the newspaper *Politiken,* asking me to call on the city editor immediately. I hurriedly answered the summons and was told the sensational news that a cable had just arrived from Scotland stating that Dr. Frederick Cook had discovered the North Pole and was now on his way to Denmark on board the Danish steamer *Hans Egede,* which had picked him up in Greenland. It was a tremendous story, but as there was nobody in *Politiken*—then the largest newspaper in Denmark— who had the faintest knowledge of the Arctic, the editor asked me to help them out.

I was flattered and pleased to enter into journalism this way, and I assured the editor I could whip off an article for him in no time. I wrote about the North Pole, mentioned the many unsuccessful attempts to reach it, and made some careful speculations on the basis of the scanty information in the cable. I was very satisfied with my story when I was interrupted by a visit from the editor in chief.

"This North Pole affair seems to be quite a sensation," he declared. "Cables are pouring in asking for details. We need a few more columns. Make up something about nature up there, traveling conditions, and stuff like that. I'll kill some book reviews to make space."

I was bursting with pride as I continued writing about my own experiences for two and a half years in the Arctic, quoting freely from encyclopedias for additional facts.

"More copy!" I was told, and I went on writing.

Around midnight the paper went to press and I thought I was through. But at the last moment the editor announced that he needed more material. But I had dried up, I could write nothing more about the Arctic regions. Suddenly I noticed the date. Cook claimed that he had been at the Pole on the twenty-first of April. In my confusion and weariness I thought this date was that of the vernal equinox, and I wrote another piece in a highly poetical vein about the dramatic coincidence of Dr. Cook's arriving at the Pole on the very day when the sun for the first time in six months sent its golden rays over the icy wastes.

Imagine my humiliation when I discovered the following morning what I had done. The afternoon papers were already making fun of the young explorer who had postponed the equinox from March to April. I felt very small when I went to see the editor.

"Congratulations, my young friend! You did a great job and I am well pleased with you," he said.

"That's very kind of you," I answered, "and I want to assure you that I am truly sorry about what has happened."

"Why, what has happened?"

"It was all my fault, please don't blame anyone on the paper." And I told him of the mistake I had made and that the whole town was laughing at his newspaper.

"Is that all? What is a month one way or the other?" he said. "We all make mistakes sometime, and in your case you have shown yourself to be a man with imagination. Would you like to join the staff of *Politiken?*"

After this surprising start I was put on the payroll.

The steamer carrying Dr. Cook was now approaching Denmark, and a great many foreign journalists came to Copenhagen to interview him. I was very flattered when I was approached by Philip Gibbs of the London *News Chronicle* about the discovery. Among other things I told him that Knud Rasmussen, who was then in Greenland establishing a missionary station in the North Star Bay, had sent a letter to his wife in Denmark on Cook's steamer. And if we could get hold of that letter we might find out what Rasmussen had to say about Cook and make a scoop.

We persuaded Mrs. Rasmussen to go with us to Elsinore where
the ship would dock, and she promised to show us the letter if
it contained any news about Cook.

We made the trip by car, quite a stunt in those days, and
arrived at the dock ahead of the other journalists who were coming by train. We asked the harbor master to let Mrs. Rasmussen
board the ship with Gibbs and myself. Unfortunately a man
with him when we made our request turned out to be Captain
Bang, whose fireman I had been on my first trip to Greenland.
The result was that permission was granted Mrs. Rasmussen and
Gibbs but not the former fireman.

I had no intention of being left behind and managed to get
into the coast-guard cutter going out to the steamer and to sneak
on board the *Hans Egede.*

Dr. Cook received the press in the dining room. I don't know
how it happened, but after the first few minutes I was convinced
that something was seriously wrong with his story. At first I could
not believe he was simply making it all up, but as the press conference proceeded I was certain he did not know what he was
talking about. I did not dare say anything since I was not supposed to be there, but I listened carefully to his every word, and
when we were on deck again I asked Gibbs for his opinion. He
also felt something was wrong.

Philip Gibbs began a series of articles in the *News Chronicle.*
His newspaper had certain traditions to live up to. Its editor
had been the first man to see through a famous hoax a few years
before—a best seller called *Thirty Years Among the Savages* by
Louis de Rougemont. The *News Chronicle* had proved that
this man's dangerous journeys in uncivilized regions were
wholly imaginary. Gibbs at once set out to expose Dr. Cook.
Lacking any knowledge of the Arctic, he pumped me dry. And
we wrote a daily article charting the travels of Cook, who had
already begun publishing his diaries. We found in these half
a dozen claims obviously contrary to facts as well as many
dubious statements. And I decided there was no reason to believe
the rest of it.

I did not hesitate to state my conviction publicly. I gave several lectures, and I wrote an article presenting all the evidence
against Dr. Cook. But my editor refused to print it. "We cannot
wine and dine a man one day and call him a fraud the next,"
he declared.

So I took my article to another paper and was received with open arms by the editor, who did not use it.

During the height of the strife Roald Amundsen arrived in Copenhagen. I went to his hotel at one o'clock in the morning and talked to him for five hours. There had been mention of sending an expedition up to Etah, in northern Greenland, to search for the two diaries Cook claimed to have left there. I felt that I must join this expedition and asked Amundsen to help me. He promised to do what he could for me, but he expressed his faith in Dr. Cook. Amundsen liked Cook and, consequently, believed in him. In any case the expedition to Etah never materialized, partly because there was not sufficient financial backing and partly because Cook himself advised against it, a position that should have caused some suspicion.

I tried to launch an expedition of my own. I suggested going up to Greenland by steamer, continuing north by dog sled across Melville Bay and up to Etah, finding Cook's two Eskimo companions, Itukusuk and Apilak, and bringing them back to Denmark. At first the *News Chronicle* was willing to finance me, but when my plan met opposition in Denmark they gave up the idea. My own newspaper turned thumbs down on the scheme, as did all the other papers I tried.

My one consolation was that my article exposing Cook finally did appear in print. I was paid three dollars for it by a small newspaper, but it did not make a great stir.

The Cook case went on and on. The university finally ordered an investigation with Knud Rasmussen as one of the commission. The investigations were shrouded in secrecy, and the results were awaited anxiously. Then one morning all the newspapers had extras in the street: "The University of Denmark had found no evidence supporting the claims of Dr. Cook that he had been at the North Pole!"

I rushed to the newspaper office where my editor greeted me enthusiastically.

"You must write a follow-up on your previous story when you proved Cook a fraud," he declared.

"But you never printed my story," I said in some confusion, and told him the name of the paper in which it had appeared.

"We didn't? My mistake, but nobody reads that sheet anyhow. We'll reprint it."

I had the short-lived satisfaction of having been right all along, but we soon had to close the books on the Cook episode, and I had to decide on my future. Whatever determination I might have made to complete my studies was soon changed by Knud Rasmussen. He asked me to become his partner in an undertaking to establish a trading station among the polar Eskimos in the extreme north of Greenland. It was his idea to exchange our modern tools, equipment, and weapons, to which Admiral Peary had introduced the natives, in return for their furs. Since Peary's return these Eskimos had had no contact with the outside world and were once more dependent on their ancient tools and the occasional supplies brought them by whalers, who drove a very hard bargain.

I agreed to this plan immediately, but there was a big obstacle as usual, the lack of financial backing. From his latest trip to Greenland, Knud had returned with a load of furs that he had sold for the magnificent sum of twelve thousand kroner—an enormous amount for a young man's use but sadly insufficient for our purpose. We tried to get a government grant, but had no success, in spite of the assistance given us by a wonderful fellow countryman, a civil engineer by the name of M. Ib Nyboe.

He was an adventurer like ourselves and a real pioneer. He had been a railroad engineer in the United States, had done great construction work for the Russian government, and now he was interested in opening up copper mines in Greenland. But this son of a Danish shopkeeper who had performed miracles all over the world could not get us a government grant. This failure may have been due to my own lack of experience with diplomatic language. At one stage of our delicate negotiations I asked the Secretary of the Interior whether he really was "such a nitwit" as he appeared to be. Whatever the reason, we had to find another source to meet our needs.

Knud and I carefully figured out the minimum which we must have for our needs and thought we had found a way to get it. And with optimism as our only asset, we set out on our first lecture tour. The discovery of the North Pole and the whole Cook episode had aroused a thirst for knowledge of the Arctic.

But our debut was not as auspicious as it ought to have been. The scheme was for one of us to project lantern slides while the other lectured. We had bought, on credit, a well-advertised projection machine, and, as Rasmussen was to give the first lecture, he gave me the signal to begin my contribution. Something dark and messy plastered the screen. I grew overheated and swore, but that made the lantern slides no better. And Knud Rasmussen lectured on apprehensively, not knowing what to expect next, flashing me signal after signal like a madman. Finally an inspiration was born of his desperation, and he explained to the fretting audience:

"Anyone can take pictures in Greenland in the summer when there is light, but these slides are something special. They were filmed in the dark of an Arctic winter! I am happy to have the privilege of showing the Danish people exactly what it is like up there during the long night."

When I flashed a Greenland dancing party on the screen, Knud explained:

"That is a bear hunt by night. It is extremely dangerous to attack wild animals with no light to shoot by."

I found a fine slide showing a group in a skin boat. He spun a yarn about a hunter out in the cold and gloom of winter standing watch over a blowhole in an attempt to catch a seal for his starving children. The audience was deeply moved and applauded him roundly when he finished. But when I began my lecture they had had enough of midnight photography and loudly demanded to see how Greenland looked in the daytime. All of which caused us to give up our conservation program and hire a real projectionist.

We played every community in Denmark, and the experience was invaluable to us.

At last, in a small ship and with pitifully few supplies, we set out for Greenland once again.

9

WE WERE THRILLED TO BE ON OUR WAY. WE WERE YOUNG AND STILL believed that life would reward us with a reality equal to our dreams. One day we found ourselves close enough to the southern coast of Greenland to view Cape Farewell. That point is seldom seen, for ships ordinarily keep far away from the coast in order to avoid the ice. Even when the immediate water is clear the polar ice lies to the south as far as the eye can see; the prevailing wind is from the southwest, and it may blow the pack in before a ship has an opportunity to get clear. We saw the huge mountains on shore, an ominous foreboding of the sternness of the land. The sea ran high and the rocks offered no solace. They are black and towering, and there is no pity in them. As I stood at the wheel I realized for the first time that I had burned my bridges and was up against something which would demand the utmost from me.

We ran into the ice and out again. We all worked desperately; the crew—six men besides Rasmussen and myself—understood that a wreck would benefit them no more than it would us.

We landed first at Godhavn where I bought some dogs and a few supplies we had neglected to purchase at home. Knud Rasmussen refused even to look at the dogs, for he had an uncle living at a remote settlement who had a reputation for being the best dog breeder in Greenland, or perhaps in the world.

At Godhavn an elderly Eskimo woman named Vivi came to us and asked permission to join us as housekeeper. She had relatives up north among the Smith Sound people, as her mother had come from there. She was the daughter of Hans Hendrik, a renowned Eskimo who had followed eight American and English expeditions to the far north. We told Vivi we were sorry, but that we were too poor to pay her wages; besides, we did not know what we were running up against. We were going to live off the country and try to earn a livelihood by hunting.

She answered that her own condition was so desperate that any change would be for the better, and she wanted no wages. That seemed to settle the argument, and we decided to take Vivi with us. Then it developed that she had a son about ten years old, a boy she had acquired at some place or other, as she explained, "I got stuck during long time by ice conditions." We shipped him too.

Next we stopped to visit Knud's Uncle Carl. He lived in a settlement named Qeqertaq, and ruled like a king. He was an old native of superior mentality who had made himself rich and was the trader of the community. We secured dogs and dog food and clothes from him, and Knud told him to take whatever he wanted from us in return, for we had no money.

What a time we spent there! We had some gin with us—prohibited in Greenland—but we distributed it liberally, and the games and dancing lasted for days. Uncle Carl was famous for his skill as a marksman, and he always asked his guests to hang their pipes for targets on nails atop the fence posts around the dog yard. He was never happier than when he had to furnish his friends new pipes because he had shot their old ones to bits. Uncle Carl also had a two-piece orchestra—himself on a violin and his daughter on an accordion. They played for us in the sunlight all through the night.

From Qeqertaq we sailed off into parts unknown.

In order to penetrate farther north the voyager must traverse Melville Bay, a stretch of water considered by whalers to be the most dangerous in the Arctic. Ice blocks crowd the water the year round, and we feared for our ship, which was not meant to be an ice jammer. At times we had to saw docks in the ice pans and stay inside them in order to avoid the gigantic pressure from the hummocks. And we continued to forge ahead, since so long as one remains on the Greenland side of the bay the current puts him to the north. It is a well-known fact that in arctic waters the current follows him who keeps land to starboard.

We got across Melville Bay without mishap, but as soon as we had passed through this stretch which we had dreaded so much we ran into a fierce gale that whipped our sails, and our weak motor was no match for it. Where we were driven I have never discovered, and it is a miracle that we were not thrown up onto the Parry Islands or that we got through at all. In the middle of the storm our boat was tossed against an iceberg and our rudder cracked. I ran out to try to take in the foresails, but at that moment the iceberg eased over and tossed great cakes onto the deck. Chunks of ice broke from the berg and, churning about in the water, cracked off our propeller blades like the daintiest chips.

And there we were, powerless in the gale, when the wind increased suddenly, as it often does in the far north, and blew us straight into a snug little harbor, North Star Bay.

We were seen by the natives, and they ran out to greet us. They had spotted us the day before, tossing about in the storm, but thought we had surely been wrecked by now, and they had tried to figure out where they might find some of the wreckage and lumber which would drift in. "If we had known Knud Rasmussen was on board," they said, "we would have realized he would make harbor."

We unloaded our goods and settled down. We had not planned to make this our station, but we had no alternative; afterward we found it to be the best location in the whole district.

It was possible to bank our small boat at low tide and screw two new blades onto the propeller, and after a few days we watched it sail away leaving us, two lone white men, in a little world of North Greenland Eskimos.

We had brought a globe with us, and it stood on a box outside the tent in which we lived during the summer. I saw a group of Eskimos gathered around it listening to something an ancient native was saying, something I did not understand. As I was young and conceited, I approached them to explain in my broken Eskimo. Knud Rasmussen listened for a moment, and then said: "You don't need to interrupt him. He was just lecturing to them about natural conditions in the Antarctic."

Then I heard the old man—this was in 1910—tell the younger men that far, far south penguins could exist, and that seals and birds were afraid of nothing, because there were no wild animals to prey upon them as they did here in the North.

I have recalled this many times since when I have heard people asking silly questions about why there are penguins at the South Pole and none at the North, etc.

A few days after our arrival in North Star Bay a steamer put into port. It was the *Beautic*, commanded by the famous Captain Bob Bartlett and chartered by Harry Whitney and Paul Rainey.

Whitney was no stranger in these waters, as he had once wintered at Etah. He was the man who had rescued Dr. Cook, when that curious person came home from his "North Pole" trip. Cook and his two fellows had no dogs and had walked all the way from Cape Sparbo at Jones Sound, and they were completely done in. Harry Whitney was, at the time, at Anoritoq. He saw three microscopic dots far out on the ice and went to investigate. Whitney took Dr. Cook on his sled and brought him to shore.

Cook was very weak, and if it had not been for Harry Whitney, who nursed him back to health, and a gale which broke up the ice immediately, the doctor would never have been able to foist his trickery upon the world. While Whitney never believed in Dr. Cook, he did not take the trouble to go for the instruments which Cook said he had left at Etah. Neither did he question the two Eskimo boys, Itukusuk and Apilak, who had accompanied Dr. Cook. He merely took it for granted that nobody would believe Cook's story—he did not take into consideration the gullibility of the civilized world concerning events in out-of-the-way places.

Later on I got hold of the "instruments"—a common sextant, which could tell nothing. Itukusuk sold it to me, glad to be rid of it, because Cook had paid him only a few boxes of matches for a year and a half's work. Besides, Itukusuk had lost his wife during his absence to a stronger man.

He told me that he had been happily married when Cook took him on his expedition and that he had to leave his wife alone in Etah when he went away. Shortly afterward Admiral Peary was looking for Eskimos to accompany him to the North Pole, and he took Itukusuk's wife with him as a seamstress. When the expedition was stationed at Cape Columbia on Ellesmere Land, Peary gave the girl away to a young hunter in need of a wife.

Itukusuk returned from his trip more than a year later to find his wife was still at Cape Columbia with Peary's Expedition. Peary had traded all of the belongings Cook had left in Etah for furs. There was, therefore, nothing left except a few matchboxes. These Cook gave to Itukusuk as his whole reward for the trip and hurried south to avoid meeting Peary.

Shortly afterward Peary returned from his victorious trip to the North Pole. This was his last expedition, and he was saying good-by to the Eskimos whom he had known for many years. Peary never failed to pay well for everything he got, and on this occasion his rewards were more generous than ever. He allowed all the Eskimos whose marriages he had arranged to keep their women forever. And so Itukusuk was left with three matchboxes and no wife.

Before he departed Peary told the Eskimos that Cook was "no good." This was a further humiliation for Itukusuk, who had been Cook's guide, and he kept quietly in the background and did not even ask for the return of his wife.

I gave him an alarm clock for the sextant, which he immediately took apart and divided among his many friends and relatives.

10

OUR FIRST PROBLEM WAS TO SECURE MEAT FOR OUR DOGS. THAT is, in fact, the greatest problem of the North. Eskimos take great pride in their dogs and keep far too many of them. Humans and dogs eat exactly the same things, but the amount consumed by the natives is trifling compared with what the dogs demand.

It is an Eskimo custom to present everyone with a portion of meat at the killing of a big piece of game. Which means, of course, every *man* except the man who owns no dogs.

I became aware of this practice the first day we went out after walrus. They were at that time to be found directly across the fjord, and, as we had brought a sailboat along, it was comparatively easy for us to get over. Some of the men in kayaks take after the big beast and hurl their harpoons into him. The harpoon is in reality a spear with a loose point. On striking the walrus the handle falls off, but the point which penetrates the skin is attached to a line ending in a bladder to keep the walrus afloat after it is dead. Also fastened to the line is a kind of drift anchor of hide stretched across a square wooden frame, which prevents the walrus from traveling too far. After the harpoon is secured in the animal the killing must be done, for the harpoon point is only caught beneath the skin. This is accomplished by spears which penetrate the walrus' lungs and intestines, but it takes time, skill, and bravery, as the natives cannot hurl the heavy spears from great distances; and if the spear sticks into the walrus without killing it, the man has to row close enough to the prey to yank the spear out again, an extremely dangerous maneuver. Consequently, it is much better for the killing to be done from a larger boat, from which guns can be fired and a fast kill made. Afterward, the boat is of great use to tow the carcass ashore.

It is always great sport to haul a walrus to shore and cut it up. As often as possible we let the tide beach it and then await low tide to carve it. Every man receives his share, and he knows from long precedent exactly what portion is his. The man who first puts his harpoon into the animal is the owner or procurer of the walrus and gets the credit for it. As reward he takes the head, the left flipper, the guts, and especially the heart. Number two takes the right forepart, but none of the insides; number three the left rear portion, and so forth. If there are more men the whole thing is divided into more parts. If twelve boys are around, twelve parts are given out. I was lucky the first time to get a forepart, because I had killed the animal after someone else had harpooned it.

I thanked the hunter as I found myself suddenly the possessor

of several hundred pounds of meat. Later on at camp he told me
not to thank anyone for meat:

"Up in our country we are human! And since we are human
we help each other. We don't like to hear anybody say thanks
for that. If I get something today you may get it tomorrow.
Some men never kill anything because they are seldom lucky or
they may not be able to run or row as fast as others. Therefore
they would feel unhappy to have to be thankful to their fellows
all the time. And it would not be fun for the big hunter to feel
that other men were constantly humbled by him. Then his pleasure would die. Up here we say that by gifts one makes slaves,
and by whips one makes dogs."

I have come to understand the truth of his words. The polar
Eskimos were a free people when we met them.

When we had killed enough animals we stored the meat in
huge piles to be picked up later by dog sled. The piles had to
be built in a particular way so that the meat would be protected
by stones and the whole thing freeze solid in winter. Small stones
had to be placed next to the meat, larger ones outside. If the
meat should freeze to the large stones we could never get it loose
in winter. The Eskimos taught me the trick, and I was proud to
have my own meat pile from my own catch. I thought it was
enough to last forever. I had no idea how short-lived the meat
pile is when guests are free to help themselves.

The Eskimos are great visitors, and as soon as a man has
finished his caches he begins to make the rounds. Then the
simplest method of bragging is for the host to stuff his visitor's
dogs so full of meat that they can eat no more. We took our dogs
visiting.

The job of house building was left to me. Knud explained
that we must get together sufficient food for the winter, as we
had planned to live off the land. And after one day of carpentry
he went off walrus hunting, leaving me with two young boys to
finish the house. We had brought along a kind of prefabricated
house that was hard to put together and not suitable for the
Arctic. The outside walls were filled with some kind of sticky
plaster which the children discovered would hold the stones they
threw at it. In due time we managed to cover it with wooden
boards, and the house is intact today. It is the local schoolhouse,
at which I always looked with pride whenever I went back to
Greenland.

When Knud returned he organized a series of house-warming parties which lasted for two weeks. There were eight Eskimo families living in North Star Bay, and they managed to keep things going day and night. Knud could always wangle from them what he wanted, whether it was food or clothing.

He was something of a dandy and always carried a pair of scissors for cutting his hair and beard. Even in the most biting cold he washed his face every day with walrus blubber, and his footwear was the most beautiful in the Arctic.

The North Greenland Eskimos make their stockings of hare-skin and the kamiks of the softest leather with a stuffing of dried grass between the double soles. The best kamiks call for expert needlework and somehow Knud always got an Eskimo woman to make a pair for him, in spite of this violation of their matrimonial customs. Their sexual code is very strict, but there is nothing wrong in a man's letting his wife give physical pleasure to other men, provided the husband grants permission. It flatters the family if the wife is found delectable. In the matter of sewing, however, they are very strict, and it is considered worse for a woman to sew for another man than to sleep with him without her husband's consent, and she is punished mercilessly. But a man rarely gives permission for his wife to sew for someone else.

Under their system, the blame for everything always rests upon the husband, who is ruler and dictator of the household. Therefore you cannot go to a woman and order anything from her. She belongs to her husband, and he is the one to be asked. After he consents, she must carry out the task for you, but not before.

This may give the impression that the poor women are the underdogs. Quite the opposite is true, yet a rigid etiquette is preserved. A couple is a unit; the man is the mouthpiece, the woman the brains—unofficially, of course. If you want an Eskimo to do something, it is always good politics to interest his wife in the task first—then you may be sure he will do it.

In my innocence I asked several women to make some kamiks for me, and I could not understand their scornful laughter until Knud explained that I must first ask permission of the husband and then reward him. The husband would always suggest payment in the most indirect way. "A piece of straight wood may be used for a harpoon," he might mumble softly to himself. "If one had some tobacco one might smoke a pipe." Such statements of fact could not be ignored.

Knud had his own technique. He would observe the footwear of an Eskimo and then openly admire it. "Really well-made kamiks! A woman who can sew like that is indeed precious and rare." This challenge never failed. The man would suggest that his wife would be proud to make a pair for the great Knud. "It's no use," Knud would declare. "I have no skins, and you cannot be expected to have more than you and your family need." The second challenge was quickly accepted. "My poor wife is always bothered by too many skins. She envies the wives of hunters who bring home nothing from their trips. Woman, leave this gathering of men and hurry home to make kamiks for the great Knud!"

The next morning the proud husband and wife would present Knud with the result of a long night's work, and Knud would view the gift critically. "I appreciate this sign of friendship," he would say. "The trouble is I am very particular when it comes to footwear. I can only use the most exquisite kamiks. These are beautiful and it's not your fault that the seams are a trifle irregular. You have made me proud by your gift. I shall present you with something suitable in return, but I regret that I cannot use these kamiks."

With truly great heroism the Eskimo would manage to laugh at this blow to his vanity and would answer: "It has finally been proved that the great Knud has a poor sense of humor. The great man does not understand that my wife is only using these poor skins as measurements. And now that she knows the exact fit she will make a decent pair of kamiks."

Next morning Knud would be presented with the most wonderful kamiks ever seen in the settlement, which he graciously would accept. It was also typical of him that he would keep the sample kamiks as well.

Knud and I decided to make separate trips in order to advertise our newly established trading post and to let the Eskimos know their fox furs could be exchanged to great advantage at our place. In the meantime I had given a new name to our settlement. Knud thought of calling the place Knudsminde or Knudshope, but we agreed such a name would be pretentious. I suggested Thule, from the expression *ultima Thule* which means, of course, north of everything and everybody. Knud agreed, and thus our station was named Thule, since to become world famous.

Knud went south for his final trip while I went north.

11

THE DOGS WE HAD BROUGHT WITH US FROM DANISH GREENLAND STILL had full sets of teeth, and we were asked by the natives to cut them off or dull them. In the south the dogs run wild the whole summer—and winter too, when not in use—and forage for themselves, eating anything except wood and stone and iron. But where we lived the rules were different. Here the dogs were tied up so that we could leave anything about without fearing its destruction.

It is impossible to tie dogs with sealskin lines if the animals have the full use of their teeth. Therefore the long sharp teeth which the dog uses for tearing and slashing must be dulled. This is accomplished easily with puppies by using a stone or a file to flatten them. But ours were full-grown dogs, and the operation had to be performed with a hammer. To handle the poor animal for this operation, he must be stupefied—hung by the neck until he is unconscious. This state is reached when his excrement drops from him. Then he is hurriedly let down, his jaws pried apart and held by two skin lines, while his teeth are flattened with a hammer. This is, of course, a cruel operation, but it apparently does not hurt the dogs very much. Time after time I have seen them jump up and shake their heads a little, then run off to eat or fight or whatever comes into their minds.

Consequently, the dogs cannot eat frozen meat in winter, and it is always a matter of great concern to thaw it for them. They are fed mostly on walrus hide cut into large chunks just possible for the dogs to swallow. They are also fed in a group so that, in order to get enough, each animal must wolf his food without waiting to masticate it. While to the casual observer this seems unnecessarily cruel, the scheme is entirely practical. Since the animals are unable to chew the meat, it requires a long time for digestion and remains in their stomachs for several days, thus giving the dogs an impression of having been filled up recently.

On sled trips we feed our dogs every second day, and at home, during the winter when they are doing no work, every third day. Later on when it is warmer they require less food, and in summer, when they are tethered along a brook or at some pond, they need to be fed no oftener than once a week. The dogs realize that when they are at last let to food they must store up for a long interval. They are never as good on trips the days after they have been fed as when they are expecting food at night and are hungry.

This custom preserves the wild nature of the dogs, of invaluable aid on bear hunts, but has come about chiefly because of the rigorous nature of the land.

One of my tasks on my trip north was to procure some caribou skins. Since the best way to do this is to shoot the animals oneself, I set out with my dogs in company with a grand old couple, Asayuk and Anarwree.

They were childless, and she dominated him completely. Nevertheless, Asayuk was the most intelligent man I met up there. Ingenious, mild, soft-spoken, and boasting the longest hair of the tribe, he took the lead of our little caravan. His wife was famous for her sharp tongue, but was respected for her ability as a hunter and sewer. She had a reputation of having "got everything"—which meant that she had killed bear, walrus, musk oxen, caribou, seal, and all manner of birds.

We were to go inland to a nunatak inside our home glacier, and I was reminded of my experiences on the east side of Greenland. Here the crevasses were just as deep and broad, but Asayuk found a way in and out between them, seemed to know instinctively where they were, and took us safely to the land we sought.

High up in the nunatak we came upon old abandoned huts. Asayuk told me of desperate men who had run away from home and gone into the mountains to get away from their fellow men. They became ghosts or were taken by the Inland people, the Eqidleet. He told me from his own experience of one such person, a man who was driven mad by a woman.

It is funny, but it is told, he said—and Asayuk was known to speak only the truth—that there are men born who care for one particular woman, and it takes them seven years to forget her. A certain young man had taken a girl from her family and lived with her at Inglefield Gulf. He made himself conspicuous by speaking of her when out hunting with other men. When they stayed out overnight and all slept together he regretted that he could not be at home with his wife, and even mentioned her name without shame on several occasions. At last some of the dignified hunters remonstrated with him. It is well known that a man who reveals such dependence upon a woman is likely to offend the seals, as they do not care to be hunted by inferior persons. Therefore, he was told either to stay at home and sew and care for the lamps or employ his mouth for the talk of men.

But the poor boy persisted. Then one day a big hunter with many children to care for lost his wife. And while the hunter could have taken a widow experienced in housekeeping, he thought it would be amusing to take the young man's wife and see if he dared fight for her.

The frantic young husband did his best, but he was not permitted to kill the hunter as that would have been too great a loss to the tribe. He was advised to use his arms and strength, or depend upon the speed of his dogs to recapture her. Instead, he did nothing but sit upon a stone for three days and cry like a baby. Even his wife said to the other women that he had left his dignity behind in the tent where they had lived.

When the young man saw her laugh and chide him for his weakness he determined to live no longer with his people; he went inland and became a *qivitoq*—a ghost who may never return home.

He was seen once from a distance, but as those who saw him felt he was about to approach, they fled. He had not been heard of for many years until a hunter went upcountry for caribou and found his dead body in a small hut.

Asayuk had known the young man and told me that he was only a boy, but he remembered that the other men had kidded him because he was never willing to lend his wife or borrow other men's wives.

This is the story of a man who died because of his belief in one, and only one, woman!

After our successful trip we decided to visit Anarwree's brother at Inglefield Gulf. It was a long trip, especially in summer, but the brother had a number of small children who would enjoy the delicious things we had to bring them, and, furthermore, Anarwree was anxious to hear the news of the white men settling among them. Knud Rasmussen was known to everyone and almost recognized as a member of the tribe, but no one had heard of me, and it gave Anarwree a certain eminence to accompany me. Visits in the summertime are almost without precedent, and Anarwree and I set out alone. We left our sleds at a spot on the glacier close to the land we headed for.

The fall had set in, and while it was not yet very cold Anarwree and I found that we could walk across Olriks Bay on the young ice. As soon as ice turns white it will hold a man's weight if he steps carefully.

We stopped at a cache and helped ourselves to meat. It was obvious to Anarwree that the cache had been made by a certain man named Sigdloo, who always left his meat in a stone grave. As she had not thought Sigdloo anywhere near this country it caused her no little concern, and that night, which we spent in a stone hut we had discovered on the way, Arnarwree took the occasion to question her foot ghost about it. This she did by tying a string around her foot and asking it a question: if the answer was yes, she could lift her foot; if it was no, no power on earth could get her foot off the ground.

She could not get her foot off the ground, and she said she could tell by this that someone had been killed. She did not dare attempt to determine who it was that was dead, for it might well be one of her relatives, whose bereaved family should certainly not be visited in time of mourning. If we approached unaware of the disaster we could not be blamed; therefore there was no point in asking the ghost too many questions.

Vastly excited, we resumed our journey next morning. I was stiff from having slept on the barren ground but felt rested and in an hour or so completely thawed out. We passed a big lake famous for its fine salmon. The natives from roundabout were fishing. Formerly, when caribou had been abundant, fishing was a job for women and children, for it was unsportsmanlike. "Fish don't fly away," the men declared.

We walked and walked across a vast plain, dotted with small stone huts, *kramats,* where hunters had dwelt on their trips, and a few ruins of more permanent residences which had been lived in by natives who had no kayaks and must spend the summers collecting food away from the sea.

There is always ice in the big lake at Inglefield Gulf, but during the summer only a large pan of it remains, floating about and shifting from side to side with the wind. Along the shore the shallow water affords a grand playground for the children. Young salmon gather here too, seeking refuge from the large fish. The children run out into the shallows and gather the baby salmon up with their bare hands and eat them raw. They think it most amusing to feel the fish squirming about their mouths and throats.

It is amazing that the children can spend whole days in the ice-cold water without apparent harm. At least they receive the benefit of a long bath, perhaps their last, for when they stop playing with fish their opportunities for baths are gone forever.

By this time we could cross the lake on the new ice, and we felt sure that we would reach the village before the sun dropped below the horizon for the night. Suddenly we saw two people in the distance coming toward us. While no one has enemies in this country it is always a little problem to meet strangers—they may be embarrassed or not want to meet you—and we stopped to discuss our next move. While we talked the other two advanced at a fast pace; we could see that they were a man and a woman. Anarwree identified them as Odark and Meqo, the latter not his wife. Anarwree informed me of this, but when we met no comment was made to this effort.

Odark's first questions were to determine who I was and what I was doing here. He was vastly pleased when he learned that I was the partner of Knud Rasmussen, who was his best friend. After some discussion he and Meqo decided to return to the settlement and entertain us. They felt that there was a party in prospect and did not want to miss out on it.

We found Odark's two brothers, his cousins, and countless relatives at Inglefield Gulf—in fact, Odark was related to everyone. After the welcome we were fed with cooked caribou, dried narwhal and rotten seal meat. After which the conversation ebbed, though I felt that not all had been told that there was to be told. Nothing is dearer to an Eskimo than to sit quiet, knowing that he has some sensational news to drop into the conversation if he so desires.

Anarwree was at a disadvantage as I was present and she could not talk about me. But she could, and did at great length, discuss our ship and the different sailors who had been with us. Our house was subjected to minute discussions as was Vivi, who had originally come from Inglefield Gulf and was remembered by everyone. The fact that Vivi now spoke a different dialect was subjected to some friendly criticism. But after two days these subjects were squeezed dry. It was only then that we learned what had happened in Inglefield.

Three sleeps before we had arrived Odark and Sigdloo had killed a man and annexed two of his wives!

Odark and Sigdloo had both been with Harry Whitney on his trip, and from that glorious journey they had brought home loads of stuff sent them as gifts by Admiral Peary, whose companions they had been on his polar expedition. Sigdloo, as his special prize, had a cracker barrel so large that he could not keep it inside his tent. Whenever he wanted crackers he went down to the beach, where he had left the barrel.

In the same community lived Uvisakavsik, a great hunter and important citizen, but one who had lost the respect of his people after he had returned from America, where Peary had taken him following an expedition to the Pole. It was evident to everyone that the man had taken leave of his senses. When he came ashore he lost no time in telling the most incredible yarns.

He said that he had seen people living in big houses on top of each other, like auks in the bird cliffs. His audience let that pass. Perhaps Uvisakavsik had made a mistake. But he also told them that he had seen more ships in the harbor of New York than there were icebergs in the fjord. Smiles flicked the corners of his listeners' mouths. How could anybody get wood enough to build so many ships? Then he related that he had seen real houses move on two iron bars, houses bigger than any tent, with walls of glass. Inside the houses sat many smiling people not in the least worried over their fate. Suddenly the whole house began to move away, and Uvisakavsik had seen no fear on the faces of the unfortunates trapped inside. While he had meditated this marvel he had seen several wagons roll past. There were neither dogs nor horses hitched to them, nor was there any smoke coming from them to account for the movement, as there was from ships.

His people listened patiently and questioned. No animals to haul, no smoke to indicate machinery inside. That did not sound so good.

Uvisakavsik kept on. He had viewed so many houses that it was impossible to see past them into the country. The paths between these houses reminded him of clefts in the mountains. Even the roads were made by human beings and covered with a smooth material which was neither cold, like ice, nor transparent.

His audience was plainly uneasy now. This was too much. And when he persisted, on top of everything else, that he had talked into a little handle that carried his voice through a tiny thread to Peary, who was, at the time, several sleeps away, and that Uvisakavsik had spoken clearly to him without being forced to shout, his sentence was settled.

Wise old Sorqaq, medicine man of the tribe, stepped forward and addressed the newly arrived man solemnly:

"Uvisakavsik! It appears that you have been far away and no longer know the truth. Go to the women with your lies!"

After that he was never believed. A big liar, an undependable man!

Shortly after, he was forced to take the consequences of his lying. Rather than suffer the opprobrium of his people he went farther south for a while. But after some years he returned, still retaining some of the white men's habits. He wanted a flag, and, having a pole, he planted it in the ground and hoisted a bearskin to wave in the wind.

Sorqaq held a séance and discovered that this was shocking to the bears, who would keep away from the coast until the skin was brought down. Still Uvisakavsik could not be persuaded to strike his colors.

He had one wife, but he thought it would prove his strength if he had two, so he took another one, in spite of the scarcity of women in the tribe. Not to be outdone, the other hunters decided to keep two women in their houses, which made Uvisakavsik determine to have three. He could easily afford three and, since he was very strong, could steal the wife of a man weaker than himself.

At this propitious moment the Whitney Expedition came through and took with it a boy whose wife Uvisakavsik had admired. There were left in the community only two men who were unafraid of him—Sigdloo and Odark. Odark's wife was already dead, and he lived with his brothers close to the bad man's camp. Sigdloo had formerly been on friendly terms with Uvisakavsik, and the two men had exchanged wives for a while. Any woman who lived with Uvisakavsik was considered fortunate, because he always had plenty of meat for the winter.

But at length Uvisakavsik became unbearable. He had not been with the Whitney Expedition and had received no gifts. Yet he had developed a taste for white men's food during his trip with

Peary, and the only means by which he could satisfy this craving was visiting Sigdloo in his tent. Sigdloo would not have grudged him crackers, but Uvisakavsik insisted upon boasting and lying while he ate. He told of the meals he had eaten in the white men's country, of seeing piles of bread higher than the meat pile, and of certain places where no meat was eaten at all. He had seen coffee and tea served several times each day with as much sugar as anyone desired. Then he said he had seen berries hanging from trees high above his head, and he had only to shake the trees and the berries fell into his hands. Of course, everyone knew that there were tall trees, but saying that berries grew on them was absurd.

Sigdloo told him to come and have tea and crackers as often as he desired, but not to think he could make a fool of him. Uvisakavsik was insulted and said that this was the last time he would ever come to Sigdloo for crackers. Next time the crackers were to be served in his own house.

Sigdloo did not understand this, but the following day when he went after crackers Uvisakavsik warned him to keep away, as he had appropriated the whole depot at the beach. And the next day when Sigdloo wanted some of his belongings he heard a bullet whistle over his head and had to drop down behind his own boxes. Each time he attempted to get up a shot sang over his head, and he had to lie still a long time before he dared crawl home.

Shortly afterward Uvisakavsik waylaid Alakrasina, the wife he had loaned to Sigdloo, and warned her not to return to Sigdloo again. Thus the situation reached a climax, and that night, as the sultan was sitting at home with his women, Sigdloo went to his friend Odark and poured out his misery. Odark did not say a word in reply but at once accompanied Sigdloo back to Inglefield Gulf.

The next day was fine and all the hunters went out to sea in their kayaks. Uvisakavsik harpooned a narwhal, and each man took his portion except Sigdloo, who refused to accept any part of it.

"A man is scared," said Uvisakavsik. No one answered.

In the evening Uvisakavsik was observed once more helping himself at the cracker barrel.

The following day the hunters went out again in kayaks. Sigdloo, waiting an opportune moment, raised his gun, and fired at Uvisakavsik. But he was not accustomed to shooting men—or perhaps his gun disapproved—for he only wounded him in the right shoulder. The wounded man made as if to aim his gun, but before he could get it to his shoulder Odark shot him through the head and he toppled out of his kayak and drowned.

Odark appropriated one of Uvisakavsik's wives, Meqo, known as the best sewer in the tribe and an extremely humorous woman. No one had ever seen her angry. Sigdloo took back Alakrasina, who was no great prize, but he preferred her to his former wife, whom he had traded to the dead man. Her name was Atitak, and she was, I thought, the only handsome one of the lot. Meqo, the much-wanted, was one-eyed. The third was taken by a smart young fellow, Apilak, who had been with Dr. Cook and had lost his wife during his absence. Apilak was an especially fine young man but was always involved in a tangle of love affairs.

This was the story Anarwree and I heard, and we were served meat killed by the murdered man. The murderer, Odark, was one of the finest men I have ever met. He had been Peary's right-hand man at the North Pole, and he told me that Captain Bartlett had given him permission to shoot Uvisakavsik. When collecting a crew of natives for his expedition Bartlett had said he had no use for Uvisakavsik and would not have him on his boat. To Odark this seemed sufficient excuse to shoot him. He realized, however, that white men disapproved of killing one another, and he had been afraid when he first saw me that I had come to take him away.

12

ANARWREE WAS IN A HURRY TO GET BACK TO THULE. THE BROTHER of Uvisakavsik lived in our community, and she knew that the news we brought with us would be a sensation.

The way home was easier, as ice now covered the fjords and the lakes. But the uneven surface of the ice was difficult for me, especially as the Eskimo men who went back with us, as is customary in the Arctic, had gone on ahead, leaving me to my own devices. They do not do this in a manner of purposeful neglect but are afraid of hurting a man's feelings by offering help which he may consider a criticism of his ability to take care of himself.

At last, on the nineteenth of October, came the day when the
sun dropped below the horizon for the winter. One might think
the natives would regret its going, but they rejoiced instead. The
long summer, with the sun always circling overhead, is tiresome.
We live in tents then, and it is impossible to make these dwellings
dark at any time. It is broad daylight when you wake up, and
broad daylight when you go to sleep. Your eyes ache for darkness, and as soon as the sun disappears the women cry out in
pleasure:

"Oh, joy and happiness! Now at last the sun is away. Now
comes the winter when we shall hear from the other fjords, and
we ourselves shall go and visit. Now comes the time of walrus
hunting and the seals will be at the blowholes. Joy and happiness!"

The winter season must be taken advantage of from the start.
For a short period before the snow falls it is possible for the hunters to walk in their bearskin soles on the ice in perfect silence.
The hunter can then listen to the yammering of the seals at the
blowholes and walk near enough to spear them before attracting
their attention. This is the best and easiest method of hunting
seals throughout the whole year, but it can be done only when
the ice is free of snow. It is comparatively safe, too, and, consequently, many natives prefer hunting seals to risking their lives
hunting bear.

The brother of the murdered Uvisakavsik was named Samik,
which means "Left Hand." He announced that because Sigdloo
had killed his brother, he was compelled to kill Sigdloo's brother
in return. Sigdloo had a younger brother, a peaceful man who
had had nothing to do with the whole affair. Everybody felt
sorry for him, and Knud Rasmussen decided to settle the matter.
He sent word to everyone involved that he wanted to see them
in our house. They all came and we gave them coffee and tobacco,
and the atmosphere was very harmonious.

Knud opened the proceedings with a speech. He was deeply
grieved, he said, that his old friend Uvisakavsik was no more.
But grief was of no use to the living, and the whole matter must
be settled quickly. It was natural that Samik should want to
avenge his brother, but the inevitable result would be that Samik
himself would be killed in return. However, not to kill a man
when you have the right to kill is the most honorable thing to do.
That you could kill a man but deliberately neglect to do so

shows great courage. And Knud added that he could not afford to let good hunters kill each other, since we were in need of the valuable furs they would get for us.

The problem was discussed calmly, and the Eskimos agreed it might be a good idea to follow Knud's advice. Sigdloo's brother was satisfied that he was not going to be killed, and Samik was proud of his magnanimous decision not to commit murder. All were happy at the prospect of being able to live on to see the strange results of having white men in their midst.

To seal the bargain Knud decided that Sigdloo's brother should live in our house for an indefinite period and that his whole catch should go to Knud as long as he stayed with us. In addition Knud was to get five fox furs from each member of our peace council, as an expression of their satisfaction with the decision.

Rumors of what had happened traveled up and down the coast. The Eskimos were profoundly impressed by the changes taking place in Greenland.

We decided that I should try to cross Melville Bay that winter and secure from the government post at Tasiussak a number of things which we had neglected to bring with us from Denmark. The time of year was favorable because, in spite of the darkness, we had a bright moon and calm skies. Knud was to remain at the post during my absence.

It may seem strange to the average reader that Knud Rasmussen and I so constantly occupied our time with traveling in a land where travel was so hazardous. Perhaps the principal excuse for our excursions was to break the monotony which moves in like the Arctic's gray, impenetrable fog. Then one does not need much excuse to travel, or do anything out of the ordinary, conditions permitting. While we seldom went recklessly into danger, we were always aware that it might suddenly confront us if we moved outside our house, but even certain peril was better than sitting about with no prospect of change in routine ahead of us.

Besides, the more we traveled the more natives we made our friends and the better was our prospect of making our trading post a financial success.

I had new clothes, including my first, and last, foxskin coat. (Foxskin is considered very warm, but it is not tough, and unless one is careful he is apt to rip a hole in it which may result in death on the trail.) I also had new bearskin pants and several pairs of well-fitting boots. The evening before I left, a young Eskimo girl came to the house bringing a pair of mittens she had sewn, saying that "someone" had left them at her home. I wondered, but I could not understand the reason for the gift. Later I learned that she had made them in order to thank me for some pieces of bread she had eaten one day while visiting us. I did not remember ever having seen her, but young girls are not especially conspicuous in that tribe. Fathers do not want to waste their fine animal pelts on grown girls. It is up to their future husbands to dress them, since a husband is always anxious to have his wife look well and not disgrace him. Many wives wanted to trade especially fine foxskins to us for the manu-factured goods which we owned, only to have their husbands forbid it. They preferred their women to use the foxskins for their own adornment.

This girl was dressed in dogskin pants, so disgraceful in appearance that they considerably restricted her visiting. Yet nothing would persuade her to request better material from her mother. She also wore an old coat of her mother's, and most of the time she carried a little brother about with her in her hood. The mittens she brought me were none the less warm, and I bought her some fine presents in the south.

To travel long distances with new people is always interesting. I had with me four men, with old Asayuk as the leader. My way took me up across the icecap for a long distance, as the sea was still open around a few of the capes. After ascending the glacier I wondered how Asayuk could find his way. I learned later that, as the prevailing wind is from the southwest, the ridges in the snow—the so-called *sastrugi*—all point the same way; if the general direction toward one's destination is known, it is easy to hold to a straight course.

Cape York, on the route south, is the scene of many of the greatest events and much of the folklore of the Arctic. It was there that the natives first saw white men, and they still recount tales which have taken on the dignity of tradition.

At Cape York lived a very remarkable man and a great hunter—Angutidluarssuk. His house was small and did not re-veal a single sign that he was the best provider in the country. He could hardly walk, yet when the occasion demanded he could run like a deer.

One day as a number of us were standing about a blowhole

in the ice a bear approached us. Our dogs were tethered far away in order not to disturb the seals, so we all took off after him on foot. Out in front of us shot old Angutidluarssuk. Before the bear could reach open water the old man had it cornered. Instead of killing it, however, he waited until a little boy, who had never got a bear because he had no dogs, caught up with him. Angutidluarssuk let him spear it first. The boy was unable to kill it, but his harpoon was the first in the beast and the prey was technically his. Angutidluarssuk had killed the animal by the time we caught up with him, and those among the first to arrive shared in the skin. But the boy, whose pants were scraped almost clean of hair, got a whole new pair, and the rest half a piece each. There is enough hide for three pairs of pants on a bear. The meat was divided among all the others, and that evening as we camped on the ice and cooked the meat there were no words fine enough to praise the young man whose first bear it was.

As a snowstorm had made the ice bad we spent several days at Cape York passing the time in eating and visiting. Angutidluarssuk was noted for the lavish parties he gave and the excellence of his provender. One day as we were all sitting about a native's hut waiting for the meat to be cooked one of the men mentioned in passing that it was too bad the gale was so fierce that it prevented him from driving out with his dogs to secure some "oil-jammed" birds.

Apparently word of this remark spread fast, for shortly after we heard a voice outside shouting:

"Everyone is invited to Angutidluarssuk's house to eat *giviaq*."

Our mouths watered over the prospect, and we hurried to the party. It was difficult to walk in the gale, especially as the village at Cape York, Ingnanerk (The Slope), is situated on the face of a cliff. In spite of that, everyone from the village was gathered there ahead of us. The women had shed their boots and climbed back of the ledge where they chattered incessantly.

Angutidluarssuk sat at his place and asked us if it had been difficult to reach his house. He told us of a man who had fallen down the cliffs once a long time ago.

"Aye, aye, he thought he could jump from one step to the next. But he stepped on the air. And that was the end of Kimik, the man who walked on air."

This witticism fell rather flat, and he tried again to start the conversation rolling. But none of us was much interested in talking. Finally a great idea came to him: how about having a bite to eat?

That being what we had come for, we said we had never given it a thought, but if he offered us something we knew this was the place to find the best food in the world.

The old man laughed. "Well, there are some people who don't know much. I never have a thing fit to eat, and I am only happy when I eat in your houses. But, as I am a bad entertainer and you have witnessed my poor attempts, you may as well know the whole truth—I have nothing to offer. Still I understand Pita likes to view our squalor, and he may as well have his chance now."

After saying this the old man picked up a sealskin line and went outside. The rest of us sat about telling each other what an extremely talented man he was, and one man related how Angutidluarssuk never slept during the summer season when the seals basked on the ice. He came in with his sled loaded only to go right out again, and only rested when the weather was so bad that it drove all the seals into the water.

A few moments later we heard Angutidluarssuk's voice:

"Somebody would be of great help! This weak man cannot even haul in his own food."

Several youngsters leapt to their feet, ran out, and returned tugging at a line. The rest of us hauled too, exclaiming over the great weight of the thing on the other end of the line and doubting that we could possibly get it in the house. Finally a big poke of sealskin, frozen and covered with snow, came through the door, followed by our host, taking off his coat so that it would not thaw and become wet. His head was sprinkled with ice and snow, and he smiled his broadest, all-inclusive smile. As he entered he explained that he had gone out after some small birds as everyone had been talking about food:

"The thought then came to somebody that there was a poke of birds in a cache near here. And as the weather was favorable for bringing supplies, one took the dogs and went for it."

Of course, before he had even invited us to the party he had driven to the cache for the poke, and left it just outside on the ice.

We told each other that this was too much hospitality. Here

was something we could talk about for years, and we were sorry
he had to waste his food upon such poor, undignified folk. The
great Angutidluarssuk! Who had ever heard of his equal?

Angutidluarssuk straddled the poke on the floor and grabbed
an ax. We kept silent, for nothing is more interesting than
watching someone else work for one's benefit, and Angutidluarssuk chopped up part of the poke. All of it was frozen solid.
After half the thing was split to pieces he sat down and took a
portion of the mess—birds and feathers—in his hands, broke it to
bits, removed most of the feathers, and commenced to eat.

"As I said and as it was foreseen," he said, "the taste is awful!
Hereby everybody is asked to get out. My poor dogs will refuse
to eat this, and my reputation is ruined forever."

At this signal everyone jumped at the savory delicacy. Those
who had wives handed portions to them on the ledge. An eloquent silence, broken only by the crunching of bones, ruled over
the whole house.

I must tell you that we were eating little auks. These birds,
hardly bigger than starlings, live in such great numbers in the
cliffs nearby that the mountains seem alive. They come in early
summer and hatch their eggs. At that time the country is quite
different—the flutter of wings, song and babbling are over the
earth all day long. When night settles down the birds fly out to
sea and return to the cliffs at daybreak. They lay only one egg
each among the stones. These birds play an important part in
supporting life in the whole district. Their skins are used for
clothing, and shirts made of them are soft and warm. Auk meat,
too, is delicious. But they serve principally as a lure to the foxes
that haunt the same cliffs and collect caches of the birds during
the summer to last them through the darkness.

But here we were consuming a special delicacy—auks pickled
in oil. This is done by killing a seal and skinning it through its
mouth without splitting the skin. Not every hunter can do this,
but when it is accomplished satisfactorily it makes a magnificent
poke, because most of the seal blubber still clings to the skin.

The person intending to fill the hide takes it along with him
to a spot where the birds are thicker than fish in an aquarium
and, with a net attached to a long stick, he catches the auks as
they fly past, often bagging enough in one day to fill his sealskin,
which is then latched and covered with stones. The sun must not

reach it or the oil will turn rancid. During the summer the blubber turns to oil and soaks into the birds, which decompose slowly without interference from the air.

This makes a dish which tastes like nothing else in the world, and one loved by old and young alike. The white feathers turn pink, and may be easily plucked out. The birds are often eaten frozen, as we ate them, but some connoisseurs say they are better warmed up. In fact, frozen meat never tastes as strong as it does when it is thawed out.

After our hunger was dulled we had time to laugh and joke, and search among the remains for the viscera, especially the heart and the blood around it, which is frozen very hard and glues the teeth together as it thaws.

Angutidluarssuk and his charming old wife were glowing from their social success. The women on the ledge began to ask for more and now, when their husbands took them second helpings, they were particular, and sometimes refused: "No, I don't want this one. Give me that piece over there and cut off some of the feathers." They compared their birds and told stories of catching them in flight last summer, and as their spirits rose they became more demanding, some of them asking for water. Finally Qolugtinguaq jumped to his feet.

"What!" he exclaimed. "Can Angutidluarssuk furnish everything? Can he bring the spring into the house? It sounds to me as if the auks are back in the cliffs . . . Oh, I see that it is the women who jabber so loud. Let the men come outside so that the women will have room to do their talking!"

This quieted the more hilarious spirits for a moment, and some of the women were overcome with embarrassment. But not for long, since everyone was happy and the party had devoured more than a hundred pounds of meat.

One of the most talented visitors belched and nearly lifted the roof off the house, and all the others followed his example to prove to their host the enjoyment of his feast. Some others belched in quite another way, and this caused screams of merriment.

Angutidluarssuk was now a great man of the world, beaming at his good fortune in having pleased his guests. As soon as he made sure that his friends had eaten plenty, he plunged the dipper into the water bucket and passed it around. Every man filled his mouth, then bent forward to wash his hands in the

water trickling from his lips, and wiped his mouth and hands on
a fine blue foxskin. Angutidluarssuk said:

"Your hands may smell of my awful stuff and my shame endure longer than necessity demands!"

Now came the time for storytelling, but we were satiated
with pleasure; besides, we had a real job before us to reach home
again. As we left, Angutidluarssuk's old wife said:

"Somebody in this house is sorry that the children cannot
come and have a bite"—knowing full well that all the children
would visit her tomorrow.

I learned more about the old woman, Itusarssuk, and why she
was so fond of children. She was one of the great ladies of the
community, a worthy soul, gentle and kind and meek. Realizing
this, it came as a shock to me to discover that she had once killed
four of her own children.

A long time ago she had lived on Herbert Island alone with
her former husband and their children. She suffered the terrible
fate of watching him drown. He had been out in his kayak for
many hours and had fallen asleep. Itusarssuk could see him, but
he was so far out to sea that her voice could not reach him. Suddenly, as she looked at him, a wave upset his tiny craft. She saw
him threshing around in the water for a few minutes, and then
drift away, face down. She was alone and could do nothing to
rescue him. She was left to provide for her five children.

The summer was not far advanced, and they had not yet
brought their spring catch to the island, so she had little to eat.
There are almost no auks on Herbert Island, and she had to kill
and eat the dogs, hoping that some help would arrive. Once she
saw a dead whale float by the island, but she had no way of getting to it. Another time she saw two bears on an ice pan, and
in the far distance specks that were kayaks from other islands.
But among them were no relatives of her husband, and they did
not come to her.

She had to make her own house for the winter, and it was
hard for her, being only a woman. The children cried for food,
and when their eyes were not upon her, she cried too. Finally
they ate their clothes made of animal skins, and when nothing
more was at hand she knew that she had to end the pain for the
small children, so she hanged them. The oldest girl, about twelve
years of age, helped her mother hang the younger ones. After
three of them were dead, the eight-year-old boy refused to die.

He said that to die looked very unpleasant, to judge by the expression in the children's eyes. And he said that he would look out for himself until he was ready to die.

After he had run away, the girl herself fastened the noose around her neck, and said that perhaps after a while she would not feel the hunger. Her mother tightened the line, and soon the girl's misery was ended.

Itusarssuk's strength was entirely gone, and she could not even cry any more. After a while she took the bodies down and buried them. The girl's hand was raised, and refused to allow the mother to place it alongside her body. This was because she had never been possessed by a man.

Iggianguaq was the boy. He lived the whole summer on grass and the excrement of rabbits. Occasionally he killed a young gull, and he and his mother both held onto life. In the fall when the ice formed, Angutidluarssuk, then a young man, arrived and took her to his home. He never beat her, for he realized that she had had a hard time when she lived for so long with the specter of death.

This was the story told me of Itusarssuk, and was the reason she could never punish a child for anything he did, but took care of all the young people of the settlement.

13

THERE HAD BEEN A GALE. NEXT DAY, THOUGH THE WIND WAS STILL strong at Cape York, the experienced hunters knew that a few miles offshore the weather would be fine and calm. So, loaded down with meat for our dogs, we resumed our journey toward Tasiussak.

At that time it seemed to me a human impossibility to start out in a storm. The sleds were full of snow, and the helpers had to hang onto the supplies until they were lashed to the sled. It was difficult to get the dogs under way. The poor beasts, so close to the ground, had to face the stinging snow from which we could protect our faces.

But old man Asayuk swung his whip and off we went, and after an hour's drive we reached the calm, only to be confronted with a new difficulty—the darkness.

So long as one can follow old tracks he is safe, but we had to seek out new routes and try to avoid bad ice at the same time. The ice was still thin in places, the current shifting it to and fro, leaving great areas of open water so that we constantly had to shift our course. We tried to remain close to shore, but at times open water stretched between us and the dark mountains, so the wise old guide found it better to keep outside. Occasionally two pans of ice had separated for a long stretch, and then we could only follow the gap until we found a place where they came together.

I trusted Asayuk and followed him blindly, but the other three men felt that they could shift for themselves and go so far behind us that, after we had crossed a crack in the ice, the two pans yawned apart before they could cross over and we were separated. Still, none of them seemed to mind, for they knew that we would very likely come together again soon.

The dogs tired easily, for they do not like to run on ice which is not covered with snow. Salt-water ice is always wet and covered with a layer of moist salt. This eats into the dogs' paws, causing stubborn sores which are slow to heal. The dogs also needed water.

After a while even Asayuk did not know where we were. Then unexpectedly I saw an iceberg looming up directly ahead, and my head dogs fell into open water. Icebergs in the Arctic are always surrounded by clear water or very thin ice, even in the dead of winter. I was frightened and dared not run forward to help the dogs out, as the ice would not have supported me. Meanwhile Asayuk had disappeared. With the help of my harpoon stick I got hold of the traces, but they were in such a mess that it was impossible to haul in the swimming dogs by the lines. Then I tried to pull the sled backward, and by using all my strength got the animals out of the water.

After I had assured myself that I was in a safe place I untangled the traces. The sealskin lines had been in the water and instantly froze solid, and I had to use my bare hands to get them straight. The dogs, wet and shivering, tried to climb off the ice onto the sled, and it was almost an hour before I was ready to start off again.

And I started. But where?

The whip was now frozen and unwieldy, and the dogs were uneasy, as I was a poor driver and they had no confidence in me.

Where I went I do not know, but I trusted to the instinct of the dogs—in this instance a misplaced trust. Soon I felt a sickening movement, a tug at the runners, and discovered that the left sled runner had cut through the ice. When I tried to get off the sled my foot broke through.

One is helpless on new thin ice. I tried to make the dogs pull ahead, but they could not move the sled. I was lucky enough not to have everything, sled and all, suddenly vanish. Presently I discovered that the right runner had cut through also and that I sat upon a sled resting entirely on the crossbar. The dogs were sick of the sticky ice, and I could not get to them or even get off the sled.

There was nothing for me to do but wait. My mittens and boots were wet, yet I was afraid to move to keep myself warm. All about it was dark and quiet as the grave, and I could only sit, hoping that after some hours the ice would be thick enough to support me. I had not the faintest notion of what had become of my fellow travelers, nor did I care much at that moment. Finally I became so cold that I dared stand erect on the load—I might as well die one way as another—and swung my arms and even moved my feet, but each time I did so I could feel the movement of the sled settling into the ice.

I had no way of knowing how long I stayed there. But at last I could bear it no longer and decided upon a desperate plan —to cut the dogs loose so that they could save themselves, and then with my harpoon try to walk out of the thin ice. This would have been certain suicide, and I was saved from it by the long and despairing wail of a distant dog. I figured that the sound had come from one of the other teams. I answered by pulling in one of my dogs and beating him until he whined and his teammates let out a ululation of sympathy which could be heard for miles in the calm night. Then I listened attentively; after a few moments there was an answering howl.

After what seemed hours I saw a tiny flare in the darkness— the light of a match! But I could not answer it. Again I swore because I did not smoke and carried no matches. I saw six matches flare and die, and I could only beat a dog each time and try to make myself heard. But I received no answer, and the signals ceased. More than anything I wanted to hear a voice, but the only sound was the crashing of the ice pans as they were thrown together by the currents below us, currents which might send us all to hell at any moment.

More hours passed, and I almost lost the spirit the sight of the matches had given me.

And then, from far off, I heard a shout. I eased myself to my feet and answered:

"Naw! Naw!"

I yelled louder. Nothing happened. Then I heard the voice again. Apparently the man was trying to explain something to me, but I did not understand Eskimo any too well and his voice was almost drowned in the voice of the sea. I sat down again. From time to time I stood up and shouted, and sometimes received an answer, sometimes not.

Several more hours passed, and at last I could distinctly hear the voice shouting, the voice of my friend Asayuk:

"I am coming."

How his message warmed me! And yet it took many hours before he came near.

Finally he was within talking distance, and I knew the reason: he was in the same state as myself. I yelled:

"How is it, then, that you are coming nearer to me?"

"I am drifting!"

Fortune then, and not any of our efforts, was bringing us together. We could hear ice crashing around us, but we did not care much. Asayuk told me he had been in the water, but was not seriously wet. Then I thought I could see him, but I must have been mistaken, for he said he could not yet see me. He asked me to light a match, and I told him I had none.

He decided that he would sacrifice his last matches and let me try to walk over to him. I was to tie my harpoon line to my leg and thus have a means of returning to my sled.

It worked as we had planned, and the ice did not crack beneath me now. But I could not see Asayuk when I was at the end of my line. I added my whip to the harpoon line and from the end of this I could just make out his dogs, and I dared drop my guiding line and struggle out to reach him. He assured me that we could easily find my tracks back to the sled as it would soon be daylight—by which he meant a dull red glare on the horizon to the south, against which it is possible for a few hours to see the silhouette of a man.

We were overjoyed to be together but had no time to waste in congratulating ourselves, for we must immediately try to get off this wretched ice. I helped him pry his sled runners loose. We accomplished it by unloading and distributing the load over a large area of ice, and then pulling the sled up. We reloaded and got his dogs going. They were wet through and thirsty, and could scarcely crawl. Then we drove to my sled, but we dared not go too near as the ice would not permit it, and we had to approach with the utmost care.

At last we were ready to travel—but again, where to go? Asayuk went out to investigate the ice. When he returned he said we must wait, and meanwhile we had better eat some meat and frozen bear fat. It was fine, and gave us courage.

We could feel that we were drifting. Asayuk said that we could not expect to remain long where we were and should place our sleds a short distance from each other so as not to put too great a load upon one section of the ice.

The wise old man was an authority on natural science in his own country. Not a secret was hidden from him. He explained to me that salt-water ice is tough and flexible—it can bend under a sled and not break. You can see the ice bending under your team, a wave rises between the dogs and the sled, and the sled will skim along in the trough of the wave. The great danger is in driving so fast that the sled runners cut through the crest.

He also told me that so long as ice is black there is no trusting it, but when it turns white it can usually be depended upon. Therefore traveling in the dark of winter is dangerous because the dog driver cannot detect the shade of the ice.

As I sat waiting I realized that already I had spent almost twenty-four hours on the ice.

Added to this, it was Christmas Day!

I had hoped to reach Tasiussak this evening and would have done so if we had not landed in this predicament.

I watched the silent stars glow brighter over our heads—that meant cold weather and the ice strengthening. I have no idea how long I celebrated Christmas in this futile fashion, but at last Asayuk said he thought we could go on. I don't know what had decided him, but I thought I would go crazy if we did not do something besides sit and wait for the ocean to freeze over.

We got our dogs in order, and Asayuk insisted on walking ahead, stepping in his padding, soft-footed fashion, cautious of his way and testing the ice now and then with a spear. He walked, and I envied him. My feet were numb, but I had to sit still and follow him with my team, cracking my whip to the aft in order to prevent his dogs from running ahead of me to catch up with their master. Presently he came back, jumped on his sled, and drove off in a straight line. I followed close behind, and I could finally see that the ice was a bit more solid.

Asayuk stopped a couple of times but never let me know what was on his mind. He only smiled when I asked him, and drove off again. Suddenly I heard him yelling at his dogs to stop, and I noticed at the same moment that my own team were leaning into their traces. They might have smelled something—a bear possibly—and this was dangerous. If it was a bear, they would bolt after it, and there would be no stopping them. But we quelled their eagerness, and the weight of the sled, heavier when there is no snow on the ice, dampened their enthusiasm. And then I saw a huge mountain looming up out of the darkness.

"What is that?" I shouted at Asayuk.

"Yes, what country can it be?" was all the answer I got. But it was something solid and substantial, and it looked particularly beautiful to me.

Unfortunately we found a broad streak of water between us and the shore. We followed it for a distance, and then Asayuk decided that we would have to go to the opposite end of the island. It was Sagdleq, he said, which is the native name for Bushman Island in the northern end of Melville Bay.

We finally reached a point opposite a cave. And we saw people there ahead of us—the other three members of our party, who had found this place and had been there for three days. We could still not reach them, as high tide laid a broad band of water between us. The ice, by rights, should have driven in to shore, but there were so many icebergs stranded here that the ice was firmly fastened to them and did not drift.

We shouted back and forth to our friends, and they told us how comfortable they were. There was nothing for us to do but await low tide—and since it was not yet at its height, I knew that it would be at least six hours before we could land.

Asayuk endeavored to make a float from a number of ice pans and ferry across. It took us several hours to hack loose first one pan and then another. After we had maneuvered the first one under the second, we found that it would not float with a sled

on it, so we had to cut a third and get that under the two already
fixed. At last it was ready, and it looked fine. Asayuk tried it first,
and his dogs all leapt on with him. Naturally they did not know
enough to spread themselves about the pan, but all huddled together on one corner, which tipped the float so much that the
lowest pan slipped out from under and shot up like a cork. The
next one did likewise, and Asayuk plunged into the water with
his dogs threshing about him. I finally managed to get hold of
him, but he had discovered that during our efforts to construct
a ferry the tide had ebbed and he could now stand on the bottom,
the water reaching only to his waist. The dogs swam back and
broke the ice before them in trying to crawl up. The whole thing
was a terrible mess.

I was thoroughly wet by now, and Asayuk stood before me
with the water dripping from him. Worst of all, his sled had
been in the water, too, and the bottom of the load was soaking
wet. But he was born to the North, and he took it like a man.

Then I saw a man loom out of the darkness. He was Mitseq,
one of our boys, and he had found a spot at a short distance
where the ice reached shore at low tide. We walked there and
found a perfect passage.

We hustled into the cave and found everything in the greatest
confusion. Even the fire was out, and there were no matches. We
decided that we would attend to the dogs first, and ourselves later.
The animals went madly for the snow, and had tangled their
traces into unbelievable knots. Trying to untangle twelve dogs
in complete darkness and Arctic weather is a job for any man.

But at last it was done and we could take stock of ourselves.
The three boys had been in great trouble. They, too, had been
separated and had had to waste their matches in locating each
other again. In searching for us they had been lucky enough to
run into Sagdleq in the dark. There they had stayed for the
first night, and after that the moon was gone and the ice so
treacherous that they had decided to remain until either the ice
was thicker or we turned up. In which event they could go on or,
at any rate, go bear hunting so that they would not return home
empty-handed. But at last we were all together, and the reunion
was pleasant.

But what can you do in a black cave without a light? There
are different methods of making a fire, of course, but here we
attempted the simplest one. We extracted the lead from a car-

tridge and divided the gunpowder, pouring half of it back into the cartridge. From the boxes we cut a number of sticks and arranged them in a pile over the other half of the powder, then discharged the blind cartridge directly into the powder on the ground. There was a blinding flash, and the sticks caught fire. After they were blazing steadily we added blubber, of which we had plenty, and soon were warming ourselves.

Old man Asayuk had to take off his wet clothes before the fire and had nothing to put on, as his sleeping bag was also wet. I offered him mine, and he was too miserable to refuse. We pushed the sled into the cave and stuffed his stiff body into the bag. Finally he thawed out, and we made hot soup for him and got him feeling well enough to smoke a pipe—and then everything was fine.

There was a fire for light and for cooking, and at last we could open our Christmas box and feast to our rescue from the ice.

The cave was dry and cozy. Outside the storm roared, but it did not concern us.

We added more blubber to the fire, and the boiling bear meat, covered with a thick, succulent layer of liquid fat, made us forget our troubles. When we had finished the food, our palates craved more delicate nourishment, and Asayuk suggested that we make tea. I filled the pot with ice and hung it over the fire, and soon the steam rolled forth in a white, hospitable stream. I poured Asyauk's cup first, he being the oldest and most dignified member of the party. Once more there was a tingling in his feet, and he began to feel better.

He sipped the tea, spluttered, and made indignant protest. I defended my way of brewing it, but when I tasted it I had to admit that the flavor was peculiar. I turned to the three boys, and they explained that, since they had no pot for boiling meat, they had been forced to use the teapot. This naturally had not improved the flavor of the tea, but furthermore Itukusunguaq had left the mittens which he used for handling dog food on top of the pot, and one of the fingers, well soaked in rotten blubber, had fallen into it. I had not seen it in the darkness.

Asayuk was furious and demanded fresh tea, but the boys kidded him and told him to take what was coming to him or make it himself. The latter he was unable to do, as he was without pants. But soon the first brew was drunk, and when I rinsed out the pot to make more I found, besides the mitten, two chunks of dog meat. That is never good for tea. In fact, tea is a refined drink even requiring clean water.

Sleeping in a cave in midwinter is not the most comfortable thing in the world, for the largest wall is made of wind and the floor of stone or ice. Asayuk was in my sleeping bag, but I could not justly complain of that, since Mitseq had brought no bag at all with him. We pushed our sleds inside and laid our skins on them. A rule often forgotten is that one must have a good, warm layer beneath him in order to rest well. If you have but one caribou skin for the night, put it under, not over, you. We piled up our skins and talked and drank chocolate and ate crackers and loads of food from the Christmas box. I remembered that this was my mother's birthday and told the men about her. Our fire blazed high, and presently I felt so warm that I took my coat off— the beautiful foxskin coat of which I was so proud. Twelve fine blue foxskins had gone into it, besides the white hood and blue tails about the face.

While I sat there and worked to get the ice out of my whiskers the cave suddenly rocked with thunder and a great stone was hurled out of the wall. Had it struck us, we should have been killed. I leapt to my feet and away from the fire, for I realized that the heat had caused the stone to drop. I explained this to Asayuk, but he said that the spirit of the mountain demanded darkness for his slumber because it was winter. He would not harm anyone, and if we left some meat for him when we departed, everything would be all right. I protested, but Asayuk read into the fact that none of us had been hit the proof of the friendliness of the spirit. If the spirit had meant to kill us he could have done so quite effectively by closing the mouth of the cave.

After the excitement was over I went back to my coat; it was frozen stiff, and I could not get my arms through it. It had been wet from my sweat. Unfortunately I tried to force my way into it, and my left arm broke through the thin skin. I found a needle in my kit and stitched it together, but I woke up during the night with the frost biting into my shoulder. Everyone else was asleep, and there was nothing I could do. I tried to put my mittens in the hole, but they only made it worse. When I finally fell asleep I dreamed that my shoulder had turned to marble.

In the morning I was unable to move my arm at all, and even after it had been warmed beside the fire I did not have complete use of it. We mended my coat again, but I was not used to the thin foxskins and my movements were apparently too vigorous, for it ripped over and over again, letting more and more of the frost into my shoulder. After struggling with it for two days I could sew no more. Asayuk patched it with a piece of sealskin which kept the wind out, but let the frost in, and during the whole trip I was conscious of the pain.

When we left our cave we had no choice of a place to go. Old Asayuk had to be dried out thoroughly, and the nearest settlement was Savigssuit, Meteorite Island, the island from which Robert Peary took the famous meteorites which had formerly been the source of all the knives and tools of the natives.

There were only three houses on the island, and we approached them while everyone slept. The ears of the natives, however, are attuned to all noises, and they hurried out to see who was coming.

A certain ritual has to be observed when arriving at any place in the Arctic. From the ice the visitors shout out:

"*Sainak Sunai! Sainak Sunai!* [Wonderful pleasure and happy to be here!]"

"*Assukiak, assukiak!* [Same to us, you are right!]" is the people's answer. They know immediately who is approaching.

It is a fact that everyone is known by his voice. It was annoying and troublesome to me at first when I met someone only to receive the answer: "*Oanga.* [It is I.]" And when I would repeat, "But who are you?" "*Oanga!*" was all he could be induced to say. No one would mention himself by name, and in a country where four months of the year are spent in total darkness—and most of the visiting is done during these months—it is difficult to recognize the natives by their voices. But I learned very soon. I had to.

We arrived at Savigssuit at a peculiarly embarrassing moment. A wife-trading for the night had just taken place, and the men could not decide whether or not to return to their own homes and entertain us properly. The three men of the village had encountered bad luck on their last hunting trip, and they attributed it to the fact that some of the women had offended the bears. Therefore, to fool the cunning animals, the men had decided to change wives for a night so that the bears could not possibly know which hunter to avoid.

The wise man of the community, Ulugatoq (The Man with the Big Cheeks), finally solved the whole problem: Nobody should go to sleep at all for the night, but we would all spend it together feasting and singing. And so we fed our dogs and gathered at Ulugatoq's house, the largest in the place. After the host had assured us that he was unable to serve anything that was edible he happened to recall that someone had left a piece of meat outside. "It might," he said, "still be there, as it has been refused by the dogs several times." This, of course, was such a hearty recommendation that our anticipations rose to the sky.

A short time later Ulugatoq returned, and we helped him bring in a great quantity of narwhal skin, or *mattak,* which is one of the delectable dishes to be had in the North. This piece had been preserved for two years, and the thawing and freezing had cured it beautifully. The epidermis was almost free from the leather underneath, and the blubber turned green as grass.

Standing over his precious food, Ulugatoq chopped the skin in two with his ax and then cut out the blubber to be used as oil for the lamps, stretching out the process as long as possible in order to give everyone the opportunity to tell him how fine his party was going to be. He complained of the dullness of his tools, stopped to sharpen them, and, when finally ready to proceed with the apportioning, sat down and looked up with an embarrassed smile:

"How can I serve such a thing for the big white man? I had better take it away and ask him to help himself from the sublime food he has brought from his own brilliant countries!"

Everyone assured him that no one in the world would enjoy his food more than I, and, like a miserable man being carried to the electric chair, he chopped the skin into pieces as large as the palm of his hand. Meanwhile Asayuk informed me that Ulugatoq was a famous social light and that his standard of behavior made him a lion at parties. I was witnessing a sample of his man-of-the-world manners, and I told him how amazed I was to find such a person in the North. He smiled cunningly and sampled the food himself.

"I was right!" he said. "This food tastes of nothing but dog excrement and urine."

After this recommendation Asayuk had to step onto the ledge to take off his boots and pants, and the women hung them over the lamps to dry. The rest of us grabbed the food spread out on the floor. It was delicious.

At Savigssuit lived Iggianguaq, son of Itusarssuk. As already related, he was spared when his sisters and brothers had been hanged. He was a small but vigorous man, and noted for his excellence as a hunter. He explained that he was really larger than he looked: he had been stunted from having insufficient meat in his childhood. And he had learned from this that pups must be fed well from the very start so that they may develop into big strong dogs. Later on they can endure privation.

Everyone knew that Iggianguaq was the best singer in the community—in fact, the only singer. Arctic music unfortunately requires a team—two must sing together. Iggianguaq said that he was in no mood to sing, and would have to go out to untangle his dogs. However, he made no move to go, so we renewed our entreaties. I told him that his reputation as a musician had reached as far as North Star Bay, but he merely sat still, looked at me fishy-eyed, and asked if I thought North Star Bay was very distant. Realizing my mistake, I said:

"It would give me great pleasure to hear you sing."

He answered: "Peterssuaq! In this country, though you are big and tall, you are but a newborn baby. You seem not to know that if a man does not feel like singing he cannot be made to do it. And I do not sing tonight!"

Naturally, I took this as final, but Ulugatoq dragged a drum from under the ledge, tightened the skin on it by licking it with his tongue, and handed it to the reluctant performer. Iggianguaq took it and cried:

"Oh, why do you give it to me? I don't know how to sing! Must I use a drum for it? I really don't know, for I never tried before."

Everyone encouraged him: "Qa, qa, come on. Let us just this once hear a really fine song. Oh, how happy we are that we have this famous singer in our midst!"

He looked bewildered and embarrassed; then it occurred to him that he could not sing alone, and he invited Mitseq to accompany him. Mitseq, not to be outdone by his southern contemporary, demanded an equal amount of coaxing. After an interminable discussion of which one was to play the *ayayut,* they at last began to sing, a modest little tune that amounted to nothing.

Only one man sings at a time, dancing as he sings. We would hardly call it dancing, for he is not permitted to move his feet. He sways from side to side shaking his head, emphasizing the rhythm of the song with his voice, body, and face. As he sings he invariably becomes more and more excited and forgets everything about him. Across from him stands his partner, stiff and stern, gripping the *ayayut* in both his hands, awaiting his turn.

The chorus sits grouped about the singers and joins in little by little. In this the women may also take part, and finally the whole room surrenders to the song. There are seldom any words, nor is there even music from our point of view, for they utilize half and quarter tones which torture the uninitiated ear. The singer repeats his rhythms several times, each time ascending the scale a little until his song ends in a wild shriek. The whole audience is possessed by the song, and emotions are whipped up to a frightening pitch. Realizing this, the artist must always end his song with something to make his audience laugh. He bends closer and closer to his partner and stops beating his drum, or quickens its pace, at the same time diminishing its accent, and his partner grips his little stick and brandishes it before the singer, waiting for the proper moment. Then when the singer has nearly finished, the partner grasps the stick with both hands, rotates it round and round, while he takes up the wail:

"Ay! Ay! A-ay—aa-a-a-a-ay!" The singer yells the same vowels, and as soon as he is completely exhausted both men laugh, and the audience laughs until the house rocks.

The *ayayut,* the only Eskimo instrument, is made from the skin of a walrus throat stretched over a frame of bone to which a handle is attached. The frame, rather than the skin, is beaten, and the drumstick is usually of bone or wood. The drum is only a means of setting the tempo, but its solemn booming in the tiny houses adds to the spirit of the scene. Before the singing begins all the lights but one small candle are extinguished. The two men stand in the middle of the floor, and the audience sits in the darkness, their bodies swaying from side to side and back and forth, hypnotized by the voices and the dull throb of the drum—boom-boom-boom, boom-boom-boom—always three beats in succession, its volume dictated by the different passages of the song.

When the first man has finished the next takes his place and sings one; then the first man sings three and the other three. Again the first sings seven, and the partner follows him until both are so exhausted they can no longer stand. At this point someone else is always so excited that he jumps to his feet, grasps the drum, and challenges another man to match him. They remove their coats, as the air is usually hot and close by this time, and stand naked, their fine tanned bodies rigid with muscles, their long hair switching from side to side. After hours of this they often slaver at the mouth, but no one seems to mind, since almost everyone is equally moved.

After two pairs of singers had been worn out two women jumped to their feet and asked to be permitted to sing. They acted as if something long buried in them could be released only by yielding to this moment of ecstasy, and the men asked if I would mind.

"You see," said old Asayuk, "we are only a few of us here, and we are all friends. Of course, it should not be, but we understand it is not to make us ridiculous, and the poor women seldom have an occasion here to sing."

My permission was granted, and Kuyapikasit and Sivaganguaq began to sing and dance. They were two passionate women, neither especially young, but both vital and fervent. Sivaganguaq had once been married to Tatarat, a lame man, but after the accident which made him lame she had been taken by so many men that her husband suggested one of them keep her for good, and Ulugatok had brought her home.

Sivaganguaq had a nickname—Ingminik—which means "spontaneous," but it was not used in her presence for it had been given her as the result of an incident in her life so scandalous that she would never live it down.

Her home had been at Cape York when the whalers used to call there to trade with the natives. The whalers were all strong men and, being without women for many months, were always crazy for girls. The Eskimo men, realizing this, brought their wives aboard the ships and managed the women's accounts. While the women went below to entertain the sailors the husbands stayed on the upper deck. Afterward the faithful wives would come up to their patient husbands, bringing with them the rewards of their charms, and there was always a certain amount of good-natured competition between friends, exhibiting the amount of sugar and tea and crackers they received. "Look at what my wife got!" one would say. "It doesn't look as if your wife is in favor down there. Oh, my wife is such a wonderful woman!"

But it was always a little strange to the natives that the white men misjudged the values of the women. A splendid, and very popular, girl might find slight favor among them, while it often happened that the whalers went wild over a woman who amounted to nothing, could hardly sew, and was traded from man to man because she was of no account at all. White men are funny!

One season, however, Ulugatoq had gone off on a long journey, leaving Sivaganguaq alone with the children, and while he was gone the Upernadlit—"Those Who Arrive with the Spring"—sailed into Cape York.

Sivaganguaq was in a dilemma. She was a woman of strict morals, and, as her husband was not present to take her to the ships, she dared not go out by herself and bring shame to their house. But the children, seeing other mothers return from the ships laden with sugar and tea and crackers, could not understand why their mother denied them such luxuries. Sivaganguaq and her unfortunate children wept together.

A few days later another whaler swung along the edge of the ice and signified his willingness to trade with the natives. Still Sivaganguaq had no husband to take her aboard, but she had three dogs and she decided that this time nothing was going to cheat her of her just due.

She did well and returned with bags full of the most delicious food, as well as a mirror and a pair of scissors, and she found that she had received more in a single visit to one ship than a number of her neighbors had in two.

But after a few days her nemesis in the person of a severe and offended husband returned. He had hurried in order to beat the spring thaw, and certain gossipy persons on the route had related to him the horrible thing his wife had done to his honor as a man. Of course he must avenge it, so he called her out of his house and beat her before all the natives in the settlement. Sivaganguaq was a polite woman, so she did him the favor of screaming and crying for mercy. But later she told everyone that she had been deathly afraid he would not beat her, for if he had not it would indicate that he placed small value on her. But now she was sure of his love, his honor was vindicated, and both of them were delighted with the gifts she had received from the boat.

Nevertheless, the name Ingminik followed her through life.

She could sing like a bird, her screams and yells trailing off like the cries of an eagle, and such a passion for song and excitement I would never have suspected in any of these silent, patient women who sit all day long on the ledge sewing and cooking.

It is impossible to keep the nights separate from the days. If anyone is tired he goes to sleep, and when he wants to get up he does so, regardless of the time. The beauty of it is that no one needs to wait for a meal to be served; there is always plenty of dog meat hanging outside the door, and the owner never cares how much anyone appropriates.

I walked out of the house. It was day; along the horizon to the south I could see a dull glow. I decided to walk up to the spot where the two famous meteorites had been located before they had been taken to the Museum of Natural History in New York.

One of the young natives accompanied me to the spot, though no one could miss it, as the great Peary always did a job thoroughly. In order to get the meteorites down to the ship he had built a road on which to haul them, a road that will never be used again. The road is made of stone and is quite a landmark, and takes anyone interested directly to the spot where the stones dropped from the heavens.

When we were ready to resume our journey Asayuk came to me and said that he could not accompany me farther, as he had been warned in a dream that he had a number of enemies among the natives south of Melville Bay; he went on to explain that the people from the south had been ill treated by his forefathers when they had last come north to trade. I finally got the story out of him:

The Tasiussak Eskimos lived where they could purchase wood for sleds and kayaks from a tribe farther south to whom it was carried by ocean currents, and these people had formerly driven north to trade their wood for sealskin lines, bearskin, and dogs. This would have been a great favor to the northerners, but the southerners were unmitigated beggars and asked for everything they saw.

Asayuk's forefathers' people grew impatient with the methods of the southerners and decided to be rid of them once and for all. It was the time of year when the birds lay their eggs in the cliffs at Saunders Island, and the only way to reach the eggs was by means of ropes let down from the top of the cliffs. The northerners managed to send all the southerners down the cliffs for eggs, and then dropped the lines, leaving the troublesome strangers marooned on the face of the cliff. This seemed an effective method of doing away with them, while at the same time obeying the letter of an agreement not to kill any traders.

Sitting in their tents, the northerners heard the poor beggars wailing in the cliffs for several days and then at last the noise ceased. Everyone thought they were dead. The perpetrators of the plot went to the cliff to view the bodies and found all the strangers gone. Apparently despairing of help, the southerners had at last decided to chance the descent of the cliff rather than submit to starvation, and by some miracle, or perhaps with the aid of a magic formula, they had reached the ground safe and driven off with their dogs. Since then, oddly enough, there had been no word from the southerners.

I tried to convince Asayuk that this had all happened so long ago that no one would remember or, in any case, blame him, but he was convinced that the many discomforts he had already suffered on the trip were proof that he was not wanted. He also said he had remembered that his wife, Anarwree, did not know where to find his cache of auks from which she was supposed to make him a shirt, and when I promised him shirts to burn from the store at Tasiussak he was all the more anxious to return.

"If this is true," he said, "one would not want Anarwree to waste her time sewing birdskins."

I realized that he was lost to the trip and let him return.

14

OUR COURSE TOOK US INSIDE ANOTHER ISLAND, CAPE MELVILLE, AND we made good time, spending our nights in the open sleds as the weather held good. There are so many icebergs after one has passed Cape Melville that it is easy to find shelter from the wind.

Sleeping on the ice requires a certain technique which must be learned and followed exactly. One must protect his head from the cold. To do this a big skin is laid half under the pillow and bent forward so that it will hang down over the sleeper's head and the aperture into the sleeping bag. Beneath the bag is placed the skin which the driver sits on during the day, and his bearskin pants are tucked between it and the sleeping bag to keep them from freezing. His boots are also stuck halfway into the bag, only the feet protruding, to keep snow out of them. On the other hand, the coat is never taken inside the bag. If warmth penetrates it, the snow on it will melt, wet the coat, and next morning it will be frozen solid.

There is quite a trick to getting into a sleeping bag when it is forty below zero. It takes a long while for the bag to warm up, but even if a fellow cannot sleep because of the cold, he can at least lie quiet and feel slightly rested in the morning, when comes the task of dressing again in the open.

On the fourth night out of Savigssuit we were awakened by strange noises from the dogs. Eskimo dogs never bark unless they scent a bear, and then the noise they make is a cross between a growl and a bark. Because of their ferocity toward bears, the dogs must be tied at night when traveling; otherwise, if the dogs have happened to smell a bear during the night the owner will wake in the morning and never see his animals again.

Our three dogs teams signaled for bear, and like puppets on strings my two companions shot from their sleeping bags, dressed, cut their dogs loose, and dashed after them. I dressed as fast as I could and followed them, because not far off I could hear the yips of the dogs, the roars of the bear, and the shouts of the men.

When I reached the scene Mitseq shouted to me that he did not have enough dogs—it was too dark to shoot—and that he would have to go back to camp for mine and for his spear. He dashed off and I stood by with Itukusunguaq. When the bear got away from the dogs Itukusunguaq merely followed and waited. Shortly all my dogs arrived and immediately leapt into the fight. Each time the bear tried to escape several of the dogs jumped onto his back. At times he circled, agile as a cat, but he could never get more than one dog under him at a time, and the rest of them would be all over him like ants. He could, of course, wound this one dog terribly, but while he was doing so he would have thirty-five others biting, snarling, and tearing at him. So he would hurl the dog into the air and try to defend himself in some other way. Once I saw my king dog tossed high above my head and thought he would be killed when he landed, but he gathered himself into a ball as he lit, and without a second's hesitation tore at the bear again to give him what he owed him.

The two brothers, Mitseq and Itukusunguaq, decided they would have to spear the bear in order to kill him—it was unthinkable to shoot into the swarming hive of animals. Itukusunguaq offered me the first opportunity. I refused, since I valued my life, and told him I would rather an expert did the killing. He charged into the mess and hit the bear. Heretofore the bear had not seen us at all, considering the dogs his only antagonists. But now he felt the spear and saw the long handle protruding from his hindquarters.

Bears are "so constructed that they do not like to have a spear in them." That is the Eskimo way of expressing it, and even if it is understatement, it is true. This one forgot about the dogs and pulled the spear, handle and all, out of his body. How he managed it is almost inexplicable, for the stick is made to break easily, leaving the spear in the flesh. But he did so and left us weaponless as our guns were still of no use. Again the younger brother, Mitseq, ran to the sled for the other spear and his mittens, which he had forgotten in the excitement. In no time at all he was back, and now it was his turn to try to kill the bear, weakened a little by loss of blood. Mitseq landed a blow squarely between his ribs. The bear surrendered at last; he went down with thirty-six dogs snarling over his body. But the dogs annoyed him even in his last moments, and he raised one huge paw to wipe them off his body. Then he rolled over, driving the spear farther into his ribs, and died quickly.

Strangely enough, dogs recognize a fallen enemy. They can be savage and dangerous even to their masters while they are in combat, but the moment the bear is defeated they loose their grip and lie down to await their reward—the warm, fresh meat.

It was only when the excitement of the kill was over that we had time to realize how cold we were, and how much colder we were going to be before we had finished skinning the bear. The temperature was fifty below, and in the darkness the skinning was a ticklish job, the white pelt covered with snow.

Whenever one of us could endure the cold no longer he would thrust his knife into the muscle of the recently slain beast, carving a hole large enough to bury his hand in the warmth of the meat. It is amazing how long meat will remain warm. I have had to leave animals exposed overnight a number of times in temperatures worse than fifty below, and next morning found all except the outer layers still unfrozen. The brain, especially, often takes days to freeze.

Next day we had an added burden of bear meat, but our stomachs were full and we did not care. We had fine, well-fed dogs, and though our course took us over good ice and bad ice, we could already see the crimson flush of day eating higher into the southern sky, and the moon rose to show us the way. The beginning of January is great.

After some days the sky became dull again. The stars grew fainter, and we noticed the ominous drift of snow on the ice—the natives call it "floor sweepings." Soon the wind struck our faces.

This is always the question at the beginning of a storm: how long should one try to keep going? You can stop early and make an igloo and meet the gale prepared. But then you have to be ready to swallow the blame that follows if the gale grows no worse. I made a rule to keep on until the dogs balked. In this instance we had no choice, for we were in the only section of Melville Bay where there are no icebergs. At the lee side of the icebergs there are always huge drifts of snow which one may cut into blocks for snowhouses.

So we kept on, and we had to drive much too far before Itukusunguaq stopped and told us that we might make camp. We tied our dogs as quickly as possible, took our knives and saws, and went to work. In the Thule District the natives use common wood saws to cut out the blocks of snow. When later I visited Hudson Bay, where I learned to build real igloos, the natives there saw me work with my saw and smiled, and did the work with their knives twice as fast.

We made the house as comfortable as possible and covered the ledges with skins. The lamps we placed on a tripod anchored in the snow and over the fire we stuck long sticks into the walls to serve as a rack for the clothing, which is first brushed free of snow with a *tilugtut,* a wooden saber, one of the most practical tools to carry on a trip in the Arctic.

At last everything was brought inside and the door closed from the inside. The last man out cuts a block of snow large enough for the hole, which serves as an entrance. This is carted inside, and then, after everyone is in, plugged into the opening. Snow is chinked into the fissures along the sides. The occupants are then in a cozy room and the howling of the gale is only a pleasant reminder of their own comfort. The dogs never make trouble so long as the snow drifts. They merely curl up, their noses buried in their tails, and let the snow furnish a warm, comfortable blanket.

We remained inside the igloo for three days. It is fine to lie down and listen to the gale, but a time comes when it is better to poke your head out and find that the wind has abated and the drifting ceased.

We had to excavate our sleds, and the dogs popped up like subterranean beings discovering that air as well as snow can be inhaled. They stretched and ran about to get the rigor out of their bodies, and then pulled to the extreme lengths of their traces to relieve themselves of three days' accumulation. Dogs are, in their own way, very hygienic animals.

It is sometimes quite a job to pull up stakes after a snow-storm, but we knew where we had left everything and merely had to dig down to it. The snowhouses are rather difficult to enter with all the goods, as the entrance is very small, but leaving the house is another matter. Then one may cut an exit as large as necessary.

The very last thing to be done when leaving a snowhouse is to walk inside and empty oneself. One is thus protected both from the cold winds and from the dogs, for nothing is dearer to an Eskimo dog than fresh human excrement. In fact, it is often necessary to protect oneself from them with a whip or, if the act is being performed by a number of persons simultaneously, to describe a circle, each man facing out. The most comfortable method, of course, is to get a boy or girl to stand over you, whip in hand.

After some days the dogs had forgotten their rest and slowed down to their usual speed, which is not convenient for the driver if he runs alongside, for he can neither run nor walk, but must run two paces, walk one, and repeat over and over again.

Suddenly our dogs sniffed the snow and turned at a right angle from the course. Running full speed, it was impossible for us to turn them. I jumped on my sled and did my best to keep it right side up. Ahead of me I saw Itukusunguaq struggling with his dogs to stop them, and finally he brought them under control. I drew alongside and the three of us ran ahead of the dogs with our whips to head them off.

"What is it?" I asked. "A bear?"

"We don't know," Mitseq answered, "but it is not a bear."

"But why are the dogs so crazy?"

"It is something we cannot tell."

I found some matches and struck one. We examined the snow and found ahead of us a great trough like no track I had ever seen.

"What is that?" I asked.

The boys were still at a loss. Mitseq suggested that it might be better to turn back. We were outside our own territory, and perhaps the spirits of this part of the world employed such tracks as this to mislead the unwary traveler.

Of that I had no fear. Then Itukusunguaq, the oldest of us all and an experienced man, shouted at the top of his voice:

"*Paunguliaq!* It is a wanderer! Some people on this journey are three lucky boys. It is a wanderer!"

With no more explanation both boys shrieked with joy, leapt to their sleds, and cracked their whips. There was nothing for me to do but follow, and I did so, confused and a little angry. I felt that the boys should show a little respect for their employer instead of screaming a word I did not understand and then rushing off. They could not know whether I wanted what we sought or not.

I had not much time to think, since my dogs were streaking through the darkness, and it was all I could do to stick on the sled. Occasionally I caught a glimpse of the track we followed. I could see no marks of any claws in the snow, only a depression as if a boat had been pulled along with the oars dragging. I noticed, too, that the thing had never changed its course for any obstruction, but had passed directly over ice hummocks and all. I was mystified.

By great effort I caught up with the boys and shouted at them again. Their only answer was:

"*A paunguliaq!* A wanderer!" But from their faces I could see that we were on the track of something as exciting as a gold strike.

Then suddenly I saw the thing—a huge, black mound apparently without head or tail. The dogs swarmed over it—we had to use our whips to get them off. I approached closer to discover that it was a huge walrus apparently driving straight across the ice to find open water.

Itukusunguaq was the first to draw his gun, and he shot the beast in the head. It died without a struggle. We stood beside almost a ton and a half of meat, an unparalleled and undeserved cache.

Before we could slice it we had to fasten our dogs. This was done by chopping two holes which slant toward each other in the ice and meet at the bottom. The hitching strap was then hooked through this, and no dog in the world could break from such a mooring.

We camped on the spot that night, gorged ourselves on the meat, cached the rest, and let the dogs drink deep of the gallons of blood inside the carcass.

Itukusunguaq told me that such a *"paunguliaq"* is the dream of every dog driver. The *paunguliaq* is a walrus that has been caught above the ice for some reason or other. Walruses have almost no nails on their flippers and must trust to their blunt noses to keep their blowholes open. They can stay beneath the ice only so long as it remains thin enough for them to break it. During the winter many of them remain close to the icebergs where the ice is always thin and trust to the sea floor to furnish them food. But occasionally they find the surface growing too solid, and then they ponderously drag their great bulk across the ice to a more advantageous wintering place. A walrus has an amazing instinct for scenting open water, but once in a while he may select the wrong route, as this one obviously had. But no matter what direction he chooses he sticks to it and allows no obstacle to deter him. He waddles across somehow, though his method of locomotion must be a terrific handicap above water. Often he must stop to sleep along the way, but the cold apparently does not bother him much. Both front and rear flippers of this animal were frozen badly, and the layer of fat under the skin was unusually thin. The stomach was entirely empty—the poor walrus had evidently been a long time on his last trek.

15

IT WAS STILL MANY DAYS BEFORE WE REACHED DANISH TERRITORY, and during the last miles we followed tracks already made by native sleds. These tracks we hailed as Columbus must have hailed

the first birds flying about and the twigs floating in the water
when he approached America.

Finally many tracks converged into what could almost be
termed a road, and the dogs grew excited and broke into a run.
We jumped onto our sleds and cracked our whips to gather
speed for our last dash. We wanted to look impressive as we drove
in. At last we could hear the dogs of the settlement howling their
distrust. The natives were warned, and we saw two boys suddenly
shoot out of the twilight as if discharged from a bow. They were
Kale and Isak, the young sons of the great Itué, called Simon the
Bearhunter by all the Danes from near and far.

More men and women and children rushed out to meet us
and we stopped to greet them. Mitseq and Itukusunguaq were
embarrassed by the practice of taking off the mitten and extending the right hand to be shaken. They had already mentioned it
to me, and the much-traveled Mitseq had explained that it was to
indicate that if the right hand was tired the strangers would help
to support it.

Still, it seemed awkward. I, too, had almost forgotten this
manner of greeting. All of us talked together in the usual manner,
but suddenly an enormous voice from the shore reached us:

"Halt! Stop and listen to the one who speaks here! This is
the country owned by the king, and he has ordered me to stay
here and look out for those who enter his royal land. Nobody
may come with dogs unless he has read this paper and answered
yes to it."

It was Itué who spoke, the famous ruler of Denmark's northernmost territory. He had been unable by circumstance and
neglect to learn to read, but as he saw a white man among the
strangers he brought forward a lantern with a candle in it and
told me to read the paper which he handed me.

I glanced at the paper. The text was written in Danish and
English, and was merely a warning not to bring diseased dogs or
Eskimos suffering from venereal or other contagious diseases into
the territory.

I looked it over carefully and handed it back to Itué.

"Yes!" I shouted like a stentor. "I am your man. I will obey."

As if these were the magic words of the Sultan of Baghdad,
Itué's manner changed. His strong, stern face suddenly broke into
a smile and his mitten was snatched off. He grasped my hand as
if we were lifelong friends who had been separated for years.

"I guess you are Peterssuaq," he said. "We know of you and you are our friend! Kunuk [Knud Rasmussen] is back, we have heard, and has brought you along. So you belong to us!"

I visited his house, a small but extremely clean hut with whitewashed interior and a ledge groaning under feather cushions. It was evident that Itué and his family were above the use of skins for comfort or decoration. On a shelf were several colored cups and gewgaws, and pictures with religious motifs covered the walls.

Itué's wife, a slim, neat woman, with his whole family greeted us. There was about them an air of prosperity which I had not observed before in any of the natives. Their speech was colored with an accent unfamiliar to our ears, and we had trouble in understanding them at first, but we got along famously.

Itué informed us that we were not allowed to leave our dogs without a night watch, and delegated his two sons as watchmen. This was a salaried job, of course, and, not unlike the majority of businessmen, he felt that his own relatives were better fitted for the work than anyone else.

He also impressed upon us that we would most certainly need a guide the rest of the way to the trading post at Tasiussak, and none other than Itué himself would guide us. He was an excellent host, but he complained bitterly the whole evening that he had no coffee to offer us and had had none himself for the past week. Finally I donated some of our own coffee, and he chose to see in our arrival the generous benevolence of the God to whom he had prayed ever since his coffee had run short.

Only three families lived in this community, and the other two resided in a house even smaller than Itué's. He, of course, was the big man of the community, but there was one who ran him a close second, Pele. Pele was not noted for his strength, but he was of tremendous importance in this northernmost Danish district because of his ability to read. This accomplishment made him both preacher and teacher. These dignities not only gave him a handsome salary—thirty-six kroner a year, or about sixty cents a month—but made him God's spokesman on this part of the earth.

The hearty natives from the north were used to much more food than was offered by these southerners. Kruaq—frozen meat and blubber of the narwhal—was served but there was almost no blubber attached to it, and the meat was cut into small pieces with a woman's knife wielded by one of the sons. And then, what seemed unique to us, the major portion of the meat was taken out of the house again. This was recounted later by Mitseq and Itukusunguaq as the strangest experience they ever had.

The southerners were also great competitors at parlor games, and the two brothers from the north were invariably losers. By the time we were ready to leave they had almost no tobacco, knives, or small accessories left.

Nor did we sleep comfortably. The ledges were shorter than ours, and, as I am very tall, my head protruded beyond the support, even when I curled up like a cat. There beneath my nose was the huge container of family urine—a sure indication of wealth and affluence—and the stench was that of some specially noxious form of ammonia. My eyes ached terribly by morning, and I was delighted to start early in an attempt to reach Tasiussak the same evening.

Itué was afraid we would be unable to reach Tasiussak if he could not see the moon, for the current is swift there and shifts the ice about treacherously. We would, he said, have to stop with either Solo in Sarfak or Abel in Saitoq. Since I knew neither of the men, it made no difference to me where we stopped.

We reached Sarfak safely, though the current ran close to the land and, as I was the last to cross the passage, I had barely made it when the ice entirely disappeared behind me.

Sarfak was in an unusual state of turmoil. The arrival of visitors in a community of four or five houses is always an exciting event, but we had come on a very special occasion. Solo himself explained it after we tied our dogs:

"We are having an important election; the king has ordered us to hold it today, so I cannot delay until tomorrow and treat you as you should be treated."

It was the first real election to be held in Danish Greenland. The new law gave the natives the right to vote for members of the commune council, and as this was the very first election it was especially solemn. They considered me a man of great intelligence because I could read, and Solo asked me to help them out of their difficulties and supervise the proceedings.

Sarfak, with its five houses, was quite an important community and entitled to select one member of the council.

The hunters were uncertain as to what was expected of a member of the council. They only knew that the office paid no salary and the members were entitled to only fifty ore (ten cents) for one meal each month on the day of meeting. As it would often take several days to travel back and forth, the hunters quite naturally, and sensibly, decided they could not waste their time at lawmaking. But the king had spoken, and somebody had to be elected.

There was in Sarfak, however, an ideal man for the office— Abelat by name. He had formerly been a big hunter, but was now old and useless. His knees were weak and his eyes could no longer see to hunt. Occasionally he could walk to the seal nets close by and catch a seal, but he was definitely on his relatives' dole, so he was instructed to become a member of the council.

Abelat had neither political talents nor ambitions, but he was forced into the latter at any rate. His son, Gaba, was supporting him, and Gaba thought this might be a way of getting the old man off his hands for a few days each month. Abelat had cried and protested, but he knew full well that there was nothing else he could do, for he was old and accustomed by now to bend to the will of others.

So Abelat was made the candidate for councilman. To avoid further confusion no one was permitted to run against him. But there were to be five voters, excluding Abelat himself, and it was easy to see how confusion would arise in spite of anything that could be done. Especially as it was impossible to depart from the clearly expressed letter of the law which demanded that the election be held in secret.

Solo's house was the largest and therefore the one most worthy of such an unusual honor. We all trooped inside and searched it carefully for plotters, though what or who might be hidden in it I never could understand since it was a single room with no furniture, no tapestries, and no alcoves.

After we were assured that everything was as it should be we went outside and Solo, the greatest hunter of the place and thereby entitled to all privileges, prepared himself to enter the secret ballot booth. This brought up an unforeseen problem. The law plainly stated that the voters should write the name of their candidate on the ballot, and only two of the voters were able to do this. I suggested, as a way out, that since there was only one candidate, the uneducated voters should merely make a cross on the ballot and I would later translate these crosses to the name "Abelat" and thus come within the law.

Solo wiped his hands carefully and, grasping a box of matches, crawled through the tunnel into the house to do his duty to king and country. Inside he lighted a candle, voted with the pencil and paper which had been provided, blew out the candle again, and came outside. The others followed him one by one, each returning to the out of doors much heated and excited by the ceremony. Finally, after they had all accomplished their duty, Solo repeated three times in a loud voice—still according to the dictates of the law: "Does anybody else want to vote?"

There was no one else to answer, so the election was pronounced at an end and we all went inside to discover two names and three crosses. Abelat had been elected unanimously!

This surprising result was greeted with shouts of delight, and we were told that in honor of the day Solo would celebrate and make coffee.

The following evening we reached Saitoq, where we spent the night in the spotless house of another great hunter, Abel. Next morning Abel served as our guide, and after a number of hours we reached the point from which we could look down into the sheltered settlement of Tasiussak. A swarm of natives streamed out to meet us. There were six or seven houses here, and their lights made the impression of a city of considerable size. My two boys, Mitseq and Itukusunguaq, were impressed.

We were asked about the trip, and a tall native inquired after his "countrymen" to the north. He was Tobias, the schoolteacher, and his voice proclaimed his dignity. He had been taught far to the south, in Godthaab, the capital of Greenland, and had received a degree from the high school there. After we had talked for a few moments it was suggested to me that I had best get along to the trading post, as Nabaja—Mr. Nielsen—knew we were coming and his wife would most likely have coffee ready for us.

16

IN MEETING NIELSEN WE MADE OUR FIRST ACQUAINTANCE WITH A family which, for many winters to come, was to be our host year in and year out. We took possession of their house as if it were our own and filled it to overflowing with our friends. Yet never did I see anything but smiles on their faces nor feel anything but extreme pleasure in their greeting.

Nielsen was married to a half-breed woman, Dorte, an extremely clever person. They had four fine children who were soon like brothers and sisters to us. We were given coffee and cake which tasted better than any cake I have ever eaten before or since. What a meal Mrs. Nielsen could lay upon the table! I was given the second room to use as my own, Nielsen gave me my mail, and I was in paradise.

In the evening a ball was given in my honor. The largest room was jammed with all the villagers, and an ingenious member of the tribe played an accordion. Only a tiny space, as small as a modern night-club floor, was left for the dancers, but their enjoyment was boundless. Everyone was prepared for such a jam, and there were no flimsy dresses to catch and tear. The girls laughed and screamed with delight, but my two boys were extremely embarrassed. They had never witnessed such a celebration, and they realized that they did not yet know enough to criticize. Yet there was nothing I could do to induce them to take part in such a shameless exhibition as traipsing around the floor with a girl.

"Especially as I do not know which one to take after the dance and where to take her! We only do our women plays in the dark where people can hear but not see," was Itukusunguaq's comment.

We danced until my shirt was wringing wet and my feet scorching. Nabaja's daughter, Jacobine, squealed with pleasure and was so delirious that she kissed me for being the cause of all this.

Ten o'clock was Nabaja's bedtime, and he had a most effective way of ending the party. He did not go to each one and tell him that the host was sorry he must be going, but merely stood in the center of the room and raised his hand. He did not speak a word, but his guests melted away like chickens before a fox.

Nabaja and I went outside and walked up and down in front of his house. He paced there for hours each day like a lion in a cage. He suggested that we remain outside for a while, as his wife would make us some real coffee and, besides, it would give the air in the house a chance to clear. When the natives dance in their heavy clothes they perspire, and this intensifies the odor of urine in their pants and boots. His windows were sealed for the winter, and fresh air could only circulate through the door.

Nielsen attempted to instruct me in my dealings with the

natives. "So long as you are going to stay here for many years, you might as well profit by my experience," he said.

His wife never threw away coffee grounds. They were always kept frozen outside the house and, after they had been used once, were fine for coffee to serve customers who came to trade. The customers were delighted with it, and often brought a piece of meat or a bird to express their appreciation.

After this warming over, the grounds were still not discarded, but used to furnish refreshment for dances and parties. Meantime, of course, the residue had been frozen again. But thawed out, and a pinch of salt added, it was always splendid for dancers. After this third brewing, the beans were given to poor women who could use them a couple of times more before they ate the grounds with a spoon or chewed them like tobacco.

Greenland teaches economy.

We gave our dogs a few days' rest, enjoyed ourselves thoroughly, and then said good-by to the Nielsens over a last cup of coffee. The weather was fine, the ice much better, and we knew that we could get back to Thule in a hurry, not stopping at all until we reached Ituisalik.

We found Itué in the midst of great tragedy. He had gone home the day after we arrived in Tasiussak, carrying fourteen pounds of coffee. Now, only one week later, it was all gone. He was humble and apologetic about it, so I paid him for the next year's piloting to Tasiussak at this time. If I had not he would have been unable to buy more coffee until the seals came up on the ice and he had more blubber and skins to trade.

His son Kale, a splendid young fellow, and Markus' son Tobias thought it would be great sport to follow us for a couple of days on the trip north. We knew that their motive was other than mere sport; they had heard about our cache of walrus meat, and they wanted part of it. They were also anxious to get a bear and have us divvy up if we bagged one. As for them, they never divided portions. They did not cut up the skin for pants, but sold it in one piece to the trader.

We were anything but eager for them to come along, but we could not say no since we did not want to get a bad reputation. The Eskimos south of Melville Bay, unlike our own, are terrible beggars, fill their cups with sugar, eat everything in sight, and have abominable camping manners. The worst thing about them, perhaps, is that they never tie up their dogs at night and these dogs, still possessing all their teeth, eat the traces. Our sealskin lines were especially tasty to them, for they were not tanned in urine.

But they were impressed by the great people who came out of the mysterious north every year. We built a snowhouse and the two poor boys had no sleeping bags but showed up with, of all things, feather pillows. These are, of course, no good for sleeping in snowhouses, so instead of sleeping quietly they never tired of pestering us with questions about the north.

Unlike the polar Eskimos, the southerners are also braggarts. We might not call them by such a harsh term, but Mitseq and Itukusunguaq were embarrassed for them when they told stories of adventures in which they admitted they themselves played heroic roles.

We liked Kale, but when he asked us about the bear we had killed on the way down, he compared it with a number of bears he had shot himself, and went into great detail about his heroism in getting his own first bear. Itukusunguaq listened patiently for a while, but finally even his stoical politeness was tried.

"How many bears have you killed in your time?" he asked Kale.

Kale figured carefully, and admitted to five. This was too much for Itukusunguaq. Grinning at Mitseq, he said:

"Well, well, here is a man who has killed five bears!"

"Naw! Naw!" exclaimed Mitseq. "Can you imagine!"

This sarcasm went over Kale's head, but Itukusunguaq finally told him in disgust that he had better keep quiet until he had something to boast about.

But next morning when we emerged from the igloo our dog traces were gone. I was disgusted and told both Kale and Tobias to return home, as we could not afford to have them with us any longer. Their own traces were eaten, and we had to make them new ones from our harpoon lines before we could get rid of them. The leftovers which we were going to throw away the cousins begged to keep. This was even more disgusting to Mitseq. "If one's dogs had to run in traces caught by someone else, one would rather they were all dead, and never raise his whip again," he said.

Finally we were alone and delighted when we saw Kale and Tobias disappear in the low-hanging mist to the south. Lucky

we were to be rid of them, too, because an hour later we sighted
a bear and killed it. Had they been with us they would have
been entitled to portions, and would doubtless have asked for the
whole skin. And, said Mitseq, we should have been forced to give
it to them in order to avoid the name of "those who are close about
bearskins," a horrible stigma indeed.

At last the light was returning. It was almost the end of January, and we were as pleased to greet the coming of day as we had
been to see the sun disappear months ago. One morning we could
detect the colors of our dogs. During the long night we recognize
them by their individual shapes, and now it was almost a surprise
to remember that some were red, others black and white and
spotted. Day by day the period of light lengthened and its intensity
increased.

At Cape York we met our friends, and visitors from the north
told us that Kunuk was preparing to cross to Ellesmere Land
to hunt musk oxen, and was only awaiting my return to take
charge of the post in his absence.

The ice round Cape York was now excellent and we made it
home from there in two days.

Knud Rasmussen's welcome was heart-warming. He should
have been an organizer of parties. In fact, he was the Arctic Elsa
Maxwell, for he was never happier than when he could celebrate
something or other, and I never knew a man who could find so
many occasions for celebration. All the natives were summoned
and our stories and laughter rang out until morning.

Yet in the group there was one face I missed—that of a certain young girl. I inquired about her, the stepdaughter of Uvd-
luriak, and all the natives were amazed and wanted to know why.
I explained that I had brought something to pay her for the
mittens she had given me. Everyone snickered, and I realized
I had done something that was simply not done: I had mentioned
and asked for a girl.

But next day I met her as she walked on the ice with her
little brother slung on her back. When she saw me she hid behind
an ice hummock. I started round to find her, but she ran as fast
as she could go. She was hampered by the child on her back, and
it was easy for me to catch her and hold her.

"Why do you run away?" I demanded.

"I don't know."

"Are you afraid of me? You need not be!"

"No, I am not afraid, but someone told that you had inquired for me yesterday before everyone. Therefore I was embarrassed!"

"I forgot your name—what is it really?"

"Oh, I am nobody, just the most ugly and foolish girl in the tribe."

"I don't think so, but what is your name?"

"I don't know."

"You mean you don't know your own name?"

"No, I never heard it."

"Nonsense," I persisted. "Of course you know your name. Why won't you tell it to me?"

"Others can tell it to you, but it is not important."

"I brought something back for you, something you will like."

"Oh, no, don't give me anything," she begged. "Give it to somebody worth giving things!"

And while I looked about me in desperation for a means of breaking through her self-abnegation, she made a quick movement and disappeared in the dark.

Later on I asked one of the girls at our house about her name. She, too, refused to tell me, explaining politely, "You are making yourself ridiculous asking for a young woman's name."

We had in our household three women—Vivi, whom we had brought from the south, Arnajark, an elderly woman, and Aloqisaq, a strong woman who had recently lost her husband.

Arnajark had been Knud Rasmussen's servant during the previous winter he had spent with these people, and was utterly devoted to him. She found it difficult, however, to compete with Vivi, who had been baptized and carried her nose in the air as a result. Whenever Vivi found herself left out of a conversation she revenged herself by taking out her psalm book and screaming her faith at the top of her lungs.

One day Knud Rasmussen asked Arnajark to count the fox-skins in the attic. Vivi overheard his request, and laughed: "These people cannot count at all. They only know up to twenty, and there are many more skins than that."

Knud called her bluff and told her to go count the skins herself. Vivi tried to get out of it, but he would not let her off. She spent hours in the attic, and then came down to ask for a pencil and paper. After many more hours she returned with a paper so littered with numbers that we could not make any sense out of it. If we had owned as many foxskins as she had computed, we would have been millionaires.

He looked over the figures, and then asked Arnajark to go up and count. In a half hour she was back.

"There are now four piles with ten coats in each," she said. "Then there is one pile with three coats, and six foxes left over."

A coat is ten foxskins, and the stupid woman had figured correctly. We actually had four hundred thirty-six skins.

Everyone in the village visited us daily. When a man did not come we could be sure he was out hunting. Strangers came from great distances to trade goods and stories. Our stock of trading material was limited, as we had little money to fit out our post, but everyone was happy to have us whether we had anything or not. "Now we are like the southerners and have a store nearby," the natives would say. Some even questioned our prices: "People never appreciate things if they can buy them for nothing." And others insisted upon paying more than we asked so that they could boast of the value of their belongings.

The actual trading always followed a certain polite ritual:

I would ask the man casually if he had been successful in his fox hunting. The man would look at me with surprised regret. "Foxes? Oh, my dear Pita, you must mistake me for someone else. I cannot tell you anything about the foxes. They are too swift and too sly to be caught by a slow fool like me."

"But I was told that you are the one man in Greenland who knows how to outfox the fox. There was mention of a supply of furs you have brought along."

The man would laugh. "You are out of touch with reality, my friend. My foxes are few and not worth having."

"But what have you got in the bags you left outside?"

"You put me to shame. I hoped you had not seen them. The contents of the greasy bags were fox furs once, but we have had to use them on our way. They are full of soot and grease and dirt. I wish you had not seen the bags."

"I might be allowed a look at the furs?"

"I would blush from shame if you should ever catch sight of them."

"The shame is mine—I have been misinformed. I was told by some ill-advised gossip that we might have an exchange. The misunderstanding gives me cause for deep regret."

And we would continue at great length until the man finally would bring in his bags. Then he would be joined by his wife so that they both could enjoy the triumph when I saw their matchless collection of perfect furs. And now it would be my turn to be shy and reticent.

"This beautiful sight will never be forgotten. I am truly grateful you have let me see your treasures. Please pack them up again. I have nothing with which to pay for such beauty. I have some supplies which are used for payment for ordinary furs, but I do not want to suggest that they could possibly be exchanged for the least of your furs."

"Oh, Pita, you are teasing me! You don't think for a moment that one would demand or even accept any payment for this filthy mess you are kind enough to call furs. If you will consider accepting them as a gift, we will be rewarded far beyond what we deserve."

I would finally agree to take the furs and then the real bargaining would begin.

The Eskimo always mentioned first the smallest of his needs, such as a box of matches or a file. As I produced these things he gradually moved up the list until we finally got to the gun and ammunition—the main items. Once he was through, his wife would be asked to mention her needs and finally, after a whole day, the bargain was complete. But their greatest pleasure was to "forget" things.

After the sleds were all loaded with their supplies they would keep running back. "In my stupidity I forgot to mention some tobacco." Or it would be needles or thread or one of a dozen items. I had to let them get away with a certain amount of "forgetting," after the bargain had been sealed, since this was supposed to prove they were smart traders, but I learned to fool them by including most of the popular items before they could begin their "forgetting."

Aloqisaq was the strongest woman I have ever seen. She, as I have said, was a widow, but her husband's story is one of the most amazing I have ever heard. It is a true story, yet I wonder whether any doctors will credit it.

Agpaleq, the husband, was an old man before he owned his first gun. He was so childishly delighted with it that he wanted several different-sized cartridges, "just to fool the gun."

One cold, fall day he went out after caribou. He took two

boys with him to carry back the meat he was sure he would get, and all the way he boasted about his fine gun. How much better this was than sneaking up on a caribou with a bow and arrow!

They spotted two caribou across a creek, and Agpaleq had such confidence in his weapon that he determined to get them both with one shot. Carefully he loaded the gun, and then dropped a smaller cartridge down the barrel. The caribou stood one just above the other, and he felt sure that the small lead would carry higher and hit the upper caribou. He instructed the boys to hide while he inched forward to get in position.

At last he was in the right spot, and he eased the gun to his shoulder. He never remembered pulling the trigger. The gun, however, went off with a fearful crash, exploded in his hands, and a splinter of it flew back and crashed in the left frontal bone of his skull. The boys rushed forward, thinking him dead, but he commenced to move and talk crazily and to roar like a bear. When they looked more closely they could see his brain beating in the open wound.

They dared not stay with him and went home to call for help but found only his wife and one other woman when they arrived. Aloqisaq, however, packed their heavy tent on her back and walked out to her husband. I know of no man who could have performed the feat, and it was only her great strength which saved them both.

He was still alive and inquired why she had come. He remembered nothing that had happened. Aloqisaq pitched the tent over him—she dared not move him yet—and there they stayed for several days eating the meat she had brought with her. When rescuers arrived to bury the body they found Agpaleq still alive, though his feet had been frozen and gangrene had set in, and, most amazing of all, part of his brain had poured out of the wound.

This I was told by other witnesses than Aloqisaq. These people are familiar with anatomy, and are certainly able to recognize brain matter when they see it. They all assured me that at least a cupful had come out, and they had cleaned out more with a spoon. After which Aloqisaq sewed the skin together.

Agpaleq's recovery was slow, but almost complete. The accident resulted in peculiarity of habits rather than invalidism. During the remainder of his life he could sleep for a week or more at a time, and remain awake an equal length of time. When asleep it was almost impossible for him to be awakened, and it became quite the custom for his neighbors to walk into his house and help themselves to whatever they might desire, including his wife. Agpaleq slept soundly through it all and never knew what practical jokes were played on him.

He could still hunt in his kayak, though, and was useful until the time of his death, after which his wife came to us and brought her son with her.

I came home late on the night after Aloqisaq and the boy had arrived, and Knud suggested that I fit the lad out with a shirt. I was tired from a day of walrus hunting, but I complied. The lad seemed frightened and embarrassed, and would not say a word. I told Knud this, and he translated it to the natives in the house at the time. They all roared with laughter, and I was finally told that he was deaf and dumb. Aloqisaq tried to excuse herself for bearing him but said that she had not discovered his affliction until he was two years old, and then she loved him so much that she could not bring herself to kill him.

I adopted him as my own, taught him to speak, and he stayed with me for many years.

Aloqisaq had formerly been with Peary's expeditions and had learned how to wash clothes. This was a lifesaver for us, as Vivi already had enough to do. Aloqisaq got along famously with her work until one day I tried to find a suit of underwear I especially liked. I searched all over for it and finally asked her if she knew what had become of it. Shyly she said she would bring it to me next day. Upon further inquiry I learned that she had not thought it dirty enough when I discarded it, so she decided to wear it and make the washing really worth-while.

17

WHEN KNUD WAS FINALLY READY TO LEAVE FOR ELLESMERE LAND I decided to accompany him part of the way. A number of years ago Asayuk had found musk oxen across Smith Sound, and since then the natives made a yearly pilgrimage to secure meat. We sent out word to the north and south that we would both be gone for a while and set out with Uvdluriark, our good helper at the post.

The ice was solid and we made Cape Parry the first day. Knud's dogs were fine, but vicious, and he could hardly approach them himself. But this served a double purpose—it made them excellent for hunting bears and keeping old women off his sled, for when an old woman asks to ride it is impossible to deny her. One may be sure that if he refuses to let her ride she will spread scandal about him and his team.

The first night we slept in a cave and next day reached Netsilik, a famous Arctic community around which countless legends and traditions have grown up. No other place has so many murders to its discredit, and upon the big stones outside the houses may be seen the footprints of the famous conjurer, the angekok, who is believed to have come here to escape from the devil, Tornarsuk. He had such power and strength that his feet made a deep impression in the stones for the skeptics to view.

Mayark was my host at Netsilik. Knud told me that he combined more good and bad traits than any other man in the North. That evening we had a long talk, and Mayark advised me to marry, since everyone knew that no man should be without a woman. He, it seemed, had just the girl for me. Over my protests he brought her forth.

In a whisk Arnanguaq was completely undressed, and her master stood her before me and pointed out, like a slave trader, her especial qualifications, leaving nothing to my imagination. It was a great recommendation, of course, that she was cross-eyed, which would make her the more valuable to me—I would not have to waste my time fighting over her. Her body was not without its virtues, and her manager would have us marry immediately.

I was both young and bashful, and was more embarrassed for the girl than for myself. Without giving too much offense I tried to explain my reasons for not wanting to marry her, and finally lay down to sleep. Later I heard the girl whisper to her protector: "Do you think I should stay here, or get out and let him come to me?"

She went away, and I did not go to her.

My reputation as a doctor unfortunately followed me. But I was glad to be of such service as I might. I was asked to go to Ulugassat (Northumberland Island) to take a look at Sigdloo's wife. Sigdloo had been "number three man" with Peary, was one of the murderers of Uvisakavsik, and had taken Alakrasina, the worst of the murdered man's wives. She was an ill-tempered, hysterical female, and now, it seemed, her right arm was paralyzed. What could I do for this?

She had been Uvisakavsik's favorite wife until he grew tired of her. While she had lived with Uvisakavsik she had become pregnant, but foolishly denied it to the other women. Even long after they could see her condition she refused to admit it and bragged that Uvisakavsik was such an excellent provider that she was merely growing fatter.

When her time came she had given birth to a boy, but to give truth to her lie she had strangled the child.

After her marriage to Sigdloo her arm commenced to wither and lose its vigor—it was the arm with which she had killed her child. I recommended massage, but at this she scoffed. While she had learned to sew with her left hand, she was such an unpleasant woman that Sigdloo had tried to get rid of her and given her away to other men. They always sent her back and finally, in order to avoid her, her poor husband spent most of his time with his neighbors. His beautiful hair and pleasant manners made him popular with the ladies, while his prowess as a hunter and his reputation as a companion of Peary made him a favorite with the men.

At this time of year nearly everyone for many miles around was gathered at Pituravik and Karrat, an excellent locality for spring walrus hunting. We stopped and talked and bargained with the natives, and while there Ukuyak and his wife, Atitak, came rushing up from the south. Ukuyak was in a hurry to reach home in time for the birth of his child. Women in the Arctic never know when their children are due, but there were unmistakable indications that Ukuyak's wife did not have long to wait.

We set off for Neqé, our final destination, Ukuyak and his wife as well as several other travelers in our party. We were now in the northern reaches of polar Eskimo land, which is divided into three sections defined by their relation to the southwest wind which prevails over the whole of Greenland. The Eskimos who live at Cape York and in Melville Bay are called Nigerdleet —"Those Who Live on the Windy Side." Immediately north are the Akuarmiut—"Those Who Live in Between." This section includes the land where our post at Thule was situated. And north of Cape Parry live the Oqonermiut—"Those Who Live on the Leeside."

Those terms are definite and characteristic, but there are many severe gales on the leeside. Without warning one intercepted us on the way to Neqé. There were no clouds in the sky, but suddenly far out to sea the snow was whisked into the air, and before we had time to make any preparations the storm was upon us, the atmosphere an unbreathable mixture of snow and blinding ice. My dogs were whipped off their feet and, in spite of my frantic efforts, gathered about the leeside of my sled. My companions were blotted out by the storm, and I crouched there quite alone, wondering what to do. At last I crawled—it was impossible to stand—ahead and came upon the rest of the party. They were all gathered together holding a confab. When I was near enough to make them hear I yelled as loud as I could to ask their advice.

They had no time for my troubles. Atitak was in labor.

We tried to build an igloo for her, but the snow was so thin that as soon as blocks were cut they were worn out by the wind and blown to pieces. Somehow I got a glimpse of poor Atitak's face, and I saw on it all the pain and distress a woman feels under such circumstances. She seemed to expect me and Knud to do something for her. And yet what could we do? There was no hope of building a shelter, and it was out of the question for her to undress.

It was a desperate moment and we had to employ desperate measures. We placed Atitak on the leeside of the sled, and a number of the men grouped themselves upon it to break the wind. We split the woman's pants only as much as was necessary. The bag of water had already broken, and I knew that the moment had come.

Eskimo women always stand on their knees when giving birth, their husbands supporting and embracing them from the back and helping to expel the fetus. This was Ukuyak's first child and he had no experience, so Qolugtinguaq, who had several children to his credit, took over the task and pressed the baby out in no time at all. Atitak snatched up the child inside her coat, wrapped some skins about him—it was a man-child—and soon had him warm and snug. The storm abated somewhat; we emptied the load from Knud's sled and bade him drive Atitak across to

Neqé at once to get her inside a shelter. When we finally reached the village we found her well and gay, and the boy already slung in her hood.

Neqé is the gayest place in the Arctic during the walrus-hunting season. When we arrived the sea was open after the storm, but it would freeze over again in a short while.

At Neqé lived a remarkable old lady, Kullabak, who was the talk of the village. She had been married to a very poor hunter who had fortunately died, and she had moved in with a much younger and better hunter. But before she could make this advantageous change she had to do away with her son.

I never saw the boy, but from what I was told he must have been a holy terror. At any rate, no one blamed her for the drastic measures she had resorted to.

The boy's debut in terrorism had taken place at Cape York where he collected a load of rotten birds' eggs and hid them high up on a hillside. Then one day he became loudly hysterical and shouted: "A ship! A ship! A big ship is coming!" Magic words, of course, to natives who were seldom visited by outsiders.

They all hurried up on the hillside to get a look at the boat. Meanwhile the boy crouched behind a rock, and when his friends were close enough he jumped out and pelted them with his peculiarly offensive cache. This naturally reflected upon Kullabak's house, and she had tried to apologize, but since she was a lone woman without a husband there was not much she could say to re-establish herself.

So she asked Mayark to help her get rid of the boy, and Mayark took him up onto the glacier and pushed him down in a crevasse. That, by all rights, should have been the end of him. Kullabak went into traditional mourning, but her mourning was pretty effectively interrupted when the boy came walking into the house. By some miracle he had escaped death in the fall and had followed the crevasse to its portal near the sea.

After that no one dared touch him, and the boy played all manner of tricks to revenge himself. He was a big, strapping youngster, but he had no hunting gear of his own and had to borrow what he wanted from the hunters while they slept. One day, while Mayark was away on a hunting trip, he went to Mayark's house and told his wife that he had followed Mayark some distance and that when they had parted Mayark had told him that he might stay in his house and take all a husband's privileges. Mayark's wife was an obedient, loving wife, and not until her husband returned home did she realize that she had been tricked. All the villagers had the laugh on Mayark.

The boy also helped himself from various caches and never took the trouble to close them. His mother was at her wit's end and finally decided that if she wanted to save the honor of her house she must do something desperate. One night while he was asleep with his head protruding beyond the end of the ledge, she made a sealskin-line noose, slipped it over his head, and pulled it tight.

Thus ended the criminal pranks of one young man, and his mother was highly honored for her good deed. Now she was remarried, and her great, booming voice was always an asset at parties.

18

KNUD RASMUSSEN LEFT ME AT NEQÉ WHEN HE WENT NORTH FOR musk oxen. Two brothers were to have accompanied him, but at the last minute the elder discovered that his dogs were in no condition for the strenuous trip. His wife, however, had been counting on the trip and the musk-ox skins resulting from it, and, rather than disappoint her—he was much in love with her—her husband sent her along with his younger brother, Inukitsork.

This so-called wife trading among the Eskimos is an interesting custom. Most persons believe it results from a lack of morality, but this is decidedly untrue. I have never met a people with a more strict moral code, though it is a different code from that of the white race.

An Eskimo's love for his wife is quite apart from the urgencies of his sex life. If a man desires a woman and has no wife of his own, he may borrow another man's wife. It would be impossible for him, however, to go to a married woman and suggest that she sleep with him without first consulting her husband.

There is also a purely practical and economical advantage in wife trading for the hunter. If he goes alone he must spend a great portion of his time building an igloo, cutting ice, and melting it. At night he must return to a cold shelter, and he has no means of drying and tanning his skins. Instead, his evenings must be spent mending boots and drying clothes, and he must carry plenty of spare clothes with him. However, if he brings a woman along all this is quite different. He builds her an igloo, and she takes care of everything else. She has the house warm when he returns, and his food steaming hot. His boots and mittens are dry and soft and mended, so that he need not cart along many changes. And while he is out hunting the woman dries the skins on a frame inside the igloo, scrapes them and removes all fat and meat, so that they can be folded together and he may return home with thirty or forty instead of the ten raw skins he would otherwise be able to haul. This is perhaps the greatest advantage in having a woman along—besides this, she can hunt rabbits and take care of the meat caches. Oh, there are many fine things about a woman.

Now, it may happen that a man needs skins, and his wife is unfit for travel. She may be ill, or pregnant or caring for a tiny baby. How much better for him, then, that he arrange to leave her with a friend while he is away and, in exchange, take his friend's wife along with him.

When the hunters come home the wives return happily to their own husbands, who listen with amusement to the stories the women have to tell of the trip.

Furthermore, I have never heard any obscene talk or unclean stories, because everything that is human is natural, and the refinements and perversions of sex have never occurred to anyone.

After Knud left we learned of a horrible disaster which had befallen our friends Pualuna and Qolugtinguaq.

At Sarfalik, where they lived, a little glacier slopes down to the sea, and from days of old children have used it for coasting. The sea is never frozen over there, as the current is swift around the point. It is especially exciting for the boys and girls to slide to the very edge of the glacier: the girls scream out at the danger and the boys feel proud and strong in turning and averting disaster at the last moment.

Qolugtinguaq had a fine son, a really beautiful boy, who had just killed his first seal—the first step toward becoming a man. Pualuna's two daughters had reached the age at which they began to look at a boy with quickening interest. Meeting at Sarfalik after a long separation, the children, who were cousins, were de-lighted to see each other. The boy took the girls to the top of the hill and put them on his toboggan—a sealskin. The girls held up the forepart so that they could stick on, and they slid down the glacier over and over again, the girls yelling and the boy roaring with delight. Each time they came nearer the brink, but their parents stood by and, remembering that they had done the same thing as children, did not interfere with the pleasure. Instead, they hailed the children and shouted, "Fine! Fine!" which, of course, made the boy all the more daring.

And then, with the parents looking on, the boy decided to show the girls his best stunt, and not turn the sled until he reached the very edge of the ice. He either forgot, or lost con-trol, for the three children shot into the water and were never seen again.

When we heard the news we were all silent, though such disasters are far from uncommon where the natives live always on the very brink of disaster and sudden death.

Poor Qolugtinguaq! He took his dogs and, at the end of the prescribed mourning period, drove away.

"I am going far to forget my sorrow," he said. "I felt last night that I did not care for my other children, and I had better leave!"

Months later we heard that he had been seen by bear hunters in Melville Bay, and next year that he had traveled far south and was living at Ikerasarssuk. He lived for a while with an elderly, good-for-nothing woman who bore him a child. The child was black, according to rumor, and died at birth. After Qolugtinguaq finally returned home, and I mentioned the incident to him, he said that he was not surprised. "I was in a fog the whole time," he said. "Perhaps she is not the only one who had babies. I have been at many places and there were many women everywhere."

Eskimos always remain in mourning for five days. The women sit with the pants of the deceased on their heads, never sleeping, never lying down, so that if the departed children return they may find their way home. The children did not return, and after the five days I went to visit the bereaved people.

Alinaluk, Pualuna's first wife and the mother of the two girls, stood upon the slope where her children had coasted to their deaths.

"Don't pity me," she said. "I cannot bear it. I am born to unhappiness and am empty of tears. Talk to me of many things, but do not pity me."

Her sorrow was touching, and her people tried to comfort her. Pualuna's second wife cried ceaselessly, as though she could not understand that the days of mourning were over. That night Pualuna came home bringing a barbed seal and gave me a piece of skin for lines. He told of his experience in musk-ox hunting, and of having lost six dogs. Then he looked at the weeping woman and the one without tears. He sighed and asked me to be patient with his women: "They are great followers after women's ways, but I am not in a mood to blame them." That was his only reference to what had happened.

In the other house Torngé, Qolugtinguaq's wife, sat sewing when I entered.

"Hereby somebody comes visiting," I said.

"Oh, is somebody out to look at people? Unfortunately you did wrong coming in here. Nobody at all is at home—only women, and you had better get out as soon as possible."

"Are you alone?"

"The Terrible has gone out hunting," she said. Dutiful wives always refer to their husbands as "the Terrible," "the Dreadful," "the Frightful," etc., to signify how frightening and impressive their husbands are.

Torngé asked if I desired anything to eat. I said no, and we sat silent for a while. Then she said: "No one wants to talk in this house. No words are to be heard here and only tears to be seen. That can be no pleasure for a mighty man."

When I left she said: "I thank you for coming." The fact that I could say nothing to comfort her was proof to her of my own grief and sympathy.

After her daughters' death Alinaluk never smiled again. She still had one baby daughter who was learning to walk, and a few weeks later she asked her mother-in-law to look after the child as she wanted to drive to Etah for some things she had left there. She took seven dogs and drove off. Everyone knew she was an excellent driver, but she never returned. After a while one of her dogs came back, the dog which belonged to the baby.

It seemed to be written that this should be a season of dreadful accidents. While we waited at Neqé for the ice to improve I learned more of the people and their folkways than ever before.

a. Knud Rasmussen. b. G. Thostrup and Peter Freuchen on their way home to Denmark. c. Odark.
d. Peter Freuchen. e. At Thule, setting out on an expedition.

f.

g.

h.

i.

j.

k.

f. Home of a Greenlander family. g. Henrik and Tobias. h. Cleansing and cutting a seal. i. The young Knud Rasmussen coming to Bergen to greet his friend Peter Freuchen and the Denmark Expedition. j. Polar Eskimo studying the newspaper in Peter Freuchen's house at Thule. k. Navarana, Pipaluk, Peter Freuchen and Mequsaq.

After all, this was a large community and something seemed to be happening at every hour of the day.

Among the natives was the man Angudluk who was lame as the result of once freezing his legs. He could go out in his kayak in the summer, or drive his dogs if there was someone along to untangle his traces. His wife, who was a clever driver, often accompanied him and, when the two were in a party of hunters, collected her share of the game.

One day while the two of them were out together they left their thirteen-year-old son at home. A favorite pastime of the children is to hang themselves by their hoods. When the hoods tighten about their necks blood is kept from their heads and they eventually lose consciousness. The other children in the house take them down as soon as their faces turn purple.

The state of unconsciousness is so delightful, the children say, that they play this game at every opportunity, over and over again. They played it on the day Angudluk and his wife were away.

Angudluk's son was the largest child in the group. One after another he hung the smaller children up, lifted them down when they were purple, and laid them on the ledge to recover. When all of them had had their turn he helped them to hang him up. Eventually he grew purple in the face and kicked his legs as the signal to be taken down. The children tried to lift him off the hook, but he was too heavy. They made every effort and still could not lift him, and, as he soon stopped kicking and threshing about, the children forgot about him and ran out of doors to play, leaving him hanging in front of the window over the door.

When the sleds came home the mother cared for the dogs and Angudluk, cold from sitting all day, hurried inside. He crawled through the tunneled entrance and saw the feet of his son hanging down over the doorhole.

There followed another five-day period of mourning. No one was allowed to leave Neqé, and all the sleds were turned front end toward the houses so that no one could be suspected of leaving.

We saw the sad little funeral procession. Only the best skins were used as a coffin. The father drove the dogs up into the hills, and some of them turned stubborn and bolted. Everyone had to stop and punish the dogs, whose howling added to the dolefulness of the occasion. The poor family, whose privations were stringent enough already, left many gifts for the boy, especially a little gun he had wanted, a big knife, and the pipes and tobacco belonging to the whole family—he would be there a long time and need all these things. All the mittens which had been used in constructing his stony grave were left also.

The old man, Sorqaq, who was also hunting in the district, announced that he would attempt a journey to the nether world to ascertain the reason for the tragedies. Sorqaq was believed to have put an end to the last epidemic before it had destroyed the whole tribe. He had met the devil and conquered him—perhaps he could do it again.

At any rate, his preparations for the descent proved his honesty. He fasted until his interior was completely cleaned out, examining his excrement until he was satisfied with his state. After three days he announced himself ready for the journey, and the time of departure was set for the following night. The old man meanwhile climbed high into the mountains seeking solitude to formulate his speech to the spirits and to train himself to swim through the rocks—which he would most certainly have to penetrate in order to meet the devil.

A huge igloo was constructed by adding many blocks of snow to the largest house in the settlement. Several men worked at it, and the snow blocks were cut by the elders who realized the seriousness of the undertaking. After it was finished the inside was draped with a tapestry of old tent skins. Sorqaq inspected the stage which was to witness his marvels, said nothing, and departed for further meditation.

Presently the natives were requested to gather and were led to their places by Krilerneq, Sorqaq's assistant. Krilerneq himself was an old man, but with the aid of a cane he was as strong and spry as anyone. His eyes burned with his fervor, his gestures were quick, his walk nervous.

Like a stage star making an appearance in an ancient vehicle, Sorqaq was the last man to enter the house, and he was announced three times before he finally arrived. He greeted us all by saying that we were a pack of fools to have come: what he proposed to do was nothing, and furthermore he could not even do it.

We all accepted this as the modesty it undoubtedly was; then he walked up to me and asked me to leave:

"This is nothing for a man like you to look at. I am only a big liar, and even if these idiots are stupid enough to believe in me, I never expected you to stand for it. I am only a foolish old man, and what happens here has nothing to do with the truth."

"Even so, I should like to listen to your wisdom."

"Well, well," he replied, "if a man is born white he may still be born stupid."

I assured him of the truth of that statement, but he shook his head sadly and went over to the ledge.

"Oh, only a little lie is on my tongue," he murmured. "A funny little lie that I may give sound to and try to fool you with!"

He peeled off his clothes, which were taken by Krilerneq, and sat stark naked. Krilerneq then took up several sealskin lines and bound him tight, tying his arms beside his body and binding his legs together, the thongs cutting deep into his muscles. The old man held himself rigid during this process. Occasionally a deep sigh escaped him.

When there were no more lines at hand, Krilerneq placed his drum and a large section of dried sealskin beside him on the ledge. The lights were extinguished, and the only illumination came from one tiny flame. We could barely make out each other's faces; we could see nothing distinctly.

Then Krilerneq took his place among us to make sure that no one approached the angekok, for it would mean death.

After a few minutes of utter silence we heard Sorqaq's voice in song. It was weak and quavery, but slowly grew stronger and seemed to emanate from different parts of the igloo. After a moment we heard the voice of the drum, as if beaten by a padded stick, and slowly its sound, too, grew in volume, until the house was filled with the song, the crashing of the drum, and the rattling of the dry skin, now over our heads, now beneath our feet!

The noise was almost unbearable, and I took hold of Krilerneq's arm, pretending fright. Actually I wanted to ascertain whether or not he was contributing to the noise. Obviously he was not.

How long the din lasted I am unable to tell. I remember that when it finally calmed I felt as if I had been dreaming. By now all of us had joined in Sorqaq's song, but slowly it seemed that the voice of the angekok was fading away. At last I definitely

felt that it reached us through the walls of the igloo, perhaps
from above or below. And then suddenly we could hear him no
more.

None of us realized what had happened or when it had happened, but when Krilerneq turned up the flame so that it was
possible to see a little clearer—there was no Sorqaq on the ledge.

All of us sat there singing as we had before. Ecstasy was upon
the face of every man and woman. Their cheeks were swollen,
their eyes bright and shining. Their mouths hung open, and
their bodies were naked from the waist up in order to endure the
heat. They swayed back and forth to the rhythm of the song, and
their heads marked the double beats. No one seemed to see anything, but merely to use his eyes as beacon lights. In the middle
of the floor was Krilerneq writhing and twisting like a dancer.

Beside me sat a young girl, Ivaloo. Her naked body was
pressed against mine, and her strong young scent swept over me.
I tried to speak to her, but she did not hear. Instead, her eyes followed Krilerneq directly in front of us. Her long hair sprayed
loose from the knot on her head, and swung from side to side as
she sang. The rhythmic swish of her hair made me as senseless
as the rest of them.

Ivaloo was married to a clever young hunter, and while he
was away she played the whole day long with her friends. Now
she was no longer a child, but a grown woman endowed with the
witchcraft of her tribe. Her face was a mask, and occasionally her
voice rose above the song in a wild screech, her eyes always upon
the swaying Krilerneq whose madness drove the audience into
the hysteria of cattle before a pack of wolves.

Suddenly one of the men, Krisuk, went out of his head. Unable to contain himself to the regular rhythm of the service, he
leapt to his feet, crying like a raven and howling like a wolf. He
ran amuck, and the audience had to defend itself against his at-
tacks. He rushed at me, I pushed him away and he fell over
Ivaloo. With a quick move of his hands he tore her boots and
pants completely off, but she, almost as wild as the man, screamed
not in fear but in ecstasy. They began to yell in a tongue I could
not understand—certainly it was not the usual Eskimo language.
Angekoks are not permitted to employ the commonplace terms
for things and people, for it would bring disaster upon the objects mentioned. But everyone seemed to understand what was

said—and if there is such a thing as speaking in tongues I heard it then.

No longer able to bear the confinement, Krisuk dove straight through the wall of the igloo, leaving a hole for air which was much needed. We could hear his shrill voice far out on the ice. Someone shut the door, and soon everyone in the room was stripped.

The song continued and I fell completely under the power of the spirit. No longer was I able to observe dispassionately what occurred. Ivaloo lay naked across me, and I could feel someone else chewing my hair, clawing my face. The noise, the odor of bodies, and the mystery of the moment caught me completely unprepared.

Then suddenly all was changed. Krilerneq, who had been the leader of the madness, announced that Sorqaq was trying to return.

He beseeched us all to take our original positions and told us to sit up and sing. No thoughts should concern us but those of the angekok who was at this moment fighting his way up through the granite beneath the igloo. We were as yet unable to hear him, but Krilerneq, who had himself made the pilgrimage a number of times, said that he could feel his imminent arrival, and complained over the suffering he was undergoing. Krilerneq, being the assistant, shared the travail of his friend who had to swim through the rocks as if they were water.

We all listened, and as from far off we could hear Sorqaq's voice. Krilerneq extinguished the light completely, since no one must look upon the angekok "muscle naked"—he has been forced to leave his skin when descending into the ground—lest he die.

And now there was pandemonium. None of us knew which was up and which was down. I remember it all as a black fog which engulfed me.

Krilerneq told us that Sorqaq was coming closer and closer, and we, too, could hear the angekok's voice. Krilerneq explained to us that Sorqaq was having difficulty in finding the house, as someone had left in it in his absence and returned.

But magically we knew at last that he had returned—from the sky or from the depths his "shadow" had "ripened." The igloo reverberated with the noise of his drum and the rattle of the crackling sealskin sometimes over our heads, sometimes under our feet. I raised my hand to try to grasp the skin and received such a blow on my arm that the bone was almost shattered. Hell itself had suddenly come to earth.

And then it all stopped. Krilerneq murmured a long rigmarole, and the igloo was quiet save for the crying of the children. They may have been crying the whole time, but no one had known it. Krilerneq's droning voice prayed to the supposedly present angekok to learn what secrets he had learned concerning the cause of the accidents.

Sorqaq's voice answered: "Three deaths are still to come. The Great Nature is embarrassed by the white men who have come to live with us, and refuses to betray the real reason for its anger. But no great disaster will come to us if the women of the tribe refrain from eating meat of the female walrus until the sun sets again in the fall."

The angekok had done his duty and the performance was over. I had no idea how long it had lasted. Someone brought fire from the next igloo and lighted the lamps.

There was Sorqaq sitting on the ledge still wrapped in his many strands of sealskin. I did not have the opportunity of examining him to see whether he had been free and bound again. He was extremely weak, covered with sweat, and spittle ran down his chest. Krilerneq warned me not to touch Sorqaq, as the fire from the earth was still in him and would be until he moved again.

He sat quiet until Krilerneq removed the lines, then fell back and lay in a coma. At last he opened his eyes. His voice was weak and his mouth dry. He tried to smile as he saw me.

"Just lies and bunk, the whole thing!" he said. "Do not believe in anything. I am no angekok. I speak nothing but lies. The wisdom of the forefathers is not in me!"

He fell back again, and we all assured each other that we had indeed witnessed an amazing thing and been in the presence of truth itself.

Next day I tried to talk with the natives about yesterday's performance, but they were mute. Ivaloo and my hostess, Inuaho, said it made them realize I was a white man—an Eskimo would not want to discuss things which were never mentioned, only done.

19

IT WAS ALMOST SPRING WHEN KNUD RETURNED TO NEQÉ FROM THE
north, loaded with skins and enough musk-ox meat for the whole
tribe. His cries and his laughter preceded him and resounded
over the whole place. We all felt that we were better off when he
was with us. His was a tangible force to which we might cling in
the wilderness. We played games in his honor, and he was
always foremost in every kind of sport. Unfortunately we had a
near accident.

A boy walked far out to sea and hid behind an ice hummock.
Then he jumped up holding a bearskin over his head with which
to tease the dogs.

Such excitement I have seldom seen. Here was an opportunity to prove to the womenfolk who had the best dogs. The
animals were hurriedly hitched to the sleds—probably thirty
teams in all—and we were off, shouting our bear signals and
laughing and lashing the dogs. My team got tangled up with two
others, but finally we neared the camouflaged young man.

The boy was to keep the bearskin over him until the first
team was almost upon him, then discard it and save himself. But
he wanted to give an especially fine performance, and ran about
with the pelt still over his head, dogs hanging onto it ferociously.
Many of them bit through it, and the blood streamed from him.
I finally got him free and drove him home while the others remained and watched the dogfights which resulted. As soon as the
boy's wounds were healed he was at it again.

Among all his myriad activities, Knud was writing a book
concerning the traditions, myths, and folklore of the natives.
Born in the Arctic and familiar with the language, he was better
fitted than anyone else for the work.

Before we returned to Thule he wanted to talk with a certain
old woman, Semigaq, who was wise in the ways of her people—
and a great gossip besides. "Where is my old sweetheart?" he
asked, going from house to house. No one would answer him
until he inquired at a big gathering held at one of the homes.
One of the men answered:

"You see. it is like this: Old Semigaq has very few relatives
here and she is alone most of the time. She went out to trap foxes

some time ago, and her traps are a long way from here. She walks with a little sled, using it both as a support and as a conveyance for her pelts. We all like Semigaq and pity her because of her age. When she did not return after the last gale we talked it over and had great pity for her, but we decided that instead of going to find her we had better use all our pity for her now and then never feel sorry for her any more."

This haphazard method of caring for old, lonely people was not in accord with our scheme of things, and we hurried out to look for her. The snow had begun to drift and my dogs were difficult to manage, so after a while I decided to seek shelter in a cave along the cliffs where Semigaq was known to keep her traps. I drove my dogs up over the ice foot and into the cave, and there I found the poor old woman.

She had not been especially comfortable, but she was at least still alive. She had caught, and eaten, three foxes which she was very sorry had been dead when she found them, since she had torn the pelts in skinning them. She had wanted them for her grandson. She had no sleeping bag, but was thankful for her sled; she could sleep on that. Her strength was exhausted, but her appetite was enormous, and the casual observer might have thought she had only been out for a walk and got a little chilly.

She had not, however, wasted her time during the storm. All her life she had been a great angekok, and here in the cave she had heard many voices and talked with the spirits of people long dead. She had gleaned much information about the living which would enable her to shame them.

When I brought her back to the settlement Knud Rasmussen was angry because of the natives' treatment of her and ordered all the women to sew her a new dress. She was overwhelmed with new clothing and said that she could never remember having looked so well.

Next day we started for home, and Old Semigaq, perhaps because we had rescued her and expressed more concern over her than had her own people for many years, decided to go with us. She climbed on Knud's sled and refused to get off, sitting upon, and smashing, his camera. When he seemed perturbed over this she immediately took the offensive and scolded him for fooling around with things which could not bear the weight of an old and half-starved woman.

Meanwhile our dogs had become sick, and in order to cure them she arranged a séance and so learned that the dogs were sick because they were harnessed in reins that had not been made for them.

It was a fact that we had bought ready-made harnesses. Semigaq also announced that our dogs would spread the infection; and so she drafted the entire male population of the settlement to sew new harnesses for us, and we got these free of charge; oddly enough, the dogs got well.

She lived with us for many years. During the darkest days of the winter months she would collect all the boxes and bags she could get hold of.

"I collect shadows and darkness," she said, "so that the world will get light again, and I keep it all locked up here in these boxes." And every spring the sun came back.

Many sleds followed us to Thule. The natives were on the way to their summer places, and wanted to trade with us. We had few things left with which to trade, but everyone was satisfied.

Old man Panigpak, a man with a reputation for ingenuity and long trips, came from a great distance to trade. He secured what he wanted and, as I had a few knives left, asked for one of them. In exchange he took five fox pelts from his bag and gave them to me.

"You are mistaken," I said. "A knife does not even cost as much as one fox!"

He smiled in his mild way: "I am sorry. My tongue is going to protest against a white man. Perhaps it may fall out, but nevertheless I am right and must speak. You cannot know that I have been without a big knife for a whole year and have been missing it terribly. That is why I give you so many skins."

We continued the discussion in our sitting room. In line with Eskimo logic, goods possess a value according to the need of the buyer rather than the scarcity or abundance of the supply.

"A thing may have no value," he said, "but I need it, and I pay for what I need."

The inhabitants of Thule must travel to the coast in order to catch little auks, and since there is one special season of the year for it nearly all of us went together. Vivi and Aloqisaq went along with us, but life in the open did not agree with Vivi, the southerner, and she returned home.

I stayed with the family of Uvdluriark, whose young stepdaughter, Mequpaluk, had given me the mittens. She repaired my boots and mended my clothes when necessary. She was a handsome girl, but her own clothes were so shabby that her body showed through in many places. It was strange to see her in a household which, aside from herself, was so affluent. But her father would have it no other way. "When she is married," Uvdluriark grinned, "it is up to her husband to dress her." She was an excellent worker, and her devotion to her younger brothers was touching. Whatever I paid her for her services she always gave to them, and she would never eat at my house without hoarding the scraps for the small ones at home.

The song of the auks is sweeter than anything else to the natives. "Pi-u-lee, Pi-u-lee-pi-u-lee," they cry, flying out to sea in living clouds at night, and early in the morning assembling in the cliffs once more, singing the whole day long. Each time a man swings his net through the air he captures seven or eight of the small birds. The net is then quickly turned so that they may not escape, and they are hauled in. The auks are killed by placing the finger on the chestbone and moving the heart a fraction of an inch. The bird dies instantly, and a delicious collection of blood clots around the heart, to be eaten later when the meat is frozen.

But many birds are eaten immediately. They have just migrated from the south and their skins are lined with a thick layer of fat, so that those fond of good food pluck, rather than skin, the birds and boil them in a pot. I was too lazy to do this, but little Mequpaluk plucked them for me. Never would she eat any of the fresh meat herself. She said she had plenty of the skins to chew at home, and they were good enough for her.

The old women chew the skins day in and day out to remove the fat so that they can be used for clothing. After many years their teeth wear down to the gums, and it is difficult for them to digest their food, but their jaw muscles are in fine condition as long as they live.

The dullness of their teeth makes it possible for the old women to chew the delicate auk skins without cutting holes in them. The skins are so small that a grown man seldom has clothing made from them, though it is said that occasionally a young woman without babies is so fond of her husband that she chews sufficient skins to make him a shirt.

When we were ready to return home the ice was bad, and I had to take Uvdluriark's stepdaughter along with me. It was then that I discovered what an extraordinary person she was.

There was no laziness in her; to work was her pleasure. When we halted to rest the dogs she always untangled the traces before the animals had a chance to lie down. Whenever I needed anything she foresaw and, if possible, fulfilled my need. She was the only girl I ever met among the Eskimos who really cared for flowers and birds.

We drove home in the night, though it was daylight. We could see the moon, but it was pale and unreal before the sun. I looked at it and remarked that when the moon was only half as large it was easier to examine it with my field glasses. She looked at it carefully through my glasses. I have always been too proud of my little knowledge, and I started to tell her about the mountains on the moon which she could see through the glasses. She stopped me:

"Mountains? The man, you mean?"

I smiled down upon her from the great height of my learning and told her that there were indeed mountains upon the moon.

"But then," she asked, "what about the man up there?"

"There is no man in the moon."

I was surprised that anyone should really believe the myth, but she explained that her grandfather, who was a wise old man, had told her there was a man in the moon. Her mother believed it too. How could one believe anything the angekoks said if they lied about the man in the moon?

This she asked in a very modest way, and as sincerely and simply as possible I assured her that they were wrong—there was no man in the moon. From that day forward there was a secret bond between us. I was to her the man who knew everything, and I tried in every manner possible to live up to the great faith and trust of her clean and innocent soul.

When we reached home we parted—she to run to her mother's tent where she spent more than twenty hours a day caring for her small brothers and keeping house.

When the time for walrus hunting arrived many more natives joined us at the island. Walrus come up from the south and pass Melville Bay as soon as the water is open. On their journey there are no clams or oysters for them, and they feed on the seals. When they arrive at Cape York, where they never halt, their stomachs are full of seal meat and skin. At Parker Snow Bay, the first place where they find a tasty menu, they stop for a few days. When they reach Agpat, they settle down to feed for a long time.

Many of us went out on our boat, which was a great boon in
towing the carcasses, but for real excitement you must hunt the
great beasts from a kayak. You get no impression of their fierce-
ness or strength if you stand on the deck of a big ship. But in a
kayak the hunter is on the same level with the walrus.

Walrus must dive to the bottom to secure their food. With
their long tusks they plow up the dirt and shells, then take the
soil and mud and shells between their foreflippers and swim
upward. The dirt washes out in this process, leaving the stones,
clams, and oysters. Then they rub the shells between their thick,
scabrous flippers and crush them. The heavier portions sink, the
meat floats, and the walrus opens his mouth and swallows it.
Consequently one never finds shells of any sort in a walrus'
stomach. Many uninformed writers have expressed surprise at
this.

The period of time the animals remain submerged is determined by the depth of the water. At Agpat they stayed down for
seven minutes; at Pituravik, nine. They always remain for a short
while on the surface, heading into the current, which permits the
kayaks to approach from the rear.

The hunters must try to judge where the walrus will next
appear in order to be in the immediate neighborhood. At the
moment the hunter sees the head of the beast emerge his arms
dart like lightning. His kayak shoots forward straight as an arrow,
and when he is close enough he hurls his harpoon directly at the
animal. If he makes a hit the bladder attached to the rope is
dragged out of the boat as the walrus dives, and is often pulled
completely under the surface for a long period.

As soon as the bladder is visible again the men in the big
boat rush toward it and the real battle begins. Nowadays guns
soon end the fight, but in former times the hunters had to finish
the walrus with their spears. That process was often cruel, and the
beast floundered about in the water for hours until it had bled
to death.

The stomach is always the prize portion, since it is usually
filled with the most delicious clams and oysters, and the stomach
juices serve as a tantalizing sour dressing.

If one has been eating meat and nothing but meat twice a
day, a feeling of lethargy eventually overcomes him. But immediately he has eaten these clams it is as if he had taken a magic
potion of pep and energy. If anything is left over, the two open-

ings of the stomach are tied up and the rare article brought home
to the women who use it for making soups.

It was at Saunders Island that I got my first walrus. I had
been out in a kayak numerous times and was anxious to get one,
but never had the opportunity. Now it was my turn, and I was
lucky enough to be directly behind the beast when he came up
for air, so I rushed ahead.

Never had any animal looked so enormous to me, but I could
not turn back without looking ridiculous. I was almost upon the
walrus before I had any plan in mind. It was breathing deeply,
preparing to go down again for more oysters. Now was the time.
Suddenly my harpoon flashed through the air. Without waiting
to see whether it had struck home I whipped my kayak around
and made off. My little boat trembled, and I hoped I was not
being attacked. It was, however, only the bladder being dragged
from the boat.

And the first thing I knew men were shouting and hailing
me from the other kayaks and the boat. I had got my first walrus!

I was "newborn in the land"—as the natives put it—because
harpooning a walrus is the first step toward becoming a hunter. I
was *somebody* now. The Eskimos even have a special word for
"killing the first walrus," so important is that event in the life of
a man.

20

~~~~~~

SOON AFTERWARD I DECIDED TO GO NORTH WITH A LARGE SUPPLY OF
goods for the Eskimos. Before I left, my friend Tatianguak came
to see me.

"It has been noticed that Peterssuak travels without a woman,"
he said. "My wife, Ivaloo, has relatives in the north and would
like to visit them. She might conceivably be of some use on the
trip. She may be of help in cooking and in drying clothes. Also
the traveler enjoys his nights more when they are shared by a
woman."

Since I had now decided to settle down for good and live like
the Eskimos in every respect, I thought, why not accept the offer.
And Ivaloo and I set out together across the Wolstenholme Fjord
and into Granville Bay. Our conversation the first few hours was
neither fluent nor romantic.

"Are you afraid of me, Ivaloo?" I asked her.

"No pleasure is felt."

"Do you know the way across the inland glacier?"

"There is no desire to cross the glacier. It's cold and windy there."

"But we'll have to. There is no ice around the cape."

"Your words are wasted. Let men talk to men and keep their silence when they are with a mere woman."

I kept quiet but after a while the silence became oppressive.

"Are you afraid of me, Ivaloo?" I asked her.

"Why should I be afraid? Please do not talk unless reasonable words are spoken."

A rather cold response, particularly since the temperature was thirty degrees below zero and the wind was sharp from the north.

I jumped off the sled once in a while and ran next to it in order to keep warm while the girl remained seated, freezing in dignified silence. Every time I asked her if she was cold, I got the same reply:

"Keep quiet. One thinks!"

I hoped she was thinking of me and the many nights we were going to spend together. Finally I asked her what she was thinking about.

"Meat!" she answered and I stopped the dogs to prepare a meal for us.

In the evening we arrived at the bottom of Granville Bay where we met an Eskimo family on its way to Thule. We spent the night in a cave there with them. There was no sign of surprise when they met me with the wife of a well-known Eskimo as my single companion. We ate our evening meal with them, and Ivaloo proudly served them tea from my supplies.

We prepared our bed in the cave by placing a large mat of dried grass on the rock, then a sealskin, then a bear skin, and finally my sleeping bag. Ivaloo had brought no bag of her own. We removed our fur coats and rolled them up as pillows, and finally we undressed. In such a sleeping bag the best way to keep warm is to be naked. There were two of us in my bag, and it was not hard to keep warm.

Our trip lasted several weeks, and I visited all the northern settlements I could reach and traded guns and ammunition, knives and other tools for furs until I had nothing left to give them. I was sincerely sorry the last night when I knew I had to return Ivaloo to her husband the following morning. And I was wondering just how to say good-by to her after all our days and nights together. I need not have worried.

Crossing North Star Bay in the evening, with Thule a short distance ahead, I had a hard time controlling the dogs, as they were impatient to get home. When I finally had them in hand I tried hesitantly to talk to Ivaloo. There was no reply. I looked around to discover that she was no longer on the sled behind me. I could see her in the distance—a small dot on the ice close to shore. She had calmly jumped off the sled to take a short cut back to her husband, without a single word of farewell.

In the following months I turned more and more into an Eskimo. It happened every now and then that Ivaloo returned to me for a night, but I cannot claim she was my only companion.

Ivaloo was a great beauty, and she was well aware of her charms. She and Tatianguak, the adopted son of the murdered Uvisakavsik, were newlyweds, and they said they wanted to remain close to us in order to avoid any grudge fights which might arise.

The young husband came to me several times and confessed that, since he was a very bad hunter, he had no business being married to such an attractive woman. He said he thought he had better leave her and let me marry her—perhaps I would give him a gun and wood for a sled in exchange. I courteously declined his offer.

He sat quiet for a few moments and then walked away. I watched him as he explained the conversation to Ivaloo, who listened interestedly. It was obvious that the scheme had been hers. I remembered her actions during the séance at Neqé, when she had been wild and positively out of her head. Now she was coldly calculating the advantages of belonging to a white man. She had evidently told Tatianguak that the marriage might not last long, and she would eventually return to him a much richer woman.

Ivaloo was remarkable to look at with her clothes off, for on her shoulder and, extending along the upper side of her right arm to the hand, lay a huge red birthmark.

I was told that there was a very special reason for this—Ivaloo was one and the same person as her grandmother!

The old woman had been living in an igloo with the family near Parker Snow Bay when a snowslide crushed the dwelling.

By a miracle everyone but the grandmother escaped. The whole family had suffered severely from exposure as the catastrophe had occurred at night and found them all naked.

The body of the grandmother was not discovered until the following spring when hunters found her right arm and shoulder protruding from a snowdrift. The gulls had eaten the flesh away to the bone.

Shortly after this event Ivaloo was born—and on her right arm and shoulder was a mark in precisely the same position as the scar left by the carrion birds upon the old woman. Consequently it was quite evident that Ivaloo was the old woman reborn.

21

KNUD RASMUSSEN RETURNED TO THE HOUSE WITH THE THREE OLD hags, and we stayed on to collect eggs and catch walrus. Then one morning I was aroused by an ear-splitting yell. Everyone was apparently going crazy, shouting and screaming, dancing and howling. What they were saying I could not ascertain, but finally I heard the word *"Oomiarssuaq!"* and a few moments later made out the masts of a ship sailing round Cape Athol.

A ship at this time of year was totally unexpected, and I realized instantly that this one belonged to whalers, the Upernadlit—"Those Whose Arrive with the Spring."

Everyone leapt into our boat and proceeded to hurl the meat out of it in preparation for the trip to the vessel. It was amazing to discover that the natives still had fox pelts to trade—the women had kept some for their personal use—now that the trading fever possessed them.

The ship was gradually approaching, and I induced the natives to wait until it was near before we set out. I must admit that the sight of its masts against the snow and ice was a welcome one to me.

Before we got into our little boat I told the women that they could accompany us on only one condition—that they promise to keep away from the sailors. I explained that I had nothing to say concerning their morals, but that they might very well contract venereal diseases and contaminate the whole tribe. The women all accepted the conditions, and we put our oars to the water. The ship turned out to be the *Morning of Dundee* and its Captain Adams an old friend of mine.

We spent several pleasant hours talking, after our meal in the cabin. I told him that I had found a dead whale with his harpoon buried in it during the last summer, and we both cursed the American who had invented artificial whalebone.

I must confess that I had forgotten my natives entirely, and when I prepared to leave I remembered them with a start. They had, it seemed, been enjoying a hearty meal in the crew's quarters and had had the time of their lives. When I called to them to get into the little boat the women were the last to arrive. They were grinning, either in amusement or fear—those that came at all. I demanded to know the trouble. One innocent soul, whose innocence empowered him to tattle on the others, informed me that Aloqisaq had lost her pants.

This was a rather delicate predicament for a lady—especially one who has no skirt—and I went down to the men's quarters to try to find out what had happened.

"Well," she said, "the pants simply disappeared." She could not understand how it could have happened. I questioned the sailors, but none of them had the pants. I asked which bunk she had been in, but that got me nowhere, as it appeared that she had not restricted herself to one bunk, and she could not identify her particular hosts. I gave up and handed her a big red handkerchief to tie around her middle like a diaper. She did not look very pleased—or very stylish—but it served. The *Morning of Dundee* sailed away north, and I never saw it again.

Captain Adams had brought us our mail, among other things. I saved the letter from the girl I had left at home until the last, partly to tantalize myself, and partly because I feared the news it might contain. I had not dared ask her to share my present life, yet secretly I had hoped she would. When I finally opened the letter, I could have cried with joy—she was coming up to join me, probably on the boat that was to bring us fresh supplies this summer!

She wanted to share my life, whatever it was. She wanted to live in my house, wherever it was, and become an Arctic woman. Together we would make life gayer and pleasanter than it had ever been anywhere in the world!

I was in the skies and set about making preparations for her arrival. As a letter from Knud's wife told him that he was the father of a newborn daughter, both of us were so excited that we scarcely knew what we were doing.

But while we waited for our boat we had to keep up our daily tasks. Summer came. We hunted in kayaks and sailed to nearby communities in our little boat. And on one day during that summer Knud gave us the fright of our lives.

We were after narwhals, which are amazingly fast. Knud was persistent to a fault, and when one came up on the left side of his kayak he threw his harpoon into the animal, though he knew that the whale should have been on his right side. When the whale dived it pulled the line attached to the bladder round Knud's body, capsized the kayak, and hurled him into the water. He was an excellent swimmer, but the line was twisted about him, and he disappeared below the surface in the wake of the wounded narwhal. The rest of us sat in our kayaks, absolutely helpless. For once, I knew what it meant to feel my blood run cold.

After an interminable interval Knud came up far away, gasping for help. We rowed frantically, but long before any of us reached the spot where he had appeared he was down a second time. I was afraid he was done for this time, but a second later he bobbed up again. This time he stayed up and we hauled him out of the water.

Not for a moment had he lost his nerve. He had merely hung onto the bladder, he said, as he figured his weight would quickly tire the narwhal and the animal would come to the surface.

"You'd better go home for a change of clothes," I said.

He eyed me reproachfully. "Don't you see that this is our chance for a big killing?" Later on I asked him if he did not at least want his clothes wrung out.

"Why?" he said.

"Because you're wet as hell!" I roared.

"By God, I forgot that!"

That's the kind of man who makes a real explorer.

But our ship did not arrive. The harbor at Thule usually remained open for only twenty-five days each year—from August 1 to 25—and already it was the middle of September. We were nearly out of supplies, especially matches and nails, and must do something to replenish our store before the winter closed in on us.

We decided that I, being the sailor, should try to make a voyage across Melville Bay to the Danish settlement in our sailboat, stopping at Saunders Island to pick up supplies for the trip from our caches there. But as we reached the island we saw a small schooner already there in the harbor. It was our ship; it had spent forty-five days in crossing Melville Bay!

My girl was not on it!

For me that was all that mattered. Born a lady, and reared in a large city, she had decided at the last moment that she could not face such an existence. I had known all along that it was asking too much of her, and I could not blame her for changing her mind. But at the time it was the worst blow that had ever hit me.

How empty my little preparations for her arrival! How much more empty the house than it had been before.

22

AT CAPE YORK WE RAN ACROSS MINIK, A BOY WHO HAD CAUSED MUCH trouble on an earlier trip. He was living there in one of the houses reserved for the young people of the community.

There are such houses in most of the larger communities— dwellings which have been constructed many years before and now in reality belong to no one. During the summer anyone may appropriate them. The roofs must be taken off so that the sun will have a chance to thaw the ice and dry the walls, and in the fall the stones and peat must be replaced. In these houses the boys and girls may live together without censure or obligation beyond the demands of the night.

The Eskimos take a wholly natural and practical view of sex. They consider no marriage happy unless a sexual affinity exists between the two concerned, and therefore they believe it most important for the man and the woman to test and establish this affinity before they undertake a permanent union.

Unfortunately two families of missionaries had come north. Both were natives from South Greenland, and were sincere believers in their doctrine and their God.

I never like to say too much concerning Christian missions among pagans. I have seen all manner of men and women missionaries, and many of them were unfit for the task they elected to perform. At home no one is able to judge whether or not these persons will make successful missionaries, and those who donate to the cause always believe in the benefits of carrying the word of God to the pagans—it is natural for anyone to assume that his charity is not wasted.

We must realize that missionaries are going to violate all manner of racial rules and traditions, and even trample upon what the pagans have always believed to be decency. Such a program requires tact and infinite patience.

Usually they set to work on the question of sex. It is strange how sex has always interested the church. Of course, sex has always interested everybody, and if the church is able to control it, the church is immediately an important factor in the life of a people. But I have always been a little embarrassed for preachers, who seem to wield such small influence over their own flocks at home, daring to interfere with the ways of an alien race.

Arnanguaq, the young lady who had been offered to me last winter, was now living at Cape York. She was the joint mistress of four young men who lived in one of the youths' houses, and Knud asked me what we should do about it. I told him that I would not mix up in her affairs, but he said it was our duty to support the missionaries. He went to talk with the girl.

"Don't you think," she said, "that I would rather marry one single man? This is the only way I have of getting in touch with them." What a natural and innocent thing to say. And how clean, after all.

That same evening Minik came to me and said he wanted to marry Arnanguaq. He had no house, but if he might move in with us he could offer her a shelter for the winter and in the spring build her a home.

We thought it over and decided to let them move in with us—thereby saving Minik, who was probably a good enough fellow and only needed a break, and the girl. We would also be supporting the work of the missionaries, and each of us would feel like a hell of a fine fellow. Minik left the next day with his bride. There had been no ceremony. I followed, alone, since Knud had decided to go south after more bear meat.

I reached home and was more satisfied than ever. I saw Minik working at last, adjusting to conditions and trying to make a living for himself and his wife. He had exaggerated his own importance, he said, when he was one of six selected to go to New York, and had been the only one of his people to survive the journey. But now he was back in the North, and he promised to begin over again and forget the outside world.

He and I built a small house beside our larger one. I moved in with him and his wife, as, in the Arctic, it is difficult to separate night from day and the natives are apt to run in at all hours to talk. Knud could stay up for twenty-four hours and then sleep almost as many, but I liked to go to bed at a regular time. We agreed that our old house would be office, dining room, dwelling, and trading post. Knud would sleep in the attic, and I would stay with Minik.

Minik's wife was not, unfortunately, much of a housekeeper. Her patience was inexhaustible, and there was not one ounce of bad intention in her. As a matter of fact, there were very few intentions of any sort in Arnanguaq, for she was as resourceless a girl as I have ever met. She could never think of anything to do. It was not long before Minik began to remain longer and longer away from the house on his hunting trips.

One day he announced to us all that he was going north, and he was going alone. He did not know how long he would be gone. I made no move to prevent his going, and he set off, leaving me alone with his young wife.

To circumvent any whisper of scandal Arnanguaq invited Mequpaluk to spend the nights with her. Each evening after the girl had done all her chores at home she came running down to the house. Her clothes were still disgraceful, her boots almost soleless, and her stockings furless. But she was always in the best of humor, and our room became a cheerier place when she entered it. She had a trick of recounting her experiences so quaintly that everyone laughed with her, and each night we awaited her arrival with impatience.

Finally one evening when she came Arnanguaq was absent, and I told Mequpaluk that she had better stay with me. She looked at me a moment and then remarked simply:

"I am unable to make any decisions, being merely a weak little girl. It is for you to decide that."

But her eyes were eloquent, and spoke the language every girl knows regardless of race or clime.

I only asked her to move from the opposite side of the ledge over to mine—that was all the wedding necessary in this land of the innocents.

Next day she wanted to know whether she was to return to her home or not, and when I said no, that was final. A few hours later one of her brothers came to ask why she had not come home. She said:

"Somebody is occupied by sewing for oneself in this house!"

The boy was startled but said nothing and turned on his heel to race from house to house with the news. After a few hours sleds hurried north and south to tell what had happened and to hear firsthand the comments of the neighbors.

Again I was amazed at the discretion of these wonderful people. Not one of them spoke a word to either of us which would indicate that the girl had not always lived in our house. Visitors came as usual and talked as if she had been my wife for years and they had been her guest many times.

The next evening my little wife asked me to come down to the beach with her so that we could talk alone without a roof over us. She said that she had spent the day in speculation, and she had decided, now that she was married to a white man, to use one of her other names. (Also, Odark's wife, Mequ, had died recently, and the name "Mequpaluk" could not be spoken any more.) She had been too frightened, however, to change her name without consulting me.

I agreed that she should take another name, and from then on she was known as "Navarana" over all Greenland.

The first thing was to secure a wardrobe for her. Now she had plenty of furs to select from, and she hired several friends to do the sewing. There was no thought of actual payment as, Navarana told me, the sewers were delighted with the privilege of sitting in our house and listening to everything that was said. Their reward was in being able to tell what they had seen and heard.

We fixed up our room considerably, and when I came home with my first seal after our marriage, we invited all our neighbors to a feast. Still not one word was said of its being an unusual occasion.

Shortly afterward walrus were reported at Dalrymple Rock, and, the ice being favorable, I left home with a number of the villagers to drive out and get a few. It was too far to return home each night, especially as it was light for only a few hours now, so we slept on our sleds. In the evenings we built big fires, cooked the meat and made hot soup, and one of the men had a great idea.

"Let us boil some eggs," he said, and was applauded for his ingenuity. This concerned me more than the others, since I was the only man who had eggs cached on the island. However, caches belong to the community, and I could not refuse to bring them out. The caches may not be carted away, but as much may be eaten on the spot as is possible.

Frozen eggs are among the finest of God's gifts. In freezing, the shell always cracks, but the white of the egg that escapes freezes and dries, and is delicious to the taste. The shell is removed after holding the egg between the palms for a few moments, and then the egg itself is eaten like an apple. The number each man could put away was almost unbelievable, especially as these were eider-duck eggs, almost twice as large as hen's eggs.

After we had consumed many dozens the pot was filled and dozens more boiled—and I was the one man who had gathered any eggs.

When I returned home I began to appreciate the woman my wife was going to be. She still wore her rags, but her new boots were finished, and she looked incongruous in pure white, long boots with bearskin emerging from the tops and giving way to pants which would scarcely hold together. But the next day the pants were replaced with fine new ones, and then she boasted the best raiment in the tribe.

I related the egg episode to Navarana, and she promised to put a stop to it. I was a little apprehensive lest my honor as a hunter be tainted, but she was far too clever for that. "Do you really think," she said, "that I would do such a thing to you? Oh, no!"

She merely remarked to her mother that she was afraid we would have no eggs when she came to visit us this winter. Her mother, a fine, intelligent woman, then dropped a kernel of suspicion into the community. "Perhaps," she ventured, "the walrus-hunting season may not last as long as usual this year, since someone has dropped eggshells on the ice and the walrus may take offense." The women carried this gossip to their husbands, who discussed it at length. Finally the elders of the community decided that, even if they could not be certain, it might be just as well to refrain from eating eggs while hunting walrus.

Thus I reaped my first material reward from marriage.

I quickly came to love and admire my young wife and to laugh at our initial difficulties. She was thunderstruck the second day after our marriage when I told her to get washed in the morning.

"Your memory must have deserted you, Pita," she said. "I washed yesterday!"

She doubted my sanity when I insisted that she must wash every day, even have an occasional bath. But in later years she came to be one of the warmest advocates of cleanliness in Thule.

PART II

~~~~~~

1

AN ENTIRELY NEW LIFE OPENED UP FOR ME, ONE WHICH BOUND ME
closer than ever to the Arctic.

Many years later I heard the term "going native," but it did
not occur to me then that that was what I was doing. I did
know that my marriage to an Eskimo girl made a final breach
with the world I had known as a young man, but I had already
left that world far behind. Navarana was immediately accepted as
my wife wherever we visited in Greenland, and no one worried
over the duration of our union. Not until long afterward, after
our two children were born, did any of the natives admit to me
that they had not at first taken our marriage seriously. Even
Navarana's mother had thought it but a casual arrangement and
that Navarana would soon be sent home.

Navarana's own life had been a blood-curdling saga of the
Arctic. As a small girl she had lived with her parents on Salve
Island. One of those inexplicable epidemics that so pitifully rav-
age a primitive race struck the people, and on the island where
they lived only Navarana, her mother, and her small brother
were spared. They had no meat to eat and were forced to butcher
their dogs for food. When this source of supply was exhausted
they ate their clothes and dog traces and anything available. The
little boy was about three years old and was still nursing. The
mother soon had no milk left, and the child in a frenzy of hunger
bit the nipple off her breast. Then, seeing no hope of keeping
him alive, she hanged him while Navarana looked on. The
mother's grief, Navarana told me, was worse than the sight of the
dead child, and she swore to her mother that she did not want to
die, no matter how hungry she was, but would remain to comfort
her.

Navarana told me that she ate grass and the excrement of
rabbits and chewed on the tatters of old skins, and, with the fall

ice, Uvdluriark arrived on his sled and took them both to his house.

After a couple of years Navarana went to live with her grandfather and grandmother. Her grandfather, Mequsaq, was a veteran of great dignity and experience, and he lavished all his affection upon her. While living with Mequsaq she had the good fortune to escape a siege of starvation which wiped out thirteen others at Cape Alexander. This had occurred the year Mylius-Erichsen and Knud Rasmussen were there for the first time.

The old man and his wife and Navarana at the last found only two others alive, Kullabak and her son, Kraungak. They took the boy along with them (there was not room on their sled for Kullabak) and when they reached the next community, left Navarana and Kraungak in a shelter while they went out to look for walrus. They got one, rescued old Kullabak, and saved all their lives. Navarana told me that she remembered only one incident of this experience: While she and Kraungak waited for the old people to return, the boy, whose feet were frozen, cut off one of his little toes with a knife in order to impress her. He said it didn't hurt, but she could never forget it.

I had thought I was well acquainted with the people of Greenland, but now their lives became doubly rich for me. Navarana told me countless tales I would otherwise never have heard. The Eskimos, great gossips about surface matters, are remarkably close-mouthed and conservative concerning anything that really matters.

Navarana's grandmother had died, and we wanted to find her old grandfather, Mequsaq, and suggest that he come to live with us. We discovered him living with some of his other relatives, but he was delighted that his beloved granddaughter was now in a position to offer him a home. He had been dreaming of this for years, he said.

Once, when Mequsaq was in a talkative mood he told us about some of his background. At the time I had only a vague idea of the strange experiences he had lived through. During the next few years I was to become quite familiar with his history as he chose the more gory details of his life as bedtime stories for my two children in Thule.

"We came from far, far away on the other side of the water," he now told us. "We came from the west when we had to leave our settlements because there was great famine in the land. Our

leader and guide was the great Kritlak, who understood everything, who could ask questions of stones and water, and make
use of the answers he received."

"What did this great Kritlak ask about?" I asked.

"He asked them where to go, where to find better hunting
grounds, and the answers proved right. We left starvation behind
as we crossed the ice and found a new home. Kritlak knew the
spirits and his power was so great that there was a shining light
around his head when he traveled at night."

I have often since heard stories about Kritlak and his halo.
Navarana was convinced that the stories were true, and she
pointed out that Kritlak's son and grandson had been marked
for life, to prove that they were the offspring of Kritlak the spirit
man. The halo had been so strong that for generations the heads
in the family had been unable to grow hair! It is quite true that
Panigpak, the grandson, was bald—the only bald Eskimo I have
ever come across. This rare baldness, combined with the pictures
of "Jesus" that the missionaries had shown the Eskimos, had
probably created this story about the halo.

Around 1864, Mequsaq had come to Greenland with his
family. He was then a young boy. Exceptionally severe winters
and poor hunting had resulted in widespread famine in northern
Canada, and with other Eskimos Mequsaq's tribe had left their
settlements in Baffin Land. They had made their way across
Devon Island to Ellesmere Island and crossed Smith Sound over
to Greenland, where they found better living conditions. They
had done so well for themselves that some of them wanted to
return to their old settlements and tell their friends and relatives
about the new and happy land they had found. It was on this unsuccessful return trip that young Mequsaq lost his eye.

They had spent two winters in Greenland when they set out
on the long sled trip back to Baffin Land. They ran into terrible
snow storms, and since they had not been able to carry much food
with them they were soon starving. At first they ate most of their
dogs, but they had to save some if they were to continue their
journey. Soon they were so weakened that they could not go on
unless they caught sufficient game to regain their strength. They
built their igloos and settled down where they were to wait for
better hunting luck.

In the traveling party were two men, Milik and Mattak, who
were stronger than all the others. They were good hunters, but

they also took a larger share of the catch and ate more than anyone else. They did not obey the rules of the tribe, they were not satisfied with their just share and took by force whatever they wanted. As the lack of food continued and their sufferings got steadily worse, the two men became more and more brutal.

One day when Mequsaq's father was out hunting with the other men, Milik and Mattak suddenly forced their way into the igloo where Mequsaq's father had left his family. It was obviously their intention to kill them all in order to satisfy their hunger. Mequsaq's older brother defended the family valiantly, and young Mequsaq himself put up a brave fight. The two men fell first on the mother. They killed her in front of the boys and carried her outside the igloo, but they were not through. They returned at once and assailed the rest of the family. Mequsaq fought for his life. During the wild struggle one of his eyes was gouged out and he received a serious knife wound in his neck and another in his back, the scars of which I had often seen.

Mequsaq saved his life, but he lost his mother and his sister, who were both carried off by the cannibals.

When the father returned he decided at once to go after the two men in order to avenge his wife and daughter. He set off, but his dogs were too weak and he himself was without much strength and had to give up the chase before long. He returned to the temporary settlement where all the survivors moved into one large igloo to be better prepared to defend themselves against the cannibals in case they should return.

One night they were aroused by the sound of sleds outside. Milik and Mattak had returned, but when they realized that the men were at home to defend their families, they gave up their attack. Nobody dared leave the house until morning when they found traces of the gruesome acts of the cannibals. They had gone to a burial place where three women, who had died from starvation, had been put to rest under some loose stones. Milik and Mattak had removed the three corpses, put them on their sleds, and disappeared. That was the last they saw or heard of the cannibals, but they were nervous about them for a long time to come.

After all these misfortunes they had no desire to continue the return trip to Baffin Land. There were plenty of women left in Greenland whom they could take for wives, and so they turned east once more, crossing from Ellesmere Island to Etah.

They settled down at Etah, but soon Mequsaq and his best friend, Asayuk, were on the move again. The young men were eager to learn the ways of the Greenland Eskimos, who were different in many ways from their own people in Canada. They had no kayaks and they were not familiar with the bow and arrow. They could catch the animals of the sea only when the ice was solid, and in the summertime they moved from their settlements to the many small islands with bird mountains. When the sea was open and ice-free they had to live off the birds. And Mequsaq followed them with his friend to Saunders Island, which was a paradise in summer.

They had both been lucky enough to get hold of one of the rare steel knives that had been brought to Greenland by the whalers. At the time the Eskimos had only the clumsy small cutters which they carved from the meteorites found in the extreme north of Greenland. These cutters were poor tools, but better than the stone knives used in Baffin Land. Later on the great *"Piuli"* (Admiral Peary) brought the meteorites back to his own country and, in return, gave the Eskimos all the steel tools they needed.

The first steel knives they had ever owned caused them a great deal of trouble. The leader of the tribe that settled down on Saunders Island for the summer was a great hunter and a powerful man—and the only one in the tribe to own a steel knife. He was furious when he saw the two young strangers in possession of this symbol of his wealth and authority, and one day, when they were both asleep in their tents he got their knives and dropped them in the sea.

Mequsaq and Asayuk were enraged. They decided at once to kill the old man. They had never liked him; he had been an old tyrant and they had rebelled against his leadership. They would make him pay with his life for the injustice and they would do it right: They would kill him with the clumsy cutters they were now forced to use instead of their knives. But they were not sharp enough to penetrate the thick fur and skin of his clothes, so one day in the fall they caught him an an unguarded moment. The men were making ready for winter and had to look after their sleds. Like other sensible Eskimos, Miuk had stored his sled on top of his meat rack where the dogs could not reach it. The young men had planned for the moment when Miuk would take his sled down. He had to stretch his arms as far as he could in order to reach the top of the meat rack. As he did so, his shirt pulled up and exposed part of his stomach. At that moment Mequsaq and Asayuk jumped on him with their clumsy cutters. They stabbed him with all their strength and the dull knives easily penetrated the skin. They cut open his belly and the old man died in a matter of minutes.

Mequsaq was stronger than Asayuk and they agreed, therefore, that he should keep the dead man's knife until the sun disappeared and Asayuk should have it as long as the next sun lasted. Thus they would take turns and have it one year each. The two friends would have had no trouble keeping the bargain, but the sensible Asayuk felt that it might be too much of a temptation. Murder went with the knife, he said to Mequsaq. After a year Mequsaq might be so fond of the knife that he might kill his friend in order to be the sole possessor of the precious tool. He would rather make a gift of it to Mequsaq so they could remain friends.

In due time they decided that Saunders Island was too small for both of them and Mequsaq went south for further exploits. He traveled all the way down to the great bay where he went bear hunting and nearly lost his knife. He had an encounter with a huge beast that seemed indestructible.

In spring his travels took him to Cape York where Mequsaq discovered to his regret that the knife was not so precious any more. Several whalers had visited the settlement and had left behind a number of good steel knives. Several men in Cape York now had the precious tool which had been such a rare sight in Greenland only a year before. But Mequsaq was greeted as a great man anyhow. He was highly respected as the killer of the great hunter on Saunders Island, and his fame had preceded him to Cape York. On his arrival he was asked to act as policeman, or avenger, for the settlement. The whole population was in an uproar.

Shortly before his arrival one of the strongest men in the tribe had committed a shameful act for which he had to be punished. Tulimak, as he was called, had broken into the house of another Eskimo who was away on a hunt. He had stolen all the man's possessions, taken away his wife, and run off to the south, across Melville Bay. Nobody had dared to go after the strong Tulimak, and nobody was quite sure where to find him.

Mequsaq was asked to take care of the community and punish

the crime. He did not quite know how to tackle the problem—
how to find the guilty couple or how to handle the strong man—
but he had no choice. With his great fame he could not afford
to refuse the people's request.

The next day he set off across the bay, and all the men in Cape
York followed him with their dog sleds as a respectful distance.
The second day out Mequsaq was lucky enough to come across
the tracks of Tulimak's sled which took him straight to the hiding place of the lovers—Bryant Island.

The bold Tulimak had taken his girl straight to the small
island and had built an igloo. He had been fortunate to catch
a number of seals, and they had enough food and blubber for
their lamp and the fire. The girl had not been at all reluctant
to go with him; she was very much in love with the wild man and
their romance might have turned out quite differently if
Mequsaq had not happened to visit Cape York at the time. In
fact, Mequsaq's own life might have been quite different, too.

Mequsaq approached the island at night when the amorous
couple was resting in each other's arms. The girl heard the sound
of his sleds when he was already quite close to the igloo. She took
one peek outside into the night where Mequsaq was hurrying up
from the shore, and brusquely roused her lover.

Tulimak jumped up and at once realized his helpless position.
He slept naked, like all Eskimos, and had left his tools and
weapons outside by his sled. He did not dare take time to dress.
He scuttled out to get hold of his harpoon or some other weapon
to defend himself and his happiness, but he was too late. Mequsaq
might have had trouble if the man had been properly armed. As
it was, he caught the naked man just as he crawled out of the
igloo. He did not even give him time to get to his feet. With
one powerful thrust he sent his harpoon right through the man,
pinning him to the ice below him.

"You might have let me put on my pants first," were Tulimak's
last words before he died outside the igloo, Mequsaq told us—
still pleased with the memory.

"What happened to the woman who had run away with Tulimak?" I asked. "What did you do with her?"

Mequsaq smiled. "What does one do with women? Her husband had asked me to take care of the wicked Tulimak, but he
had said nothing about his plans for the woman. When he had
shown his own cowardice by his inability to fight for his wife I

decided to let him keep the dead man's belongings, which I did not need, but I kept his woman. She stayed with me through all those years, she became the mother of my children and gave me much happiness as long as she lived."

The woman who had run away to Bryant Island had been the grandmother of my wife, Navarana! I had never heard this secret.

"How did it happen that you left Canada and came all the way over here?" I asked Mequsaq.

"That was all because of the caribou," the old man explained. "The great Kritlak made the decision for us, as I told you. I was only a small boy at the time, but I still remember the settlement where we lived in Baffin Land. I can also remember that the caribou left us. Every year there were fewer and fewer of them, and there was great hunger in the tribe. Finally Kritlak, who knew the spirits, went out by himself, far away, to ask them for help. When he returned he explained to us the reason why the caribou stayed away from us."

Kritlak had met the spirit of the caribous, and he had told him that the Eskimos had offended them deeply. When they killed the animals and brought them home they let the women cut off the heads which they threw away so carelessly that dirt and gravel got into the eyes of the animals. Such treatment was a grave insult to the caribous, and they stayed away from the tribe. In the future only men should cut off the heads, Kritlak decreed, and they should treat them carefully.

The next year the caribous returned—great herds of them. One day such a herd got into a very narrow, steep valley when the Eskimos came after them, and they had no way of escape save through the water. They crowded down on the beach and were finally forced out into the icy sea—and now the Eskimos came after them in their kayaks. They could kill them off at will, and they continued the slaughter until their arms were worn out.

Finally the dead caribous were all driven ashore and there were so many of them that the men could not handle them alone. They asked the women to help them with the animals—forgetting the warning of Kritlak. Two women—a mother and her daughter —were too greedy for the delicious caribou tongues. When they had cut them out they were so eager to eat them that they threw away the heads without watching how they fell—and once more there was gravel in the eyes of the dead caribous.

When all the animals were cut up and eaten the men went caribou hunting once more—but there was not another animal to be found. The caribous had left their country and they never returned. Too late did the Eskimos remember Kritlak's warning. They realized that the two women had caused the famine which followed, and they decided to punish them in order to placate the caribou spirits and tempt them to return. The women had to be treated exactly the same way they had treated the caribou—their heads were to be cut off and rolled on the ground until their eyes were covered with dirt.

The mother and her daughter knew what was coming and tried to escape, but the men were too fast for them. When they found the women gone they set off after them.

"I still remember Kritlak and the other men returning from the chase," Mequsaq finished. "They called out to all the women in the tribe to watch as they threw the two heads on the ground. Kritlak asked us all to kick the heads in order to demonstrate properly to the caribou spirits that we were truly sorry for the insult against them. It was no use, however—the caribou stayed away. They are like the wind, nobody knows where they come from or where they go. We suffered a great deal from starvation until Kritlak finally decided that we were to break up, leave Baffin Land, and go to the east."

Navarana gloried in her new eminence, and was delighted to be able to repay her grandfather for the countless things he had done for her. We had many provisions with us, and she was at her best when acting as hostess to a group of people. It is wonderful what responsibility and affluence can do in a short time for a person who has never before had anything. She was a little confused at first but soon became mistress of every situation.

Navarana and her grandfather were always recalling something that had happened a long time ago. The first time she handed him the sugar box, she said:

"Do you remember when somebody got all the sugar in the house?"

This was enough to set him off. Navarana had been the pet of the household, he said, and he himself the greatest man of the tribe.

Once, during an affluent period, he had brought home, among other prizes, a large box of granulated sugar. Navarana, then a child, took possession of the box and would permit no one to

come near it. She ate it with a spoon and developed an acute
stomach ache. But even this did not stop her, and she ate until
it was all gone. Only then did she say: "Oh, why did I not save
a little until later?"

Many of the people who came to visit us remembered this
episode. They all said that they had never expected, after the
little girl's greediness, to find her the keeper of a whole box of
sugar.

2

IT GREW DARKER, BUT WE WANTED TO DRIVE FARTHER NORTH TO TELL
more of the natives that we would soon be going south to Tasiussak for mail, and suggest that they accompany us. We had to
round a cape where the ice was not yet thick. It began to give
way under us, and finally, when we reached a pan which seemed
a bit safer than the last, we stopped. We sat on the sled and
peered ahead into the darkness.

"Are you afraid?" I said.

"Is a woman afraid when she is driving with her husband?"
she countered. "Doesn't she trust her worries to him?"

Such talk encourages a newly married man and makes him
feel that he amounts to something. I did my best, but the ice was
so bad that we had to try another route, one that took us up over
a section of the icecap. When we reached it the dogs were too
exhausted to pull us and we both walked between the upstanders
of the sled. I whipped the dogs in order to impress upon Navarana that she had married a man who could bend dogs to his
will. I swore and yelled, but our advance was embarrassingly
slow. Occasionally the dogs stopped and I ran forward to grab the
animals by the necks and beat them for their laziness.

I had been afraid to admit to Navarana that I was worried,
but after some hours I was exhausted and we seemed to be getting nowhere. We should have been down on the other side long
since, so I said:

"Let's go back. These dogs can't take the load across!"

"You don't want to turn back and admit to people that we
could not cross, and listen to their laughter. The women will

make fun of me for not getting where we wanted to go. I do not like to hear that."

"To hell with the women's kidding!" I shouted. "You can see for yourself that the dogs can't drag the sled along."

She looked up at me shyly, as if afraid to say what she knew she must: "It is not impossible that maybe something could be done to make them try it?"

"What would that be? Show me what you suggest."

She mumbled something and asked me not to think badly of her. Then she took my whip and started for the dogs. They perked up at this new voice of authority, and instantly Navarana had them on their feet. She was a fury turned loose. From the shy, sweet little thing of a moment ago she was transformed into a mad witch. The crack of the whip was like ice breaking; her voice echoed over the icecap, and the dogs leapt into their traces.

Away from the merciless lash they tore, the load as nothing to them. The animals instinctively knew that authority was in the hands of a person who knew how to command.

We dashed toward the highest point in the passage as if we were on the heels of a bear. So fast did we go that I could hardly keep up with the sled, and I looked with admiration at my little wife with the big whip in her hand; she was more beautiful than ever, and I forgot everything in my awe of her.

When we reached the top she halted the dogs and handed me the whip:

"They only felt ashamed because they were driven by a poor woman, and hurried so that they might not be offended any more."

I knew that I had coddled my dogs too much, but I told her that in my country we did not use dogs for hauling and it was difficult to learn to drive them. She explained that she had gone hunting often with her grandfather, and she had learned to drive from him.

"But don't tell anybody," she warned, "that I took the whip while driving with you. I do not want the women to say my husband is not the best dog driver in the country."

What the women would or would not say was, for a long while, our court of last appeal.

When we were ready to return to Thule old Mequsaq followed us with his seven dogs. They were excellently trained, but so vicious that no one could come near his sled. No one but

Navarana, who, though she had not seen the dogs for two years, could untangle their traces and fondle them as if they were puppies.

"One is not afraid of one's grandfather's dogs, of course," she said.

We camped in the open, and Navarana made our bed with skins laid between the stone of the cliff and our sled. She knew how to make it warm by gathering dry grass from the slopes which thousands of birds had fertilized during the summer.

Before we had finished our meal we heard sounds of dogs and men approaching, and soon a whole party of travelers drove up— several sleds, men and women and children. They were on their way to Thule to trade with us, and Navarana became a bit excited as the duties of hostess weighed heavily upon her. All the other women were superior to her in age and experience.

Nevertheless, she let it be known that she had tea to offer them with sugar in it, that she slept at the side of the white man, that she could open his stores of supplies, take out a pipe, carve her own tobacco, fill her pipe, and pass the plug to whomsoever she desired before returning it to the box. Later she explained to me that she did this because there was a certain woman in the party who had always been especially cruel toward her. Navarana had been at her house a number of times and seen others fed but had never been offered anything herself. She had been ordered to come and care for the children while the mother was out visiting, and had overheard herself discussed as if she were little better than a dog. So she dared to boast in order to impress this other woman. Still, she had not been certain that I would stand for it, and she had been ashamed of herself.

When we reached Thule, Knud Rasmussen was there before us. He had, of course, already heard that I was married, and he met us with the warmest congratulations. He told me that there was no other girl, from Cape Farewell to Thule, who was good enough for me.

Knud brought with him the lame man, Tatarat, and his mother. I protested vainly that our house was already over-crowded, but since I had added to its congestion with a wife and her grandfather, my protests bore little weight. Besides, Knud needed the poor man to furnish him material for stories.

Tatarat had once been the most famous hunter in his tribe,

but now his whole body was crippled. All his joints were stiff, and he could move only his jaw, and that with great difficulty. When he went on visits he was pulled around by his old mother, who took care of him. He was always in the highest spirits, and he was the best storyteller of the tribe. His useless limbs were withered and terrible to behold, but his mind was in perfect condition.

We had first met him at Natsilivik. We were with our host, filling ourselves on delicious whale meat, when we heard the dogs barking, which announced visiting sleds.

We ran out and shouted "Welcome," but among the shouts and cries reaching us from down on the ice was a voice which was cursing and raging most dreadfully. It was Tatarat's voice. We got the explanation later. They had been coming down the mountain slope to the settlement, and his nephew, who was driving, had lost his grip on the uprights of the sled, which had then gotten away from him and overturned. Both his legs were broken, and he was furious, so furious that he could hardly think.

I recall asking him if his broken legs were giving him great pain.

"Oh, no," he said. "What do I care about my miserable legs that I can't even walk on! My legs have turned to wood, and wood can't feel any pain, but it drives me mad that that miserable fellow can't even drive a team of dogs properly. When I was that young I used to drive at full speed down that slope, and he can't even run behind and hold on to the uprights!"

Tatarat's mother left shortly on a visit to another fjord, allowing him to remain only on the condition that Knud personally would look after him. Soon the other residents of the house complained of Tatarat's odor, and it must have been high indeed to elicit comment from people who dress in skins and eat nothing but meat. Knud decided to give his friend a bath, and Tatarat made no serious objections. He had had, he said, many strange experiences, and he might as well try bathing for a change. I refused to touch him when I saw his body, which was not like a human body at all, but matted with long black hairs. Knud and Arnajark threw him into the tub and worked on him with brushes used, on pleasanter occasions, for scrubbing the floor. My only part in the whole thing was to carry away the water, which resembled a thick sauce. As his skin broke through the dirt, Tatarat's expression changed from one of surprise to delight. In later life he took several more baths and became a great propagandist for soap and hygienics.

Poor Tatarat also had other problems. His jaw became calcified. We had to pry his teeth apart with a piece of wood, which was very painful to him. But Knud figured out a solution. With a hammer he knocked out the man's two front teeth, upper and lower. We could then give him his food through the opening thus created, and also set the stem of his pipe in through the opening. His spirits were always very high. He was the local wit, and he knew all about scandals and never forgot anything, even the sayings of the little children.

Sometimes he would summon us with loud shouts of "I've lost my pipe! I've lost my pipe!" It would be lying an inch from his lips, and we would have to insert it again. He always laughed very heartily about this.

3

NAVARANA WAS ALMOST AS HAPPY AS SHE COULD BE. ALL HER clothes were ready for her now, and she was easily the best-dressed woman in the tribe. There was only one fly in the ointment: when certain women came to trade they recognized the skins they had traded to me in her garments, and they never neglected to tell her how happy they were at being permitted to furnish her with clothes. Mayark's wife remembered the circumstances of catching this fox, and Amémé told Navarana that she had been in a quandary whether to keep that one—"that one on the left sleeve"—for herself or sell it. Then she had caught one she liked much better, so she had sold this one.

This, of course, was not to be endured by any housewife, especially the wife of a hunter, and Navarana decided to trap her own foxes. She had already trapped a number of foxes but had never before been permitted to keep the skins for herself. Now she had a team of her own dogs, and she visited her own traps and had great good luck. Very often I drove out with her, and she taught me how to outsmart the animals. Sometimes we rode together from early morning until late at night, and she regaled me with tales of her own life and the lives of the natives whose joys and scandals few men of the white race are ever permitted to glimpse. She was also intimately informed concerning the various Arctic and polar expeditions, from the point of view of the natives.

One day I was sitting on my hilltop, staring out across the sea and ice for a ship, when Navarana joined me. I heard her footsteps approaching me, nearly inaudible in her kamiks. She thought I was hurt by something that had just happened and she had come to comfort me.

"Do not think about it, Pita," my wife told me. "When the food is good, people eat and eat. Their stomachs do not ask where the food comes from. It is all forgotten, Pita."

I had already forgotten the episode, but her words showed me that she was still hurt. Now she was doing her best to make me feel better, to make me forget her own humiliation and mine.

When I did not answer, Navarana pointed to the binoculars I held in my hand.

"Just look at your glasses," she said. "They are enough to prove your superiority. Who could ever make such a wonderful thing here in Greenland? Black pipes with little glasses that make you see great distances."

I looked through the binoculars once more. I did not want to admit that I was looking for a ship, and had to pretend searching for something else.

Suddenly Navarana jumped up and stared intently across the ice in the direction of Saunders Island and farther north.

"What do you see?" I asked her.

"Can a woman see anything when her husband sits next to her?" she returned modestly, but she did not move her eyes. She kept on staring.

I did not want to say any more and risk being further humiliated, but without saying a word I held out the binoculars to her.

"One is born with eyes," she said quietly and sat down again next to me. Surreptitiously she pointed her finger, however, and once more I held the binoculars to my eyes. There was nothing to be seen. Ice, ice—nothing but ice. Some large floes had turned upside down and looked like weird figures, a few icebergs loomed large on the horizon, otherwise there was only the flat pack ice. I stared until my eyes started watering.

Our harbor at Thule had open water that summer, but outside

the pack ice closed all approaches both from Smith Sound to the north and from Baffin Bay to the south. When we went hunting we had to go deeper into the fjord from Thule. In the late spring we had settled down at Ugdli, where there were many narwhals and where we lived happily in our tents.

Navarana was very proud of ours. There is an old custom among the polar Eskimos that while the men, naturally, build the stone houses, the women make the tents that they use in the summer, and they alone decide the size of the summer home. Sometimes a husband may force his wife to limit the size of the tent, but only if he is an unlucky hunter and unable to provide enough skins for the tent. Such a thing never happened in our fjord where the seals were abundant. If one of our tents was small, it was only because the woman was lazy, or perhaps had too many children to look after and did not have time to sew a large one.

Enlarging a small tent involves a great deal of work—as well as a number of skins—since the skins have to be added to the bottom of the tent where the circumference is largest. If a woman has any pride she will always do this work, provided she has the necessary poles to support a large tent. All the poles, and particularly the central rafters, have to be very long. They are the pride of a polar Eskimo and they stay in the family for generations, always being handed down from mother to daughter, never from father to son. Navarana had provided me with very long poles and we had a large tent.

We had a wonderful summer in Thule and Ugdli that year. To Navarana, there was only one drawback: Her husband was of course not so good a hunter as most of the men in our settlement. I had never been lucky enough to catch a narwhal from my kayak, and thus I had never been able to serve our guests the much desired tail piece—the most festive food that is reserved for guests of honor. I knew that Navarana was unhappy about it. She could always offer tea and sugar, or even pass around a large tobacco pouch—all precious and rare in Greenland. Such treats added to her prestige, but they could never take the place of a tail piece from a narwhal caught by her husband. A few times we had served a fabulous meal, offering all the things I had brought along from Denmark, delicacies our friends had never even seen before. They were grateful, they admired the taste and quantity of the food, they ate enough to satisfy three times their number in any other part of the world. But the end was always the same: They asked politely for permission to boil some meat in order to appease their hunger and feel that they had something substantial in their stomachs.

The day Navarana joined me on the hilltop to comfort me I had taken pity on her and managed to serve a tail piece of a narwhal. Navarana's mother was visiting Thule, and my wife wanted to honor her with a great party. I got hold of a narwhal which had decomposed to exactly the right shade of green and yellow, indicating that the blubber would have a superb taste. My friend Asayuk had caught the whale, and I had bought it from him for a stiff price in tobacco. I had looked forward to Navarana's triumph, but my efforts proved a complete failure.

When the guests were assembled and Navarana—according to the ritual—asked me if I had anything edible to offer I went outside to get the tail piece. I tried to keep the solemn expression on my face which the occasion called for, and walked out slowly and indifferently while my guests watched in silence. When I began pulling in the enormous piece of meat some of the younger men came to my assistance, groaning under the weight in order to demonstrate my wealth and hospitality to the other guests.

Asayuk was one of the guests, and he stuck to his bargain, never revealing the source of my meat. Unfortunately he had brought his wife, Arnawree, and she could not control herself. When she saw the delicious tail piece she announced in a loud voice:

"I am proud to see, Pita, that you have found some use for the whale my husband caught. It gives great pleasure to be able to provide a festive meal for your party!"

The whole event was ruined for Navarana. All of the guests had of course known that I had not caught the narwhal myself, but there are no people in the world more tactful than the Eskimos. They had all been prepared to keep a straight face and not humiliate me by showing that they knew the shameful thing I had done: offering my guests another man's food. Only Arnawree had not been able to keep it up. She was too proud and, perhaps, too jealous of Navarana. There was no longer any happy pride in the voice of my wife as she begged the guests to eat more. To make matters worse we had no more tea or coffee left. We had run out of supplies while waiting for the ship. For the hostess, the party was a miserable failure. And now that we were alone, with no Eskimo to listen, she wanted to tell me that she was sorry for me.

"But you are such a great man," she told me. "You should not go away by yourself to the mountain and thus show the whole tribe that you are ashamed and wounded by the words of a mere woman."

We sat there for a long time without talking, two young people in love. Love cuts across all barriers of language and race, and yet it is impossible fully to understand some of the deep emotions in a person of another race. One can only realize that there is a feeling which is common to the whole race, and accept it as such. Navarana was convinced that I was in misery because I was an inferior hunter. It would only hurt her still more if I were to tell her that I was utterly indifferent to the scornful words of an old woman, to the insult wrapped in poisonous pleasantry.

"Pita, you are good to a woman who worries when you are sad," Navarana told me with a shy smile. "You are a wise man, and you bring new thoughts into the head of an ignorant woman."

We fell silent again. I toyed with my binoculars as I watched my wife. Her eyes did not move from whatever she thought she saw far, far out on the ice.

My eyes had become tired from the strain of watching day after day. And I knew that the moment a ship did appear it would be impossible not to see it, that it was stupid to wear myself out looking for something I knew was not there, could not be there. Navarana seemed unable to wear out her eyes, and she had no need for the binoculars. She was born with keen senses that she put to good use. She had certainly seen something, but she did not want to claim the discovery for herself. Her husband had just suffered a defeat, this was his chance to rehabilitate himself, to regain the admiration of his friends. Even to me she would not say a thing or admit that she had seen something before I did.

I admired her self-control as I used the binoculars again. She did not help me, she did not explain. She wanted me desperately to be the first to see it.

"There is nothing there, Navarana," I sighed at last. "What on earth are you staring at?"

"A little to the left of that dirty iceberg," she whispered. "A trifle beyond it."

Now she was tense with excitement. I looked again. I was prepared to discover at least a herd of walrus on the ice, or perhaps a flock of birds—but there was simply nothing. I readjusted the glasses, I polished the lenses—all in vain.

Finally it was too much for Navarana. She could not control herself any longer.

"*Inuit*—people!" she exclaimed. "People from the north are coming to visit us. They are moving. Several people! Perhaps it might be useful to call down to our friends that visitors are coming. Most of them are asleep after their great meal."

My good Navarana had worked it so that it would help restore my reputation if I proved myself alert when others slept, the one man to discover the arrival of many people from the north. It would, of course, never dawn on anyone that she, a mere woman, had the better eyes and had made the discovery first.

At last! I could see something like tiny ants against the snow. They were obviously not seals or birds, they moved in a different way. When Navarana said she saw people I was quite sure of it, but I would never have seen it myself. She had seen them with her naked eye long before I could discover them with my binoculars. But once I had finally seen them she agreed to look through the glasses. She stared for a long time and at last she announced:

"It is possible that the travelers are white men."

I was getting impatient with her. "How do you know?" I asked her. "They are much too far away, you cannot possibly see what kind of people they are. Let me have a look."

They were still only dark spots on the ice. If they had not moved it would have been almost impossible to distinguish them.

"There are movements different from ours," Navarana answered calmly.

All the Eskimos came running up the mountainside when they heard our news. And Navarana, of course, let me take all the credit. "One has seen people," she announced calmly while I was shouting in my excitement. She explained to our friends just where her clever husband had discovered the visitors. They were easily seen with the naked eye now, but they were heading straight for Umivik and would soon be out of sight. They were clearly making for Saunders Island and our spring camp which faced the open sea. They would find all the food they needed in the depots we had left behind—meat and eider eggs and other delicacies.

We discussed the great news for a while. It was as good as the arrival of a ship, perhaps even better, the Eskimos felt. There might be news from the north, from friends and relatives. And they were all eager to meet the travelers.

"One might like to taste some eggs again," one of the young Eskimos remarked casually. "The sight of strangers brings to mind the eggs that are stored on Agpat [Saunders Island]."

"Agpat is a bad place to leave meat too long," said another. "How often one has left good supplies there, only to please the bears. Perhaps one left too much there in the spring."

The travelers out there may have forgotten that kayaks may get ruined in the ice," Aviangernak mused. "Such travelers often forget to take along supplies for sewing and mending their kayaks. One might bring them what they need."

All the Eskimos were eager to make the trip to Saunders Island, but they knew that they had to wait for my decision. I had the only available wooden boat which could be pulled across the ice without being damaged when there was no open water.

Finally I announced that we would use my boat for the trip but that we would take along one or two kayaks for the hunting on the way to the island. I uttered the decisive words with the proper indifference and the Eskimos listened with an equal lack of apparent interest.

"It might be necessary to go along with Pita in order to bring back some walrus teeth left on the island," one of them said calmly.

"A leather bag was forgotten this spring when we left the island," said Uvdluriark, my step-father-in-law. "It might be picked up again if there is an opportunity."

They all made similar casual statements, since none of them wanted to ask for permission to come along. If the request was refused it would mean humiliation and ridicule. The more eager the Eskimos are, the more indifferent they appear.

I did not commit myself. I simply stated that it might be good to get some sleep before we returned all the way to Thule. I knew, of course, that nobody would sleep, but I wanted to be left in peace for the trip back across the mountain, down the valley.

4

WE ALL SET OUT TOGETHER. A FEW OF THE OLD WOMEN WERE LEFT behind in the summer tents to look after the dogs, but all the children ran on ahead of us. I set a reasonable pace since not only all the other women came with us but also old Mequsaq. He was a wise and honored man, but his legs were getting weak although he would never admit it. He was as eager as the rest of us to find out what we had seen far out on the ice—if we had seen anything.

"If there is nothing we would be able to laugh for days at the funny joke," said old Mequsaq. In case it turned out to be a mistake the old man wanted to protect his granddaughter and her husband who had announced the great news.

Our crossing from Thule did not call for any elaborate preparations although it would not be an easy expedition. None of the women was allowed to come along. There were eight of us going, and the boat was not particularly suitable for the trip. It was a clumsy, heavy whaleboat with four pairs of oars. It would be no easy task to pull it any distance across the pack ice, but between the eight of us I thought we would manage. Three of the Eskimos brought their kayaks, and at first we did not see much of them. They paddled ahead of us searching for seals, or they served as scouts looking for open passages when the ice seemed to close in on us. Whenever it proved impossible to row the boat and we had to pull it up on the ice, the three of them were out of sight.

Mequsaq sat stolidly at the tiller and saw more with his one eye than the other four pairs of eyes together. We trusted him and knew that he would find the safest and quickest way through the ice. Sometimes he would keep us rowing when there did not seem to be any way out of the ice, sometimes he would stop us for a moment to confer with the men in the kayaks. Once in a while he had to admit that there was no alternative—we had to get up on the ice and pull the boat across until we found the next open channel.

We were only a few hours away from Thule when we caught the first seal, and the Eskimos, of course, wanted to eat it at once. If I had tried to protest I would only have spoiled their happy

mood, and they would have lectured me on the advisability of
eating the seal while it was still warm. The Eskimos are convinced that the sooner the animal is eaten after the killing, the
more strength and energy it will give. After a solid meal of raw,
warm meat one can go hungry for a long time and "the stomach
will not get bored," as they express it. Anyhow it was a small
seal; we could finish it up in one meal and would not have to
carry a still heavier load.

The meal was quite a treat since, during the spring and summer, we had nothing but narwhal. It may be stored for any
length of time and it is delicious as *niko,* or dried meat, but when
it was fresh we always ate it raw.

The good meal made us lazy, but why should we hurry? The
strangers might already have reached the island, but we would
find them whenever we got there. The time of the ice breaking
was near, however, and deep below us there was a hard, relentless pressure against the ice although we could not see any movement. But suddenly, while we still dawdled over our meal, the
ice floe on which we were resting broke in two. It happened so
fast that old Mequsaq did not have time to get away. The rest
of us jumped to our feet and ran over to the boat before the
water separated us, but Mequsaq moved more slowly, and all at
once he realized that there was no support for his left foot. Before he managed to step back there was none for his right foot
either, and the old man was thrashing around in the icy water.

He did not utter a sound, but I could see a silent appeal in his
eyes. I threw myself down by the edge of the water and grabbed
him—but not before he had ducked once or twice. I pulled him
safely back on the ice and everybody laughed at the episode,
including Mequsaq, who was dripping wet. It was out of the
question to express any sympathy or to suggest that he should
put on dry clothes. The summer day was reasonably warm, and
in a day or two his clothes would be dry.

At last we broke up and launched the boat once more.

We were in a narrow channel, and before we could begin rowing there was suddenly no water to dip the oars into. With frightening speed the ice floes closed in on us and we were lucky to
save the boat before it was crushed by the screw ice. We had to
put Mequsaq in the boat since we had to move at a moment's
notice because the screw ice was in violent movement all around
us.

While we waited the ice seemed to grow around us. There was no noise, only an invisible relentless power beneath us. In a few seconds a tower of ice loomed above our heads, completely closing off our view. We no longer had to worry about the direction we were taking—our only concern was to save our lives. Samik, one of the men with a kayak, was making his way carefully across the ice to join us, carrying his small craft on his shoulder. Suddenly it was as if an unseen hand grabbed his kayak and pushed it under a block of ice the size of a small house. Samik did not move fast enough, probably the kayak had blocked his view. He wanted to save his craft and nearly lost his life in the attempt.

We had to ignore him for a moment while we struggled to rescue the boat, without which we would all be lost. When we looked at him again he was sprawled on his back, with one leg pinned under a mass of ice that moved closer to him like the foam on the crest of a wave. We ran and managed to pull him out from under the ice, but his leg was broken and his kayak was completely out of sight.

The screw ice seemed to boil around us and we carried Samik back and lowered him into the boat. Mequsaq apparently drew new strength from this mishap, and as we could not carry both of them in the boat he jumped out to help us, suddenly as strong and nimble on his feet as the rest of us.

After a while we could notice some sort of a system in the apparent chaos. The ice seemed to settle down in enormous stripes with narrow channels of open water between them. Only one such stripe moved at a time. After a while the stripe we were on calmed down and the movement traveled farther toward the shore. At the same time the whole mass of ice was moving out to sea and each separate floe was spinning slowly around in the water like a merry-go-round. Several times there was open water all around our ice floe, but before we could move the boat and get it into the water the ice closed in again and piled up like a solid wall around us.

As soon as the ice wall receded the floe which held us and the boat seemed frighteningly small. If we had not had a sick man to care for and a boat to hold onto in order to save our lives we might have stopped to enjoy the splendor and beauty of this fantastic spectacle, the incredible power of the water hurling around icebergs like nutshells and shifting floes large enough to stop a ship and crush smaller craft.

The two kayaks we had left were thrown on top of the suffering Eskimo as the boat was tossed from side to side, no matter how hard we tried to keep it upright.

During a momentary lull we became aware of the wind and noticed the first clouds. A southwester was coming up, the prevailing wind in western Greenland. We could always tell a change in weather by looking at the two mountaintops behind Thule, the Pingos. Every morning we invariably looked up at the Pingos to see what kind of day it was going to be. Now the clouds gathered around them, indicating a strong southwesterly wind. The ice had already carried us beyond the mouth of the fjord, and now the wind began moving us north.

The southwester proved to be a blessing because it did not take long before we were close to the goal of our journey, Saunders Island.

I could not help wondering about Navarana's insistence that the travelers were white men, and I mentioned it to Mequsaq, asking if it was possible to tell the difference between the movements of Eskimos and white men at such a distance.

Before Mequsaq could answer, Samik broke in:

"One has not seen the strangers, Pita. Only you and Navarana watched them. But there is a hope in me that they are Eskimos. We are happier in Thule without white men."

Samik was a quiet, silent man, and I was amazed at his strong words. The Eskimos were usually far too polite and tactful to criticize the white men to my face.

I tried to reason with him, but Mequsaq interrupted:

"Pita does not know what happened to you, Samik," he said. "It was a long time ago, before Pita came to us, and we have never told him what the white men did to you and your friends. Pita will understand it better if you tell him the things I heard about when I first came to know you, Samik."

"I still remember the day you came to us, Mequsaq," Samik said. "That was the day I told you about Flaming Water. There was a hunger in our souls because we had experienced much and longed to tell about it. Many wrong things had happened because we let anger possess us. It is not our custom to fight, we are not like white men who go out in great numbers and shoot each other like rabbits or caribou. We find such behavior shameful for human beings who should help each other get food and find happiness. But the search for Flaming Water made us fight too, and now I'll tell Pita about it—just the way I first told Mequsaq."

5

THE WHOLE THING BEGAN WITH A PLEASANT SURPRISE. LIUK, THE OLD woman, had gone up to our mountain to set her traps because she was out of rabbit fur for stockings. When she had climbed high enough she suddenly discovered a ship far out by the mouth of our fjord. She rushed back to our village, flushed with excitement and pride because she, a mere woman, had been the first to know about such great news.

"Ai, ai! The great hunters are still asleep in their houses, and a poor woman has to climb the mountain and serve as their eyes when a ship arrives!" she shouted proudly. Tornge, her husband, told her to keep quiet, as a woman should, unless she wanted a beating. Liuk obeyed, but she had already had her say and her eyes beamed with pride. Her voice carried so far that we had all heard the news and could not ignore it.

Old Ehre announced casually that he thought he might take a walk up to the mountain, but he was too excited. He did not give a reason for his walk, and he did not proceed calmly and in the proper dignified manner. He hurried, and he was back in a very short while.

The ship turned out to be much smaller than the ones that sometimes came by in spring, the whalers that carried a great number of men. There were only a few white men on board, and they did not carry as many supplies as the larger ships. At first we felt a little sorry for them, as they apparently came from a poor country and did not have enough wood to build a well-sized ship. But we were happy to see them anyway, since we never had any visitors coming in the fall.

And we were all the more pleased when it appeared that the white men planned to stay with us for a long time—all through the winter. Their decision proved their good sense, we told each other, for our place was a good place.

The strangers had peculiar names and manners. They carried with them thick piles of extremely fine, thin skins on which they had marked tiny signs and symbols. The skins were made in such a way that they contained words in the human tongue instead of the strange and twisted language of the white men.

Even so they spoke without modesty and were not ashamed of using their own names. We felt pity for them but could not help laughing when each man pointed to his own chest and exclaimed: "I—Gogol!" "I—Semede!" We realized that they wanted us to know them and be their friends and we got used to their foreign ways.

When we had settled down for the winter Semede asked the two oldest women, Ivaloo and Saigak, to come to him every day. He explained to them that he wanted to hear them speak and tell all the stories they knew from ancient days. At one time our men were bigger and stronger than they are today, and they performed astonishing deeds which our fathers had told us about. Semede wanted to hear all about them. By making small signs on his thin skins he seemed to be able to remember all the words of the old women.

At first we laughed at his ridiculous desire for the company of the toothless, senile Ivaloo and Saigak, but he turned out to be a generous man. He gave them many small gifts and even some tobacco in return for their words.

The other white men were of a different kind. Sometimes they seemed weak and useless to us, and we wondered how they had acquired their wealth. They must have been good hunters once although they were still young in years. They had apparently given up their hunting, and in their younger days they must have worked so hard that sleeplessness had robbed them of their sanity and their sense of values. That was the only way to account for their strange behavior.

One of these men had the peculiar idea that a man can spend his days with flowers and grass and lichens without losing his dignity and honor. He picked all the plants he could find and collected them in strange, small boxes.

Another man was always on the spot when we had caught some animal. His excitement at the sight of a dead seal was something to marvel at. He emptied the intestines and studied their smelly contents. Not only seals and walrus—he did the same with auks and rabbits and all other animals.

The only white man who showed ability and good sense went by the name of "Doctor." In many cases he knew how to exorcize the spirits. When one of us got sick he knew how to chase the disease away.

There was one man who did all the thinking for them—and he was the strangest of them all. His name was Gogol, and his words and deeds were worthy only of contempt. His greatest pleasure was to play with rocks and pebbles. He carried a hammer and a pickax, he knocked pieces of rock out of the mountainside and put them in beautiful leather bags which his women must have spent days preparing for him. He filled one sled after another with his foolish stones and pebbles.

Semede explained to us: It was Gogol's desire to get as many different kinds of stones as possible to see how our mountains were built. We politely ignored the insanity of the man, and Ehre told him that there were white and black stones right there in the settlement. We even had some red ones, and perhaps he would enjoy the small, soft stones from the great glacier.

The color of the stones did not interest him in the least, Gogol explained through Semede. But he was interested to hear that some of them were hard and others were soft. I told him that I might bring him some of the stones which were so soft that we could even cut into them with our knives and turn them into dolls for our children. It was my intention to insult the fool by comparing him with a child, but he did not even understand it. He would go on collecting stones, he said, but he might be interested in seeing the small soft ones some day.

Some days later Gogol came unexpectedly to my house. Semede was with him, as always, in order to make his words intelligible. My wife pulled on her kamiks to go outside. I felt like boasting, so I told Gogol and Semede that the three white men who were good hunters had expressed their desire for my wife. Her beauty had made them eager for her company, and they had asked her to visit them when the moon stood over the mountain as it did that evening. They were through with their work for the day, they were ready to enjoy themselves, and I sent my wife to add to their pleasures.

I told it to Semede in order to make him explain it to Gogol, hoping to give the strange and foolish man some desire for the company of women. Semede never got around to telling Gogol— something happened to stop him. As my wife left, our little daughter woke up. Arona missed her mother and started crying. I had to think of something to keep the girl happy and quiet.

Under my wife's bed I found the leather bag where she kept her sewing things, needles and sinews, and I pulled out of it some of Arona's toys. I gave the child a couple of dolls I had once made for her, carved from the soft, shiny stones I had found by the large glacier.

Soon Arona forgot her tears and her mother. She played happily with the dolls I had given her so that the men could ignore the little girl, but the effect was the opposite. Gogol, who never showed any dignity, made himself the laughingstock of the men by turning around and staring strangely at the child.

After a while Arona felt his eyes upon her and in her confusion she lost one of the dolls. The little toy clattered to the floor and rolled to Gogol's feet. He quickly stooped and picked it up. I thought perhaps he liked my daughter and wanted to give the doll back to her, but he did not let go of it. He seemed to forget our presence as he stared at it with eyes so intent that I thought the man was angry. At long last he took his knife and scratched the surface of the shiny stone.

Semede noticed the strange behavior of his friend, but when he moved closer to take a look at the doll Gogol quickly tried to hide it. We thought there would be a quarrel, but Semede was too fast for Gogol. He snapped the silly toy out of the fingers of his master and studied it carefully. Now it was his turn to act like a madman. He looked up, beyond our heads, with dreamy eyes, and seemed oblivious of time and space.

For the first time we heard a word which was to become all too familiar to us. The two white men whispered it to each other as if it were a magic secret, a word which must not be spoken aloud:

"Gold," they whispered hoarsely, their faces purple with excitement, the sweat pearls shiny on their foreheads. "Gold . . . Gold . . ."

At last Semede turned to me and asked me where the toys came from. I told him the truth. They were just a pastime, something I had made for my girl who did not know or care whether her toys were of any value. Semede did not seem to understand my words. He and his powerful friend behaved like fools or children. We showed them our contempt quite clearly, but they continued playing with my daughter's toy. And they insisted on knowing more about it. They wanted to see the place where I had found the yellow stones.

Patiently I explained to them that it was beneath the dignity of grown men to bother with pebbles and toys. The stone was quite worthless, although pretty to look at. We had noticed that it never lost its color no matter how long it lay beneath the water. It would sometimes shine like the sun—a glittering fire through the waters of brooks and rivers. That was, of course, the reason why we called it Flaming Water.

Gogol spoke again, and Semede explained his words: "Take us to the place where you find the Flaming Water!"

The yellow stones could only be found by the great glacier, I told him. They were visible among the pebbles and the clay which the ice spits aside as the glacier moves to the sea to satisfy its thirst for salt. And Flaming Water was found only in summer when the ice had melted below the glacier and the river ran out from beneath the ice.

Gogol and Semede wanted to have all the toys made from the yellow stones. Every single one, they insisted, and nothing must be kept from the white men. They seemed to realize, however, that their hunger for toys was a shameful thing, for they asked us not to tell the other men on board the ship about the Flaming Water. It would be better, they said, if only these two knew about the dolls that they called "Gold."

In the meantime Arona had become impatient and wanted her doll back, but Gogol at first refused to return it. I was amazed to discover that the white men apparently never grew too old for toys, but I was determined that Arona should have her favorite doll, which was as large as her own hand. I made a gesture to reclaim it, but the white man held on to it as if it were really important to him. I had to laugh in spite of my anger as I took it from his fingers which were without strength.

No sooner had Arona begun to play once more than Gogol tore the doll out of her hands. We could hardly believe our eyes. Old Ehre whispered to me that Semede had meanwhile found two small toy dogs which he had already put in his pocket. Arona could not understand why the visitors took her toys away, and she was soon in tears again. I told Semede severely that men never before had been seen playing with toys and that the property of my daughter could not be taken away from her without her consent. She might be just a child but she was my only one, and I insisted on the return of the two dogs as well as the doll.

When Semede reluctantly produced the dogs from his pocket

Gogol seemed to be ashamed of his friend. He talked to him in a loud voice, Semede talked back, and it looked for a while as if they were going to disturb the peace of my house and begin a fist fight. Thus we realized the power of the yellow stones to cause strife among white men.

In the end they settled down peacefully and told us that all the children who were willing to part with their toys would get sugar and tea and biscuits in return.

Soon my house was filled with merry laughter as the men sent for their children and told them to bring their toys. Gogol and Semede were all smiles as the little dolls and dogs and bears piled up on the floor by their feet. The children were promised great gifts in return as Gogol left for the ship to get a wooden box for the toys and bring back tea and sugar. It was explained to us, however, that Semede would remain in my house to guard the yellow stones and make sure that none of the children repented and ran away with their toys. Some of us resented this insult—as if we would take back a gift already given!

As it turned out, Gogol should have left someone to guard Semede if he was so worried about his toys. When he returned from the ship with his gifts and his wooden box, the two men quarreled violently. Semede had planned to fool the other man by hiding some of the dolls inside his high boots, but Gogol was a great man with numbers. He had counted the toys before he left, he knew just how many there should be, and he ordered Semede to return the dolls he had removed from the pile. We had never seen white men so angry nor heard them talk in such loud voices.

Still Gogol was not satisfied. His thirst for toys seemed to be unquenchable. He asked the men to go back to their houses and dig through their garbage piles in search for old toys and pieces of yellow stones. My friends answered, of course, that they were not dogs and would never stoop to picking in the garbage.

The white men were not ashamed to crawl in the garbage. They would return the next day, they assured us, and they asked us again and again to leave the refuse intact. And they waited until all the men on board were asleep before they returned to the ship with their box, their toys, and their childish excitement.

In the morning the two of them returned and without blushing went about their task. They had brought tools and dug up the piles of garbage behind our houses. They kept at it until a storm one morning covered everything deep under the snow and they had to stop for some days.

We were happy to see an end to the digging. We were tired of their quarrels—and we did not like to let our children see white men, grown men, behave like beasts. Some of our women disliked it so much that they complained about it to some of the other white men. They were visiting the three strong hunters who lived in the fo'castle of the ship. Since these men had shown themselves to be less foolish and weak than the others the women asked them to teach Gogol and Semede not to go digging in the garbage like animals. The women did not have the right words to describe the yellow stones that Gogol and Semede were looking for, but under her clothes one of the women wore a necklace made of yellow stones.

When the hunters saw the trinkets they, too, became childish. They forgot their old desire for women. They grabbed the yellow stones and began quarreling for the possession of them. They asked the women for more and instead of spending the night with them as men should, they wanted to go with the women to their houses and search for more stones.

Insanity seemed to grip them all at the thought of Flaming Water. There was great anger in them, their faces were red and their voices loud as they talked and pointed toward our houses where Gogol and Semede had once more resumed their doglike search in the garbage. Suddenly they all left the ship and ran to the settlement as if the evil spirits were chasing them. Even "Cook," the fat man who was the master of all the food and had never before been seen on the ice, ran like the rest of them. We thought that the yellow stones had made them murderous and that there would be a fight among the white men, but their fury spent itself in loud talk.

When their shouting was over and Gogol's words had brought some order into their confusion Semede was told to explain to us the desire of the wild white men. They wanted to see the river that ran out from the great glacier—and they wanted to see it at once. They realized that it was still frozen, Semede admitted, but they would like to make their preparations so that they could spend the summer by the glacier looking for yellow pebbles.

Alas, it was no use explaining to them that winter was no time to look for doll material. The ground was frozen and covered with ice and snow, but Gogol refused to wait until another

moon had come and gone. After the big quarrel he had once
more taken command, and the men accepted him reluctantly as
their leader. Gogol decided that they would dig through the
soft snow at once and then light bonfires on top of the ice. When
it thawed and the ground softened from the heat they would
be able to find their "Gold." After long arguments they agreed
to go back to the ship—all of them, since they no longer dared
to be alone—to get the supplies they needed: shovels for digging,
food, sleeping bags and wood.

The following day we all had to work hard to satisfy their
hunger for Flaming Water. Back on the ship they piled up
wooden boxes, tools, and supplies on the ice. We were told to
get our sleds and carry the big piles to the glacier. As soon as
we arrived there and the white men had shoveled away the
snow, we saw a terrible thing happen: The precious wooden
boxes were put on fire! "Doctor," who knew about wounds and
diseases, the other man who only cared for plants and flowers,
the fat "Cook"—all of them built bonfires and watched with
greedy eyes as the ice melted. They did not seem to be our
friends any more, they would not even listen when we told them
how much the wood would mean to us. We could use it for
barter, wood was our greatest need, our most valuable possession.
We spoke to deaf ears.

At last the bonfires died down. They had burned all their
wood, and now Semede came to me with the request that finally
caused great anger among us and led to the terrible event which
will never be forgotten in my tribe. The white men demanded
that we give them all our whale oil, all our supplies of blubber
and fat. They planned to use it for more bonfires and more
pointless digging in the ground. They did not seem to understand that we needed our fat and oil, that we had saved it for
fuel and light and for eating.

We considered their demand offensive and unworthy of grown
men. We all turned our backs to them and to the glacier, and set
out for our village. Gogol and Semede ran after us, however, and
soon the other white men followed, for they all clung together
since they had found the yellow stones. To get rid of them we
gave them some of the oil we had with us. As this was enough
to light a few bonfires it satisfied their immediate need and they
all returned to the glacier. In the evening, however, they came
to talk to us again.

Semede explained to us that they were all grateful for the yellow stones we had given them. They wanted to show us their appreciation, he told us, and we should all come to the ship and receive gifts from Gogol. There would be a party and we would all have hot tea and good things to eat.

We all laughed happily as we went to the ship, even the old women who had told their stories to Semede before the doll madness took hold of the white men. They had been away from the ship for so long that there were snow drifts in front of the doors on deck. We had to shovel the snow aside before we could get inside, but soon we were all seated and a fire was going in the stove. Now even "Cook" was smiling as he boiled tea for us and "Doctor" showed us one of his many marvels: he had sugar not only in lumps, but also in a bottle! Liquid sugar, he called it, as he poured it into our cups and showed us the bottles.

We could not read, of course, but he told us that the name of the strange sugar was "Rum." This liquid sugar made the tea taste much better than any tea we had ever had—and it made us much warmer. We all felt happy—and very sleepy. When we woke up the room was cold, the fire had died in the stove—and all the white men were gone!

As we stumbled toward our houses we slowly realized what had happened. The white men had not given up their doll madness after all. When the party was over they had all left us to return to the glacier. In the distance we could see small pinpoints of light from the bonfires. We wondered what they had found to burn.

As soon as we were back in our houses we knew how they had made their bonfires. Arona was the first to cry out. Our house was in wild disorder. The white men had thrown our belongings about and had taken all the little girl's toys. All the houses had been searched, and every single piece of yellow stone had been stolen from the children. And the worst was yet to come: our oil was gone, our lard, our entire fat supplies! That was how the white men had made more bonfires.

Some of our men felt that the honorable thing to do would be to kill all the white men, but the older ones among us, who knew the wisdom of our fathers, warned us to be careful. If we killed there was the danger that the curse of the yellow stones would move from the white men to us and cause strife among us. We followed their advice and agreed to move away from Pilik—the good place which had been cursed by the white men.

We were fortunate in not having many possessions that might tie us to a certain place. We owned no more than we could easily pack together, and thus we were always free. Before leaving for the north we decided, however, to talk once more to the white men and get some of our oil and fat back. Spring was still a moon away, it was too early to replace it and we would suffer without it.

We all went down to the glacier, and as soon as they saw us the white men came to meet us. I could see that they were ashamed of what they had done for their faces were dark and angry and some of them carried guns as they stood close by their little piles of Flaming Water. They had divided the yellow stones among them, it seemed, and it looked as if they were guarding them. They were afraid, perhaps, that they had given us the curse of the yellow stone and that we, too—grown men—might try to take their worthless pebbles away from them.

I told them calmly that we were not interested in Flaming Water.

At this the white men relaxed and I went on to talk about the fat and oil. We could not catch any more narwhals and walrus until spring came, I told them. We needed our supplies and had come to take them back.

Gogol and Semede talked a great deal together, and it seemed to me that Gogol had some justice in him. I did not understand his words, but I could see that he wanted us to have our oil. The other men began shaking their heads and shouting angrily, pointing to their bonfires. At last Semede turned to me and explained that they could not do as I asked, since they still did not have enough pebbles.

Arona had become impatient with all the talk. Like the child that she was, she had wandered off by herself with some of the other little girls trailing behind her. Suddenly she jumped toward one of the little piles of yellow pebbles. She had caught sight of her little doll and she wanted it back. The other children who had perhaps seen their own toys followed her toward the piles.

Arona was just a little girl and she was in her right—but her action had terrible results. The white men ran for their yellow stones and one of them jumped on Arona. He tore the doll from her hand and hurled her far out on the ice. Arona lay still, she never moved again. The fall had broken her neck.

At first we were all so horrified that we could not move. The white men did not seem to realize what had happened, or they did not care. They only thought of their yellow stones which they tried quickly to hide in their clothing. I could not believe my eyes, and my arms were too heavy to move, but my brother Agpalerk forgot his fright of the white men. He was always more quick-tempered than I, and now he grabbed his harpoon and sent it flying through the air. The sharp point pierced the chest of the man who had killed my daughter. It seemed to go right through him, and the man fell dead on the snow.

Now, at last, the white men forgot their toys. They ran for their guns—and there was more killing that day. My friend Mayark was shot to death, and two of our men and three women were wounded. We had no guns, but two more of the white men lost their lives before the rest of them fled. In spite of their guns they were afraid of us, since we outnumbered them.

We buried our dead that night—Arona, my only daughter, and Mayark, my best friend. With heavy hearts we moved away from Pilik and went north to Pituravik and friendly men of our own kind.

Spring came at last, and with it good hunting, which almost made us forget the toy-crazy white men. But among us there were two young hunters who could not forget. They decided to borrow a sled and go back to the white men, to find out if they had come to their senses.

And they saw that the obsession was still with the white men. Their camp was by the river, which now ran freely from under the glacier, and they still seemed to be digging for Flaming Water. Most of the men were sitting down by a fire, for it was late in the day and time for food and sleep.

The two men decided to stay on the mountain overnight and visit the camp in the daytime. They found a place that was sheltered against the strong warm wind blowing out to sea and there they settled down for the night. They did not sleep long, however, for in the middle of the night they were awakened by a thunder that seemed to shake the entire mountain. Powerful forces were at work in the night and the men were afraid. When they looked out from behind the large boulders they could see that the whole edge of the glacier was moving, pushing its way to the sea. The solid ice covering the fjord broke up as if it were the first brittle ice of the summer's end.

When it finally calmed down they looked down over the edge to see what had happened to the white men. They saw at once that there was no trace left of the camp. Nobody had survived the calfing of the glacier. The huge ice mass that had broken off and fallen into the sea as an iceberg had crushed everything under it. The river of the yellow stones, the white men, and all their belongings had been buried deep in the ice. This was the punishment of the white men for their greed, for their obsession with pebbles that shine through the water.

They had their punishment, we had our revenge—but we no longer talk about these terrible events, although they will never be forgotten in our tribe.

6

WE WERE ALL STRANGELY SILENT AS WE MADE READY TO LEAVE Dalrymple Rock. The usually taciturn Samik was tired out from his long story and in considerable pain from his broken leg when we carried him into the boat and set off once more.

The other Eskimos had obviously heard the story of Flaming Water before, but they had listened as quietly and eagerly as I. They were all my friends, the best I ever had, and now they were wondering if I was hurt by this tale of evil caused by the greed of the white men. But they were too tactful to comment further on the story.

Much of the ice had disappeared by now and there was open water along the shore. We had no trouble rowing as the ice floes we came across were easy to get around and we made good progress. Two men were waiting for us on the shore.

I could see at once that Navarana had been right—the strangers were no Eskimos. They were white men, and we were anxious to learn how and why they had come to Saunders Island, but to the Eskimos any show of haste would be unseemly. We made leisurely progress toward the strangers as I wondered who they could possibly be, what condition they were in, and what assistance they would need.

Our visitors turned out to be five in number, not two. They had made camp quite a distance away on the shore, and these two had left their companions in order to climb the mountain and search for some birds. They had seen us on the ice and had been waiting impatiently for us.

They were all whalers who had been separated from their ship, we found out. They were stranded on Saunders Island, and their rowboat could take them no farther. The two men who met us on shore were Bill Rasa, the whaler's first mate, who was in command of the rowboat, and a Norwegian by the name of Semundsen. He was a huge, blond man with an enormous beard.

I asked them first if the two of them were alone, and they explained that there were three more left behind in their camp farther up the coast. They were utterly exhausted and in need of rest. But above all they needed warm food, as they had nothing but raw seal meat to eat for a good many days.

They were all from the Scotch whaler *Horticula,* and they had lost their ship. It was the same old story: In their small rowboat they had left the mother ship and gone after the whales. Before they caught any the fog set in—the terrible, heavy Arctic fog which can last for days. One can see the sunlight above the dense fog and one can see the peculiar rainbow made by the ice crystals in the air. They had been helpless and could do nothing but wait.

In addition to Bill Rasa and Semundsen, they told me, there were three others—a Danish whaler by the name of Tom Olsen, a Portuguese by the name of Pablo, and Rockwell Simon, an American.

Semundsen and Rasa were in poor shape, and we made slow progress toward their camp as they told me the rest of their story. Left alone on the small ice floe, they had repaired the broken boat as best they could. The boat carried the usual tool chest, and somehow they had managed to rearrange and saw off enough wood to replace the broken sideboards. With great ingenuity and labor they had turned the boat into a smaller, clumsier craft which leaked like a sieve but could be kept afloat for a short while as long as three men kept bailing out water while the other two rowed. They would stay in the boat for nearly half an hour at a time before they had to get up on the ice again and thus they had been drifting around helplessly.

At last they sighted the island in the distance. They had used their boat a few times to move from one ice floe to another in order to get closer to the distant shore, but they realized that they would never get there unless the ice carried them close enough. They had waited in a state of unbearable tension until Saunders Island was at long last within reach.

When they reached the shore the three other men had collapsed, but Bill Rasa and Semundsen had gone off in search of food. They had "heard" the bird mountain in the distance. There is always movement on such bird cliffs. Small and large pebbles and rocks, upset by the hundreds and hundreds of birds, start rolling down the cliffside, and the resulting avalanche can be heard far away. The rolling stones usually take some birds along on their way down. The birds get killed by the rocks and can be picked up at the bottom of the cliff. They are always freshly killed and can be eaten without danger since they never remain on the spot for any length of time. It seems only a matter of minutes before foxes or the huge Arctic sea gulls pick them up. They appear to be on the lookout day and night; they rush to the spot so fast that there is usually a fight, with the fox most often carrying off the prize.

The two men had found two birds which I now offered to carry for them. They were tired enough to give them to me without a protest as we trudged along the shore. All my Eskimo friends came with me, of course, eager to help the strangers. After two hours of slow walking we reached the small camp and the three other men. One of them was livelier and smaller than the other two, and he got up to greet us:

"I am glad to see that there are other people in the world than the five of us," he said in a tired voice—and burst out laughing. The sound seemed loud and strange, and the man became embarrassed. He calmed down until suddenly his laughter turned into loud sobbing and the tears were running down his cheeks.

Tom Olsen was a giant of a man and did not act as if anything out of the ordinary had happened. He had been sound asleep when we turned up, and he greeted me like a long-lost friend. The last of the five was a middle-aged Portuguese who went by the name of Pablo. He did not speak much English; in fact, he did not speak much at all, but from what little he said he seemed to be an experienced sailor who had come up to Greenland for many years.

The boat they had hauled on shore was in a sad state, but

we could not help admiring their ingenuity. It had served them well even if it could not stay afloat for more than a few minutes. On their way across Baffin Bay they had had to be on the move constantly, changing from floe to floe as the ice broke up, and the craft had undoubtedly saved their lives. Now Bill Rasa agreed with me, however, that they had no further use for it. We cut it up and soon we had a roaring fire going. The five men gathered around it to keep warm while the Eskimos helped me prepare some food.

Once they had eaten and settled down by the bonfire, they all decided that the future was up to me. They gave me all responsibility and gladly put themselves under my command. I might have appreciated their touching confidence more if I had known what to do next. We had no supplies with us and not much food beyond what we could catch. There were eight of us from Thule, in addition to the five men who could not talk with the Eskimos and who in their present state could not be counted on to provide any food for themselves. I had to take care of them all, and it might not be easy.

The Eskimos are masters at making a pleasant shelter with small means. They salvaged one half of the whaleboat which we did not yet need for firewood, turned it upside down, and built a supporting wall of rocks around it. By extending the stone walls they made room enough for our five "guests" to stretch out under the boat where they were protected against the wind and the rain. The rest of us gathered around the bonfire trying to keep warm. Even if it was summer we were pretty far north and the sharp southwester lashing the rain in front of us was bitterly cold—the nastiest of all Arctic weather. We had been lucky for too long, and now the weather gods decided to make us pay for it.

The strong wind, more like a gale, brought the ice with it. The waters outside Saunders Island were soon completely blocked by ice as far as we could see. It was constantly churning and piling up, and the prospects were none too good. We could not get back to Thule before the ice cleared up.

We put my boat opposite the wrecked one and built a wall of rocks and turf between the two. Finally we put the mast cross-wise from one boat to the other and hung the sail over it, weighing it down with rocks and large pieces of walrus meat to keep the violent wind from tearing it down.

We spent some hours building this elaborate house—always a pleasant task. In the Arctic I have sometimes spent hours preparing a good place to sleep, perhaps only to have no more than an hour or two left to sleep there, once the shelter was ready. The pleasure of making a shelter is often more valuable than the rest itself.

We had not planned on a long stay on the island and had brought no extra clothing—something we bitterly regretted during the many cold and rainy hours. Soon we ran out of wood, we did not have much left of the walrus, and our guests complained of the lack of tobacco, the first thing they had asked us for. In summer we had no tobacco until the first ship from the south turned up.

The gale continued, the rain never let up, and we were all impatient to get going, particularly the five whalers.

I had to explain my situation to them—that I lived alone with my Eskimo wife among the Eskimos in Thule. We would be very glad to take care of them and help them in any way we could, I assured them, but they had to realize that my wife who would be their hostess was an Eskimo—like every other living soul in Thule. And I warned them that they would have to treat the Eskimos the way Knud Rasmussen and I did—as their equals in every respect without any kind of discrimination or condescension.

Rockwell Simon, the American, answered for all of them. He was grateful for my assistance and hospitality, but although he had come to the Arctic to meet adventure he felt that he had had enough. He wanted to get home as soon as he could and would prefer to go south at once if I could lend them a boat. Rasa and the others agreed with him. They were in a hurry to return—if possible to their ship and if not, to their homes.

While we were still considering the best course of action, one of the Eskimos interrupted us:

"Sigdlartupok!" he cried jubilantly. "Change of weather, clearing up!"

He had been up in the mountains, and now we could see what he had discovered higher up. It did not look too promising, but the wind had died down. The rain was still pouring and the clouds seemed impenetrable, but there was one spot that appeared a little lighter.

The Eskimos made ready to break camp. They knew that the

weather would be all right, and before long they had cleared up our shelter. The rain stopped and there was a pale glimpse of the sun. We finished our last meal of walrus soup and were ready to leave. The ice was still heavy, but we had no doubt that we would make it back to Thule now that the gale had changed to a sudden calm. We got the boat back in the icy water and some-how found room for everybody—the five strangers, my seven Eskimos, and myself.

The crossing took us more than twelve hours, twice as long as it normally would, but on the way the first hint of the warm southeast wind told us that the ice would soon again be on its way out of the fjord. We had been more often on the ice than in the water and all of us had fallen into the icy fjord several times. When we entered the Thule harbor we were once more utterly exhausted, but the sight of our houses with the smoke coming up the chimney revived us. All our tiredness was for-gotten when we saw the Eskimos standing on the Thule shore waiting for us—the children down by the edge of the water, the women in a group a little farther back, and the men at a proper dignified distance where they would not seem too curious.

As my wife, Navarana was the hostess in charge, and she handled this sudden invasion with ease. The only problem was to supply the guests with the necessary clothing, otherwise their presence caused no immediate complication. There was food enough, and even if we did not have beds for them all, we had a large attic where the five whalers would be comfortable with polar-bear furs and caribou skins to keep them warm.

While I set about at once preparing for the long trip to Thom Island the five guests enjoyed their long-needed rest. The Eskimos were all disappointed because the whalers did not speak "the human tongue," as they called their own language, but they visited us every day and crowded into our small house, staring at the guests and asking questions about them.

The five whalers did not know their way about, and I provided a special guide for them, a young orphaned boy whom I had taken under my wing—Qupagnuk, or Snow Sparrow. Although he was still a youngster he was a master at handling the dogs and would see to it that the strangers did not get into any trouble with the huskies. The boy was originally called Ungarpaluk and was used for odd jobs by everybody in Thule. He had been left to fend for himself at a very early age. He was dressed in a curi-

ous collection of clothes. Someone might give him an old pair
of kamiks, another would donate a worn-out pair of bearskin
pants, and the boy was always so full of lice that nobody would
have him in his house.

The boy did not care. He had a wonderful time and was everybody's friend.

If our five guests were at all tempted to get into trouble it was
with Aloqisaq.

Aloqisaq was put to work preparing the skins and furs we
needed to equip the whalers for the trip south. They all had to
have new leather kamiks and pants, and Navarana was in charge
of the sewing.

"It might be a good thing to have Aloqisaq stay in our house
until the visitors leave," Navarana told me. "She has nobody to
look after in her own house, and she can stay up nights with the
sewing."

Aloqisaq was delighted with the arrangement, but she had a
different program in mind for her nights.

"Remember that I am a widow," she smiled. "I have to be
satisfied with the men who visit me occasionally, and I'll be glad
to take care of the white men. I want to show them true hospitality!"

But Navarana was a firm guardian of virtue—not so much for
moral as for practical considerations. She needed the widow to do
the sewing, not to entertain the visitors at night.

I had made up my mind to take the whalers down to Thom
Island, where we might be fortunate enough to meet the whaling
vessels—if not *Horticula,* at least one of the others that might
take the five men south.

With the five whalers and myself already in the party I decided
to take no more than three Eskimos along. The first choice was
inevitably Mequsaq.

I discussed the second choice with Navarana and we agreed to
pick Kraungag, an old childhood friend of Navarana—the one
who had cut off his toe. The third man I picked was Itukusuk.

With this crew I was confident that I could get to Thom
Island. Mequsaq would again be at the tiller and the three of
us at the oars. The five whalers were of course also used to
handling an open boat. I had sails, but they would not be of
much use because there would be too much ice for any convenient sailing even if the wind should be favorable.

When the time for departure approached it was obvious that some of the whalers did not mind their stay in Thule at all. They had recovered sufficiently to have strong desires beyond mere survival, and they had evidently enjoyed the companionship of Aloqisaq the widow. She knew how to please them, and although some of the younger Eskimos were deprived of her pleasant company they did not mind this sacrifice on the altar of hospitality.

"The white men are strong and have great demands," Aloqisaq explained. "Their long absence from women makes it our duty to pity them and be helpful to them!"

As we made ready to leave Bill Rasa and Semundsen tried to thank Navarana for her hospitality and help, but an Eskimo woman does not want any gratitude. It would only embarrass her if the men should publicly acknowledge that the help of a mere woman had in any way been needed. She calmly urged them to get going and hurriedly gave their equipment a last-minute inspection.

When everything was checked I casually mentioned to Navarana that the weather seemed good for a little boat trip. That was the only good-by. The Eskimos feel that any sign of emotion may be a bad omen for the trip. Instead of saying good-by, Navarana smiled to me and said that she suddenly had a great desire for fresh salmon. She would go up to the lake behind Thule and try her luck, she told us, and while we boarded the boat she and the other women walked up the hill without a backward glance.

The men we left behind in Thule pretended not to notice our departure—as if we were just crossing the harbor. The only person to say good-by and wish us good luck was Aloqisaq the widow, and the Eskimos roared with laughter as she was left behind on the beach.

"Poor Aloqisaq," one of them exclaimed. "She forgets her manners because she is afraid she'll never again invite a white man to her bed!"

7

IN WOLSTENHOLME SOUND OUTSIDE THULE A BREEZE FROM THE north enabled us to put up the sail and take it easy on the first lap of our long journey while we made things as comfortable as possible in the boat.

At first we sailed easily enough and made rapid progress. But then the ice began to close in all around us. Whenever Mequsaq saw some kind of channel ahead we had to row for all we were worth to get there before the ice closed in again. And once we moved too fast. The boat shot ahead with such speed that it crashed against the ice and the kayaks caught the full force of the blow. One was ruined completely and had to be thrown away. The other was badly damaged and could not be used before it had a new cover. And this would have to wait until we reached Cape York, because preparing the skins for a kayak cover and sewing it is a job for women.

"What did I say!" exclaimed Thomas Olsen. "I told you we should have brought Aloqisaq along with us!"

He had been unable to forget the hospitable widow in Thule, but we reassured him that we would soon meet other women in Cape York who would be able to repair the kayak for us. And the Cape York women were hospitable, too, Mequsaq promised him. They might do more than repair a kayak in order to please the white men.

As we moved slowly south the floes and icebergs got so large that they hit bottom before they reached shore and thus left a channel of open water close to the beach.

By now we had very little food left and our evening meal consisted of seal fat and tea, but I think we were all too tired to care. And we were quite glad to spend the next day in Kangek, resting and stocking up on food. We caught a few of the large Arctic sea gulls and some rabbits.

I was glad that there was nobody in the settlement when we passed by Sarfarik and I was glad to leave Parker Snow Bay behind. Although the wind was not yet very strong it brought mild weather and that night we reached the famous Agpat cave, the halfway mark between Thule and Cape York. On Conical Rock just outside the cave we caught several eider ducks and had a luxurious evening meal. Before settling down for the night Itukusuk and Kraungak set out on an inspection tour and soon brought back the report that there were strangers in the neighborhood. They had found well-stocked meat depots which had been built since the last frost. The strangers could be only a few hours away.

"We are likely to meet Kridtluqtoq tomorrow," Itukusuk announced.

"Why Kridtluqtoq?" I asked. "How can you tell who has built the depots?"

Kraungak explained that every man builds in his own peculiar way and might as well leave his name behind because his identity is clearly revealed by the depots.

We broke up early next morning to see if they were right. We seemed to inch our way down and Mequsaq made us follow the shore as closely as possible. He had the fear of the old kayak man for the open water. If we forced him, he would reluctantly cross a bay or an inlet, but when we did not watch he followed every small indentation, every zigzag in the shore line.

Some hours beyond Agpat we came across a small camp, just as the Eskimos had predicted. In a narrow valley with a steep glacier Kridtluqtoq had settled down and I had the impression that he had recently moved away from Cape York to this remote and lonely spot where nobody ever stayed. We did not ask him why he was there, and all he volunteered was that he had obviously chosen his camp site wisely since it was honored by a visit of white people. This rather far-fetched explanation of his choice sounded more like an apology to his wife, Arnaluk, who was still young and gay and good-looking. She probably hated living in such a lonely place.

They had two small children with them and Kridtluqtoq had brought along old Semigaq.

I was surprised to find something odd in Kridtluqtoq's manner. He seemed to be on his guard, and if I had not known him so well I would have said that he was afraid of something. At first I thought it was simply the strain of this sudden meeting with his beautiful wife's first husband. (Admiral Peary had given her away to Kridtluqtoq while Itukusuk was away with Dr. Cook.)

I told the whalers about the situation, and they were eager to see how the main actors in this Arctic triangle would carry it off. The men were too tactful to refer to the old conflict, but old Semigaq had no such restraint. She was bursting with excitement and eager to fan the flame. When the men had greeted each other politely she was quick to speak up:

"In a dream last night strange things were predicted and now they seem to come true! A man has come accompanied by strong friends in order to get his woman back. Since she has proved herself able to bear sons there is likely to be a fight in this valley tonight!"

This insolent challenge went unanswered by the men, but Arnaluk seemed pleased and flattered by the prospect of a fight between her two lovers. She studiously ignored them and pretended to find the view particularly fascinating as if she had never before seen the icy fjord.

The Eskimos were getting tense, but Rockwell Simon, who did not realize the seriousness of the situation, pointed to Arnaluk and made some remarks to the other whalers. Arnaluk took this as a sign that she was now the center of attraction. She felt compelled to follow Semigaq's lead and fan the flames of desire still further.

"One is not used to being the only woman among so many men," she said with a bashfulness that was not entirely convincing, since she was obviously enjoying herself. And then, with a quick look at her two men: "But nobody here bothers to notice a mere woman, of course, particularly such an ugly one as I!" And turning to Semigaq: "Such great men will hardly notice whether a woman is here or not. She might just as well not be here."

To her obvious regret there was still no reaction from the men, but her bold words demanded action. Reluctantly she turned to the tent and disappeared, followed by the excited old woman. In the silence that followed I tried to relieve the tension by telling Kridtluqtoq about the ordeal of the whalers and the long journey ahead of us to Thom Island. Kridtluqtoq was an experienced traveler, and from his trips with Peary he had learned some English. He told us that he would have liked to go with us across Melville Bay and that he was sorry he was encumbered with a family he could not leave behind. He asked us to stay overnight in his camp and not leave until high tide the following morning. He had recently come up from Cape York and assured us that the ice would not cause us much trouble from there on.

When we had finished the substantial evening meal he served us and there was still no hint of a fight between the two Eskimos, the whalers asked me if they could spend the night in the tent in order to get a comfortable rest for once. Since the main attraction in the tent obviously was Arnaluk and not the prospect of sound sleep I told Rasa instead to take his men down to the boat and spend the night there.

Kridtluqtoq seemed more relaxed once we were alone, but the

Eskimos were still waiting to see what would happen between the two men. I tried my luck as a peacemaker.

"There is a pain in my ears," I told Kridtluqtoq. "They still hurt from the stupid words of your old woman."

Kridtluqtoq looked quickly at Itukusuk but said nothing. Mequsaq and Kraungak were still apprehensive until Itukusuk finally broke the silence and decided the issue:

"It gives me cause to wonder, Pita, that you can still feel pain. There must be a long memory in your head. Even if one could understand the idle chatter of an old woman, her words are long since forgotten!"

Once more the good man had preferred to keep the peace. He was not going to fight for Arnaluk, and we could all relax. I mentioned to Kridtluqtoq my surprise at finding him in this lonely spot. But he had been wise to stay by himself since such a great hunter never left any catch for other people, I said, intending to flatter him. He was known to kill anything that crossed his way.

He did not like my words and looked at me nervously as if he had found some hidden meaning in them.

The next morning ice conditions had improved greatly. Kraungak climbed up the mountain for a good view and told us that there was open water or at least ice-free channels all the way down the sound. We said good-by to Kridtluqtoq and his women and left with the high tide.

Our host was still nervous, and I noticed that he never let go of his gun as long as we were on shore. He did not relax before we had all boarded the boat, and I wondered if he was still afraid that Itukusuk had designs on his wife. Many months went by before I finally discovered the reason for his strange attitude— and the explanation was much more dramatic than I had imagined.

8

ADMIRAL PEARY HAD GREAT FAITH IN KRIDTLUQTOQ BECAUSE OF HIS many outstanding qualities: he was a good traveler, he had great stamina, knew some English, and was exceptionally good-natured and helpful. When Peary made the final preparations for his dash

to the North Pole he put Kridtluqtoq in charge of the Eskimos
going with Professor Ross Marvin to establish food depots for
the return trip. This team under Professor Marvin had to go up
to the last outpost before the final journey into the unknown and
leave vital supplies there to keep Peary and his companions
going on the way back from the Pole.

Professor Marvin was not well liked by his three companions
—Kridtluqtoq and Aqioq, who were both seasoned travelers, and
Inukitsorkpaluk, a much younger Eskimo (and cousin of Kridtluqtoq) who made up in strength and toughness for his lack of
experience.

Many times the three Eskimos wished they had been in another
team, but they realized that Marvin himself was also unhappy
on the trip. He had no one to talk to. He did not understand the
Eskimo language, and Kridtluqtoq had only a limited and strictly
utilitarian vocabulary in English. Whenever the Eskimos talked
together and laughed Marvin would ask what they were laughing at. Since Kridtluqtoq was unable to translate he shrugged
his shoulders and told the poor American that it was a trifle too
unimportant to be translated.

On the return trip they ran into several fresh wide cracks in the
ice. They were usually covered, since it was extremely cold, but
the ice was not always thick enough to carry them. Marvin knew
nothing about the dangers of such fresh ice. A few times the
Eskimos stopped and explained to him that it would be dangerous to continue and that they either had to detour or wait until
the ice was more solidly frozen. Marvin got angry and insisted
that the ice was strong enough. He was convinced that the
Eskimos were simply lazy, and he urged them on with angry
words. When they had their first argument Marvin finally gave
in, but the next time he wanted to demonstrate to them that
they could not possibly judge the safety of the ice simply by
looking at the color. He left the Eskimos behind and walked
boldly out on the black ice. He had walked only a few steps when
he crashed through.

The Eskimos pulled him out without difficulty. Marvin did not
say anything further about the ice. He was satisfied to let the
Eskimos build an igloo and remain there until they could proceed safely. The following day they ran into more fresh ice,
but Marvin had apparently not learned anything from his experience. Once more he impatiently urged the Eskimos on until

Kridtluqtoq found a safe passage by detouring the crack, and Marvin reluctantly accepted the compromise.

They quarreled again several times during the day, and there was not much left of the team spirit that night—when Inukitsork-paluk fell sick. He could not digest his food and was very weak in the morning. Kridtluqtoq knew that he would be all right in a day or two and explained it to Marvin, but he refused to stay over. He ordered the Eskimos to let the sick man stay behind. They could leave his food rations with him in the igloo, he said, and as soon as he regained his strength he could follow their tracks. If he did not recover . . . well, then he had to die alone in the igloo. And since the man would be unable to handle a dog team Marvin would take his sled from now on.

At first the Eskimos could not believe that he was serious. When Marvin began loading the sled of the sick man, they were finally compelled to realize that he meant what he said.

Kridtluqtoq did not waste another word. He walked over to his own sled, pretended to rearrange his load, and when Marvin did not watch him he got out his gun. Without further argument he shot Marvin through the head.

The Eskimo left the white man where he fell. He calmly returned to the igloo and told the other two that a man was going to be left behind in this camp—but a white man, and not an Eskimo. They decided to tell the Americans that the professor in his ignorance had tried to cross dangerous ice, had plunged through, and drowned before the Eskimos could help him. It might well have happened that way, they assured themselves as they tied Marvin's gun and scientific equipment to the body, made a hole in the fresh ice and watched the weighted body sink rapidly.

The three Eskimos settled down in the igloo, fell asleep at once, and slept all through the day. When they awoke they had a substantial meal, eating more than Marvin had ever allowed them to, and fell asleep once more. In the morning a blizzard raged outside and they had to stay over another day. The rest and food gave Inukitsorkpaluk new strength, and as soon as the storm abated they were ready to leave.

When they approached the ship at last, they had to honor the dead man and announce his death in advance. As soon as the ship was in sight Kridtluqtoq began beating his dogs to call attention to their arrival. When the Eskimos in the distance could be seen running out on the ice they knew that they had been discovered and the three of them sat down on their sleds with their backs to the people who came to meet them. In this way they made it clear that someone in the team had died.

The man in charge of the base camp in Peary's absence was Bob Bartlett, "The Great Captain." He asked them at once what had happened to Professor Marvin. Kridtluqtoq spoke for the three, since he was the oldest of them and also because he was the one who had saved his cousin from being left behind on the ice. He explained to Bartlett that Marvin had insisted on crossing the thin new ice in spite of numerous warnings from the Eskimos. At last he had fallen through and before the Eskimos could reach him the poor man had drowned.

Bartlett was very angry with them and refused to believe their story. A man falling through the ice would not sink so quickly, he insisted, and he accused them of having caused Marvin's death deliberately. He knew of course that the dead man had not been especially popular with the Eskimos.

The Eskimos had all been told the true story, and they agreed among themselves that Kridtluqtoq should stick to his official version. If he changed his story and explained to "Piuli" that they had shot Marvin in order to save Inukitsorkpaluk, the white men would say that the Eskimos no longer knew the truth and then they would no longer visit this part of the country.

Kridtluqtoq was praised by all the Eskimos for the brave way in which he had saved his cousin.

Soon the triumphant Peary returned with his companions and told of his successful trip to the "Navel of the Earth." He left Greenland shortly afterward, never to return to the Arctic, and the truth about Marvin's death remained Kridtluqtoq's secret for a number of years.

I did not know all this when I met Kridtluqtoq that fall on our way to Thom Island with the five whalers. I was only bewildered by his odd manner. He seemed nervous and restless as long as the strangers were around, and he kept his gun close at hand. The poor man had obviously been afraid that the white men were going to take revenge. He must have been greatly relieved to see the last of us as we went on our way down the sound toward Cape York.

9

WE REACHED THE WIDE OPEN SEA OUTSIDE CAPE YORK WHERE WINDS
and currents are always unpredictable and treacherous. A sudden violent gust had shifted the boom, and we could hear
splintering wood as it hit the water on the leeside. The heavy
boat settled down so the water came pouring over the side. Even
after the boat righted itself every wave drenched us and added
to the water we were desperately trying to bail out. The sea that
had been so calm minutes before was now churning viciously all
around us. There was no more solid ice in sight, but there were
enough floes to make it dangerous to race as fast as we were
going. Mequsaq clung to the tiller, but he had not the faintest
idea how to handle the boat. As long as he was there, we were
at the complete mercy of the wind.

It was my boat, I was technically in command, and I thought
that I had better take over although I was no expert sailor myself. The wind seemed to increase every minute, and while I was
still debating with myself what to do Thomas Olsen suddenly
and dramatically relieved me of further responsibility.

Seemingly in one single movement the otherwise quiet Dane
moved from his seat, pushed old Mequsaq aside, took the old
man's seat, and grabbed the tiller. Just looking at his sturdy hand
and the way it took hold of the tiller gave me confidence. He sat
there as solid as a rock, and it was obvious that here was a man
who was used to being in command.

In a booming voice he ordered us about, and without the
slightest hesitation or indecision he told each man what to do.
Automatically I obeyed as he roared at me to let go of the mainsail line. Keeping up the sail with a broken boom in that
terrific wind was sheer suicide, but no one had thought of doing
anything about it. I let go of the line, but the mainsail would not
come down. We had strengthened the mast with a couple of guy
wires, and the canvas got entangled in them. Willing hands were
ready to obey his angry orders and somehow got the sail out of
the mess before it could cause any more trouble.

The jib was being whipped by the wind and looked as if it

would be torn to shreds any moment, but Olsen got the boat under control, came about, and sailed with the wind as long as the boat was so dangerously low in the water.

The gale was of incredibly short duration. It disappeared as suddenly as it had come, and when the wind calmed down Olsen told us to hoist the mainsail again. We had to get it up fast if we wanted to stay afloat, he warned us. He alone had realized that the boat was leaking badly. During the storm we must have been hit by an ice floe which had broken one of the clinker boards, and the water was still coming in as fast as we could bail it out. We covered the damaged part with hunks of seal meat and let two men sit on top of them. In the meantime Bill Rasa and Semundsen had managed somehow to splice the splintered boom. We got the mainsail up, and with Olsen in command we headed for the cape so many sailors had used for a landmark, the profile which is always etched in the memory—Cape York.

The sun was low behind the mountains when the dogs in Cape York discovered us. They set up a concert of howls that brought all the Eskimos from their tents to welcome us as we approached the shore. I was surprised to see nothing but women in the settlement—although the sight of them seemed most welcome to some of my whaler friends. Apparently all the men were out seal hunting and the only male left was poor Usukodark, who was deaf and dumb. He was the most useless man in the tribe, since his double handicap kept him from all hunting.

The seal hunter must be able to hear the animal approaching the breathing hole and he must not make any sound to scare away the seal. Usukodark could not tell whether he was making any sounds or not, and he was unable to hear the seal. He could not be used in a kayak, since he did not realize that the sound of his oar hitting the water might be enough to put the game to flight. The poor man could not even join the children in their rabbit hunts. Usukodark made so much noise that the rabbits were warned off long before he could catch sight of them.

Now that all the men in Cape York had gone away Usukodark was left behind, as usual, and he was delighted to be the host and the man in charge. He motioned to the women to bring us food, and he made some incoherent sounds which the women strangely enough understood and quickly obeyed. They lit a bonfire outside their tents and served us an overwhelming meal. Due to the presence of so many white men, the women even obeyed him when he motioned them to retire and not offend the great guests by sitting down to eat with them.

We had to stay overnight in the settlement—to the delight of the whalers and the women of Cape York. I was determined, however, to leave the next morning no matter what urgent reasons Pablo and Semundsen and the rest of them might find for staying on.

The whalers were most reluctant to leave in the morning, but I got them together. They had to say good-by to the hospitable women, and we were off once more. We were already a distance away from land when I suddenly noticed that Usukodark had casually settled down with us in the boat. I wanted to return to get rid of the poor man, but he protested so vigorously in his own peculiar way that I gave in.

After a few days' easy traveling we were once more surrounded by moving, cracking ice. Just then, Usukodark saw a seal and got wildly excited. We were tired and had no need for another seal, but he would not give up. If we would not kill it for him, very well—he would do it himself.

He ran up to me—his good friend Pita who always spoiled him —and grabbed my gun. In his sign language he explained that he wanted to shoot the seal, and to humor him I gave him a couple of cartridges. He had never fired a gun before, but he had seen others do it and apparently was confident that he could do as well.

He walked off and we forgot about him. Once again all our attention was focused on the ice. The wide rift which we had crossed with so much trouble closed again. The ice was rumbling and groaning all around us; the pattern changed; existing channels disappeared; new ones opened up. One of these new rifts approached our boat, and we had to interrupt our meal to pull the craft further back on the ice and throw all our belongings into it before they disappeared in the water. We slaved over the heavy boat and did not remember Usukodark until there was a thunderous noise from his direction.

Heavy ice from the south was pressing relentlessly forward, pushing small and large floes in front of it. Some of them were piled up in a horizontal position before they crashed down again. We saw Usukodark outlined against the backdrop of such an ice floe. He could, of course, hear nothing. He was solely concentrating on the seal he was going to shoot. We saw him lift the gun to his shoulder, his back to the ice mass towering above him. My dog stood next to him, equally intent on the animal in front of them. Instinctively we shouted to him at the top of our voices, forgetting that the poor man could not hear us.

There was nothing we could do, the tragedy was unavoidable— although another man could have saved his life simply by running a few steps. He gave us a look over his shoulder and saw us waving to him. Apparently he thought we were cheering him, praising his ability as a hunter. He gave us a happy, proud smile, and turned back to his seal. That was the last we saw of him. The ice mass crashed down. One moment he was there with the gun to his shoulder—the next there was only ice. When we reached the spot there was nothing but water where Usukodark and the dog had been.

Usukodark probably died at the happiest moment in his life. He drowned as a proud hunter with a gun to his shoulder.

Mequsaq had been helpless all by himself. He was now busy trying to save all the equipment we had left in the boat while the ice was slowly but surely enveloping it. The entire rear of the boat was covered, the ice moved forward, imperceptibly but with relentless pressure. There was nothing we could do to stop it. When we reached the boat, or what little was left of it above the ice, Mequsaq had saved most of our clothes, food, and equipment.

"An old man could do very little alone," Mequsaq apologized, and smiled. He was not greatly upset. He was a fatalist; he took things as they came, and he had often before in his life been stranded on drifting ice without a boat. Most of us had not, but we tried to take it as graciously as Mequsaq.

"Well," Semundsen sighed. "We are right back where we started when you found us—except that now we don't even have a boat!"

I decided I would try to take us first to the only island close by —Bryant Island, an isolated dot in Melville Bay, hardly more than a single huge rock standing straight up from the ice. We would be safe there until we formed a better idea of the weather and ice conditions. I explained my plan to the others and told them that I thought we should split our forces. We might have to walk for hours through the ice field before we reached the island, and I felt we would do better if we walked in three separate groups rather than all nine of us together.

I decided to keep my wife's grandfather with me on this hike, and asked Thomas Olsen to join us. Bill Rasa and Pablo would go with Kraungak, and Semundsen and Rockwell Simon would team up with Itukusuk. Traveling in this manner, we had one Eskimo in each group. We would stay fairly close together, I explained, but we would obviously have to take different routes from time to time, and the two white men in each group should stick with the Eskimo.

Finally we divided all our belongings, leaving behind the things that were useless or too heavy to carry. Each group had a makeshift toboggan consisting of sealskin and pulled along with lines taken from the boat. On these toboggans we piled as much as they would carry. The rest we made up into bundles that we carried on our backs. The harpoons, although heavy and clumsy, served us as walking sticks, very useful to test the ice as we went along.

We kept walking for several hours, but the ice was by no means like a skating rink. For a few minutes at a time it might be level, but most of the time we had to travel across rough screw ice, climb uphill, and slide or crawl downhill. Once in a while we had to scale icebergs so steep and high that we thought we would never make it. And every now and then we had to walk around open water—if we discovered it in time. Sometimes thin, new ice that was not solid enough to carry our weight would cover the water. Twice Olsen stepped into slushy snow and ice that turned out to have no foundation, and plunged into the water below. We were right behind him and got him out before he suffered any ill effect—except for his soaking-wet clothes which we could do nothing about.

As we came closer to Bryant Island we had more and more trouble with the water. We were forced to make long detours to work our way around wide rifts, and soon the solid ice changed into loosely packed ice floes growing smaller and smaller in size as we approached the island. We were in for one more disappointment before the hike was over. Between the ice and the shore there was open water, several hundred feet across. We had been jumping from floe to floe for the last hour when it looked as if we were finally going to be stopped by water, but Itukusuk took command.

He was an experienced ferryman, and he did not hesitate to take us across on an ice floe. All nine of us gathered together on one floe that was barely large enough to hold us and began peacefully rowing across. The sun was very low on the horizon, it was probably close to midnight, and we were utterly exhausted but in surprisingly good spirits. I think we all had a feeling of pride in our accomplishment, our successful crossing to the island.

Rockwell was in top form. He sat quietly for a long time, lost in contemplation of the Arctic scenery, and finally he sighed deeply and said:

"This is even better than Arizona. And I always thought Arizona was the most beautiful spot in the world!"

The final crossing was strenuous, but compared to the rest of our long journey from Saunders Island it was an anticlimax. We split up in three groups as we had the previous day, but we moved with considerably less speed—partly because we were in poor condition but mainly because of our feet. The many hours on the ice had ruined our kamiks. Some of them had sizable holes in their soles. Every now and then we had to stop and cut out small pieces of sealskin to put inside the kamiks. They protected the feet for a while, but they never lasted long and could not keep the water out. They had to be changed constantly, and all this patchwork on the kamiks delayed us.

Once again we were stopped by water, an open rift stretching in both directions as far as we could see and much too wide to jump across. The ice was thick and smooth, the edges sharp and clean, with no small ice floes broken off to be used as a ferry. Our goal was clearly visible within a few hours' walking distance, but we seemed to be stymied.

Farther out in Melville Bay the rift probably ended in open water. How far it reached we had no way of telling; there were no icebergs we could climb for a better view. If we had to detour in the hope of getting to the end of the rift we might have to walk for days. We might also stay where we were until the rift closed again, but that might take hours or days and we had no assurance that the ice would remain stationary. We might be carried with the ice back to Cape York!

Suddenly Kraungak called out to me. He was running along the rift with Itukusuk, and when I caught up with them I realized that they had sighted another polar bear. I could not quite share their excitement but was nevertheless ready for a bear hunt. It would at least make us forget our predicament for a while.

The bear was on the other side of the wide rift, beyond the range of our one remaining gun. The huge animal had seen us and was very curious, like most bears. The only way to lure it within range was to take advantage of this curiosity, as I had done so often before. I flopped down on the ice close to the water, waved my arms, and kicked my legs wildly. The bear stopped at once, watched me for a few minutes, and decided to investigate further this strange creature on the ice. Gently it slipped into the water and began swimming across the rift. Apparently afraid that I would try to escape if I became aware of the approaching animal, the bear swam very slowly, mostly under water and practically without a sound.

At last Itukusuk could wait no longer. When the bear surfaced for the last time the Eskimo sent a bullet right through its head. Never have I seen a bear with such shocked astonishment so clearly expressed in its face, and we could not help laughing as the proud animal sank. In a moment it came up again, floating, like all dead bears. This one was a very fat specimen and was high in the water.

The sight of the floating animal gave me a great idea, probably the only good one I had on the entire journey. I could now discard all my plans to set out for Seddon, we did not yet have to admit defeat. The polar bear might ferry us across the rift!

I did not tell my friends what I had in mind. I asked them quickly to gather our belongings which they had scattered all over the ice when we were stopped by the rift. Kraungak brought his harpoon, and I used it to pull the dead bear close to the ice.

We still had the two oars we had used for our makeshift toboggans. I now put one on each side of the bear, tied the front and hind legs of the bear to the oars, and thus had a fairly stable "ferry."

When I had completed these preliminaries I motioned to the others to stand aside, pushed the bear halfway out in the rift, and stepped back a few yards from the edge to gather enough speed. I started running before the others realized what I planned to do, took off from the edge with all my strength—and for once thanked the Lord for my long legs. I landed with one foot on the floating bear and hurtled off again, the wildest jump I ever made.

I stumbled on the ice, rolled over several times, but I made it without touching water. When I got to my feet the others were cheering me.

Itukusuk was the first one to follow me. The bear sank deeper under the weight, but it carried him and I got him safely across. When he jumped off he was soaking wet up to the hips, but I was vastly relieved to have at least one companion—and an Eskimo is used to being wet.

The oldest white man among us, Thomas Olsen, was next to cross over. While the others continued chopping through the ice, he calmly began undressing! When he had removed every stitch of clothing and stood naked in the snow he bundled up his clothes, held them tightly on his shoulder with one arm, and jumped on the bear ferry. Clinging to the neck of the bear with his free arm, he shouted to us to pull as fast as we could. The crossing did not take very long, but he was half-frozen when we pulled him up on the ice on our side and put him down on a sealskin to keep his feet warm and dry. He quickly dressed and assured us calmly that he was now really warm for the first time in days.

Rockwell Simon was ready in his birthday suit with all his clothes on his shoulder. Again we pulled, but were interrupted by a wild shout from Itukusuk. The Eskimo had used his eyes while all the rest of us were watching the ferry, and he roared with laughter as he looked at the rift a little farther out. While we were frantically trying to complete the crossing the rift had closed again a few yards away from us.

We were furious because we had not had the patience to wait, but we laughed with relief—and promptly forgot about Rockwell Simon, who was still clinging to the bear halfway across. We watched the other four men walking down to the covered passage until Rockwell screamed at us. As soon as we stopped pulling the line the ferry sank still deeper and the poor man was just about going under when I began pulling again. The water reached up to his neck, and he held his clothes on top of his head. As soon as he was close enough I relieved him of the bundle on his head. I meant well, but the immediate result was that Rockwell lost his precarious balance and plunged into the water.

When we pulled him up his naked body inevitably scraped the sharp ice. When he finally stood up he was bleeding from cuts on his chest and stomach, hips and thighs. They were only surface cuts, but they must have hurt terribly in the icy air, and he looked quite a sight.

The poor man swore and cursed. He threatened us with the most vicious retaliation for leaving him in the water, and he was so infuriated that he forgot to put on his clothes. Naked and bleeding, he danced around on the ice, shouting and screaming at us. He became even wilder when I suggested that he put on his clothes before he froze to death.

"That's none of your damned business," he yelled. "I'll get dressed when I'm good and ready!"

I could not help laughing at his helpless fury and his refusal to dress. The others joined me, and after a while even Rockwell realized the humor of the situation. He howled with laughter while we helped him get dressed. In a few minutes we were joined by the others, who had calmly detoured and walked across the ice while we nearly lost our lives in the water. As soon as we had skinned and cut up the bear we were ready to cover the final distance to Thom Island without further interruption.

We were triumphant when we stepped ashore. We felt as if we were already in safe harbor with all our troubles behind us, although we had no good reason to believe that we would be any better off on the island, or that any ship would call for us. My only thought was a certain satisfaction because we had accomplished the seemingly impossible: losing a boat in the middle of Melville Bay and crossing safely on the ice in the month of September when the sea should normally be ice-free. I do not think it had ever been done before, and I doubt if anyone has ever done it since.

After many days of waiting a ship finally arrived and we said good-by to the five whalers. To tell the truth, I was not too unhappy to see the last of them.

10

A FEW MONTHS LATER, AROUND CHRISTMASTIME, KNUD AND I DEcided to go to Tasiussak together. Navarana was to come with us.

We suggested that, since the trip would be a cold one, Navarana wear a man's costume. She was violently opposed to the

idea at first, but when Knud assured her that in southern Greenland the colony managers' wives all wore men's clothes she finally
consented. The man's costume is much warmer, consisting of a
long coat and bearskin pants reaching to the knees. The woman's
pants are made of foxskin and are much shorter. Their boots
extend to the crotch, making walking difficult, and running
almost impossible. The men wear a string of foxtails around their
knees where boots meet pants to fend off wind and catch drifting
snow. Secretly Navarana's friends laughed at her when they first
saw her in a man's outfit, but later she told them how comfortable she was, and within two years all the smartest girls in the
tribe provided themselves with such a traveling costume.

The day before we decided to go on we were all awakened
by an ear-splitting yell and an answering roar from the natives
on the ice. A young fellow had been sent up from Cape Melville
to tell everyone that a great narwhal stake was in progress at
Imnalugssuak.

It was a fantastic experience. The sea was boiling with the
frantic animals fighting for air. The fountain of water they blew
up every time they breathed would fall down on the edge of the
breathing hole where it would freeze and make the hole still
smaller. And there was a constant stream of whales desperately
struggling for air. They showed no fear of our harpoons, and no
matter how many we caught there seemed no end to the mass
of swirling, fighting, slippery bodies.

The Eskimos were in ecstasy as the dead whales were piled up
on the ice. The blood bath lasted for four days and four nights.
Bonfires were lit, and together we watched the men dancing
wildly on the blood-covered ice as the killing went on and on.

Suddenly the whales disappeared, having found a narrow strip
of water under which they could swim to freedom in the open
sea. By then more than two hundred dead whales were on the
ice, and probably an equal number had escaped our harpoons.
The moon and the northern lights disappeared the moment
the whales were gone, and suddenly a storm hit us.

We all rushed to shore, and most of the men were so exhausted
from the blood bath that they went to sleep at once. And as they
slept the ice broke up and went out, taking the mountains of
meat to the open sea!

When they woke up the Eskimos were wildly amused. They
had thought they would not have to go walrus hunting in the

north that year because they would have enough meat to last them until summer—and suddenly they had nothing. "We have fed the polar bears far out at sea," they laughed. "They can live on our meat now and won't have to come to shore where we can kill them this winter!" It tickled their peculiar sense of humor.

The rest of the trip was tiresome and uneventful. At Bjoerneborg we found provisions which Nielsen had cached for us during the summer, and Navarana commenced to worry over her debut in the outside world. Should she wear her man's costume or should she go back to her own decent way of dressing? We assured her we still had a long distance to travel, and the people she would meet would not be judges of style. Still the entrance into a new country excited her so much that she did not sleep at all the last night. She saw her first completely wooden house and was sure that she would soon be in contact with people, all of whom could read and write.

When we approached the first settlement all the men ran out to greet us, shouting: *"Kuisimangitut tikeqisut."* [The unbaptized are coming.]

The polar Eskimos did not know the difference between "baptized" and "unbaptized," but those who had visited in Danish Greenland had always been looked down upon by the baptized southerners because of their natural status, and so they resented it. Navarana had heard the term used belittlingly, and now that it was applied to her she tilted her nose in the air and sniffed.

"One gets the idea here that something smells of urine!" she remarked.

Their emancipation from the urine bucket was the polar Eskimos' triumph over the southerners. The northern people carry it from their houses as quickly as possible, while the southerners use it for everything from driving ghosts out of their dwellings to washing their hair, and keep it inside until the stench brings tears to their eyes. Still, Navarana was a bit premature; before she entered any house she had used the retort which she had planned to give when anybody called her a pagan.

The Nielsens were prepared for our arrival by runners who had gone ahead to tell them of our coming. To my great surprise Navarana was greeted with a certain aloofness, especially by Mrs. Nielsen. Later I learned the cause of it:

The Nielsens had selected me for their son-in-law. Their

daughter, Jacobine, was as yet unmarried, and in Danish Greenland marriage is much more of a business proposition than in the
Far North. My qualifications were nothing to brag about, but
when there was only one unmarried white man in the community I suppose I was a catch. Among the educated natives
and half-breeds the parents arrange the marriages of their children, and the young people are fairly content. They know they
must marry young, or else suffer the jibes reserved for spinsters
and bachelors, those ridiculous figures of Eskimo folklore. The
entrance of the bachelor or spinster is always the cue for laughter.

It took Mrs. Nielsen two days to get over her pique, but she
soon became one of Navarana's closest friends. Until then she had
been living in a splendid social isolation, as she was the only
native woman married to a white man—now she could share this
questionable distinction with Navarana.

We learned that an expedition under the explorer Ejnar
Mikkelsen had started for the Thule District via the north coast
of Greenland and had never appeared. Knud and I decided
to search for Mikkelsen and his men.

We set out, and the water was as calm and free of ice as it
would be in summer. The sun was returning, and by noon it
was already fairly light. Several of the natives accompanied us
to bring the boats back.

One incident occurred en route to Tasiussak which boded ill
for the success of our venture. While rowing we sighted an object
in the water and, approaching it, decided that it was a sleeping
seal. One of our boys, Nasaitordluarssuk, had his harpoon ready
before anyone else and hurled it at the very moment I discovered what it was. My shout was too late, and the harpoon
struck the body—the body of a drowned man, Peder Lynge, a
good friend of ours. He had gone out to shoot seals from the ice
and had worn new kamiks with slick soles. Apparently he had
slipped and fallen into the water.

Now we had mistaken him for a seal and harpooned him
which, to a superstitious people, is worse than killing a man outright. The native minister refused to tell the wife, and we had
to turn back with the body. The poor boy who had harpooned
the body was told to cut off the handle of the weapon and leave
the point in the dead man, and he was forced to give the stick
to the widow to be buried with Lynge.

On our trip back to Thule a child was born at Saitoq with a

tooth already in its mouth. This was also a sign to the old women that the world was going to end unless something was done to prevent it. The poor natives were frightened lest the minister hear of their bargaining with the devil, but they managed somehow. The devil, once called upon, stuck around.

He approached in the evening from the ice foot in the shape of a black dog. The natives called our boys and Navarana to look at the devil, but they were unable to see him, and felt ashamed because the others, the baptized, could. Sometimes the devil was heard outside the houses, one night just outside Abel's door. One of the girls, braver than the others, poked her finger out through the hole in the skin window, but she pulled it back in a hurry; it felt, she said, as if she had plunged it into boiling water.

Worst of all, the devil ran into some of the houses and had sexual intercourse with the young girls. They could hear him approaching, but they dared not light a match as death would come to them if they did. The poor girls admitted their submission, because they dared not resist the devil. Or so they said!

We reached Thule without further undue interruption and found a great many customers waiting to trade with us before we set out on our trip to locate Mikkelsen. We took care of them as best we could and then began our preparations for the expedition.

We were to take with us my father-in-law, Uvdluriark, and a fine young fellow, Inukitsork. They were the best men available and both volunteered to make the trip, not as hired men, but as Greenlanders whose unique privilege it would be to take a look at the other side of their country, and make their own observations.

We planned to follow the sea to the north coast and then go east until we met Ejnar Mikkelsen, or came upon traces of him. We would return—well, when we returned. We might be forced to spend the winter on the other side, but what of that?

The day before we intended to leave I was called to a conference. Uvdluriark had been looking at the map, along with a number of the other natives who had been with Peary, and he thought it would be a waste of time to follow the coast around to the east.

"Why can't we go straight across?" he asked. "It looks as if it would be a short cut."

I tried to explain to him that such a course would lead us

directly over the icecap—that we would encounter no land, and
no game!

"The icecap is only a road without rough ice," he persisted.

We all talked it over and argued the possibilities. Then
Knud joined the discussion and asked me if it would not be
possible.

Thus did we plan our inland ice voyage in the year 1912.

There was nothing to prevent our trying it, except that we
had insufficient provisions, no goggles to prevent snow blindness,
and we knew we would find no wild game until we came down
on the other side.

"If you can navigate us across," Knud said, "we'll look out
for the food!"

And so it was decided.

I went to my igloo to check my figures once more and could
find nothing amiss. I had my theodolite, and my two watches
would be of no more aid one route than another. I determined
to try to drive straight across the icecap and descend on the east
coast at the head of Denmark Inlet. At any rate, all I had to do
was guide the party up to the right latitude and then continue
eastward. We would in time be bound to strike land and could
later ascertain what land it was.

11

NEXT DAY WE STARTED OUT—THIRTY-FOUR SLEDS AND THREE HUN-
dred sixty dogs. The natives would return to Neqé, as we made
room on our four sleds for the extra meat they hauled. Wise
men of the tribe told us to ascend the icecap via Clements Mark-
ham's Glacier—named for the old English admiral whose splendid explorations had been made near Neqé.

The first day we did not go far. The glacier was steep, and
the humidity and heat were exhausting. The thirty-four sleds
stretched back from us in a long, ragged column. The teams were
eager to overhaul each other, even our own dogs who did not
realize they had so far to go. We had used an old trick to advantage here—harnessing the bitches in heat among the forward
teams; then the team of dogs where they really belonged could
haul any load in order to catch up with them. It was springtime,

and we had plenty of she-dogs to encourage their teammates to superdog efforts.

We did not feed our dogs the first night, so we had the whole crew with us another day. The four who were going farthest had tea and sugar. Next morning soon after starting out we reached a spot where the going was terrible. All the snow had blown off the ice, leaving no foothold for the dogs—and we were constantly ascending. We had to unload, drive on with half our loads, and return for the rest. Late in the afternoon we reached snow again and kept on until our dogs were exhausted. The third day there were only twenty-seven teams, and we sent more home each day as our dogs consumed the walrus meat. After three more days we reached the interior dome of the icecap and bade good-by to all our helpers.

We were at last at the spot where the success or failure of the expedition would depend upon our speed. And our speed depended upon native methods, which no expedition of whites had ever used before.

The icecap is especially difficult to traverse because of the soft dry snow through which the runners cut easily. We had brought along from Neqé walrus hide sliced into long strips as broad as the palms of our hands. These we fastened beneath the runners of the sleds. Then we melted snow with our primus stoves and poured the water over the long strips, letting it freeze. It took us twenty-four hours to prepare the runners, but when we finished the sleds were almost as easy to shove as a baby carriage. With such runners much greater loads can be hauled over loose snow, and we had the advantage over sea-ice travelers that we could spread out our load without danger of its catching against ice hummocks.

At three o'clock on the morning of April 14, 1912, I took the hour angle, and we set out.

Inside the icecap the snow drifts constantly. Even when one is unaware of the wind dry snow sifts through the air covering everything, like flour in a mill. In no time the sleds were white and the loads saturated with the stuff. We looked like ghosts driving ghost dogs. When we put our hands in our pockets we even encountered the snow dust there, and it was not very pleasant.

My special job, of course, was taking observations. Knud had never learned much about astronomy, as mathematics had always been difficult for him and he had had a schoolteacher who always tried to humiliate him before his classmates. As a result he hated everything about figures, and a table of logarithms was enough to make him vomit.

So far as I was concerned I did not mind this task—at first. My talent made me especially valuable to the expedition, and in the evenings when the others were cooking I could figure out my observations. But in the mornings it took me a long time to get the hour angle, take the temperature and pack my instruments, and do all those tedious little things which are annoying for others to watch.

At night we tied the dogs with walrus hides, although they were usually too tired to try to break away and only amused themselves by gnawing at the blubber on the inside of the hide. At the time we saw no reason why they should not do this—it even lessened the load—but later we became so ravenous for fat that we wanted nothing else, and by then there was no fat left.

Every morning Knud woke us with his Danish songs, and his voice was so powerful that it gave us energy to get started. Knud had once planned to become an opera singer but had met with discouragement from the impresarios. Now he declared that his voice was too good for opera. Be that as it may, his lively humor carried us through many a bad day.

All of us soon looked terrible. We were at an altitude of six thousand feet, and the sun's rays were white-hot metal in our eyes. Everywhere we looked the landscape glittered, and at the same time it was so cold that our faces froze and our skin burned under the ultraviolet rays. It commenced to peel off. The skin on Knud's and Uvdluriark's cheeks hung in ragged splotches, and my nose was raw and bleeding.

We could not have endured water, even if we had had any, and soon we had no fat to apply to our affected parts. Our craving for fat became an obsession. Each man carried his own food, and I remember that one night all four of us sorted out clear blubber and cooked it. The soup was nothing but liquid fat, and we drank it like sweet milk. To swallow lean meat was as difficult as eating dry flour. The dogs were similarly affected. They refused to eat meat, and if they tried, it stuck in their throats. Whenever possible we thawed out pieces of walrus hides and cut chunks for them. There was much fat on it, and it satisfied them. But soon there was no more blubber for our lamps—we had eaten it all.

The worst calamity of all—for all of us—was that I was slowly falling a victim to snow blindness. Unless a person has experienced it he cannot appreciate the torture. Your eyelids feel as if they are made of sandpaper. Knud Rasmussen, who had much dark pigment in his eyelids, was not troubled, but I am rather light. Added to this, I had to take all the observations. Each time I shot the sun a hot poker seemed to be plunged into my right eye—a rather unpleasant feeling. I tried to shift over to my left eye, but it was soon as irritated as the right. The lids were so inflamed that I could scarcely open my eyes at all.

But my observations must continue. Now that we were nearer land it was all the more important that we know our approximate position. Each night I painfully made my calculations. And how I blessed a howling gale which kept us inside the tent for a day or two! I would pray that the storm would continue, but since we had decided that unless we traveled we did not eat I was torn between the gnawings of my stomach and the scratching of my eyelids.

We traveled whenever humanly possible, and I continued to make my observations as accurately as ever.

One day I proudly announced that we would "see land" the following day. My prediction was partly guesswork, since I had no way of knowing just how far inland the coastal mountains would be visible before the icecap covered everything—but I was right. In the morning the glacier began a gradual decline until we could finally see mountains in the far distance.

I had to stop as usual at noon to take my daily observation. I told the others not to rush on before I had plotted a safe course, but once they had seen land they would not stop. When I caught up with them they had finally halted far down the glacier. We were not driving any more, we were falling. We did not know what lay ahead, but we knew we could not retrace our steps. The glacier was so steep, so slippery, so steel-hard that the exhausted dogs would never be able to climb back again. We had to continue cautiously down the incline.

Before long we discovered the glacier ended in a vertical drop of more than seventy feet. In order to reach solid land below one must go down over the precipice edge which stretched in both directions as far as we could see. We tied together our sealskin harpoon lines, not bothering to remove the harpoon points, and cut a deep hole through the edge of the ice to make a pulley arrangement. I was to go first, being heavier than the others, and if the lines would hold me they would hold the rest.

A sealskin line is slippery and hard to hold on to. I grabbed the line with both hands, wound it once around my thigh, and crawled over the edge. I closed my eyes and moved down slowly. The lines were strong enough, and I thought all was well until I felt a sharp harpoon point penetrate my thigh. I let out a yell which made the three on top pull sharply on the rope and drive the point more deeply into my flesh. The pain was terrific, but somehow I managed to tear out the point and descend quickly. I was bleeding freely, but the steel had not hit the bone or any major nerve or artery.

The others managed to get most of the dogs down and soon joined me below the glacier. But three of the dogs refused to be carried down and jumped to their death. We cut them up and fed them to the other dogs, and, famished as we were, we ate some of the meat ourselves although it was tough and had an unpleasant taste and odor.

We had succeeded in making our way to the east coast, but we had no idea where we were or where we could get any food. I had to stay where I was. My snow blindness had become so bad I could not see at all. My eyelids were swollen as thick as my lips, and I could hardly endure the pain. I was also weak from loss of blood and had to keep quiet until the wound in my thigh healed.

The other three set out to explore the land and look for something to eat. We had seen traces of musk oxen, and they hoped to get fresh meat by killing at least one. They left me behind with a few of my dogs, and I was hardly conscious of the passing of days and nights until they returned five days later after an unsuccessful trip. A heavy wet fog had covered everything, and they had managed to catch only a couple of rabbits. They had had to kill a few of the dogs to feed the rest of the dogs and themselves.

After another day I caught up with the others. They were as exhausted and starved as I was and had found no game of any kind. Then Knud remembered he had put in his bag some of the walrus-skin strips we had used under our sled runners on the glacier. We had to boil them, but we did not dare use any more of the kerosene which we had saved for the return trip across the icecap. Fortunately we found enough of a small Arctic plant—

the *Cassiope tetragona*—to make a fire. It is found everywhere in Greenland and burns easily even when it is green and in bloom. We boiled the abominable skin from the sled runners and ate it.

My eyes were improving steadily, and I was soon able to move about without difficulty. While Knud and the two Eskimos rested after this grand meal I decided to set out on my own— and luck was with me. After three hours of skiing I ran across the fresh tracks of three musk oxen. I got all three of them, cut out their tongues and some breast pieces, and hurried back to camp. I did not take time to skin them; I only cut open their stomachs to let out the gas which would, otherwise, have made the meat decompose in the space of a few hours. This gas has a horrible odor and gives the meat a peculiar acid taste if the stomach is not opened at once.

The three animals I caught saved us. We were soon strong enough to continue down the river and finally reached Danmark Fjord. It was easy going for a while with plenty of musk oxen to feed us well.

By the mouth of the fjord we suddenly noticed something shiny on the shore one morning. It turned out to be a sled runner glittering in the sun. It had been put up as a marker for a depot, and we thought it must have been the summer camp of Mylius-Erichsen, Hagen, and Broenlund, who had lost their lives during the *Danmark* Expedition. But there was no writing—no diary or letter or any kind of statement as evidence.

When we returned to Denmark later on, we learned that Mikkelsen had taken Erichsen's diary without leaving any written record. This omission was contrary to tradition and cost us a great deal of trouble. If Mikkelsen had left some kind of document we would have known where to look for him and his companion. As it was we had nothing to go by—and we continued our search.

We entered the Hagen Fjord, searched through Independence Fjord, and crossed over to Peary Land. The weather stayed clear and fine and I made observations everywhere, measured distances, and took notes. While we were looking for Mikkelsen I drew maps as best I could, since this was all new territory. We continued into Independence Fjord, reached Cape Knud Rasmussen and entered Broenlund Fjord. The farther in we went the poorer the ice became, and soon the going got pretty rough. I wanted to recross to the southern side of Independence Fjord for the sake of my observations, but Knud insisted we had to make speed and gave me just twenty-four hours to cross the fjord and return.

I could clearly see Academy Glacier, and I was convinced that I would find traces of Mylius-Erichsen there and probably some sign of Mikkelsen. Knud refused to be sidetracked and continued on his way with the Eskimos while I tried to cross the rotten ice on foot. I lost sight of the others, and soon plunged into the water. I got back on the ice safely enough, but I had lost my theodolite, my most precious instrument, which I must have to find our way back across the icecap. I could see it on the bottom of the shallow water, and I decided to dive for it. I was terrified lest the current should pull me under the ice, but I was able to retrieve the instrument after three dives.

When I caught up with the others they had already reached the bottom of the fjord and made camp there. We explored the land to the north and finally established the sensational fact that there was no such thing as a Peary Channel, a natural surmise of Admiral Peary, I later understood. Instead of a channel, there was a glacier which we named for our friend Nyboe, one of the men who had made possible our expedition to Thule. Nyboe Glacier was incredibly steep, and we could not climb it. Instead, we had to make our way up the mountains at the bottom of the fjord.

When we had climbed more than three thousand feet we reached a glacier which took us down into a valley that had to be crossed before we could reach the inland ice to the south. In the bottom of the valley there was a roaring ice-choked river we had to traverse, and again my size proved a handicap to me—I had to carry the others across. First I took Knud to the other side, then I returned for the Eskimos, but the current was too strong for me, and I had to have Knud as ballast. In this way I finally got all of us over.

We continued on the glacier until we found our way into a valley to the west—an incredible oasis in the middle of the ice. We promptly named it Poppy Valley. Planted in the green fields of soft grass, beautiful poppies bloomed. We found musk oxen for food and *Cassiope* for fires. We stayed in the valley several days until we were well fed and rested.

We continued climbing the glacier until we reached the region Peary had visited twenty years before with Astrup and Matthew

Henson. We decided to look for Peary's cairn and to take home his written report. Once again we found plenty of musk oxen, and everything would have been fine if it had not been for Knud. He woke up one morning with a yell of pain, complaining of a cramp in his leg. He could not stand up, and the pain turned out to be a bad attack of sciatica. So he had to stay where he was while we went hunting. There was an abundance of musk oxen to feed us and the dogs while we waited for him to improve.

Inukitsork and I set out to find Peary's cairn. We located it without trouble, as I had plenty of time to make all the necessary observations, and from the top of a mountain we spotted it with our telescope. Down valleys and up mountains, across rivers and lakes we made our way until we got to Navy Cliff, where we found the cairn.

We could see the depressions in the ground where once had lain the small stones Peary and his men had used for building the cairn. Their footprints were no longer distinguishable, but we could see where they had walked. Several of the stones in the cairn had been put there with the underside up, and they were bare and shiny while the lichen on the underside was still alive. In the polar regions lichen grows so slowly it may take a hundred years to reach the size of a half dollar. In the soft gravel we found several matches Peary had dropped, and in the cairn we found the bottle containing his report. I wrote a short report of our trip and left it in the cairn. I took Peary's bottle back to our camp to let Knud open it.

We found Knud in agony when we returned. It was obvious he could not return to Thule under his own power, and that same evening he told me he had decided I was to go back to Thule with Inukitsork while he would stay behind with Uvdluriark. I was to send off a report of our unsuccessful search and let the world know we had found no trace of Mikkelsen. He said he would stay in the camp until winter was over, when I could come back and get him and Uvdluriark.

His plan was quite insane and I told him so. Under no conditions would I leave him behind. I knew we could manage to get him safely back with us. We were now reduced to two sleds which we carried up to the icecap from our camp a few miles down the valley. Then the Eskimos carried our gear and food up to the icecap, while I took Knud on my back.

At last we were ready for the long trip home. With Knud lying on Uvdluriark's sled we set off across the inland ice. He fainted several times from the pain during the first few days, but he refused to cut down on the distance we expected to cover each day.

The weather very soon turned bad, and we were forced to slow down anyhow. I walked ahead on my skis, the dogs following. But soon the dogs got sick. They were used to the fat walrus and seal meat and could not manage on the meager ration of lean musk-ox meat. One by one they collapsed and had to be killed until we were reduced to eight dogs.

That last part of our trip was pure torture. We had absolutely no meat left and had to eat more dogs until we finally had only four left. I developed an inflammation of the tendons above my heels and was in constant pain. Fortunately Knud was now able to walk, otherwise we would never have made it.

All pain and hardships were forgotten when finally we reached familiar landmarks and could see Thule far below us. Knud and I sat down on a sled for a while to gaze at the beautiful view. Without saying a word we looked at each other and shook hands. We had lived through something we would never forget—a great and unbelievably strenuous journey that cemented our friendship.

At that moment I was ready with my great surprise. From my bag I pulled out a tiny supply of tobacco I had saved for this great day. I divided it between Knud and the Eskimos who decided, with true heroism, to save it until our arrival in Thule the following day. They wanted to enter the settlement with their pipes in their mouths. And when the first Eskimo came running out to meet us Inukitsork, with unspeakable pride, said to him in a casual voice:

"Have a smoke?"

After five long months we were home again. Navarana had spent her idle time in making me a new set of beautiful clothes as evidence of her confidence in my safe return.

12

WE CONSIDERED THE CROSSING OF THE INLAND ICE—THE FIRST THULE Expedition, as we called it—quite a feat and we decided to make a trip home to Copenhagen to report our findings. We were the first people since the Norwegian explorer Fridtjof Nansen to complete such a crossing, which never before had even been attempted so far north. We settled once and for all the controversial question of the Peary Channel, and we added considerably to the map of northeastern Greenland. But before we could return to Denmark we had to regain some strength, and I had to recover from my inflamed ankles.

We were eager to get home to tell the world about our expedition and enjoy our fame, and finally we set off in January 1913. Navarana accompanied us as far as Tasiussak where I left her in the home of the post manager, my good friend Soren Nielsen. The minister from Upernivik was there at the time, and he offered to teach her Christianity and to baptize her when she was ready for it. I told him that was up to Navarana, who assured me she had heard a great many wonderful things from her converted Eskimo friends about Jesus and she was eager to learn what it was like to be a Christian. With the post manager and the minister to take care of her needs, I left her in safe hands, I thought, and Knud and I hurried on to the south.

We entered the harbor with all flags flying, ready for the great welcome we confidently expected. A crowd of reporters met us and gave us a great display in the newspapers the next day, but we waited in vain for the banquets and receptions. On the day of arrival Knud and I gave a tremendous dinner for our friends in Copenhagen, but the following evening we walked alone in the streets.

It did not matter much to me, since I was mainly interested in seeing my friends and family after the long absence. The first person I went to see was my friend Magdalene, whom I had met during our lecture tour three years before and of whom I had grown fond. I found her sick in bed with a nervous breakdown, and after we had a long talk her nurse told me not to come back again as my visit had excited her patient.

The next few days I spent at home with my parents while I worked on my maps which I had to complete before we returned to Thule. Knud and I applied to the Carlsberg Foundation for financial aid to cover the cost of our expedition. The total amount we asked for was only seven hundred dollars, but the foundation hesitated because it had never before been asked for so little. When we had convinced them that the modest request was well founded it was finally granted.

After five weeks in Denmark I was ready to return to Greenland. During our stay we had purchased a small vessel which could be used in the coastal trade of Greenland and to supply our station at Thule, saving us the many long trips down to Tasiussak. We named the small craft *Cape York* and engaged as its master a young and able sailor, Peder Pedersen, who became known from one end of Greenland to the other as "Cape York Peter."

The day before I left Copenhagen, Magdalene came to see me at my hotel. Sick as she was, she had made the trip in order to say good-by and to reproach me for not having called on her again. Her nurse had never told her I had been ordered to stay away.

In Tasiussak I found Navarana patiently waiting for me. She had had a very bad time there because we had been gone so long. She had been told not to expect to see me again, and, since I had not paid enough in advance for her room and board, she had been ordered to go to work for her lodging. She had been made to help with the tanning process which consisted in washing the skins in urine, and her hands were swollen and sore. When I asked her about her instruction in Christianity she told me it had come to nothing because the minister had showed her quite a different kind of attention. She knew how to defend herself, but in the process she had lost her interest in his religion.

A few days after our arrival in Tasiussak the *Cape York* turned up. The season was too far advanced, however, to try to get through the ice to Thule, and our good captain was told to unload all our goods, which we were allowed to store in the attic of the local church house. In small stages we took the greater part of the supplies up the coast as far as we could go by motorboat— to the southern end of Melville Bay. On the last trip we left Knud to wait for the first chance to cross the new ice over the bay, while Navarana and I returned to Tasiussak where we spent a few peaceful weeks and celebrated Christmas together. When the new year of 1914 dawned we set out on our sleds for Thule and finally got there after a year's absence.

But we were no longer alone in the Thule District. A group of American explorers, the MacMillan Expedition, had arrived in Etah and had built a house there for headquarters. And not many

days went by before we received the first visitor from the Mac-
Millan camp, the American geologist Elmer Ekblaw. We naturally invited the guest to stay with us, but our house was
bare of food. The only thing to eat was a rotten walrus quarter
—delicious when it has decomposed just the right length of time,
but nauseating when it has gone for more than a year like this
one. Before I could explain the situation Knud took care of it
with his usual presence of mind.

"You have picked an exceptionally fortunate moment to visit
us," he told Ekblaw with a straight face. "It so happens that we
have the most marvelous delicacy which we have saved for a
great occasion like this. I am sure you will want to sample this
Eskimo specialty if you have never had it before."

I brought in the monster, and Knud served Ekblaw a huge
piece—green and smelly from age. Knud and I set a good example by eating the foul thing, and Ekblaw had to follow suit.
His face turned the color of the meat, but he managed to get it
down—only to have Knud serve him another portion. The poor
man was in a cold sweat when he was through, and his face lit
up when Knud said:

"Do you think a cup of coffee would be the right thing now?"

I knew—and Knud knew—that the nearest coffee was at least
a hundred miles away.

"Please," said Ekblaw, "that would be just right after such a
good meal!"

"Ah, but that is where you are wrong, my dear friend," Knud
said blandly. "It would be a great pity to ruin this fine taste by
coffee. You must finish the meal in true Eskimo fashion. The
taste is supposed to stay with you."

Ekblaw spent the night, and he hastened to return our hospitality the next morning before Knud had a chance to offer him
any more delicacies. He announced that after the festive meal
we had given him it was now his turn to do what he could. And
from his sled he brought in the best he had of everything—
coffee, biscuits and marmalade, and other rare treats in return
for our nasty walrus meat.

In the following months we filled our storerooms, however,
making a great many round trips to the south to bring home our
supplies. And we were soon to need them, for it turned out that
the MacMillan group—or the Crocker Land Expedition, as it
was called—was not too well equipped. They came to us for tools,

cooking utensils, warm clothes, and many other things. I felt it was my duty to lend support to the Americans, and in early spring I went up to Etah to meet the members of the expedition and to take them more supplies. MacMillan was on a trip to locate Crocker Land, but I met the other men and got the impression there was little harmony among them. Ekblaw and Dr. Tanqueray seemed eager to get away for a while, and I invited them to come down to Thule with me. In the meantime Knud had left me in complete charge in Thule while he made another trip to Denmark.

In a letter dated October 1914 he wrote about the terrible war which looked as if it might last for three more months! And he warned me that there might be a shortage of many things and that there would be no market for our fox furs for a long time to come. He asked me to be saving with all my supplies, especially ammunition.

That winter was hard and game was scarce. Navarana and I made a long trip to the north during the early winter and found many Eskimos near starvation. Once after a visit to a settlement where there was nothing at all to eat we started north for Neqé where we hoped to find food for the dogs and ourselves. Halfway there a snowstorm forced us to stay overnight at Igdlorssuit, a deserted settlement, where we spent the night in an empty stone hut. Next morning I set out to catch some rabbits and spent the whole day without success. But Navarana was waiting for me in the moonlight outside the hut, happy just to have her empty-handed husband back again.

Next day the same thing happened. I returned with empty hands in the evening to have Navarana meet me with a smiling face. She said she had searched the empty huts while I was gone and had found two frozen seal flippers. She apologized for having eaten one of them without waiting for me. The meal was ready, and I gobbled it down. Starved as I was, the disgusting meat was a treat. When I was about through I became aware of her large eyes following my every bite, and I suddenly realized that she had lied to me. There had been only one flipper which she unselfishly had prepared for me. When I reproached her, she answered that I had been out hunting all day while she had only rested in the hut and was in less need of food. Besides, she was used to starving since childhood, while men must have their food to act like men.

I felt deeply humiliated because she showed me that a woman is stronger than a man and that an Eskimo is made of so much sterner stuff than a Dane, a proud white man! My only way out was to scold her for deceiving me and to prove my manhood right away. So, tired as I was, I put on my kamiks again and set out in the moonlight.

I was so weak I could hardly keep on my feet, but after an hour or two a miracle happened. I ran across two fat rabbits and hurried home with them. We ate the livers and hearts raw, gave part of the meat to the dogs, and boiled the rest. It was one of the best meals I had ever tasted.

13

ONE DAY FITZHUGH GREEN TURNED UP IN THULE AND ASKED ME IF he might move in with me. I had no objection, especially since he brought along a great deal of food. I might have turned him away if I had known why he had left Etah. The reason his American colleagues treated him as an outcast was due to the fact that he had shot and killed Puivatsork, an Eskimo he had taken along on a trip, in order to take over the man's wife. I had been told only that Puivatsork had lost his life under an avalanche. Once I asked Green what had happened to his Eskimo companion and he turned pale and asked me never to mention the man's name. I thought his reaction meant that he had taken the man's tragic death to heart.

Years went by before I learned the true story which was revealed by MacMillan in his travel diaries. Once the truth was known, Denmark demanded reparation from the American government on behalf of the widow and the children who had been left without support. In the meantime Green had won national fame as an aviator and was quite a hero. But something had happened in Thule which took care of the reparation demand.

The Eskimo Kridtluqtoq became a Christian and as soon as he was baptized he went to confession. He told the minister that he had shot and killed Professor Marvin, in order to save the life of his own cousin.

As soon as it was known that Marvin had not drowned, as we had presumed, but had been killed by an Eskimo, the American

government made a counterclaim and it was decided to let the
Green case cancel the Marvin case. Later Puivatsork's widow
married my father-in-law, and thus the international dispute was
settled to mutual satisfaction.

Green stayed on in my house while he waited for the ship that
was to take the American expedition back home. I must confess
I was looking forward to having the district to myself once more.

Meanwhile there was a murder in the next village to occupy
us. Quanguaq, a strong-limbed but weak-minded widower, lived
near Sekrusuna and his wife at Granville Bay. Sekrusuna had
been a great one to tease poor Quanguaq; he would taunt him
by suggesting, when they were hunting together, that they go
home to their "wife" now, sometimes adding references to their
intimate relations which were almost more than the young and
wifeless Quanguaq could endure. Sekrusuna also tantalized the
poor man by promising him that he might sleep with his wife
when they returned, but whenever Quanguaq attempted to take
advantage of this favor he found the woman's lawful husband at
her side. The husband thought this a great joke. Such actions
can infuriate even more decent men than Quanguaq.

Besides all this, Sekrusuna beat his wife in order to demonstrate to Quanguaq the many advantages of being happily married. He beat her only when the widower was present.

One day in the spring the two men stood out upon the edge
of the ice. Quanguaq drove his harpoon not into a seal but
straight through the body of his friend Sekrusuna, who dropped
into the water and was carried off by the current. Quanguaq
came home with both sleds and teams. He drove straight to
the dead man's wife and told her that he was going to stay with
her and here were a few birds he would like her to prepare for
his supper. The widow meekly accepted her altered status, and
cooked for him.

When at last Quanguaq came with some of his friends to
the store I took it upon myself to speak to him and let him
know how I felt toward murderers. He brought Navarana a large
bundle of rabbits, and they recalled at length how they had
sat in the little hut starving together and the old grandfather,
Mequsaq, had been their only provider. Mequsaq loved to hear
this story over and over again.

I had to break into the recollections. My speech was prepared,
and everyone in the village was present.

"Quanguaq," I said in a stern voice, "I hear that you are a murderer."

"Let others tell of it," he answered. "One never likes to brag."

"To murder is the basest crime in the world. If you had been down in my country you would have been killed as punishment."

"Peterssuaq, you are mistaken. White men would not disgrace themselves even to look at me!"

"Yes, they would. You have ruined the reputation of the whole tribe. You are not worthy to eat with us."

"Peterssuaq, stop talking to me. I am so low that it is not worthy of you to talk to me."

He persisted in that vein. His sorrow over what he had done seemed real enough, but the more I blamed him the more he debased himself. "You don't know how bad I am. I have also committed many other crimes."

"Well," I said, "why don't you behave? You could have found other wives."

"No, no. No other women are so low that they could get along with me."

"But that doesn't give you the right to kill."

"I never do the right thing. I am awful."

If I said "terrible," he said "horrible." If I charged him with one crime he admitted it and accused himself of a worse one. It is difficult to scold a man who admits everything and thinks up added degradations. Against my will I found myself consoling him.

14

WE SIGHTED A SHIP ONE MORNING AS WE WERE WALRUS HUNTING and hurried out to meet it. On deck I was greeted by an elderly gentleman:

"Are you Peter Freuchen? Oh, thank goodness, we are saved at last!"

The man turned out to be Dr. Hovey, who had been sent out by the Museum of Natural History in New York, in order to terminate the Crocker Land Expedition, which had already cost far more than stipulated. When the museum received reports that MacMillan planned to stay in the Arctic for another year,

Dr. Hovey was sent up on a ship from the Grenfell Mission, the *George B. Cluett,* in order to take MacMillan and the rest of them back to the United States.

Dr. Hovey asked me if I would take him in to Thule, then up to Etah in my motorboat, and bring back the members of the expedition. I told him Green was already with me, and Dr. Hovey came along to my house. He turned out to be rather a difficult character. Navarana and I served him the best meal we could, whereupon he refused to sit at the same table with-an Eskimo. I pretended not to understand him, but this tactless statement was typical of him.

We went on to Etah to pick up Ekblaw, Dr. Tanqueray, and Dr. Hunt. While we loaded all the materials to be taken back to New York, Dr. Hovey inspected the belongings of the Eskimos in Etah and took away from them many things which Mac-Millan had either sold or given them. It was all the property of the museum, Dr. Hovey claimed, and in amazingly short time he managed to become sincerely disliked by the Americans, the Eskimos, and myself.

Back in Thule once more the captain and crew on the *Cluett* insisted on sailing at once.

As soon as they were gone we resumed our peaceful existence. With the first ice of the season quite a few bears came to the district—mainly at Pitufik where the gigantic American air base is now situated. The bears walk across the glacier to Melville Bay behind Cape York in a straight line to the richest seal center in the whole district. Practically every day we saw a bear. We also were able to add ptarmigan to our diet and Canadian snow geese.

Our peace did not last long. One day while we were hunting Navarana noticed a strange procession in the distance. It turned out to be Green from the MacMillan group and Davis, the first mate on the *George B. Cluett.* They brought me a letter from Dr. Hovey with the news that the proud ship was ice locked. They had had motor trouble on the way south, they had met ice outside Cape Athol, and the ice had forced them into Parker Snow Bay, where they would have to stay through the winter. There was no possibility of getting the ship out again until next year.

Dr. Hovey asked me "in the name of humanity" to come to his assistance. They had no winter clothes on board, they were low in supplies, and their quarters on the ship were cramped. I had no choice, of course, and set off at once.

It was a more modest Dr. Hovey whom I met in Parker Snow Bay. He still had not learned to be considerate, however, and he and Captain Mitchell were like cat and dog. He swore that the captain was going to pay for their misfortune, once they were back in the United States. There was nothing the captain could do about the ice, of course, but the fact that they were short in all their supplies was his fault, and he knew it. He was an old prospector from Alaska and used to taking chances. His contract had specified that he was to take along reserve food and supplies, in case they should be forced to spend a winter in the Arctic. But he was sure he could make it back before winter, and he gambled on it and sold all the reserve stores.

The captain had turned the hold into a common room for the crew, his aim being to annoy the members of the expedition so that they would be forced off the ship, thus leaving all the food to the crew. The whole crew, of course, joined this cause with true devotion. There were some terrible scenes on board, especially after I had given Dr. Hovey all of my tobacco supply that I did not need myself. I had been naïve enough to expect him to ration the precious tobacco evenly among all the crew, and I was dumbfounded when I realized he was going to keep every bit for himself. Dr. Harrison Hunt, a grand old man, calmly announced that he was going up to Thule and that he would not return to the ship even if Hovey was dying.

Dr. Hovey refused to leave the ship. He did not want to "relieve Captain Mitchell of his obligations," as he put it. But his mere presence was a torture to the men who were suffering acutely from the lack of tobacco. He would even parade in front of them with his pipe in his mouth, and whenever he emptied his pipe he would carefully throw away the last remnant of tobacco.

Finally the tobacco hunger got so acute I decided to help the men. I went on a trip to the south and found a good supply of tobacco in Tasiussak. I bought everything at black-market prices and returned to the ship. But I refused to hand it over. I knew they had thirty-five tons of coal on board which I could use in Thule, and I demanded thirty-two tons as payment. Mitchell refused, and I prepared to go back to Thule with my tobacco.

When the captain saw me getting the sleds ready he set out

empty cans all around me in the snow, picked up his gun, and
sent the bullets over my head, hitting the bull's-eye every time.
But I calmly went on with my preparations until he had to give
in. The crew had to carry the coal to land and deposit it on the
cliffs before I gave them the tobacco.

I returned to Thule, but I still had to make many trips down
to the ship with supplies. Finally I refused to give them any more
without payment. Dr. Hovey promised to send me a check when
he returned to New York, but I had no use for checks in Greenland. I told him, however, that I knew the expedition had a large
quantity of fox furs which had been traded in return for goods,
and I asked for the furs instead of useless checks.

Dr. Hovey had not known about the furs which the MacMillan
Expedition had acquired, and he now insisted they were the
property of his museum. The MacMillan group should not have
traded with the Eskimos, he claimed, but once the furs were had,
they would have to be used to help cover the expenses of the
expedition. MacMillan had, however, planned to keep the furs
for himself.

I had also counted on these furs. Navarana had told me where
they were stored. The Eskimos knew, of course, that MacMillan
had hidden them in the cabin of his motorboat, which he had
pulled on shore for the winter. One night I calmly brought the
whole load to Thule, where I stored it.

In MacMillan's absence Dr. Hunt was in charge of the expedition. I told him that I expected to be paid for all the supplies I
had handed over to the Americans and that I did not consider
American checks suitable payment in northern Greenland. He
agreed and told me he would see to it that I got fox furs in return. When I told him I had already taken charge of the collection
he laughed and assured me I had done the right thing.

Toward the end of the winter the Americans finally decided
to return by way of Danish Greenland, instead of waiting to go
with the ice-bound vessel, and I took them down south as far as
Egedesminde. The going was slow in the deep snow, and I had
to spend many days and nights with them, learning to like them,
in spite of the great difference between us in attitude and out-
look.

Shortly after my return we moved out to Saunders Island to
spend some happy weeks at this favorite spot of ours, now that
Navarana was expecting our child. And while we were still there

we were suddenly surprised one morning by Knud Rasmussen. Knud, who was supposed to be forced by the war to stay in Denmark, had caught a vessel from Copenhagen to southern Greenland and had traveled up the coast at a time of the year when no one else could do it. And here he was back with us in Thule.

15

WHILE THE WAR RAGED AROUND THE WORLD KNUD RASMUSSEN HAD been forced to stay in Denmark in comparative idleness, writing a book and giving lectures, but this man of action was always impatient to return to Greenland. And here he was back again— but not alone. He had brought with him a young student who was later to become a great Danish explorer—Lauge Koch.

Life settled again into a routine of habits. There were many of us in the settlement now, and Lauge Koch, who slept in our attic, was youthfully excited at being with us. He told me he was happy during the first day, but that night he slept in his bag between two murderers. Later he admitted that he had never known murderers could be such fine fellows.

It was at about this time that Navarana's grandfather admitted he was ill, and gave up trying to care for himself. His life had been an exciting one. He had traveled far from his birthplace at Admiralty Bay in Canada; he had fought cannibals in his youth, had immigrated to Greenland and taught the natives here to use the bow and arrow, to construct kayaks and to eat certain meat such as caribou and ptarmigan which they had never dared sample before. He had been a great man among his people.

His last years, he said, had been made happy by Navarana and me, and he thanked us for them. He could have done nothing more to please us. Finally, with the greatest dignity, he told us that he was tired.

"It is not impossible that someone is going to sleep and keep on sleeping," he said. And shortly afterward he died.

We placed him on his sled and hauled his body to the crude stone mausoleum which we built for him. His sled still stands there, and his harpoons and tools lie beside his bones. We shot four of his dogs to do him honor, and one of mine. That is, I traded one of my old animals which had served its time for five of his good ones, which seemed to me better than permitting five good dogs to rot away beside their old hero. He had given me so much in his life that I was sure he would have been glad to grant me this last gift.

And life once more stood still for five days. There was no hunting in kayaks, no sounds of dogs on the scent of a bear.

Then he was gone and would never more be mentioned. He had been born, he had lived, and now he was dead.

Mequsaq, the grand old man of the North!

16

I HAD JUST RETURNED FROM A LONG HUNTING TRIP ONE EVENING when Navarana told me that some of the Eskimos had caught a narwhal and we were invited to a party. I told her I wanted to sleep but would join the party later. I do not know how long I slept. Navarana woke me as she entered the house again, and I asked if the party was over. She told me calmly that the party was still going on but that she had left because she had a stomach ache and wanted to go to bed for a little while. She went into the other room and I fell asleep again, only to be awakened by Arnanguaq, an old Eskimo woman, who told me that Navarana was in labor.

Wildly excited, I jumped from my bed and called frantically for Knud, who was asleep in the attic. He was an experienced father, and I asked him what to do. All he could think of was that coffee had always been served when he became a father. I told him there was no coffee anywhere in Thule, but Knud said he had saved some coffee beans for this great occasion. Triumphantly we went to the brook for water just as the Eskimo called out:

"*Anguterssuaq!* A big boy!"

We went out in the night, I with the strange sensation of being a father, Knud sleepy and sullen. "I don't know why you should be able to have the son which Dagmar has been unable to give me," he complained, thinking of his two daughters.

We returned with the water, and I went to see Navarana, who told me it was more tiring than she had expected to produce a boy and now she wanted to take a nap. Since it was only three o'clock in the morning she asked me to leave her alone until breakfasttime.

Knud went back to sleep again, forgetting all about the coffee. I went outside to sit by myself on the large boulder by our house. I was dreaming and making all sorts of plans for my boy. I decided to spend the rest of my life in Thule, to be all that a father should be—to make my son strong and brave and good and to help him avoid all my mistakes. I was daydreaming about the boy I had not yet seen when Navarana appeared and asked me to come and have a look at him. She had got out of bed to take care of the house as if nothing had happened. In the evening we gave a big coffee party for the whole settlement, and Knud opened the ball with Navarana, who danced till early morning. We called the boy Mequsaq, after his great-grandfather.

The summer was drawing to a close, and we had our first frost when the *Danmark* finally turned up with our supplies and with Dr. Wulff. The next few days the whole inlet filled up with pack ice so rapidly that the *Danmark* could not go out again. Once more we had a ship and its crew to share the winter with us. Lauge Koch went down to Tasiussak to spend a couple of winter months, and Dr. Wulff moved into my house.

We had a great deal of trouble with him during the winter. He was an able botanist and a fine man in many respects, but he had little understanding and no affection or consideration for the people he had to deal with. He never realized he could not behave in Thule as he had done in China, where he had spent many years. One evening when he returned from a sled trip the Eskimo who had been his guide told me that Dr. Wulff had hit him with the dogs' whip. Knud gave Wulff a piece of his mind, but Wulff insisted his way was the only way to deal with "the natives."

My worst experience with him was on a sled trip to Cape York across the glacier. Halfway we encountered some terrible screw ice and some large crevasses we could not cross. The going became risky, and I have seldom been as scared as I was crawling across the ice bridges spanning the yawning crevasses. In the end we had to give up the trip and try to make our way back to Thule. The distance was not great, but because of Wulff we could travel only four hours a day. He refused to go faster, declaring that "his heart was at the breaking point." I urged him on, but at last he simply settled down where he was. I could not leave him alone in the ice, with the result that he set the pace.

Finally one day I lost patience. We had a snowstorm which forced us to stay put for three days. We had hardly any supplies left and no dog food, since we had expected to reach Cape York in a day or two. Wulff had some chocolate and biscuits which he happily munched. On the third day the snowstorm abated and I decided to go on, but Wulff refused to move before it cleared up completely. He settled down once more when I told him we simply must go on. "Not I," he answered calmly. And with a smug smile he claimed that I could not go without him.

"I don't intend to," I answered. "I am taking you along."

"I refuse to move," he countered. "You had better stay here with me and let your damned dogs starve."

I took my long dogs' whip and began hitting the snow close by him. First on the right side, then on the left, closer and closer. I had learned to use the whip like a circus artist, and it struck less than an inch from him.

He turned white with fury but he was scared.

"You are not going to whip me?" he snarled.

"You bet your life I am. I am not going to stay here for your sake, nor am I going to starve my dogs because you are too lazy to go on. Get up or I'll whip you back to Thule!" And I let the whip snap at his polished boots.

When Wulff realized I was serious he got up without a word and moved his sled in line behind mine. Once in a great while he cursed under his breath. That was what I wanted him to do— it was a slight indication of spirit. When we finally got out of the crevasses I built a windbreak and we lay down to rest. Next morning the atmosphere was changed. Wulff obeyed blindly without the customary cursing and pleading for more sleep, even volunteering to help harness the dogs.

"It proved," he said, "that I could do more than I had believed myself capable of doing, and I thank you for forcing me to do it."

That gave him the victory over me—he was frank with his understanding and appreciation. And I had believed him my enemy!

17

AT THE FIRST SIGN OF SPRING THE EXPEDITION ACROSS THE INLAND ice got under way, but the plans became radically changed, to my great disappointment. In the first place Knud decided to follow the coast all the way up to the tip of Greenland and to cross the icecap only on the return trip. And secondly I reluctantly had to agree to stay at home. We still had the Danish ship and the crew with us in Thule, and we could not all leave the place, because some of the sailors suffered from venereal disease which we did not want to spread to the Eskimos. And MacMillan was still in the district. He had not forgotten the collection of fox furs I had taken over, and I could not leave it unguarded.

I said good-by to Knud who set off with Lauge Koch, Dr. Wulff, and three Eskimos, including my old friend Henrik Olsen. I felt very unhappy about staying behind, because it was the first time I had to keep out of an adventure I had been prepared to join. Fortunately I did not know at the time of their departure that they all were not going to return.

I was alone in charge of our station in Thule, and the spring and early summer of 1917 went peacefully by. There was no great harmony on board my old expedition vessel the *Danmark,* and I was glad to see the last of it. The captain and the crew were anxious to leave the anchorage where they had been forced to lay idle for so many months.

Summer passed and fall arrived. It had been a bad year. The weather had prevented our hunting in kayaks, and ammunition was low. There was not enough to waste it shooting birds, and although we did not suffer we had to resort to the ancient methods of hunting. This takes endless time and patience. To bring down a bird with a gun is much easier than waiting for it at the nest or beside a piece of meat laid out advantageously to lure it to earth.

Winter was at hand and the ice in—and still no word from Knud and his mapping expedition. I planned to go north and cache meat along the route for them, after I had secured the meat. I tried to persuade some boys to follow me north, but they excused themselves. It was the time when they had to remain beside the seals' blowholes to secure their own food. We could not yet cross the fjords, but we went after seals and managed to kill just enough to keep ourselves and our dogs alive.

Then suddenly they ceased to show themselves. We hunted for blowholes and found them all frozen over. There were no seals out in the open water, nor were there any walrus to be found.

Little Mequsaq was growing so lean that I was frightened. He still lived on his mother's milk, but she, too, was under-nourished.

In those times of stress I could not help admiring the tact of the native housewives. Each night when I returned from hunting Navarana was at the beach waiting for me. Yet never did she ask if I had brought home any meat—she had merely come to help me with the dogs, or to take my coat and put it in the store so that it would not thaw out by being worn into the house. But whenever I had a seal on the sled she saw it immediately and shouted in surprise. She called all the girls and anyone else who happened to be in the house to come and admire her clever husband and his catch.

An important event in the development of little Mequsaq occurred that fall. The widow Aloqisaq lived in a small house in front of our own. It was she who tanned our skins, thawed out the dog food, and so forth. Once the boy had been taken to visit her, and while he was there one of those sudden Arctic hurricanes had blown up. It was a devil of a wind, and no one could stand upright in it; the atmosphere was charged with needles of snow, and even small pebbles bombarded the house. Fortunately our windows were covered with a thick layer of ice and did not break.

Navarana ran to me as I sat writing, and called out that Mequsaq had been caught by the gale and could not return home. I had seldom seen her so pleased. Now, she said, she was a mother who could sit at home and await the return of her son, as he had to remain away until good weather returned.

I offered to go for him, but this would spoil her enjoyment of his "bravery." That he was completely innocent of either bravery or cowardice, being only a year and a half old, had nothing to do with the situation—this was the first time he had been hindered in his movements by the weather.

We talked of Knud and his party—we hoped they would be back soon. Old Inaluk, the most gifted conjurer in the community, suddenly left the house. A few moments later we heard her singing outside. We all ran out and saw her standing in the moonlight, her coat off, her long hair loosened and switching as her body swayed from side to side:

"Those who have been on the Eastside are back.
Those who have been on the Eastside are back.
Satok and his wife will visit us too.
His wife is preparing by taking off her pants."

That was her song, and after her first seizure had passed she went on to say that Knud and his party were now coming home, "but two of them are missing."

After we went to bed, I could not get the woman's peculiar portent out of my mind nor help feeling that there was evil in the air. Should I go up and look for the boys? I wondered. But where?

And then the head of my friend Knud poked through the door. I leaped up with a shout to grasp his hand. I shall never forget that moment, and his assurance that he had missed me during the whole summer "every, every day." The look of the icecap was upon him, months of starvation and hardship written on his face. It was several minutes before I inquired after the rest of the party.

"It has been a terrible summer," he said, "with such starvation and hardship as I have never known!"

"Are all of you here?" I asked.

"No. Two are missing," Knud answered.

He went into the kitchen to look for something to eat. Navarana and I scarcely dared ask who might have fallen. When Knud returned he said: "Henrik was eaten by the wolves, and Wulff fell by starvation. It is too horrible to think of."

We sat up all night, and Knud told me of his adventures. He laid out the whole trip before my eyes and then wanted to know if I thought him in any way to blame for the misfortune. I told him then that I did not, and I still think so.

Dr. Wulff was dead. He had been a hindrance throughout the trip. Unfit for such a journey, he had neither the spirit of adventure to urge him onward nor the co-operation of the natives, who all disliked him. It must have been a terrible experience for him—a man who is disliked always feels uncomfortable. The constant lack of food and the unexpected scarcity of game made him morose, and he had no eye for the stark beauty of the Arctic.

On the return home across the ice they had no food but the dogs which died occasionally, and Wulff was sick and could not eat. When they had to wade across the paralyzingly cold rivers on the icecap he refused to follow, lying down and protesting that he would not take another step. Twice Knud had to recross the torrents to persuade him to come, and when at last they reached the land back of Etah he was completely exhausted.

Knud and Ajago had walked on ahead to Etah so that Knud could find natives to return for the party and bring them out. Knud had given orders to Wulff and Koch and the two natives to remain at the spot where he had left them or, if they did go on, to follow a certain route. The two natives were anxious to get home to their families, and as they had nothing to eat they walked slowly on. Each time they climbed a hill they had to wait for Wulff, who was weak and could not keep up with them. Once when they killed a rabbit he refused to eat any of the meat except the liver; he must have been very ill, mentally as well as physically. Then the cold began to affect him—none of them had sleeping bags.

The natives killed two more rabbits, and these he also refused in spite of their liberal offers to give him any portions he preferred. Then he reiterated that he would go no farther. Each time they stopped to rest it took hours to get him started again. Many times he told them to go on without him, but when they disappeared over a rise of ground he would call to them to wait, and this irked the natives. Lauge Koch stuck to Wulff, but it was difficult for him to placate the Eskimos.

Then finally, after a long rest, Wulff said:

"This is the end. I will not go any farther."

They heated a little water for him. He wrote one or two letters and lay down on the grass the natives had collected for him. And they left him behind.

The natives told me later that they did not really believe Wulff was serious. He had been such a trial during the whole trip that they thought him only lazy now. Lauge Koch had exhausted his powers of persuasion, and he, also, did not quite believe Wulff would fail to make another effort. He had done all it was humanly possible to do, and was in no way to blame. Yet, as the Eskimos told me, the mere fact that Wulff did not shoot himself led them to believe he still hoped for rescue.

The natives had their own lives to consider; Lauge Koch was young and strong, and it would have been useless, and dangerous, for him to wait for Wulff to die. He had refused point-blank to go on, and Koch's waiting would only have resulted in his own death as well as the weaker man's.

We went back to look for the outfit they had brought back across the icecap. It was at the spot where they had left it at the foot of the glacier, and the courageous story of six exhausted men was written in that cache. It had been stripped clean of everything that could be eaten or thrown away, the sleds and boxes ribbed to mere skeletons and utilized for fuel.

We also looked for Dr. Wulff. He could not possibly have been alive, but I thought we might locate his body. We found the spot where the two Eskimos said they had left him, and discovered traces of the grass they had plucked for his mattress. I thought he might have crawled down to the nearby brook for a drink, but he was not there.

I am positive that he regretted his decision to remain behind and tried to follow his companions and lost his way. If he had not we would have found him.

And Henrik was dead, my devoted friend from the east coast expedition. He had fallen asleep far from the others, while he was out after rabbits, and never returned. His companions looked for him only to discover three huge wolves instead, one of them smeared with blood. The poor little fellow will always remain in my memory as the kindest and dearest of men.

18

THIS WAS THE SECOND THULE EXPEDITION, AND IT MARKED THE beginning of a terrible winter.

We had no meat, no supplies of any kind. I think it was the worst, the longest, the hungriest winter I have ever spent in Greenland. Knud Rasmussen soon recovered his full strength and decided to go south to look for better hunting grounds—or maybe all the way to Tasiussak to get fresh supplies. Koch

needed more time to recuperate, and when he was finally strong
enough Navarana and I took him along and set off after Knud.
We had to go down to Tasiussak, because there was no food
in Thule and we were getting desperate.

We picked a bad day to begin our trip. A few hours from
Thule we met the most terrible snowstorm and had to seek
shelter. Fortunately we found a large cave where we could be
fairly comfortable until the storm abated, but only fairly because
the roof was so low that we could not stand upright. Lauge Koch
and Itukusuk, our Eskimo companion, settled down in one part
of the cave, Navarana and I in the other with our little boy
Mequsaq between us. We put the big fur on top of our sleeping
bags, and I put my heavy fur pants under us to keep them from
freezing. Soon we were all asleep while the storm raged outside.

The dogs had been tied outside the cave and were quickly covered by snow. Consequently they did not notice the large polar
bear that quietly entered the cave during the night. He wanted
shelter as much as we did, and he moved softly without waking
us up. We slept on—all but little Mequsaq, who woke up and
began crawling around the way he always did at home. We had
no way of keeping him out of mischief and we used to tell him—
what all Eskimos tell their children—that if they do things they
are not supposed to a big polar bear will come and gobble them
up. Mequsaq saw the bear, and he crawled back into the bag with
such speed he woke his mother, who saw the bear inspecting
the contents of my sled.

"Pita, Pita," she cried, "there is a bear on your sled."

I was wide awake the next second and saw the bear pulling at
my last piece of walrus meat. My gun was on the sled with the
bear, but I had to do something. I jumped out of my bag, stark
naked, in a temperature of thirty degrees below zero. I had to get
on my pants, but in my hurry and confusion I pushed both feet
into one leg. The bear turned toward me and I tried to run for
the gun. But I stumbled and rolled across the cave right up to
the bear.

Fortunately the animal was as scared as I was. He jumped
toward the entrance of the cave, but in the meantime the dogs
had been aroused. They tore loose from their harness and made
a mad rush for the entrance of the cave the moment the bear
tried to get out. For a while there was complete confusion. The
bear, Koch, Itukusuk, and I, not to mention thirty-eight dogs,

were all running around in circles. The only one who enjoyed it was little Mequsaq, who screamed with laughter.

It was very hard to shoot the bear in the wild merry-go-round. Two of our dogs were killed before we could fell the large animal, which provided us and the dogs with food for several days. The moment the excitement was over I noticed I was still naked and colder than I had ever been. I had to rush back to my sleeping bag to warm up before starting to clear out the dogs and cut up the bear. Mequsaq protested wildly:

"*Adolo, adolo!*" he shouted. "More, more!"

The other men had also jumped around without a stitch on and had to go back to their bags while Navarana kept the dogs away from the dead bear. It was easy enough to keep them quiet once the bear was dead.

Finally our food supply came to an end. There was nothing for the dogs either, but we hoped each day to reach Cape Seddon where we had friends. Lauge Koch now began to feel his weakness; his appetite was enormous, and his face looked haggard. We had nothing to give him except dog meat—one was killed each night. The gales toyed with us and made it almost impossible to keep going. I do not remember how many days we were out in the open, but it was so long that Navarana started to lose her milk. We fed the boy soup brewed from dog meat, but it did not agree with him—starving animals do not make very good soup—and we gave him a bone to chew on. Still he grew weaker and weaker, and I was afraid he would die. One evening he was too weak to nurse at all, and his poor mother sat as though petrified. There was nothing she could do for him. We took him between us in the sleeping bag, but we could scarcely keep warm ourselves. Lauge Koch's hunger burned from his eyes. His poor tortured body craved food, and he hammered the skulls of the starved, butchered dogs, to secure the brains. He even picked up the bones we had thrown away and gnawed them once more. It disgusted me to watch him—I do not recall why—and I asked him not to do it.

We finally reached Cape Seddon where two of Navarana's uncles lived. They had meat and gave it to us willingly. Within a day all our travail was forgotten. The boy began to cry again—he had lain deathly quiet out on the ice—and once more there was milk and delicious food for him, and he could crawl about on the ledge.

The rest of the trip to Tasiussak was easy, and we waited there for a few days to permit Knud to catch up with us. When he arrived he tried to persuade me to go on farther south with the party. I said I would rather return home at once.

"But," he said, "it would be nice for Navarana to have her baby down here and get it over before going home."

That was how I first learned of the advent of another child. In the evening I asked Navarana if this was true, and she admitted it was. "Why did you tell Knud before you told me?"

"Because he is going to Denmark and won't hear about it there. But you have enough to worry about now with no ship and no meat, so I thought I should wait."

That night she danced and enjoyed herself for many hours, as she did for several nights following.

There was no object in our going farther. Navarana went to visit some friends at Uvkusigssat, and the rest of us went to Ritenbenk where Mr. Andersen, the best host in Greenland, lived. He was a great admirer of Dickens and cited him upon any and all occasions. He was not at home—in fact, he was on a trip to Umanak Colony with the lady who is now his wife to invite guests for Easter. His maid, a famous cook and the devoted caretaker of his property, was none too pleased to see us. "We" were fairly numerous at that moment, as Knud had invited everyone along the road to accompany us.

On the wall outside the house hung an entire caribou and two hindquarters—the reason for the invitations Andersen was issuing. First we took down the hindquarters and forced the poor maid to cook steaks. She was a fine cook even when made to perform against her will. When that was done she refused to remain in the house and walked out in protest. As a result we also took down the whole caribou and finished that as well. Knud then went down into the cellar.

"He has wine," Knud shouted, "wine in wartime!" I must admit that he had no wine when we left.

We took the road to Jakobshavn, and there was the culmination of the trip—the parties are still remembered in Greenland. First a coffee party was given for all the natives. Then a dance, and another, and so on until no one but Knud was able to dance. Then the Danes gave parties, cleaning out their stocks of provisions before Knud left once more for Denmark.

When I returned north I heard that the Andersens at Ritenbenk had spent their Easter eating hardtack and barley soup. Sofie had complained of violence, but the host thought it was a wonderful joke and regretted that he himself had never done likewise. That is the type of humor prevalent in Greenland.

I found Navarana ill. I was unable to diagnose the trouble, but I could see that she was in a critical condition, burning with fever. The doctor from Umanak Colony said it was pneumonia—and the baby might be born at any moment.

That same afternoon a little girl was born.

Childbirth is an amazingly natural phenomenon with healthy native women. Navarana wanted to get up next day and travel, but the doctor advised against it, as the ice was bad and the going difficult. We decided she should not go north until next summer, and then that she should stay a while with the Nielsens.

The little girl, Pipaluk, was very tiny, and her older brother sat the whole day long looking at her. We gave coffee to the natives in celebration, and I felt that I was leaving an important part of my life behind when I had to go.

19

I SPENT A LONG AND LONELY SUMMER IN THULE COLLECTING FURS and longing for my family.

When I finally rejoined them in the fall I met a big surprise in Tasiussak. I was told that a new man had arrived from Denmark to replace me. Jeppe Nygaard had been sent up from Copenhagen to take charge of our trading station while I went back to Denmark for one year's vacation. Wonderful and exciting news! Knud had arranged everything, and Navarana and I discussed our plans as we returned to Thule with Pipaluk and "Aipasak," as my boy and I called each other. The word means future hunting companion, and we used it in order to save the word father for great occasions.

The winter was close at hand when we got back in Thule. Fortunately we did not know that we were never again to share that happy carefree life, so we had nothing to spoil our last few months. Navarana was now a lady with a great deal of authority. She was highly respected among the Eskimos. She was the mother of two children, she was widely traveled, and on top of it all I discovered that she had taught herself to read while she was alone during the summer. Such a feat takes intelligence and energy— two qualities Navarana had in abundance.

In September 1918 we set out on our trip to Denmark: Navarana, the children, myself, and two bear cubs I had caught recently. We sailed down on our boat to Umanak Colony where a bark, the *Thorvaldsen,* one of the last two sailing vessels plying between Greenland and Denmark, was scheduled to call. It had not yet put into port, and as the wind had been against it chances for its arrival were rather slim. Since our own boat was to call in at the copper mine at Ivigtut and thence go on to America there was nothing for us to do but wait.

The *Thorvaldsen* arrived at last—a fine vessel commanded by Captain Hansen, a grand sailor of a type now almost extinct. We had a little trouble persuading him to take the bears along, but I finally told him that they were gifts for the king from the natives, and that made everything all right.

The trip was uneventful but pleasant, for me at least. Navarana thought it was monotonous, especially as our fresh water was limited, and she could not accustom herself to washing her face in the brine. One day while we were becalmed I got a small whale, and the bears had the time of their young lives.

On the eleventh of December, 1918, we sailed into the harbor of Copenhagen and the pell-mell of newspapermen and parents and relatives which one anticipates for so long and so soon wishes to be rid of. By the end of the first evening I was all for turning around and returning to Greenland.

Navarana, like all Eskimos visiting civilization for the first time, was disappointed. White men are apt to exaggerate the commonplaces of their homeland.

"Oh, I thought the houses were bigger—they are not much higher than an iceberg. I believed the horses were much higher than a man." There were few surprises for her—everything she saw was no better than what she had expected.

Only two things impressed her. First, it was winter, still the sun was shining; second, a team of horses eating from their nose bags. The horses could be driven about and still feed. This device Navarana thought a certain proof of white men's intelligence.

Next day we had an audience with the king. The ruler of our country was gracious and asked Navarana the conventional questions: What did she think of Denmark, etc., etc.?

Navarana turned to me: "Is that man really the king we have heard so much about? How can he think for everybody in Denmark if he is stupid enough to suppose I have any opinions about this magnificent land after only one day's stay?"

"What does she say?" asked the mighty man.

I translated freely: "Your Majesty, she thinks it is wonderful and grand!"

"I thought so!" said the king, and was content.

An epidemic of Spanish influenza swept over Europe, and I contracted it. I was walking along the streets of Copenhagen when suddenly I felt dizzy. I staggered up to a couple of policemen and asked them to call me a taxi. Unfortunately there was a telephone strike on at the moment, and they could not call a cab. Also, they thought I was drunk. When I denied this it only convinced them they had been right and they bundled me off to the police station where, fortunately, I was recognized and rushed to a hospital.

I was kept there for four months and for a long time was so ill that I was isolated in a ward reserved for dying patients. I remember that the room was meant to accommodate six beds, but the epidemic raged so furiously that on one morning eleven patients were brought in alive, and nine bodies carried away before evening. I was one of the lucky two who survived. The other was a champion wrestler and a devil to handle in his delirium, as, they told me, I was. It took three porters to hold me down, and I played football with them, tossing them from one side of the bed to the other.

Then Navarana came to visit me, and she was the only one who could keep me quiet. My mother and my sisters also visited me as well as a number of newspapermen. Navarana sat beside me most of the day. She lived, during this harrowing interval, in a hotel and had a long distance to walk each day, but she knew the streetcars by their color and followed the tracks between the hotel and the hospital. She said she preferred walking to riding. If she walked, she said, she could stop in wherever she desired to eat and drink coffee. I asked her how she managed to pay for what she ate.

"That is easy. They all know the price of what they sell. I give them my purse, they take the money out of it and give the purse back to me."

Strangely enough she was never swindled, and I know that

she dealt with some notorious crooks. It has been my experience, however, that the worst crook will not trick a person who is absolutely naïve—there is no sport in it for the crook.

I was so weak after being released from the hospital that I could not walk for a long while. My hair fell out, I was thinner than I had ever been, and tortured with sciatica. It looked as though I would be out of the picture for months, and Knud told me that they had decided to send another man up to Thule to replace me for a while. I protested, but when Mr. Nyboe, supervisor of our post, also agreed with Knud and the doctor I had to submit to their judgment.

This was my first serious defeat, and it was a great blow to me.

I went to a little island, Slotoe, to rest for a few weeks and also spent some time with Knud. For the next year he was planning an expedition into Hudson Bay for the purpose of studying the Central Eskimos' customs and was counting on both me and Navarana to help. He suggested that Navarana return to Thule as soon as possible and supervise the sewing of clothes for the expedition, then come back down to Umanak Colony during the late winter and join us there next summer.

We discussed this with Navarana, and she was anxious to do it, for while she had liked Copenhagen when it was new to her, now the life, or rather the lack of it, was beginning to pall. She was tired of being a curiosity. The citizens had been tactless, staring at her as she passed on the streets, offering her money and fingering her garments. She would be glad to get back to Greenland.

We decided to leave Pipaluk with my parents. Both my father and mother were anxious to keep her, and Navarana said she wanted the little girl to have the advantages of Denmark—and the safety.

One night I took her to the Royal Theater to see a ballet, which was at that time the most celebrated in Europe. She was entranced. After we returned home and I went to bed she sat looking out the window. "Tell me the truth," she said. "Were those real angels we saw in that church? If so, there must be some truth in that Jesus stuff."

I was cruel enough to laugh, and it hurt her. I explained that we had not been in a church, but a place of amusement. The leading lady was certainly a lovely person, but positively no angel, and I promised Navarana I would take her to visit the woman, who was a good friend of mine, the next day.

We lost no time in calling upon Mrs. Elna, the ballerina, who was then one of the foremost dancers in Europe. She chatted with Navarana pleasantly and gave her a large bottle of expensive perfume to take back to Greenland—it should have lasted at least a year.

Navarana was disappointed with Mrs. Elna's obvious earthly bearing and said later that it would certainly have been nice if Jesus had such a theater where the doubters might go and be given a glimpse of the workings of heaven.

We gave a farewell ball for our many friends and all the Eskimos of South Greenland who happened to be in Copenhagen. Navarana was a great success. She was so lovely and her happiness shone from her eyes. She wore the finest gown and bright, shiny new pumps.

We drove back to the hotel after the ball was over. Her feet hurt her so badly she could scarcely hobble from the car to the lobby, and when she was finally undressed she could not sleep.

I awakened after a few hours and found her sitting with her poor, swollen feet in a basin, into which she had poured all of Mrs. Elna's choice perfume. The perfume was, she said, the only thing she could feel. Water was worse than nothing.

"Whether she was an angel or not," Navarana went on, "I thank her for the bottle. The stuff smells terrible, but it is wonderful for cooling sore feet."

That was the end of Mrs. Elna's gift.

20

A FEW DAYS LATER NAVARANA AND MEQUSAQ LEFT WITH CAPTAIN Pedersen. I was still so weak that I could walk only a short distance without resting, so I returned to my island where the doctor told me that the sciatica would prevent my ever swimming again. This was a hard sentence for a former prize swimmer, so I went in bathing immediately, but could swim only a few feet. I tried to do some physical labor; that, too, was impossible. I was less help to anybody than a baby, and my disposition was worse.

But soon a telegram arrived from Knud which changed every-

thing. Since I had been in Denmark we had built a ship of
our own, the *Soekongen,* a sturdy little boat constructed especially
for ice navigation and expeditions. Its cost had been almost pro-
hibitive, but we found that, after the war, the prices of our
furs skyrocketed and we had much more cash on hand than we
had anticipated. Captain Pedersen was commanding our boat,
but word had come from him that he had run into a gale, broken
his bowsprit, and had had to stop in at Norway to have it
repaired. Both Knud Rasmussen and I were needed; there was
no doubt of that. A steamer was sailing tomorrow for Upernivik
—the last boat of the year. Could I go along?

I did not even stop to say good-by to my mother—she would
have thought it suicidal for me to travel. Within four hours I
had purchased a small outfit, and next day Knud and I were
once more bound for the Arctic.

When we reached Upernivik we were informed that the ice
to the north was worse than usual. A few days later Lauge Koch
appeared with his schooner, which had been furnished by the
Danish government, and I accompanied him as pilot across Melville Bay. The boat was overloaded, and goods piled high on deck.
Koch had brought dog food—dried fish—from South Greenland
and piled it on top of everything else. In fact, to reach the deck-
houses one had to burrow through holes.

I was a very poor helper. My weakness and sciatica made it
painful even to stand at the wheel. Often I was desperate, but
since I had got into the mess I refused to complain.

A gale blew up and the ice began to pack around us. I routed
all the men out to work, pushing and shoving, anything to save
the little ship. During the storm I fell in the water and soaked my
clothes. When we had traveled through the worst ice the snow
kept falling steadily and I had to remain in the crow's-nest for
twenty-four hours in my wet garments.

When the sun returned and permitted us to relax, my sciatica
was cured. Everything the doctor had told me to avoid as a death
penalty, I had disregarded. Since that time I have never felt a
twinge in the nerves of my leg.

We had no sooner arrived in Thule than we heard the natives
shouting. They were announcing another ship—the fjord was
filling up. This ship was our own, the *Soekongen,* with Knud,
Navarana and Mequsaq, and Hans Nielsen, the new manager,
aboard.

Seldom had I seen Navarana so happy. She leapt into the air and danced with joy to be at home once more—she could not put into words the emotions she felt.

I went on with Captain Pedersen and the *Soekongen* to the southernmost part of Greenland to investigate the old Viking ruins there. It was an entirely new and different country to me. The landscape was lush and green with excellent grazing lands surrounding the deep, silent fjords where the ancient Norsemen had settled. Over all was a hush which gave it the quality of a dream.

But the ruins themselves were disappointing. The Vikings had certainly exaggerated when they sang their sagas. I had studied the sagas on the way to Brattahlid, the spot where Eric the Red had lived and established a colony, and I remembered an episode in one of the later sagas: Two adopted brothers were attempting to revenge themselves upon each other. One of them was especially furious and for a practical joke crashed in the skull of a slave of his host during a beer party. The host heard the noise but "because of the distance and the many guests he could not see what had happened."

I measured the largest room—I supposed it to be the dining room—and found that at most eleven people could have been seated at one time. Of course, the sagas have been told many, many times and something added to them at each telling.

The Eskimos at Julianehaab are fine people and possess a certain culture. In fact, they are quite as advanced as the inhabitants of Scotland's northern islands and are sufficiently intelligent to enable them to compete with immigrants when, eventually, the country is thrown open to foreigners. They are most frugal, and that automatically gives them an edge on the newcomers.

21

IT WAS 1921, THE TWO HUNDREDTH ANNIVERSARY OF THE ARRIVAL OF Hans Egede, the "Apostle of Greenland," who first brought Christianity to the pagan Eskimos. A great celebration of the event was planned, and even the King of Denmark had consented to dignify it by his presence. As it was the first time any king had ever visited Greenland everyone was in a state of wild excitement.

The principal celebration was to be held at Godthaab, the capital. The first Sunday was to be devoted to prayer and thanksgiving. The town consequently was crowded with two bishops and a wholesale assortment of high priests, ministers, and simple teachers of the gospel.

Knud Rasmussen and his wife were there too. She had come up with Knud on the *Soekongen* to bid us good-by when we sailed for Hudson Bay. Knud was in his best humor, a brand better than anyone else's. A navy vessel represented Denmark, and Eskimos were collected from remote settlements.

At nine-thirty Sunday morning I received a message from the Supreme Bishop of Denmark informing me that he had mistakenly failed to invite me to take part in the procession at ten o'clock. Would I be sure to show up?

I showed up—perhaps more than anyone else. The truth was that I did not realize the gravity of the occasion, as I had spent few hours of my life marching in church processions. The evening before, I had worn a scarlet anorak to the party, and it did not occur to me that the same garb might be incongruous at the service.

I had had only three hours' sleep, but I leapt out of bed and made for the line of march. The procession was already under way, marching slowly and seriously, chanting as they traversed the distance between the high school and the church. I hid behind a house and waited until the first dignitaries had passed by. Then I saw the native editor of the Eskimo paper in the ranks, and I thought that would be about my place, so I joined him.

Later I was somewhat shocked to learn that the one and only discordant note in the whole procession was my blouse—the anorak made of scarlet cloth originally intended for a pillow slip. The bishops and high priests apparently could not appreciate the variation of color. I thought it relieved the monotony; they thought it disgraceful.

On the next Saturday the king arrived in the harbor. This event had been anticipated as the high point in the week of festivities. His Majesty disembarked with his whole family and was greeted at the pier by every notable of Greenland. (The authorities had made certain about a uniformity of costume this time, and white anoraks were *de rigueur*. I behaved myself and was a model of servility.)

The Danish king was a tall man, and the Eskimos had constructed a special kayak to present to him. It had been built to my proportions, and I am the only man who ever rowed in it. The king disappointed local sportsmen by refusing to try it out. I had been chosen to present it to him, and he examined it with interest.

"I see," he said knowingly. "That must be the hunting coat."

"Yes, indeed, Your Majesty," I replied. "It is certainly the bladder for hunting."

"Well, well. So this harpoon is made of narwhal horn."

"Quite right, Your Majesty. It is a walrus tusk."

It was a great day for the natives. The king had promised to dispense coffee, which everyone expected to be extraordinary. When the drink turned out to be merely plain coffee the natives were sullen with disappointment. He could not have known that the bishops had double-crossed him the Sunday previous by feeding the entire population coffee and cookies, figs, dried prunes and cigars.

Next day there was a big banquet aboard the king's transport. All the prominent Danes and natives were invited to attend, and the royal family graciously mingled with the throng. After a suitable interval the king went below and remained there. His adjutant walked through the crowd with a long paper, on which were written numerous names, and spoke to those whose names appeared on the list. One by one they entered the cabin on the starboard side. Shortly each one emerged from the port side knighted or with a medal or order of some sort pinned to his chest. Those of us who had not yet been approached by the officer stood about in nervous groups chatting desperately about the weather, our eyes following the king's adjutant.

Presently the king reappeared on the bridge, and the adjutant ceased his peregrinations. Those faces that did not beam over a cross or a medal were darkly brooding. Their hopes were shattered.

"Peter Freuchen, I want to talk to you!" shouted the king. I jumped toward my sovereign—everyone witnessed my triumph.

"I want to give you something I know you will appreciate," said the king. "Please come below."

I followed him down the stairs. I knew that I was not in line for a medal—I had only recently been decorated while I was in Denmark—but, I said to myself, I shall undoubtedly receive a gold watch or a diamond pin or something of the sort dignified by the king.

The king picked up a large bottle containing a live beech branch, a branch he had cut himself on the day before he left home. (The beech is the national tree of Denmark, and the king's love for it was well advertised.) He explained to me that each day on the journey he had nurtured it with fresh water and cut an inch from the branch, hammering the new end to keep the leaves fresh.

"And now," he said, "I shall give you one of the leaves!"

"How interesting," I replied. "How can it be that the leaf is still fresh?" I stood for a moment holding the beech leaf, and feeling somewhat ridiculous, my visions of a gold watch or diamond pin fading fast. Still, it was something for King Christian to present me with a leaf.

Next on the program was the royal buffet, which pleased the natives immensely. The king and queen themselves served the guests. I saw the king pick up a large cake and present it to one of the natives. "Very good," said the dignified Eskimo. "This is the way one expects a king to serve his guests!" He took the whole cake from the king and proceeded to eat it. The party was a great success, and the tables were stripped clean before they were abandoned.

Soon afterward the king's ship steamed out of the harbor and the colony slowly settled back into its usual monotonous routine. Still, for years they had something to talk and argue about. And that is a great boon in the North.

We stopped in at Jakobshavn, Knud's birthplace, to secure dog food and other necessities. There we learned the most exciting news that had come to us for a long time in the Arctic.

A large passenger ship, the *Bele,* chartered to carry the many Danish tourists to Greenland for the jubilee, had been wrecked just south of Upernivik. The boat had run upon the rocks during a dense fog. It was equipped with a wireless, however, and the king's vessel had picked up the SOS and proceeded from Jakobshavn to the rescue of the eighty-three passengers and members of the crew of the *Bele.*

The captain of the *Bele* was naturally in a bad mood, but when he saw the king coming to save him he burst into tears, and cried:

"You are not only a king, but you are also a *man!*"

That simple expression was perhaps the best, and sincerest, compliment ever paid to the present King of Denmark.

Navarana was already at Jakobshavn. She had traveled down on a sled and had all the skin clothes ready for the expedition, but she was not very well. She had fallen victim to a cold germ that had been carried north by a ship which had stopped at Umanak and was in such poor health that it was impossible for her to enjoy any of the parties hurriedly organized for us. Instead, she went immediately to bed.

We sailed on to the wreck of the *Bele*. The captain was still there, but he was to leave for Godhavn with the inspector and thence home. The wreck was doomed, and Eskimos from great distances had come to look at it.

I had never known the thrill of piracy, but for once I indulged it to the fill. The first mate slept on board to keep a watch over the boat, but he rowed ashore to eat and we stripped the ship of everything from a few chickens (which I had the pleasure of offering to the Swedish captain of the *Bele*) to the bathtub and table from a second-class cabin (which I gave to the manager of Upernivik colony as a birthday present).

When we had secured everything possible out of the *Bele* and I had made a number of dives into the water to hunt out a few necessary scientific instruments, we sailed to Upernivik, where we were joined by Dr. Mathiassen and Dr. Birket-Smith, who had come up to Greenland on the *Bele*.

Navarana was still very ill. It was difficult for her to walk, and we carried her in a boat from the harbor to the assistant's house, where we slept in our clothes—it was summer and one could drop down to sleep wherever it was most convenient.

It was apparent by now that Navarana had Spanish influenza, the same disease to which I had fallen victim the year before. I did not leave her side, and got our good friend Fat Sofie to help nurse her.

The next day Navarana was worse. There was no doctor in Upernivik at the time, and there was nothing more we could do for her. In the evening she asked me what I thought was the

matter. Her head was buzzing with thoughts which came unsum-
moned, she said. It was ghastly to sit helpless and watch her fade
away. I told her to try to sleep, but she could not.

I went into the kitchen to brew tea for her. As I sat and
watched the water it came over me how much I loved her and
why, but suddenly I regretted that my good friend Magdalene
had not been in Denmark when Navarana was there and that
the two girls had never met.

Navarana was so quiet that I tiptoed in to look at her. As I
watched, her lip just quivered. Then she was dead.

I would not believe it. I had somehow never thought of the
illness as much more than a bad cold, but I called the young
assistant, and he could only concur in what I saw before me.

Fat Sofie took me to her house, and she and a friend made
arrangements for the coffin and funeral. I was almost unconscious
of anything that happened and had lost interest in everything.
But soon something happened which brought me to life with a
vengeance.

The minister in Upernivik, an undersized, native imbecile,
came to me with the statement that, since Navarana had died a
pagan, she could not be buried in the graveyard. No bell might
toll over her funeral and, he was sorry, he could not deliver a
sermon.

Those were the sad tidings I had to relate to Knud when he
returned from Thule. He had always adored the happy and helpful little Navarana. She made her own memorial in the clothes
she had put together for our expedition. We had always counted
upon her for so many things. The two of us climbed up to her
grave and said good-by for the last time, and sailed away to new
chapters in our lives.

PART III

~~~~~~

1

KNUD HAD BROUGHT THREE FAMILIES OF ESKIMOS DOWN FROM THULE to be our helpers on the Hudson Bay Expedition. They were all curious about their Canadian cousins and were fine men and women, but they fell sick, probably infected by the same germs which had slain Navarana, and now were also victimized by the itch. That was a pest which we never had at Thule while we were there, but recently the bugs had infested Lauge Koch's camp, and no one knew where they came from.

Knud thought it would be a fine idea to take along a native secretary to help tabulate the traditions and folklore of the Central Eskimos. As the missionaries said that they would be delighted to have one of their number with us to scatter the seeds of religion among the heathen, Knud decided to combine the two offices in one man, Jakob. He was strong and intelligent and willing. He was also an excellent hunter, and even though he did disappoint the church (he had no inclination or interest in the missionary portion of his labors) we put him to good service on the expedition. He spread considerable seed among the different tribes, but not quite the sort the church officials in Greenland had anticipated.

The natives with us began to recover almost as soon as we sailed out of Godthaab.

Finally we sailed out of the western end of Hudson Strait, setting a course to the north of Southampton Island, and thence heading straight for Lyon Inlet where we planned to make our headquarters on Winter Island, the place where old man Parry had stopped a hundred years ago.

But we ran into bad ice—heavy and sluggish. The ice one finds around Greenland, on both east and west coasts, is treacherous and never to be relied upon. It grips the traveler, holds him, carries him about and smashes him. We made slight progress. Resorting to all the tricks we knew, we accomplished only a few miles a day through the jungle of ice. It was also difficult to ascertain our direction, for the clouds blanketed the sun and our compasses were entirely useless so close to the Magnetic North Pole.

And then one day sure enough there was land ahead—a low range of mountains materialized through the fog. I did not know where we were, nor did anyone else, but as we approached it looked like Winter Island as described in Parry's book, and the fjord had the appearance of Lyon Inlet.

The motorboat was lowered into the water and the dogs hurried to land. They were so filthy and so lean that they scarcely looked like dogs. They made a beeline for the pond and drank till their bellies bulged. Not until then did they stop to sniff and explore the place on legs stiff from long disuse.

We shared the work as usual. Knud took the natives with him and set out to determine the location of the land we occupied and also to secure meat for ourselves and the dogs. He was always lucky and I never was; therefore, I remained at home and built our house.

To tell the truth, I was a little annoyed because Knud had left me with only two scientists and a young man named Helge Bangsted, whom Knud had hired as a handyman, as helpers. They were not much help. They pounded their fingernails instead of the nails, and their backs were too weak to lift a hundred pounds unless they emitted frightful groans. Still they were so kind and interested in the task that during the whole expedition we had no quarrels and remained until the end the best of friends.

According to the map, we were building a house on the open sea. We knew, however, that there was earth under us and that the map must be wrong.

Knud returned finally with news and provisions. He had discovered that we were situated on a tiny island, and the mainland near us supported herds of caribou. He had shot twelve and a number of seals. There were also many walrus in the sea outside, so we were assured that we would not starve.

As soon as the ice was hard Knud and I and our adopted boy, "Boatsman," left to discover the native Eskimos—if any lived about. We traveled up the fjord and came to a narrow sound through which ran a swift current. It was, we later learned, Hurd Channel, which never freezes.

The next day we set out again as soon as it was light, and

before long we came upon tracks of a sled. From the tracks we could see that the sled itself was very narrow, the runners broad. Far in the distance were black dots moving through the snow.

We urged our dogs to their greatest speed in order to arrive among the natives in an impressive manner. The Eskimos stopped when they saw us coming and grabbed their guns. I was a little frightened and shouted to Knud. He yelled back that he would go ahead and meet them first.

He took off his mittens and raised his bare hands in the air. We followed his example. Instantly the natives dropped their weapons and stuck up their hands. We halted our dogs and stood quiet a few moments to give them time to look us over.

After a little while the chief stepped forward and said:

"We are only plain, common people."

"We also are only plain, common people," said Knud.

They had thought, because of our white clothes and sleds, that we were ghosts, and our whips had frightened them still more. This was the first step toward a friendship of four years' duration between the natives and ourselves. The chief's name was Pappi (The Birdtail), and the three families with him belonged to the Netchilik tribe.

It was no great treat to visit this tribe, for they had no food whatever. We brought in some oatmeal from our supply, and the woman of the house, whose body was tattooed all over, simply dumped it in her pot of old soup. The mixture was terrible to the taste. I noticed that she herself ate nothing, but she later explained to me that she was pregnant and therefore not permitted to eat from the same pot as the rest of us.

Later, when we arrived at the little post at Repulse Bay, we were greeted by a number of natives obviously cleverer and much less frightened than the Netchiliks had been. As soon as they heard us speak in their tongue they were won over. It was a surprise to them and to us how easily we could converse, and we had little difficulty in explaining to them where we had come from.

Captain Cleveland—Sakoatarnak—was quite a person and not without merit. He lived there, the only white man, and his word was law over a district larger than many states in the United States. He ordered the natives to cart our belongings from the sleds to his house and to feed our dogs. Then he asked us if there was anything else he could have done to please us. We said no, very much impressed with his grandeur. The great man then turned to the natives waiting at the door and, speaking in a soft, mild tone, said: "Well, then get the hell out of here!"

The Eskimos understood and scuttled away leaving us alone with Cleveland.

Cleveland was a great character. When we asked him, during our first meal together, whether he would object to our bringing out a bottle of our famous Danish schnapps he assured us that we could make ourselves at home in his house as long as we desired. "In fact," he assured us, "liquor is my favorite drink—any kind and any brand."

He was limited to six bottles a year "for medical purposes." But, as he was usually ill the very day after the ship arrived with the year's supply, he almost never had any left over for subsequent illnesses. After he had appropriated our bottle he opened up and confided his troubles to us.

His troubles had to do exclusively with women. "I have," he said, "been too kind to too many." And now he could not get rid of them. They hung about, their husbands were insolent to him, and the women themselves were most expensive to keep. Now if we could use a few women on our expedition he was the man to recommend some very good ones. It would also be a great relief to him to be rid of them.

There was another expedition in the district. This one, said to be under Captain Berthie of the Hudson Bay Company, was to explore Committee Bay and Boothia Felix next spring. The members of it had been caught by the winter and were lying over at an occasional harbor in Wager Inlet.

I decided to drive down and see the leader.

Berthie received me royally, as did the natives. They were vastly interested in my stories and my clothes and my outfit as a whole. They questioned me endlessly. They wanted to know if all the inhabitants of Greenland had whiskers like mine. They could hardly believe that the sun disappeared during the winter entirely, and they asked whether the Greenlanders were cannibals and did they speak the same language.

Finally one of the men asked whether the natives there conceived children in the same fashion as they did, and when I assured them that there was no difference they came to the conclusion that perhaps theirs was not the only civilized country in the world.

In the evening there was a dance, and the girls came dressed in some of the most horrible costumes I have ever seen. They were made of gingham, and apparently designed after a pattern in vogue a century before. The girls were not bad-looking, but their tattooing and the gingham dresses, which they wore over their fur clothes, made them appear monstrous.

When I returned to Repulse Bay I found both Dr. Birket-Smith and Dr. Mathiassen there. Knud had thought them in condition by now to make a visit to Captain Cleveland and secure information from him in order to plan our work for next spring.

They were both overcome with joy as I met them. "He is the most amazing man!" they said. "He knows everything! He's worth his weight in gold!" They had their notebooks in hand and jotted down every remark he made.

They were both great scientists, and suspicion was not in their trusting souls. Unfortunately I have never been a saint, but I was saved by experience from believing in the old man, and I told them that he was a damned liar, and nothing else. I recognized the stories he told as the same old ones that were always used in the North to impress greenhorns. Later I learned from the natives that Cleveland had never been north of Lyon Inlet.

Captain Cleveland boasted of his cooking and said that he would prepare a Christmas dinner of eight courses, no more and no less. At two o'clock he would start to work, but to gather physical strength and morale for the ordeal he would first have a drink or two. He gulped them down, and we listened to some of his stories. When it was lunchtime he asked me to prepare it, as he would need all his strength and enthusiasm for the dinner. He was going to cook us a dinner of five courses, no more, no less, just to show us that one of the best cooks in the world lived at Repulse Bay.

But he needed a little drink to fortify himself. And after some moments he said that he was about to prepare us a dinner, a *real* Christmas dinner, of four courses, no more, no less. But surely a man deserved a drink before he commenced work.

He was almost stiff after that, but the three-course dinner he was about to prepare would be better than anything we had ever tasted—especially as he was to serve us caribou roast. First, of course, it would have to thaw out, and while it thawed he would occupy his time with a little drink. Unfortunately he took the drink first, and the caribou meat remained outside in a temperature of forty below.

By this time the rest of us were ravenous. Captain Berthie, who had come up for Christmas, volunteered to cook the dinner himself, but Cleveland vetoed the idea. No, sir, he would cook us a real, northern Christmas dinner. He knew that we did not believe in many courses, nor did he. There would be just one course, but it would be caribou roast like nothing we had ever tasted.

It was rather difficult for him to stand now, but he asked me to help him, and I got him into the kitchen where we discovered, much to our amazement, that the meat had not come in by itself. It was still outside frozen hard as a rock, but Cleveland said, "To hell with it; we'll put it in the oven and let it thaw out while it roasts."

Cleveland proceeded with his incredible yarns, but was interrupted by the odor of something burning. We rushed out and found the kitchen full of smoke. It was, however, only the meat roasting as it thawed.

He and I now proceeded with the meal. Cleveland was actually a fine cook. Quickly he took the meat from the oven and carved away the burnt portions. By now the interior was thawed out and ready to roast.

Finally it was ready, a tender, delicious roast. And now came the time for the great Cleveland specialty—gravy. He poured the juice from the meat into a pot and stirred up a delicious fluid. I know, because I tasted it.

2

ON OUR ISLAND—DANISH ISLAND, WE CALLED IT—WE PREPARED FOR our spring journeys. I was to go north on a mapping tour while some of the others were to drive south and inland in order to visit unknown tribes.

Dr. Mathiassen was to accompany me and assist in the surveying and mapping. We divided the wasteland between us and Fury and Hecla Strait so that he should go up Admiralty Bay and I through the strait and along the west coast of Cockburn Land.

We traveled with an old couple, Awa and his wife, and their adopted boy, a child who had to be fed crackers and sugar constantly so that he would not yell and annoy us.

Then one day a man named Kutlok (The Thumb) returned
from the south where he had gone to deliver a letter. The man
to whom the letter was addressed had moved, it seemed, and
Kutlok had spent more than two years completing his mission.
While in the south he had visited a school and received a taste
of the Christian code of morals. The day after he returned home
his wife gave birth to a child.

So he became a teacher. In a short time he had won over all
his people to Christianity. The conversions took place at a meeting, and immediately all the old restrictions fell by the wayside.
In fact, it was a great relief to the natives to be able to sew all
sorts of skins at any time of day or night, to be permitted to hunt
whichever animals they needed, etc.

On the other hand, there were a number of beliefs and rules
which it was difficult for them to grasp. It was said that the missionaries did not favor wife-trading, and that would have to be
stopped.

However, not to make it too dull for the poor ladies it was
decided that Kutlok and a few of the mightiest men of the tribe
should have the privilege of entertaining the girls, as it was considered healthy for the women themselves and also for the children they would bear.

In our group were also Akrioq and his wife, Cape York natives who had come down to Canada with us. We made good
progress up the coast.

It was a joy to travel with Dr. Mathiassen. He could not drive
dogs, so he walked. His speed was an unvariable three miles per
hour. He started off early in the morning and when we caught
up with him he rode for a short distance. Whenever we stopped
he walked ahead, and toward evening he dropped behind and
caught up with us after we had camped.

We also met a party of natives on their way south to trade.
Akrioq and Arnanguaq, his wife, were interested in talking with
them so that they might return to Greenland and recount it later
in their igloos. These natives were the same mild and understanding people as those of Greenland.

A number of small boys played outside, sliding down a slope
until their clothes were filled with snow and the hair worn off
their pants. The old wife of Awa asked them a couple of times
to stop: "Don't you think of your old grandfather who has to
walk around and hunt and hunt to fetch those skins for you? Or

of your old grandmother whose eyes hurt when she has to sew pants for you?"

The children laughed and kept up their destructive play.

"Oh, how pleased one feels watching them play," she said. "It makes one think of the time when they will be older and learn how to think and behave. How wonderful it is that foolish little children turn into intelligent grown-up people who know how to care for their things."

The natives of northern Canada have developed a fine method of making their sleds easy to haul. In the first place, the sleds are quite different from ours—long and narrow, and heavy. The runners are at least two inches broad with the crossbars fastened on clumsily. The most surprising thing is the treatment of the runners: they are made of frozen mud!

If such a sled hits a stone the frozen mud may crack, but it is marvelous how much punishment a mud runner will take. It can be repaired with a piece of chewed meat plastered on the crack.

When we came to Hudson Bay we knew nothing about this practice, and though we had better dogs our old-style iron runners made it impossible for us to compete with the Canadians on the trail. We had no mud, but we found that frozen oatmeal or rye meal would serve just as well. I made a dough of the stuff and plastered it on the runners.

Later on in the spring when the rye meal was of no more use on the runners I made pancakes of it. As I said before, however, we were rather careless of what we smeared on it, and I gladly dispensed with my share of the pancakes.

We reached Igdloolik after a number of exciting hunting adventures along the way. This is the center of population in the northern reaches of Hudson Bay, a small, flat island at the eastern outlet of Fury and Hecla Strait. The Parry Expedition explored it when it was still believed possible to find a route north of the American continent to China and India. The land is all flat and almost at sea level and the waterways almost impossible for a skipper to navigate.

There for the first time we saw houses made of ice slabs. The natives had built them near a lake where they fished for black salmon before the snow was in the right condition for constructing igloos.

At Igdloolik, Dr. Mathiassen and I parted, he to go straight north across the land to Admiralty Bay, and I to follow the coast along through Fury and Hecla Strait and up the west side of Cockburn Land to the north, a stretch never before seen or mapped by a white man.

I was to take only one boy with me, while Dr. Mathiassen took Akrioq and Arnanguaq and some local natives. Unfortunately I let Awa make the choice for me, and he recommended a certain Kratalik as my companion.

Kratalik was young but said to be very clever and had only recently married. He was the son of the chief at Igdloolik, a man with two wives. Kratalik also had several brothers, and they planned to follow along after us for three days or more to an open hole in the ice where there were so many seals that one had only to stand by and slaughter them.

We reached Ormond Island to the west, the farthest point visited by the Parry Expedition. I climbed the mountain on the mainland and discovered the cairn left by Parry a hundred years before.

From Ormond Island we were to go on west. Fury and Hecla Strait, named for the two ships belonging to Parry, was filled with ice many years old, and it was plain to see that it could not be navigated.

The older brother, Takrawoaq, dropped his load at Ormond Island and set off for Igdloolik. I was occupied at the time making observations on a small island nearby, but when I returned I found my proud Kratalik weeping furiously and crying through his tears: "Look! Look! There he goes. I am alone with you and afraid to go on."

Then I made a great mistake. I should have realized that he was impossible as a helper and turned back for another man. But I thought I could manage him, and we went on. We had only one sled and my own dogs, which I drove. I also had to build the snowhouses every evening and cook the meal, besides observing the landscape and caring for the dogs. Kratalik did nothing but weep. He was the worst fellow I ever had to travel with, and, added to it all, I went snow-blind.

Kratalik then thought he could take command, and ordered me to turn back. He would leave me if I did not. I made a few pointed remarks, but Kratalik grabbed a gun and said that if I did not obey him he would shoot me. At this I had to open my painfully swollen eyelids, take the guns away from him and hide them in my sleeping bag. He only sobbed the louder and stayed with me.

We advanced along the coast and I found a new island which I named for the Danish Crown Prince, Frederick, and also a number of unknown fjords and traces of ancient settlements. But we bagged no game whatever.

Our meat supply was running low, but every other day I cached a part of the fast dwindling supply in the igloo which we deserted, so that we would have a means of returning the same way we had come.

When we turned around, Kratalik became snow-blind. I bandaged his eyes. Every time he got off the sled for exercise I had to lead him, and he cried out with the pain, believing he was going to be permanently blind. I applied a compress of tea leaves, and that helped him.

When we reached the first igloo on our way back it had been smashed in by a bear, and our meat, as well as a spare harness, was gone. The kerosene can which we had left there was upset and the contents drained.

The next caches had been visited by wolves—the meat was gone. Then we struck the track of a wolverine, the most annoying animal in the Arctic. These overgrown weasels are persistent devils, and this one had lived up to his gluttonous reputation. He had consumed the meat in one igloo, then slowly, as is usual, followed the track to the next igloo and finished the cache there.

We did our best to map the coast on the way back to Danish Island—fortunately we had made a preliminary survey on the way up and recognized points we had passed. This land, however, can be accurately charted only from an airplane. From a sled it is impossible. Sometimes we thought we were well out over the sea, only to notice grass poking up through the snow. It was difficult to tell which was land and which was water.

3

WHEN WE GOT BACK TO OUR CAMP THE HOUSE WAS COMPLETELY buried under the snow. By the use of our snow knives we cut a passage into the store and found spades to dig out the door of the house.

Boatsman scouted about to find the natives we had left to guard the house and soon ran back to tell us that they were alive, but buried under the snow.

Sure enough, Patloq, a highly esteemed medicine man, was buried in his igloo. He was, as his wife said, not a great man for talking and working, but he was a terrible man for thinking, and he took his time when he indulged in his specialty. He had plenty of meat in his house, as well as tea and sugar and flour, so he need go outside for nothing. This seemed as good a time as any other for thinking.

A heavy snowstorm had come up and the snow had buried everything including Patloq's house. But Patloq knew that someone was likely to return home soon, and they would find it much easier to dig him out than he himself would, so he decided to wait.

Our camp attracted neighboring Eskimos, as usual. Among those who settled down near us were a tall man, Akrat, and his wife and little daughter. He was an elderly man and the best igloo builder I ever met, constructing some snowhouses large enough for dancing. Another native, Anaqaq, a man with a past, determined to settle with us too.

Anaqaq was a Netchilik and came from a distant tribe whose ways were foreign. Over at the Magnetic North Pole the women are scarce, and it is considered a luxury for a man to have a wife to himself. Instead the men club together to support one woman —and the women love the idea. When a girl has two husbands she is the ruler of the house. She sleeps in the middle of the igloo, which is warmest and coziest, and she does very little sewing.

Anaqaq had been happy, but since faithfulness was one of the tenets of married life there, as everywhere, and two-thirds of his household did not observe the rule, he grew angry.

Anaqaq was both medicine man and physician. His specialty was curing indigestion; when the caribou migrated from the north in the fall many of his patients ate too much and his services were required. Which, of course, kept him away from home much of the time.

While he was absent the co-husband rented out the wife and was paid for her services with caribou tongues, marrow, etc. The co-husband and wife kept this breach of trust a secret from

Anaqaq, but the neighbors told him—they always do—and he was deeply hurt. There were but two things for him to do to restore his honor—kill the man or go away. Anaqaq was a decent sort of fellow and chose the latter course.

He merely wandered away, becoming an Arctic nomad, strolling from place to place, suffering cold and privation and loneliness. He visited various tribes for a few days at a time, and then walked on again. He could keep alive by spearing salmon in the lakes and rivers, and he caught an occasional ptarmigan, but it was a hard life. Finally he reached Repulse Bay—he had then been walking for two years.

We always had enough to keep an extra man busy, but for a few days I let Anaqaq idle about acting the summer guest. Then when the time was ripe I gave him little duties. I returned in the evening from a day's hunting and saw Anaqaq, as usual, walking about and smiling. I asked him why he had not done his work, and he answered, in a very friendly manner, that as he was an angekok he was so holy that he was not permitted to work at all.

I had to fight fire with fire. I said that I, too, was an angekok. Recently I had met a number of ghosts who foretold Anaqaq's arrival, and they also said that while ordinarily he would not be permitted to work they would especially appreciate it if he tried to be as helpful and industrious as possible while we were in the territory.

Anaqaq and I believed each other, and he plunged into the work and was most helpful. In the latter respect he was quite different from my personal servant, Inuyak, who was the most devoted and most stupid gentleman's gentleman I have ever seen. The man was a miracle of dumbness, but I liked him. He had been a poor native when I arrived, and he would doubtless be poor the day after I left.

He was a master sleeper. No one else in the world could sleep so long or so often as Inuyak—and it was impossible to wake him. In all fairness I must say that he was also a great worker. If neither intelligent nor fast, he was at least persevering. I told him to shovel the snow away from the front of the house. He made various objections and excuses, but I finally got him started and merely told him to keep at it until I stopped him.

Dinnertime came and passed, but Inuyak did not appear. The cook supposed he had gone hunting, and thought nothing of his absence. After dinner I walked outside to take my observations, and after working out the results went to bed. I completely forgot about Inuyak.

Next morning I saw, far out on the plain, someone shoveling snow like a wild man—Inuyak. He had shoveled a trench extending hundreds of feet from the house.

I hurried out and asked him what in hell he was doing.

"What you told me to do," he answered.

"Why didn't you come in to eat?"

"Because you said I was to keep on until you told me to stop."

We spent the fall of 1922 in traveling among the natives in the district and in transporting our collections to Repulse Bay where they were to be picked up by a schooner early in 1923.

I planned to make an extensive foray into the field, mapping the north reaches of Hudson Bay east of Igdloolik along the coast of Baffin Land. With me were Helge Bangsted, as assistant, and Akrioq, as headman. We were to pick up more native guides and hunters en route.

We set out immediately after the first of the year, 1923, in a terrific cold spell with the temperature hovering around sixty below zero. Unfortunately we had no concentrated dog food for such a trip, and our sleds were heavy. Our faces had become softened during the Christmas celebrations, and the north wind burned into them. This wind never ceases during the winter months.

We were about a week out of camp when we reached a spot where it became necessary to desert the sea ice for the land. The snow was soft for many miles, and we had to whip our dogs cruelly. Both men and dogs did their utmost, but it was clear that the loads were too heavy—we would have to throw off part of them and return for the stuff later.

After we had cached it the snow soon grew hard under a thin soft layer, and we managed to complete a reasonable distance. I was disgusted at the delay our dropping the loads would necessitate, and I decided to return for it myself while the boys made camp and built an igloo. I thought I could be back before they got up in the morning, and thereby reclaim a wasted day.

My dogs were none too pleased at backtracking when they had expected to sleep. They were entitled to their rest, but I was tired too and even more stubborn than the dogs, so I set off.

I made the trip well enough and loaded the boxes on the

sled, but shortly after I had turned about the wind started to blow harder, howling like a fiend. The drifts were alive under my feet, and it was impossible for me to follow the tracks. The wind turned into a storm, the storm into a gale.

I was lost. It was impossible to determine directions, as I could not see the hills. I was growing more tired by the minute, but the dogs understood me now. I dropped my load again, keeping nothing but my sleeping bag with the extra kamiks and a small square of bearskin. I walked ahead of the dogs and they followed along after me. With no load I ought to be able to get back to camp.

I had to stop now and then to turn my back to the wind and catch my breath. It was so bad that I could scarcely stand upright, and finally had to go back to the sled and hang on to the up-standers. I could not swing my whip against the gale, and the dogs refused to go ahead.

By this time I could not be far from the others, and I decided that it would be better for me to stop than to run the risk of passing them. I was hungry, too, and when I reached a large rock behind which the wind had hollowed out a depression, I stopped. The dogs dived into the hole, and I decided to spend the rest of the night there.

I set about building an igloo, but for the first time in my life I found it impossible to cut through the snow. It had been packed solid by successive storms, and I gave it up as a hopeless task. But I made up my mind to stay awake and wait for daylight.

At first I kept awake by walking back and forth in front of the boulder. When this got too boring I tried the old trick of walking with my eyes closed. I walked ten paces straight ahead, turned right, ten more paces and another right turn, another ten paces and the same thing a fourth time before I opened my eyes to see how far I had strayed from the starting point. But for once this game proved too cold, too windy, and too uncomfortable. I felt an unbearable desire to lie down and saw no reason why I should not do so without risk, and I decided to make a small cave-like shelter where I could stretch out.

I began digging in the solid snow and soon I had a depression long enough for me to lie down in. I put my sled on top of this strange bed, then I put all the lumps on top of the sled and around the sides. I had built my bed in such a way that the end opened into the cave where the dogs were asleep, and I left this side uncovered, since it was well protected by the large boulder.

On my sled I had the skin of a bear's head I had killed some days before, and I took this along for a pillow. Finally as I crawled into my snug little shelter, I pulled my small sleeping bag in place with my foot, so that it covered the opening like a door. It was a little like a berth on a ship—rather more cramped, but I had room enough to stretch out.

I was well protected against the sub-zero temperature, dressed like an Eskimo in two layers of fur—one with the hairs inward against my skin, the other facing out. I had heavy boots and good gloves. Strangely enough I have never been bothered by cold hands, not so my feet.

Warm and comfortable at last, I soon fell asleep. I woke up once because my feet were cold and I tried to kick out the bag which served as a door. I wanted to get out and run around to increase my circulation, but I could not move the bag. It was frozen to the sides of my house, I thought. In reality there was an enormous snowdrift in front of it. I was annoyed but not enough to keep me from going back to sleep.

When I finally woke up I was very cold. I knew I had to get out and move about at once. What worried me most was the fact that my feet did not hurt any more—a sure sign of danger. To get out I had simply to crawl out through my little door, I thought, and I inched my way down to the bag. I could not move it. I used all my strength, but it was obvious that I could not get out the way I had come in. I was not worried because I expected to turn over the sled which covered me and get up that way. And I managed to turn over and lie on my stomach so that I could push up the sled with my back. There was not room enough to get up on my knees, but I pushed with my back the best I could. The sled would not budge!

At last I was really worried. My friends would soon begin to search for me, of course, but the question was whether I could survive until they found me. Perhaps I could dig my way out. But the snow surrounding me was now ice, and it was impossible to make the smallest dent in the surface with my gloved hands. I decided to try digging with my bare hands. My hand would freeze, but it would be better to lose one hand than to lose my life. I pulled off my right glove and began scratching with my nails. I got off some tiny pieces of ice, but after a few minutes my fingers lost all feeling, and it was impossible to keep them straight. My hand simply could not be used for digging so I decided to thaw it before it was too late.

I had to pull the arm out of the sleeve and put the icy hand on my chest—a complicated procedure in a space so confined I could not sit up. The ice roof was only a few inches above my face. As I put my hand on my chest I felt the two watches I always carried in a string around my neck, and I felt the time with my fingers. It was the middle of the day, but it was pitch black in my icehouse. Strangely enough I never thought of using my watches for digging—they might have been useful.

By now I was really scared. I was buried alive, and so far all my efforts had failed. As I moved a little I felt the pillow under my head—the skin of the bear's head. I got a new idea. By an endless moving with my head I managed to get hold of the skin. It had one sharply torn edge which I could use. I put it in my mouth and chewed on it until the edge was saturated with spit. A few minutes after I removed it from my mouth the edge was frozen stiff, and I could do a little digging with it before it got too soft. Over and over again I put it back in my mouth, let the spit freeze and dug some more, and I made some progress. As I got the ice crumbs loose they fell into my bed and worked their way under my fur jacket and down to my bare stomach. It was most uncomfortable and cold, but I had no choice and kept on digging, spitting, freezing and digging.

My lips and tongue were soon a burning torture, but I kept on as long as I had any spit left—and I succeeded. Gradually the hole grew larger and at last I could see daylight! Disregarding the pain in my mouth and ignoring the growing piles of snow on my bare stomach, I continued frantically to enlarge the hole.

In my hurry to get out and save my frozen legs I got careless. I misjudged the size of the hole through which I could get out. My hand had, naturally, been able to move only above my chest and stomach, and to get my head in the right position seemed impossible. But I suddenly made the right movement and got my head in the right position.

I pushed with all my strength, but the hole was much too small. I got out far enough to expose my face to the drifting snow. My long beard was moist from my breathing and from the spit which had drooled from my bearskin. The moment my face got through the hole my beard came in contact with the runners of the sled and instantly froze to them. I was trapped. The hole was too small to let me get through, my beard would not let me retire into my grave again. I could see no way out. But what a way to die—my body twisted in an unnatural position, my beard frozen to the sled above, and the storm beating my face without mercy. My eyes and nose were soon filled with snow, and I had no way of getting my hands out to wipe my face. The intense cold was penetrating my head, my face was beginning to freeze and would soon lose all feeling.

Full of self-pity, I thought of all the things in life I would have to miss, all my unfulfilled ambitions. With all my strength I pulled my head back. At first the beard would not come free, but I went on pulling and my whiskers and some of my skin were torn off, and finally I got loose. I withdrew into my hole and stretched out once more. For a moment I was insanely grateful to be back in my grave, away from the cold and the tortuous position. But after a few seconds I was ready to laugh at my own stupidity. I was even worse off than before! While I had moved about more snow had made its way into the hole and I could hardly move, and the bearskin had settled under my back where I could not possibly get at it.

I gave up once more and let the hours pass without making another move. But I recovered some of my strength while I rested, and my morale improved. I was alive, after all. I had not eaten for hours, but my digestion felt all right. I got a new idea!

I had often seen dog's dung in the sled track and had noticed that it would freeze as solid as a rock. Would not the cold have the same effect on human discharge? Repulsive as the thought was, I decided to try the experiment. I moved my bowels and from the excrement I managed to fashion a chisellike instrument which I left to freeze. This time I was patient, I did not want to risk breaking my new tool by using it too soon. While I waited the hole I had made filled up with fresh snow. It was soft and easy to remove, but I had to pull it down into my grave, which was slowly filling up. At last I decided to try my chisel, and it worked! Very gently and very slowly I worked at the hole. As I dug I could feel the blood trickling down my face from the scars where the beard had been torn away.

Finally I thought the hole was large enough. But if it was still too small that would be the end. I wiggled my way into the hole once more. I got my head out and finally squeezed out my right arm before I was stuck again. My chest was too large.

The heavy sled, weighing more than two hundred pounds, was on the snow above my chest. Normally I could have pushed it and turned it over, but now I had not strength enough. I exhaled all the air in my lungs to make my chest as small as possible, and I moved another inch ahead. If my lungs could move the sled I was safe. And I filled my lungs, I sucked up air, I expanded my chest to the limit—and it worked. The air did the trick. Miraculously the sled moved a fraction of an inch. Once it was moved from its frozen position, it would be only a question of time before I could get out. I continued using my ribs as levers until I had both arms free and could crawl out.

It was dark again outside. The whole day and most of another night had passed. The dogs were out of sight, but their snug little hole by the boulder was completely covered by snow, and I knew they must be asleep under it. As soon as I had rested enough I got to my feet to get the dogs up. I fell at once and laughed at my weakness. Once more I got to my feet, and once more I fell flat on my face. I tried out my legs and discovered the left one was useless and without feeling. I had no control over it any more. I knew it was frozen, but at first I did not think about it. I had to concentrate on moving. I could not stay where I was.

I could only crawl, but I got my knife from the sled, pulled the dogs out of their cave, and cut them loose from the harness. I planned to hold to the reins and let the dogs pull me on the snow, but they did not understand. I used the whip with what little strength I had left, and suddenly they set off so fast my weak hands could not hold the reins! The dogs did not go far, but they managed to keep out of my reach as I crawled after them. I crawled for three hours before I reached the camp.

Fortunately I then did not know the ordeal was to cost me my foot.

As soon as I had been inside our igloo for a while and began to warm up, feeling returned to my frozen foot, and with it the most agonizing pains. It swelled up so quickly it was impossible to take off my kamik. Patloq, our Canadian Eskimo companion who had had a great deal of experience with such accidents, carefully cut off the kamik, and the sight he revealed was not pleasant. As the foot thawed, it had swollen to the size of a football and my toes had disappeared completely in the balloon of blue skin. The pain was concentrated above the frozen part of my foot which was still without feeling. Patloq put a needle into the flesh as far as it would go, and I never noticed it.

The only thing to do was to keep the foot frozen, Patloq insisted. Once it really thawed, the pain would make it impossible for me to go on. It was obvious that we could not stay where we were and that we had to give up the whole expedition to Baffin Land. And with my foot bare to keep it frozen, we returned slowly to Danish Island, where Knud Rasmussen was completing all preparations for his long journey to Alaska.

He was horrified when he saw what had happened to me, and he wanted to give up his trip. But I insisted I could take care of myself with the aid of our Eskimo friends, and I persuaded my companions to carry out their plans according to schedule. And after a few days Knud set off to the north with two of the Eskimos, Mathiassen to Ponds Inlet at the northeastern tip of Baffin Land, and Birket-Smith south through Canada.

I was left with Bangsted and the two Eskimo couples from Thule, who refused to leave me.

I was nursed by Patloq's wife, Apa, and I was in constant discomfort. It felt as if my foot had been tied off very tightly. The leg above was all right, but the flesh below turned blue and then black. I had to lie quietly on my back while my nurse entertained me by recounting her experiences with frozen limbs. She knew a number of people who had lost both legs, others their arms or hands, but many had been killed because they were far too much trouble to take care of. And as the flesh began falling away from my foot she tried out her special treatment. She captured lemmings—small mice—skinned them, and put the warm skin on my rotting foot with the bloody side down. Every time she changed this peculiar kind of dressing, some of my decayed flesh peeled off with it, but she insisted on this treatment until there was no more flesh left.

Gangrene is actually less painful than it is smelly. As long as I kept my foot inside the warm house the odor was unbearable, so we arranged to keep the foot outside. We made a hole in the wall by the end of my bunk, and I put my foot out into the freezing temperature whenever the odor became too overpowering. As the flesh fell away from the bones, I could not bear having anything touch the foot, and at night when I could not sleep I stared with horrible fascination at the bare bones of my toes. The sight gave me nightmares and turned my nerves raw.

I felt the old man with the scythe coming closer, and sometimes we seemed to have switched roles and my bare bones to have become part of him.

One day Apa told me that I needed a woman to take my mind off my pains. She brought along a young girl, Siksik, whose husband had kindly put her at my disposal while he went off on a trip with Captain Berthie. I felt like King David, who was given young girls to keep him warm at night, but I told Siksik that I was in no condition to take advantage of the kind offer.

In the meantime it seemed as if Apa's cure was having some effect. The gangrene did not spread beyond the toes. Once the decay had bared all five toes to the roots, it did not go farther, and the flesh stopped peeling. I could not stand the sight, however, and one day I decided to do something about it. I got hold of a pair of pincers, fitted the jaws around one of my toes, and hit the handle with a heavy hammer.

The excruciating pain cut into every nerve of my body, an agony I cannot describe. Siksik had watched me and was deeply impressed. She offered to bite off the rest of the toes, and if her teeth hurt as much as the pincers, she said that I could beat her up. Ignoring her offer, I fitted the pincers around the next toe, and this time it did not hurt so much. Perhaps one could get used to cutting off toes, but there were not enough of them to get sufficient practice.

I admit that I cried when I was through with them—partly from pain, partly from self-pity. But it was a great relief to have the toe stumps off since they had kept me from walking and putting on my kamiks. Now I could at least get on my boots and hobble around.

4

IT WAS AT THIS TIME THAT WE SAID GOOD-BY TO THE TWO SCIENTISTS. They had completed their investigations and still had a long trip before them. Knud Rasmussen also set off on his big trip along the northern coast of America. He took with him the young Kraviaq and the widow Arnalunguaq. We would not meet again until we reached Denmark.

I was left with two families: Akrioq and his wife Arnanguaq,

Boatsman and his young wife. The former couple had been married for many years and now surprised us, and themselves, by having a baby, a little girl. They named her Navarana, for my late wife, which, of course, placed the responsibility for her upkeep squarely upon my shoulders.

Bangsted was to remain at our camp through the winter and go out next year by sled. Meanwhile it was his responsibility to watch out for all the boxes of valuable collections which were to be sent home next year.

We had been informed that the steamer which visited Chesterfield Inlet every summer carried a doctor, and I decided to go down there to have my foot examined. The wounds refused to heal, and I was in constant discomfort.

I took my pal Inuyak with me. We understood each other, and he had become very helpful to me. While we waited for the steamer I dug among the ruins sufficiently to convince myself that the ancient culture was closely akin to the "Thule culture" we had encountered in all the other ruins.

After a number of days the *Nascopie,* a fine modern steamer, arrived with supplies, passengers, and, what was most important for me and a number of others, a doctor.

Douglas was assistant surgeon and anesthetized me when I was put on the table. My foot was taken care of, and I was put aside in a corner of the dining room while the doctors worked over the next case. The first thing I remember upon regaining consciousness was hearing one of the young apprentices who had come up on the *Nascopie* being asked to help with the operating. He was unwilling as, he said, he would faint if he looked on at close quarters. There was no one else, and his weak objections were overruled.

He was a youngster who spent most of his time kidding his companions, and he was not too well liked. He usually carried a bag of chocolates about with him, and munched on a piece of candy. Now he was instructed to stand with his hands at the bloodiest point. He begged to be let off but was ordered to stick to the job. He grew white while the doctor amputated a number of infected fingers and, after a few seconds, fainted and dropped to the floor.

The doctor said that he really thought he should cut more off my foot but gave me the chance first to see if it would cure up as it was. I was not to walk, however, until the wound was entirely healed. In fact, he advised me to go out with the steamer in order to save my leg. I could not do this, however, as I had to take my collections and my natives back home.

During the fall the natives turned pagan again. They had been Christian for more than a year and it had done them no good—the dogs had come down with distemper just the same. The Eskimos had even gone so far as to hang tiny crosses about the dogs' necks, but it had not helped. Then a young woman remembered that once as a child she had cured a dog by binding pagan amulets around its neck. She was a cautious, clever girl, so now she fastened both a cross and a round piece of wood to several dogs' necks, and the animals recovered. Then, by a scientific system of trial and elimination, they set about to determine which had been responsible for the cure. Half the remaining sick animals were treated with crosses, the rest with the wooden amulets. The dogs wearing the pagan wood recovered. Whereupon the natives returned to the ways of their forefathers, and doubtless remained satisfied until another problem arose.

I could do nothing but sit around and wait for my foot to heal. I read and wrote a great deal and listened to Douglas, who had many tales to tell me of his recent year at home in England. He had driven about in a little car and looked up all his old friends. His descriptions sounded so alluring that a great longing for home came over me. There was an emptiness within me, a need for something, so I wrote a letter to my dear friend Magdalene and asked her to marry me. It was strange that this had never occurred to me before. The exciting part of it was that I could not hear from her for at least a year and a half. I would have something to look forward to.

At last Inuyak and I left for Vansittart Island. A whaleboat belonging to the Hudson Bay Company took us part way but turned back when we ran into ice.

We must run and hop and leap; if we stood still too long the ice began to tip and sink under us. On certain slabs we could not land at all without getting our feet wet. This sort of thing had been my greatest pleasure as a boy, but I lost the taste for it that day and have never done it since unless absolutely forced to do so.

My foot hurt as much as it had before the amputation. Its throbbing almost drove me wild. I sat down and tried to yank off my kamik, but it was too painful. Then the reaction to our labor set in and we began to grow cold. We had to get up and walk, yet I screamed like a madman when I put any weight on my foot.

Inuyak pulled my kamik off—it was full of blood. The stitches had cut through the flesh, and the wound lay open.

This was disconcerting to look at, so I made Inuyak take needles and sinew and sew the ends together. I closed my eyes and set my teeth against the pain I knew was coming—and it did not come. I felt nothing whatever. Inuyak was a splendid surgeon. He said that it was dangerous to get dirt in wounds, and to avoid it he drew the sinew through his mouth, sucking it clean. He also rinsed needles and scissors with his tongue, and the operation did not hurt in the least.

We turned my bloody kamik inside out, and then put it back on; but it was impossible for me to walk until the next day.

That night I was awakened by Inuyak screaming out in fear. He had dreamt he was drowning. In reality we were covered by a heavy layer of snow. We wore only our summer clothes and were sure that we were freezing. We thought we might as well walk on until we came to Bangsted's camp, wherever it was. We only sat down to rest occasionally, and again found a few gulls and ptarmigans to eat. There was nothing to worry us especially, except my foot.

5

WE SPENT THE REST OF THE FALL AT THE HOUSE AT DANISH ISLAND. Practically the only break in the routine was the birth of a child to Tapartee's wife. Tapartee himself was away, and the wife had stayed with us during the summer. We were visiting her tent one day for tea when she told us that perhaps we had better get out— she was giving birth to a baby. It was a girl, which was the more interesting as she had boasted to Arnanguaq that *her* child would be a boy. Arnanguaq's child was the little Navarana.

The woman dug a hole in the ground and stood boxes beside it to support her arms. I asked her if she needed any help, and she said no, she was all right. She got down on her knees between the boxes, and we returned to our house.

Shortly afterward the woman came into the house to tell us what had happened. She had, as predicted, given birth to a boy. However, every child must have its navel attended to before a word is spoken in the room, and the mother was about to perform this rite when the boy's sister had run unexpectedly into the room shouting something about her clothes. This breach of etiquette had so embarrassed the boy that he drew his genitals inside his body and promptly became a girl.

On December 26, at daybreak, we were up and ready to start.

Bangsted took the least provisions, since he could buy more at Repulse Bay. We had our three sleds loaded, and turned north.

As usual with the Eskimos, there were no farewells. We only shouted at the dogs. But when we came to the point we stopped and turned our heads for one last glimpse of the little house. Bangsted was standing quietly watching after us. He had a long trip before him too.

There were three sleds of us: Boatsman and his wife, Akratak, on one; Akrioq and Arnanguaq with the little Navarana on the second; and I alone on the third. Anaqaq and his new wife also trailed along for a time, as we took with us the last meat from the house—he said that he merely wanted to visit a number of friends along the way. The first night he arrived in camp long after the rest of us, but he bragged that it was simple for the others to make haste with their tiny women; his wife was big and fat and beautiful, and hauling her was a torture to his dogs.

Two days north of Lyon Inlet we came upon the first native settlement, where we stopped over for a while.

We also met a number of natives whom the Greenland Eskimos loved so much that they invited them to follow us home to Thule and live with us. They were, my natives told me, fine people and not "disgusting" like most of the Central natives.

Aguano was one of these men. He was now en route to Ponds Inlet, and perhaps beyond. Who could tell? He was always traveling, his object being to find his Nuliaqatie—the man with whom he shared wives. The two were especially good friends and owned two women jointly; both women were loved equally well, so they said, by both men. Neither of the women could bear children, and therefore the men had arranged to live with one woman for a year, and then shift. They had done this for several years, and all four concerned were pleased with the idea.

Qinoruna, the wife now living with Aguano, was a clever, as well as a kind, woman. She had recently bought a little baby from another woman, who had inherited it in turn from the mother. Qinoruna had paid one old frying pan for the child, but the day after the exchange loud arguments arose. The baby was sick, but, on the other hand, the frying pan was cracked. What to do!

I was called in as judge and settled the whole matter by telling the women that, since both items in the deal were inferior, they should stick by their bargains. The baby was a poor little thing whose face was almost blue, and it was impossible to make it nurse from Arnanguaq's breast. Little Navarana was more than a year and a half old now, and Arnanguaq still had plenty of milk for a second child.

6

AT PINGERQALING I MET A REMARKABLE WOMAN, ATAKUTALUK. I had heard of her before as being the foremost lady of Fury and Hecla Strait—she was important because she had once eaten her husband and three of her children.

It had been a long time ago, before the natives had either guns or wood. Wood was the principal commodity desired, and Atakutaluk and her party were driving north across Baffin Land to buy wood for their sleds.

On the way they had to travel with such implements as were at hand. They rolled hides together and soaked them in water, then let them freeze in the shape of sled runners. As crossbars they used frozen meat or salmon. We saw many similar sleds still in use at Boothia Bay, constructed from musk-ox skin. Theirs had been of caribou skin.

Atakutaluk's party had numbered thirteen persons, and they set out with a load of raw goods for trading. On the way, however, a mild spell of weather descended—this is not unusual even in the Arctic—while they slept in their igloos, and they were awakened by the roofs of their dwellings caving in. The sleds had been left overnight on piles of snow (to keep them away from the dogs) but the sleds, too, had thawed out and been eaten.

It is impossible to travel during the winter without a sled, and they happened to be in a bad hunting district, so they had to kill their dogs and eat them. Then they devoured their skin clothing, and some of them died of starvation.

Those left resorted to cannibalism.

The next spring by chance our good friend Patloq, the philosopher, passed by with his wife. He saw a half-demolished igloo and drew closer to examine it. On the ledge inside he saw two horrible-looking hags—Atakutaluk and another woman. Neither could walk, and both had great difficulty in speaking.

Patloq inquired about the rest of their party.

"We don't know," the women answered, but indicated with their thumbs a snow pile back of the igloo. There Patloq discovered human bones.

"*Inutorpisee?* [Did you eat people?]"

"We don't know," they answered.

Patloq could tell by the appearance of the bones that they had been gnawed and split for the marrow which, I am told, is like the marrow of bear bones.

It was difficult to make the women eat anything. When a person is almost starved to death it is painful to eat. They were finally induced to try some meat, and then it was almost impossible to keep them from gorging themselves. Half a day after one has first eaten a craving for food sets in with such intensity that only a strong-willed person can resist it. The other woman could not do so, and she died three days later in terrible agony. But Atakutaluk resisted her impulses, ate only a little at first, and lived to relate the experience.

Now she was the first wife of Itusarsuk, chief of the community. She was well dressed, merry, and full of jokes. She herself told me her story, but she saw that it distressed me.

"Look here, Pita," she said, "don't let your face be narrow for this. I got a new husband, and I got with him three new children. They are all named for the dead ones that only served to keep me alive so they could be reborn."

Her skin was blue around the mouth—which was said to have resulted from eating human flesh—and it was impossible to make the Eskimos admit that she had had the mole previous to the experience.

I was sorry to leave these people of Pingerqaling, who were as happy as they were remote from neighbors. However, I had to press on.

At Igdloolik I visited my friend Eqiperiang and his two wives, who were sisters. The one in favor at the moment did all the talking and joking, treating the less fortunate sister like a servant. If one happened to pass by a few days later, the former servant might be queen of the day. Eqiperiang then slept on her side of the ledge. It is up one day and down the next for Eskimo women.

We left Igdloolik behind us and set out for Baffin Land. Now we were in an entirely new country, the very seat of all the traditions of the Eskimos. It was, in a sense, sacred ground for a student of these people.

The beginning of the trip was easy, for the country rises gradually from the south. We had trouble, though, with Qinoruna's little baby. It was weak and without proper food.

One night we were very tired after finally lowering two sleds over a steep waterfall, and decided to turn in and call it a day. I usually slept in the same house as Boatsman—the other two families each had their own igloo. I was soon awakened by Aguano crying outside.

"Pita, Pita! The little baby is dead!" It had been dead when Qinoruna tried to waken it for its feeding. Both the man and the woman cried and said they were sure it must be their fate never to have children.

The little body was sewn inside of two skins, carried out through a hole in the back of the igloo and up to a depression in the cliff where there were many loose stones. Aguano built a grave and placed the baby on it, then covered the dead child with so many stones and in such a helter-skelter manner that no one would suspect it was a grave. He did this, he said, because many Eskimos must pass here between Igdloolik and Ponds Inlet and they might be frightened if they knew this was a grave. He then asked all of us who had helped him with the stones to give him our mittens. We did so, only to see him bury the mittens too. Later on, when it was permitted her to sew again, Qinoruna made us each new ones.

I tried to go on next morning, but we had to remain there for five days. Arnanguaq complained that she was ill; Akratak did not want to drive on, as we had plenty of meat and my foot needed the rest. So we stayed and mourned the customary period, and Aguano was deeply grateful.

As we drove on Aguano stopped several times, walked back,

and swept out the tracks behind our sleds. He did this because the little child who had been so weak in life would, after death, have its full strength and might do violent injury to us if permitted to trail us. It was better to be careful and cover our tracks.

We followed a river with indifferent sledding into Milne Inlet. The inlet itself was hard to traverse, because the snow was deep and soft—the wind apparently never blows at the head of the fjord.

It was certainly a long fjord that the old whaler had discovered. It took us two days to reach better ice, and we had to walk along beside the sleds on skis. Aguano owned none and was handicapped because of it. Finally we came to a seal blowhole and stopped; Akrioq stood beside it and in less than an hour had killed a seal. We had eaten so much caribou on the journey that we were famished for a change in diet and sat down to a delicious meal.

We drove on toward Ponds Inlet.

The natives there had "progressed" to the use of wooden houses, but it was certainly no improvement for them. Nothing can be more hygienic than living in temporary igloos and tents, because garbage and filth cannot accumulate. But some of them were living in tiny houses there, and they had no idea how to keep them clean. It was obvious that a great many of them had already contracted tuberculosis. They may have had it before, of course, but their conditions now were far from favorable to a cure. The stench inside the houses was nauseating and the air suffocating. I noticed also that they had bought clothes from the store, and used filthy old rags for bedclothes.

7

PONDS INLET IS ACTUALLY THE SOUND BETWEEN BYLOT ISLAND AND Baffin Land. The island's high mountains are stately and impressive. Only the southwestern corner is lowland, a vast plain said to be excellent for pasturage.

Aguano and Qinoruna tagged along with us. They intended now to go as far as Lancaster Sound and hunt, while waiting for their partners to show up. They were supposed to be somewhere along the east coast of Baffin Land.

We had no particular adventures the first few days, caught a couple of seals at their blowholes, and encountered beautiful weather. Then as we entered Eclipse Sound a gale struck us and we had to stop for several days in an igloo. The wind was so strong that it tore a side out of the igloo and the snow drifted until it nearly swamped the shelter.

Next day we heard someone yelling at us far up the coast, and a native staggered toward us begging our help. His people were starving, he said; two of them were dead, and they had no dogs to drive for help. He was the only survivor who could move about, and he looked very ill. I gave him one seal and the food we had counted upon Aguano and his wife using. Then I wrote a note to the police at Ponds Inlet and hurried Aguano back with it.

Thus finally we parted company with the kind young couple, and never saw them again. The three girls cried and expressed their grief at parting in a manner entirely unlike any other Eskimos I had ever met. And at last we were alone and on our final stretch home to Greenland.

Suddenly Akratak yelled: "Look! There's open water right behind us!"

We turned and saw the open sea at our heels. It looked like a yawning mouth, the jagged edges of ice like teeth grinning at us. We yelled at the dogs and drove on with the wind at our backs.

But soon there was open water ahead of us. The ice pan on which we stood had revolved!

I was frightened now, and we decided to stand by and wait until the gale had blown itself out. The little Navarana needed to get up, so we cut some snowblocks and made a shelter for her mother, Arnanguaq. The two women sat together while we stood and talked about the situation. Suddenly we heard a scream. The ice had parted between the women; Akratak had grabbed up the child and had run with her. The mother's arms were inside her coat, and she could not get them out in time. Thus the two women were parted by open water, and I ran after Akratak and Navarana. I took the child—she had been lying on her mother's lap with no kamiks on her feet—and stuffed her inside my coat with her feet down inside my pants. She thought this was very funny and laughed hilariously, but her position prevented my jumping back to my friends, and after a few seconds the water was too broad to leap over.

The natives were frightened. We ran up and down the ice searching for a spot where we could cross to each other. Finally Boatsman shouted that he had found a place. I took off my coat, turned it inside out, and poured the child into it. Then I shouted to the father to come and help catch her, and I tossed her like a sack. They caught her, and the mother immediately stuffed her into her hood again. Akratak and I walked farther along the crack until I found a place narrow enough to jump.

Now we came to break after break in the ice. We had stopped thinking about our direction—we only sought to prolong our lives from one moment to the next.

After a while the snow stopped drifting, and the weather turned warmer. The wind still blew, but we could at least see where we were.

Eventually there seemed to be a lessening of pressure around us, and we thought we could get to a larger pan floating past. Boatsman and I made it across on my sled, and Akrioq was to follow immediately after. But the pressure began again; his dogs were frightened and pulled his sled back, so that we were separated after having been but ten feet apart.

We knew that we should wait and not risk our lives in trying to get together until the time was ripe. We were all dreadfully uncomfortable, our clothes wet from the warmth, and the ice wet too, so that our kamiks were soaked.

But worst of all was having to stand and wait, unable to do anything. We told the women to sleep if they could; they simply lay down on the sleds and were immediately dead to the world. We had been fighting the ice now for thirty hours, and they must have been exhausted.

I also snatched a nap now and then, until Akrioq's ice pan shrunk so small that his family could barely stand on it. His dogs whined in terror, and he knew he would have to try to get across now or never. He started over the ice wall at a spot where it looked fairly quiet, but it began to slip and slide when he was at the very top. The dogs fell and howled in pain. They can stand little ice pressure, because their feet are easily caught and crushed by the heavy, moving ice.

Akrioq saved his sled and six dogs, but more than half his load was irretrievably lost. Once more we pulled ourselves onto the middle of an ice pan and took stock of our reduced resources.

It seemed to me impossible to make it home to Greenland now. There were only sixteen dogs in place of the thirty-four yesterday. We had no kerosene and no primus stove, and in all only about thirty rounds of ammunition for each of our three guns.

We were, I thought, in about the middle of the sound. With good going we could make it to either side in one sleep. If we returned to Baffin Land we could reach a settlement within a few days; if we went on to North Devon we might be forced to stay over for the summer in an unfamiliar, uninhabited country.

Thus it meant going back to the land we had just left. I would have liked to try to complete the trip if I had had my own time, but the *Soekongen* would be leaving Thule soon, and we had arranged that, if I was not there when it left, it was to pick me up at Ponds Inlet. I had, by the grace of God, saved my notebooks. It was only my good luck that I had not lost my sled and load.

Once more we divided everything between us. The two Eskimos drove the two sleds with eight dogs each, and carried the load.

Now followed two harrowing days. There was no safety for us anywhere. We could neither cook nor dry our clothes, and, as it turned cold once more, we were all miserable. Arnanguaq rocked back and forth with her baby on her lap, wrapped in whatever we could provide, and moaned. After a while both child and mother fell asleep. When they woke, little Navarana took up her crying where she had left off. Arnanguaq then found several enormous lice in my shirt and accused all the white race of breeding lice that bit like wolverines. The situation was anything but merry.

Meanwhile we drifted about aimlessly in Lancaster Sound, and there was nothing to keep the women interested. Akrioq motioned me away from the women and said confidentially that Arnanguaq, after all, was a woman, and "she belongs to those who are angry when adrift on an ice pan if they have small babies." I admitted that one did not encounter the type every day and that if this was her specialty she might as well take advantage of it when she had the opportunity.

It took us many hours to reach shore, jumping across dark, treacherous stretches of water between ice pans, and shoving and pulling the ice together. I could not help admiring the two

women who were now in action for the fifth day with no more
than four hours of actual sleep. They leapt about like young
schoolboys, a little nervous, perhaps, but always courageous. I
especially admired Arnanguaq. She was rather small and heavy,
but she was as light on her feet as Boatsman's wife.

When we once more stepped on solid ground we were far to
the west of the place we had left, and the two sleds were still
far out on the ice. What would become of them I did not know—
and the guns were on the sleds. As we watched they drifted
westward, farther from us each moment.

Akratak offered to take the harpoons and try to reach the
sleds again while I cared for Arnanguaq and the baby, but I
considered this a challenge, gave her my matchbox, and started
for the sleds. I reached them in less than three hours, but I
was so exhausted by then—I had not slept in five days and I have
never been able to keep awake longer—that I sank down and
passed out.

When I eventually awoke I was stiff from the cold. Not only
my clothes but my limbs were rigid. The temperature had
dropped suddenly, and we could see the ice forming solid on the
water. If we had only waited a few hours we could easily have
reached shore on either side.

We drove east again to locate the women and finally heard
a voice calling to us. Akratak stood at the mouth of a cave in the
cliffs. They had discovered a wonderful shelter, and Arnanguaq
was still asleep in it but woke when she heard our voices.

We decided to remain here until our clothes were dry and
we were fit to travel again. Arnanguaq grew merry again, and we
discussed our adventures on the ice as if they had been arranged
for our pleasure. Eskimos are great people.

My foot started hurting once more. I had completely forgotten about it. When I examined the foot it looked like an old
newspaper soaked in water, a wonderful but not very pleasant
sight. The pain seemed to mount when I lay down, yet I could not
bear to put any weight on the foot.

Two days' traveling brought us back to Admiralty Bay where
we could see open water cut by the tides at the mouth of the deep
inlet. We stayed there for three days and had nothing to eat.
Boatsman and I then drove up to a bird cliff we discovered at the
eastern entrance of the bay and, using our shotgun, wasted all the
rounds of ammunition for it in killing a few gulls. Meanwhile

the area of open water expanded at the mouth of the bay, and we knew we would have to hurry.

Akrioq, who had been here before with Mathiassen, advised us to travel far down to the head of the fjord. There, he said, was an adjacent fjord leading to the east. He had hunted caribou there and had followed a valley eastward. It was his opinion that the rivers ran eastward to Milne Inlet from there, and he thought it would be safer to take an overland route.

I thought of my ill-treated foot and hoped to God that we would not have to walk. We argued for a while and then decided to do as Akrioq had suggested. The seals became more abundant as we traveled up the bay, and the immediate danger of starvation passed.

8

AKRIOQ WAS THE FIRST TO SPOT THE PEOPLE.

They looked strange to us, unlike any people we had ever seen before. Their faces were hollow and their eyes sunk deep in their skulls. They had no real clothes but were covered with scabrous-looking rags and filth.

They were starving.

Their voices were eerie. I have seen many shocking things in my life, but nothing like this. We thought them ghosts at first, but I talked to them. Thirteen of the tribe had died during the winter, and there was no prospect of anything but death for the rest of them.

They told us that they had been caught by a gale which lasted from one moon to the next. Their chief, the famous Tulimak (The Rib), had died first, and after that no one was able to prevent the weaker members of the tribe from eating the dogs. The starving animals had not been butchered—they had died off faster than the dog meat could be eaten. Eating the diseased and starving dogs had caused a plague among the natives, they told me. It was evident on their faces.

We gave them a seal to eat. Like very poor people, they did not want to take our food and cut off only a small portion and gave the rest back to us. There were twelve of them left, among them a few I had previously met in Igdloolik. After we had built a fire and boiled soup in their pots they seemed to revive slightly.

They told us that the corpses were left a little farther along the fjord. We could see the spot plainly, but Akrioq, who was more curious than the rest of us, begged me not to look at the bodies. Either the natives, or their dogs, had eaten some of the human flesh.

Our own plan was immediately forgotten in our desire to help these wretched humans. There were four families of them, though I learned that several of the families had been broken up by death. As soon as possible after the deaths they had repaired the missing links in the couples. Akratak learned that one of the girls had had four different men during the winter. She had accepted the men because it was believed that death is always a greater peril to a single person than to a married one.

I took a special fancy to one of the young men, Mala, who had lost his whole family. He and I stuck together, and he was in good shape again within a week. The men walked to their old camping place and brought up their property. Considerable property it was too, including two loads of narwhal tusks secured at the big killing last fall.

After a while we moved north. First we took two of the local natives with us, and each day when we went hunting we brought more. I gave them my sled to use, and they hauled up their belongings and settled down. They had plenty of needles and guns with ammunition.

Mala and I went out hunting alone for several days, driving up the fjords because he would not let me approach the spot where they had spent the winter. The place, he said, would be haunted all summer. Although the dead had been buried one could hear their ghosts moving about; if we drove near the ghosts might follow us and kill us.

We fed the starving people and gave them whatever we had. In return they gave us thread to mend our tents and clothing, ammunition and knives. They were not badly off, but the things they possessed could not be eaten. They were just what we needed most.

Soon afterward we moved farther up the fjord where the men could get out to sea in their kayaks and hunt.

At last I felt that it was time some of us, at least, should go to Ponds Inlet and head off Captain Pedersen. The natives agreed that it would be possible to walk across country, but we could take no sled with us, and the going would be difficult. I thought about sending some of the Baffin Landers, but we were not sure we could trust them, especially as they were afraid of facing the relatives of their dead companions in Ponds Inlet. I asked Boatsman and Akratak if they would like to go, but she was, after all, a girl and not so strong as we were; it would not look well to send a woman after help.

So I decided to go myself, and my friend Mala volunteered immediately to go along if I would pay him for the trip. He did not know at first what he wanted, but I assured him he could have any and everything he wished if we made the trip safely.

The next day was the worst of all. I shall never forget it. The clay was a slough, and we sank deep into it. We were so completely plastered with the gritty stuff that we lost interest in trying to keep clean. Whenever we stopped it was all I could do to get up. My brain felt doped, my body a dead thing. I walked ahead with the gun, and Mala plodded after with the harpoon. We dared not mention game any longer; it was too tantalizing.

If I could only lie down, I thought. To hell with everything but sleep. Every inch of my body cried out for it, but I knew what would happen if I gave in to my body. I must have slept as I walked, because suddenly I toppled over and fell face down in the disgusting stuff. I could not get my breath, yet I did not have the initiative to raise my head out of it, and only came to when Mala stood over me, shouting and yanking at my hair.

Then I thought of Mequsaq and Pipaluk. One step for Pipaluk—up with the bad leg and forward. One step for Mequsaq—the foot sank and disappeared in the hellish stuff.

One step for my mother, and my father and my sisters and my brothers. I thought of them all, and took a step for each of them. One by one. One by one.

And then I stopped thinking of them. I knew that I might as well confess that I was going through this purgatory to get home to Magdalene. I had never had an answer from her, but I was sure I would have her someday. If it had not been for the thought of her, I could never have gone on with that red-hot piece of iron hanging at the end of my leg.

I would call the whole stretch of clay and hell Magda's Plateau. As soon as the idea came to me things seemed easier. If it were named for her I could cross it somehow—there must be something good about it.

Poor Mala had to rest. The boy was young and had been through one hell already this winter. He had watched his people die of starvation and had looked the monster in the face himself. Now he had been tricked into coming along with me only to meet the old terror once more.

I sat down beside him. We were so careless of ourselves now that we flopped into the wet clay as if it were an easy chair. I let it run through my hands as children play with sand at the beach. Mala told me about his father's death.

"Did you think you were going to die, Mala?" I asked.

"Oh, no. One never thought of that. Help was sure to come —just as it is now. We, too, could die, but we are not going to!"

His confidence was a challenge. He was right. We were not going to give up!

We jumped up together. I discovered that the barrel of the gun was full of clay, but, worst of all, the sight was gone. It had dropped off and buried itself in the clay. What use was a gun without a sight? I was in such a childish rage that I threw the gun as far as I could. It sank almost out of sight.

"Come, let's go!" I shouted, and set off. I was half mad by now, and my fury possessed me. I walked on, punishing my foot, almost getting a thrill out of the daggers that pierced it.

Mala came along, and I waited for him where some stones poked up through the clay. There was even one large enough to sit on. I turned around, and there was the boy carrying both gun and harpoon, and looking like a dog expecting a whipping.

"You can take this," he said, handing me the harpoon.

He was the wise one; the gun had to be carried. I had not been myself when I tossed it aside.

And then at last we reached a more friendly portion of God's good earth. We saw no living things, but we discovered a few plants, the roots of which we could chew and digest. Besides, here was year-old dung of rabbits. If one has blubber (we did not) it can be eaten easily. We collected the excrement, chewed it, and got it down. It is hard to swallow, but at least gives one a sensation of having something in the stomach. We collected roots and grass and ate as much as we could. The new, juicy grass was not bad to taste, but swallowing it was something else.

We walked for short distances and then slept until we grew cold. Once Mala wakened me by laughing.

"What is so funny?" I asked.

"The idea comes to one's head," he said, "that after having had one tough time before, the same man runs into worse as soon as he has recovered from the first. One likes to be fat and comfortable, but this is a funny way of doing it."

The flag lay over us. It felt better to breathe against something, even if it was sleazy and almost useless.

"I want a knife, a knife of every kind," he said, and I promised them to him before we slept again. Perhaps he dreamed of all his possessions while he slept. I hope he did.

Next day we came within sight of the sea and Mala shot a rabbit. It helped some, but in order to reach the sea we had to cross a small lake by wading in it up to our bellies.

Next morning we walked out on the ice with more confidence, but when we had been walking for two hours we considered it worse than the land. But not worse than the clay—nothing could be.

There were seals on the ice, but there was also water. Mala had the first try at a seal and missed. Then I took the gun, and the seal spied me and flopped into the water.

Mala tried his luck at another seal, but it sank. I shot and wounded one, but it got away. Mala missed another, I missed another, and several dived before we could get close to them.

At last we were down to four bullets. It was my turn to crawl up to the next seal. Our bad luck had probably been due to the trumped-up sight we had attached to the gun, but now I was desperate.

The seal was no fool, and I put on such a performance as few actors have ever given an audience. I lay on my side, lifted my head and my legs like seal flippers. I rolled over and lay with my head in the wet snow on the ice—and I thought of what would happen if we died here of starvation after all our troubles. How silly we would look if we were found here on the ice . . .

Meanwhile the seal's head was up. It obviously distrusted me. Each time I crawled nearer, it grew more uncertain of my kinship. I presume I played with that seal for three hours, wallowing in the wet snow, finally realizing that I was as close to it as I ever would get. The distance between us was still formidable, but I was in a rage by now and pulled up my gun and fired. The seal flopped over dead!

We were saved. Here was a whole big seal for us, and no dogs with which to share it. We lapped up the blood streaming from the bullet hole, we stroked the skin and considered where it would be best to start eating.

It was our big day, the day that gave us back our lives. We had cared for our matches all this time, and this was the first chance to use them. We used the blubber for fuel by chewing the fat and spewing it out over some turf. We found two flat stones, placed the meat between them over the fire, and roasted it.

That is one dish I shall always remember. It was better than anything I have ever tasted in my life.

We had come down to Milne Inlet and not, as we had expected, to Eclipse Sound. We knew, however, that there were inhabitants at Toqujan, and we headed straight for that community. It took us three more days, and when we finally came within sight of the village we were received with shrieks of joy and fright.

The women were fascinated at the sight of our bodies. We were so emaciated that we could have passed for freaks in a sideshow. All of them wanted to feel my ribs and made conjectures as to my probable appearance when well fed. I said I was not going to be butchered, and they thought that very, very funny, laughed uproariously, and repeated the remark over and over.

The natives were going now to Button Point on the southeastern point of Bylot Island to hunt narwhals. I was still very weak and should not have gone, but I got a lift from a man with a good team, and it proved lucky. The man had a daughter and although she was no great beauty Mala took a shine to her—and I had promised earlier to get him a wife.

We camped twice en route. Each night I used all my powers as lecturer, advocate, and barker to convince the whole family that Mala was the one and only perfect man for a son-in-law. The father swayed like a reed in the wind. There was also a local widower after the girl—and he would give the girl a splendid wedding. The girl whispered this to me herself, and I told the family that if Mala married her while I was here they should have such a wedding as none of them had ever imagined. From my ship would be brought box after box of presents. The kettles I would give to all the women related to the family would be miracles of beauty, and I would present Mala with a boat which the Hudson Bay Company would sell. That gave Mala the advantage over the widower.

When we landed at Button Point, Mala was informed that he

was the lucky man. He took his new wife into the tent I had given him, and I lived with them as long as we were at the point. When I finally left to walk back to Ponds Inlet, Mala said he was not yet through hunting and would come along later. He needed more meat, he said, and his feet were not yet hungry for walking. Neither were mine, but it was August, and I knew I had to hurry.

I never saw Mala again, as he did not show up before I left Baffin Land. But at the 1934 annual dinner of the Circumnavigators Club in New York my good friend Reginald Orcutt screened some pictures he had filmed at Ponds Inlet. There was Mala in all the brilliant colors of the film. It was as if I enjoyed a visit with the fine boy again, and all the old memories of our struggles and companionship came back with a rush. It is to him that I owe my life—such as it is.

9

AND FINALLY THERE WAS OUR LITTLE SHIP, THE *Soekongen*, ROUND-ing the cape. It was the most beautiful sight that has ever greeted my eyes. We started back for Greenland immediately and encountered hard weather as soon as we hit Baffin Land. It was impossible to get through even to Cape York, not to mention Thule. I asked Akrioq and Boatsman whether they wanted to be put ashore at Cape Seddon, if possible, or go on down to Danish Greenland. They all preferred Cape Seddon, since people of their own kin were there, and the two men and their wives had looked forward to seeing them for many years.

We made it safely, but I was disappointed. My son, Mequsaq, was still in Thule, and I would have to return to Denmark without him. My only consolation was in learning from the natives that he was in good health, and Akrioq and Boatsman would carry my presents to him. I would come back for him later.

I said good-by to my friends there in Melville Bay to return to Denmark and become a civilized man once more, if possible.

It was a long, monotonous trip home across the Atlantic in the steamer *Hans Egede,* but I was an honored guest and it was quite different from the time years ago when I had been a stoker on the same boat. For old times' sake I went down into the hold and took a shovel in my hands, but it was no good trying to stoke any more. My foot still pained too much.

I must be a very flighty person, easily affected by the advice of others. I am sure that, had I been forced to remain in Baffin Land and never reached Ponds Inlet, I would still have my foot. But now I had doctors about, telling me how bad the foot was, and spouting Latin terms at me. Consequently I was unable to do anything but limp from one place to another and then sit down. I even considered learning to play cards during the trip. I was saved from that, thank God, and later I had no time to learn.

But everything must have an end, and on a certain day we passed old Kronborg castle, Hamlet's stomping ground. Two hours later we were in Copenhagen. The captain hoisted all his flags and stationed me on his bridge.

There was a great crowd. I saw my father and mother and little Pipaluk. Only now she was a big girl eight years old, and I hardly recognized her. There were dozens of journalists too, and I was overwhelmed by them and had to relate my story before I could go ashore. I started in on it but soon asked them to excuse me. I would be back in a minute.

I ran up on deck and glanced about me. And there she was down on the dock—Magdalene.

PART IV

1

MAGDALENE AND I WERE MARRIED, AND I BEGAN TO LOOK AROUND for a way to make a living in Denmark. I gave a series of lectures throughout the country, worked on my maps of Greenland, and wrote a short book about that fascinating country. I almost became a zoo director, a museum director, a man who lives in a castle. I did become the editor of a weekly magazine and also a regular contributor to a Copenhagen newspaper. I bought an island and settled down to the life of a farmer-cum-writer. My daughter Pipaluk came to stay on our island with us, but for Mequsaq it was not the right kind of life and we sent him back to Greenland where he felt more at home.

In 1927, I took a trip to the Faroe Islands and in that same year I had to have my left leg amputated. It had never stopped bothering me since that time I froze it in the Arctic snows.

I tried my hand at writing a novel—and was successful. *Eskimo,* my first novel, became a kind of best seller and I even sold the movie rights to it.

Gradually I became rather well known, and often I was called in to give expert advice to leaders of Arctic expeditions. I was sent to Leningrad as a delegate to the Congress of International Arctic Exploration. From Leningrad several of the delegates (including myself) were sent up into the polar region to view a mooring mast that had been built at Vardoe by the Italian explorer Nobile for his dirigible. At the time of our junket Nobile was already marooned on an ice floe, but we did not know it yet.

There is no hardship to going on polar expeditions in a Pullman car. We rolled smoothly along, had four plentiful meals a day to eat, and wonderful berths in which to sleep at night, and all along the route could listen to dignified and learned lectures. The train made many stops, too, and there was always something interesting to look at.

Along the line of the rails were great heaps and piles of logs—

trees that had been felled by gales or killed by forest fires. Large as those piles of logs were, there was no gap in the ranks of the standing timber behind them.

The first city on the White Sea to which we came was Kem. That year it had a population of about four thousand, but next year there were to be houses for fifteen thousand. There were seven hundred carpenters at work in the town putting up houses and other buildings for the population which was to follow, and nobody doubted that the anticipated growth would take place.

As we pressed forward the forest began to give way to the tundra, a land of swamps and marshes with occasional small groups of trees.

Farther north still, the people who stood and gazed at our train were Lapps. They are dependent upon their reindeer herds for their livelihood, and during the summer there was nothing for them to do, so they had plenty of time to watch the train with the same stolid faces as the Karelians. There was only enough time for me to spend a single day among the Lapps, and I did nothing for them which would have made an impression in most countries. I only told them a little something about the Eskimos and how they lived. But when I visited them in their houses I was specially careful not to laugh at them or any of the ideas they expressed, and apparently they appreciated that. Anyhow, just as the train was about to pull out of the station, they brought me as a pure gift a large basket containing several fine salmon. This was a token of their feeling toward me, and they would not accept any sort of payment in return.

Before we reached Murmansk we stopped at Kola, the place where another mooring mast for a dirigible was to be erected. All of us got out of the train and went to have a look at the site, and for the first time in my life I was grateful to mosquitoes. They swarmed all over us, stinging and humming, but when I saw how much their activity accomplished in the way of speeding up the proceedings I began to wish there had been even more of the insects.

In between slapping at the mosquitoes and scratching we took a look at the river, and to me it appeared just an ordinary one. Why this was a better—or worse—place to put up a mooring mast than any other I never did understand. By the time I was through looking at the plants and the birds the whole discussion on this point was over and we were all headed back to our car.

In Murmansk we were given an official luncheon, from which I slipped away in order to look at the town. I was impressed with what I saw. One interesting thing was the local monument to Lenin; it stood in a square at the center of the city, and instead of being a piece of sculpture it was a platform from which speeches were delivered, speeches to further the growth and development of the Soviet state. From this functional memorial the avenues of the city stretched away in what will be, in time, a series of fine vistas.

In Murmansk we got the news of Roald Amundsen's heroic flight in search of Nobile, and his disappearance into the unknown. The story came in over the cables, and like the rest of the world we had followed it with the deepest attention.

We were taken to visit the Arctic scientific station at Alexandrovsk. Never had I seen an institution like it before. It is located where it is, in part to study the natural history and phenomena of the Arctic, and also to assist the fishermen sailing out of this port. Before they leave on their voyages they pick up a trained biologist at the station. This man goes out with them and tells them where to go and what places to avoid.

As I myself had seen fleets of fishing vessels in other waters sailing about in vain for days and weeks, unable to locate the schools of fish, I could not help admiring the Russian system. The problem for the fishermen is always to find the places where the fish are feeding, and this in turn depends upon the relative salinity of the water, the temperature, and the set of the tides and currents. Codfish naturally remain in the "layer" of water where their food is to be found. Therefore, these scientific fishermen begin by sending down into the ocean sample jars and instruments with which to test conditions below the surface. If their findings indicate that there is nothing under their keel at the moment on which the fish might feed, they waste no time fishing there. The trained biologist directs them to some other area, and the central station keeps track of all the reported data and hence is able to direct the captains to the most likely feeding grounds. This technique accounts for the multitude of fish caught in these northern waters year after year. The currents and temperature belts move, and the codfish with them, and the whole cycle is interpreted at the station.

At Alexandrovsk I bade the congress farewell. Some of the members had already dropped out, but six of us had been delegated to go home by way of Norway and take a look at the mooring mast at Vardoe, the one General Nobile had used, to determine if it was still in good condition.

Our party went to a hotel in Vardoe and took baths, after which we felt more civilized, though when that thought occurred to me I had to laugh because it implied that we had been away from civilization, which was scarcely the fact.

Vardoe is on an island, so we had first to ferry across to the mainland. Then we drove by a wonderful highway along the coast, enjoying the magnificent weather and scenery. While we were stepping along I saw something ahead of us that I at first supposed was a row of bushes. Instead, it turned out to be a couple of thousand reindeer who were lying down right across the road to chew the cud. Their antlers were what I had taken for the branches of shrubs.

We were taken in a small boat across to the island on which the mooring mast stood. It was the first time in my life that I had seen one of the things, so I had no grounds for comparison, but it looked all right to me.

At Tromsoe everyone was stirred up; the town is the center of the Arctic trade and a famous place for expedition people. More than any other place in the world, her sons have aided in Arctic exploration and research. Here I ran into my old friend Helmer Hansen, who was now harbormaster in his own home port except for the times when he was away on trips into the north.

I had several other friends, too, in town, and it is the rule of the place that newcomers have to stand a round of drinks. When I told them that I was flat broke, without a single crown, they did not believe me. They wanted to know why I came to Tromsoe if I could not stand even a single drink?

One question occupied the whole thought of the place: where was Amundsen? You heard it a hundred times an hour in the hotels, which were crowded with newspapermen and Arctic veterans.

The fate of Roald Amundsen and his crew was sealed long before most of the rescuers even started to look for him, and an indication was eventually found of what that fate must have been. Quite some time after the Norwegian airplane disappeared one of its gasoline tanks drifted ashore on the northern coast of Norway. It was battered and split, as such a tank naturally would be after exposure to waves and rocks, but it had been emptied of its gasoline through the outlet valve which was soldered to it. The fact that it had been emptied through the outlet valve proved that the men themselves had done so.

At the time the tank was found it was felt that it would be cruel to let the families of the lost men know of it and its implications. They might have suffered deeply from thinking about the agonizing fight for life which must have been made by Amundsen and his men, the long hours in the cold sea while their waterlogged plane gradually sank from under them.

For a while the story was not given out publicly. But that is not the way to think about it. I feel certain from my personal friendship with him that Amundsen experienced no fear, then or under any circumstances.

So died Roald Amundsen, in an attempt to rescue other men in distress. He could not have had a finer end to his magnificent life.

Before the gasoline tank that told the tragic story had washed ashore, I went out in a whaling ship to the Greenland Sea to do the share of the Danes in the search. We sailed along the edge of the pack ice from a spot north of where Amundsen had last been heard from, and thence south, following the line of the ice. The skipper and I took turns sitting in the crow's-nest and looking out, a melancholy thing to do when human life is at stake.

Time after time you see the shape of ice hummocks take the form of the missing men. Again and again I had to rub my eyes and tell myself that it could not be they. And it was not. Ice can deceive the most experienced man when it is dirty, as is often the case, and when the shadows from the small caves in the piled-up pieces are black to look at. Each time the ice deceived us there was the instant of wild hope, and the bitter aftermath of disappointment.

We realized at last that we were searching in vain and set a course back to Tromsoe. When we returned we found the town in mourning, a strange place and different from any time when I had known it. As the boats came in they docked in silence; there were no drunken sailors celebrating their return to port, no fights over girls, and no dances in the familiar places.

I collected my belongings and continued my trip south, and home.

2

HAVING SOLD THE FILM RIGHTS TO MY NOVEL *Eskimo,* I WAS NEXT hired by John May, the film's talented and enterprising director. My work on the film included taking a trip up to Greenland to arrange for locations at which the various scenes would later be shot. I liked nothing better, especially as Magdalene had decided to come with me this time.

And finally one evening we drove down to the harbor, bag and baggage, and boarded the steamer which was to take us to Greenland. Summer days are long in northern countries, and it was still broad daylight when we embarked.

Magdalene's eyes were shining. Much as this voyage meant to me, it was still more of an adventure to her; she was happy as a child at the prospect of going to the country where I had lived so long and about which she had been told so much. (Privately I was concerned for fear she would not find it up to my own descriptions and eulogies, but time would soon settle that question.) She walked the decks of our small steamer, looking at everything with round eyes and asking dozens of questions.

Just as the mooring lines were being cast off a young engineer and a party of his friends came aboard, also bound our way. His destination was Ivigtut, the town in South Greenland where we were scheduled to make our first stop.

The group of friends and relatives on the dock began to wave and flutter handkerchiefs, and the strip of water between the pier and our hull widened irrevocably. Under our feet the ship began to pulse slowly and rhythmically as the propeller revolved beneath her stern. Now the wharf and the people on it were dwindling behind us. The thump!-thump! of the engine seemed to me to be saying, "Greenland! Greenland!"

The first part of our voyage was calm as a millpond, our course taking us through nothing but sheltered inland waters. Both Magdalene and I enjoyed it to the full; it suited me perfectly that we were not on a regular passenger vessel. Our captain was an agreeable man, at least on this part of the trip, and he had a fund of stories collected from all over the world.

As on other voyages, we put in at Methill in Scotland for coal.

Things seemed not to have changed since my previous visit. There was very little shipping business; only three boats were awaiting the high tide to come into dock.

Soon we nosed out into the broad Atlantic and Magdalene greeted the open sea with a sigh. Before we sailed many of her friends and relatives had spouted warnings and advice about seasickness in her ears until she almost turned green merely listening to them. She had brought along enough suggestions and remedies to treat the whole ship's company, and I think she had been dreading this moment ever since we started. In a few minutes now she would be laid low by the dread *mal de mer,* or so they had told her.

There was a ground swell running which moved the vessel perceptibly, but she said at the supper table that she felt still able to eat, so why not keep up as long as she could? During the night we ran into a smart little storm, and the next morning she said that of course she would have to surrender soon, but before she did so she might as well have a look at the sea and drink her morning coffee. She stayed up all day and ate her dinner like a good sailor, and never in later life has she had a thought of being seasick.

That was a great relief to me, for I had been really worried about this point. I had never had occasion to doubt my sincere love for her thus far, but seasickness might have shaken it.

The sea did not stay calm all the way. The wind shifted and came howling down at us from the north, building up to a real gale. Magdalene enjoyed watching this storm; she followed all its phases with interest. Shortly before, she had been saying that she had never seen such an easy life as the sailors on tramp steamers appeared to have, with only a few routine duties and not much hurry about those. Now things looked very different. The sea wore a far from friendly face, and none of us cared for it.

Nobody really loves a storm except the poets who sit home and make verses about the fury of the gale. Aboard a ship, small or large, existence is uncomfortable. You are rolled and scrambled around in your berth and your sleep is disturbed. When the storm is over you feel as if you have had an ungentle massage all over, and you are terribly tired. But Magdalene enjoyed the novelty of it and was not in the least afraid.

One of the people aboard our boat was an old shipmate of mine, a certain Captain Ibsen. He had been sailing to Greenland,

and along its coast, for many years, and as the waters are badly charted and a navigator does not learn to deal with ice conditions all in a moment, the Royal Company had sent him along with us as a coast and ice pilot.

While we were out on the Atlantic, Captain Ibsen had nothing to do, any more than a passenger. During the crossing he was a modest and retiring man who sat in a corner of the sofa, and ate his food without any remarks at all.

Meanwhile the vessel's regular captain had been undergoing an unfortunate change. We had liked what we had seen of him while the ship was at Copenhagen. There had been a childlike, naïve quality about him.

After we left port at Methill, though, this sweet and simple character had filled his quota of good behavior. He took to the bottles in the charthouse with enthusiasm and grew more and more intoxicated. He was most unappetizing to sit with at table, but on his own ship the captain is supreme and has a right to disregard everyone, passengers and all, if he chooses.

Nor did the storm make any difference in his conduct. He drank more steadily than ever until his face became the color of an overdone piece of salami and his eyes faded to the hue of bread and milk. The seas were boarding the vessel and racing along her decks, but he paid no attention. The young first mate showed great discretion in the way he kept his captain out of sight of the crew, but just the same everyone knew what was going on and it was bad for discipline. So far as the actual necessities of navigation went, of course, the two mates handled everything in good shape.

Another thing that worried us during the course of the storm was the fate of Captain Ahrenberg, a Swedish flier who was trying to cross the Atlantic to Ivigtut. We had followed his plans by the ship's radio. Then we got word that he had landed at Reykjavik, on Iceland, and was going to stay there until the weather reports were favorable.

Immediately after we had turned in the mate came tumbling down the companionway and yelled, "We can see Greenland!"

Everybody got up. It was rare to have a sight of Cape Farewell, which lay ahead of us, for most ships take a more southerly course till they are well past the cape and then run west to the middle of Davis Strait, experience having taught them that it pays to do so. The southerly route avoids the ice, and in these waters it is well to take no chances. But this captain of ours was different; he just laid out a direct course on the chart and plunged ahead.

We hurried into some clothes and up on the bridge. Ahead of us was a break in the clouds and through it, far out on the horizon, we saw Cape Farewell. It was not the first time I had seen it, but as always, it gave me a feeling of the hardness and cruelty of Greenland. Those high mountains, steep cliffs, and the sun behind them to the west lining their flanks with bright golden light!

The next day we had a milder sea, and after being on deck for a while I dashed down to Magdalene to show her the first piece of Arctic ice she had ever had a chance to see. It was rather too small to dignify with the name of iceberg, but it had the same general shape. In a few hours that one piece was followed by more and more ice; we had run into the drift line of the Great Ice. Immense quantities of pack ice are formed in the Polar Sea. This pack ice drifts from Siberia over the top of the world, so to speak, across the North Pole and then south to Greenland and along the east coast.

To come into the area of sea where the ice is makes an immediate difference. The roll of our ship stopped at once, and the water between the pans of ice was smooth as oil though the gale was still blowing outside the ice area. As we moved cautiously ahead the floes began to corner us more and more, and our steamer was not built for this sort of navigation. A steel hull has no chance in the ice; it can be smashed in no time and even the smallest split in the plates is fatal. The rivets will snap off, then, and the water will pour in. Wooden hulls are different and much tougher, which is why they are always used in the Arctic.

Handling a ship among great masses of ice requires real skill, and now our Captain Ibsen began to come into his own. He dropped his shy and inconspicuous manner; he seemed almost to grow in size and stature. Where before he had tied an old woolen scarf over his head, it had now burgeoned a splendid cap encrusted with gold lace; he carried himself with a new erectness, and as he paced up and down the bridge he wore a face we had never seen before. Nor was his voice as small and infrequent as it had been; it now reverberated through the cabins and the steward got his orders like shot out of a cannon. Captain Ibsen began to relate stories of his earlier experiences, and those of his friends, but if any of us attempted to join in at this game he reminded us kindly to keep quiet. His brain was too burdened with responsibility to endure talking from other people.

So Ibsen had his day conning the ship through the ice, and I suspect he was disappointed when it grew so jammed ahead of us that we had to set a course south and west to get round the blockade and out into the open sea. As for us passengers, the fair wind and smooth sea enabled us to enjoy the trip and we thought of nothing except watching the line of the coast, where great mountains stood up, one after another, their names harking back to the ancient days of the Vikings.

One conspicuous summit is that of Thorsten Icelander. As I stared across to its eternal peak, sharp and high in the air, a cap of mist began to form round the summit. It grew and grew; clouds gathered themselves out of nowhere, and I told Magdalene that a southeaster storm would be down on us inside of an hour.

The wind hit us with the solid speed of an explosion. It howled and whistled around the ship, and though it was so sudden a blast that waves had no chance to form, sheets of water were blown round us like so much smoke. The violence of such southeasters as this is a fresh surprise each time one blows up, and they are feared up and down the Greenland coast for the disasters they so often cause. Captain Ibsen jumped into command. His arms began to mill about in the air and his voice roared and bellowed. He applied no censorship at all to his language. Meanwhile the coastline had been blotted from our sight by driving spindrift and the clouds, and the wind blew so terrifically that the ship made little progress against it.

In the midst of this confusion the mate came leaping from the radio shack to the bridge, yelling that Captain Ahrenberg had started from Iceland at two o'clock and should have been in Ivigtut by this time. He was unreported, and we were all requested to keep a lookout for him.

As we headed slowly up the Arsuk fjord toward Ivigtut we all scanned the sky intently, hoping for sight of the flier. Just as it was almost dark a specially hard gust of wind snatched the hat from my head and blew it along the deck, It rolled there for some distance and then dived overboard. In the middle of my pursuit I heard the whole crew yell, "There he is!" There were other shouts, too—"The flier!"—"He disappeared over that way!"—and "He'll come down in Kunak Bay where we anchor!"

I was fortunate enough to catch a glimpse of the plane just as it went out of sight, enough to confirm the fact that it *was* a plane and hence must certainly be Captain Ahrenberg.

There was nothing for it but to hope that we should come upon the plane in Kunak Bay, where we figured it had probably landed. Because of ice conditions, and the fact that the wharf at Ivigtut was occupied by another vessel, we should merely anchor briefly in Kunak Bay, unload some of the most urgent freight by boat, and then head north. The steamer could discharge the two thousand cases of beer and other things in her hold on the return trip southward.

We reached the bay late in the evening. Here we witnessed a metamorphosis in another of our ship's company. This time it was our good friend Mr. Hasselbach, the engineer. Throughout the voyage he had been rather a silent, though pleasant, man. We had planned on having a farewell party for him, but our captain had appropriated all the liquor and drunk it himself, so the bottom fell out of that plan.

In spite of this, our engineer made us fully aware of his departure. When the motorboat that was sent to meet him came out, his voice, like Ibsen's, swelled in volume. He cursed and shouted, and made loud decisions in order to impress us. Finally he and his duffel were loaded into the launch and he left.

And yet, though it was two in the morning when he set out from the ship, nobody but Mr. Hasselbach was the man to find Captain Ahrenberg. The flier had landed safely and anchored his plane at the head of another bay; when Hasselbach came along he took him aboard the motorboat and brought him safe to the mine.

It took us most of the next day to get under way once more, and even so our voyage came close to ending right there in Kunak Bay. The gale blew up again, and it was worse than ever in that narrow anchorage, the mountain walls of which acted like a funnel for the storm. The weight of the wind was almost as solid as water as it poured down the clefts in the mountains. Sand, gravel, and even stones were blown into the sea. Our ship had both anchors out, but they were not enough to hold her; while the storm lasted we had to keep full steam ahead to take some of the strain off the chains.

As suddenly as it started the gale stopped. Only an hour after we had been staring anxiously at the taut anchor chains the

sea was as smooth as glass and the snow buntings were chirping
on the shore. Nature was peaceful and full of smiles, the sun was
shining, and it was once again the calm Arctic summer. The
change was as sudden as if a curtain had lifted on a whole new
set of scenery.

Thus far Magdalene had seen no Eskimos. Now, as we
steamed out of Ivigtut fjord, we passed close to the settlement of
Arsuk, at the entrance. Chimneys were smoking, and the natives,
gathered on the beach to watch us pass, waved at the ship. Arsuk
is the least happy Eskimo settlement on the entire coast. Inside
the very borders of the original village was found a costly and
valuable mineral deposit, cryolite. This substance is a fluoride of
sodium and aluminum; it is used in the manufacture of lamp
shades, extra-hard glass and porcelain, and various ornaments,
besides being a source material for various costly chemicals. The
natives had been mining it on a small scale, using it for snuff and
trading it up the coast.

When a Danish professor discovered cryolite's commercial
possibilities no less than three companies began to mine it in
quantity. After a while a single large concern took over the
mining operations in a large-scale way. It employed hundreds
of miners and millions of crowns in profits were made. Ships
came into the fjord and sailed away loaded down with the precious stuff, and it is no wonder that all this prosperity had its
repercussions upon the Eskimos.

They tried to sell anything they could to these wealthy white
men, and the sight of things which before they could never have
even imagined awakened in them a whole set of new desires.
The very trash the white men threw into the sea as waste would
have taken them years to acquire in the old days, when every
scrap of metal and fabric had to be acquired laboriously. And
white men waste things on a tremendous scale.

Naturally, the boom at Ivigtut attracted the Eskimos with the
prospect of easy gain (just as it attracted the white men), and
then, as they became demoralized, they got the reputation of
being a lazy, shiftless lot, and their women of being immoral.

Instead of holding up Arsuk as an example of the frailty of
a primitive people exposed to civilization, I like to look on the
population there as proof of the Eskimo character and its power
to resist temptation. Arsuk still has her hunters and fishermen,

and the volume at the trading post shows that they are still industrious, though the location of the village is not the best for this kind of enterprise.

The evil effects of the mining boom have almost disappeared. At one time there had been a certain amount of venereal disease among these people, introduced, of course, by the sailors. A government doctor was stationed right in the village, and any cases of these diseases which happened to find their way to other parts of Greenland were brought promptly to Arsuk. Now all that is a thing of the past. There is no more venereal disease in the settlement, the doctor has left, and only the old reputation for shame and weakness cling round the village, much to the regret of the people who live there.

As we went by, several of the natives were out in their kayaks. They recognized me and yelled their greetings. That gave me a warm feeling of satisfaction.

On up through Davis Strait we went. Magdalene enjoyed the towering mountains and the icebergs, and there were plenty of whales to watch.

The next port where we put in was the lovely colony of Holsteinsborg, in its setting dominated by the skyscraping peak with the odd name of Womanhood.

A motorboat came out to meet us, and in it was the company manager, Mr. Rasmussen, with his young assistant and their two ladies. We were shown every courtesy; the Rasmussens had known that we were aboard and gave us a kind invitation to come ashore and stay with them. We were anxious, however, to get on north as fast as possible because we had arranged to meet Knud Rasmussen at Godhavn. The boat in which he was coming was so small that it carried no radio, and we had to depend, as in the old days, on favoring winds and currents to bring us together.

Those days of old were not, in many respects, so good as I remembered them. I realized that when I walked up the hill to the village and met my old friends. They were worn and old, especially the women. There was Anine, with whom I had once danced till she was worn out—quite a feat that was, too! She did not look at all as I had remembered her. And Katak, the girl who was so proud of her beauty that she refused to go to a dance if certain other girls who had once criticized a new dress of hers were to be present! To tell the truth, she was now an old hag.

When a lady loses every single one of her teeth her looks suffer a certain impairment, and when, on top of that, her clothes are both poor and dirty it takes a very permanent love still to see something delightful in her.

Changed or not, their welcome was warm, with handshaking as cordial as ever, and smiles and words of greeting.

For years Holsteinsborg had been a very impoverished settlement. There were now no seals and no walruses in the waters around it. Originally the place had been famous as a stopping-off point for Eskimos, who used to travel south down the coast at one season and up again at another. Then came the era of the missions, and naturally every effort was made to keep the natives in their settlements so that they could attend schools and churches regularly. The result was that the village lost its tourist trade. Troubles descended upon it thick and fast as winter storms. The whales, which used to be numerous around Holsteinsborg, disappeared. The plentiful caribou of the region died off, and seals ceased to frequent its waters. Fish alone remained to the natives, and though they could be eaten they could not be sold.

Gradually the morale of the Eskimos began to break. From a group of gay and happy people they became morose; their lives were spent in half-starved idleness, sitting around in their small, unhealthy houses, while in the same settlement they saw the Danes going about gaily and well dressed.

Suddenly one day halibut began to have a commercial value. A specialist from Denmark came to Holsteinsborg and taught the natives how to fish; gradually he put them back on their feet. It was no small task, and he did not have a pleasant time of it. This fishing master demanded discipline, of the same exact sort which he applied to his own life. He set an hour and minute on which he would pull the dories out of the harbor behind his powerboat, and he stuck to it.

As the men of the settlement learned how to become proficient fishermen the government helped them to buy powerboats of their own. Usually groups of four fishermen would co-operate in the purchase of such craft. After a few years of this new lease on life Holsteinsborg was the only town in Greenland that could be called really prosperous.

Once more the poor natives had something to learn. The only halibut which are good enough to attempt preserving in tins are the "white" ones, the finest of all. Some halibut have black or gray bellies; the meat of these varieties is too soft to use. Accordingly, the canning factory was ordered not to buy such fish from the natives, and the Eskimo fishermen were informed of the ruling.

Great disappointment and indignation followed this edict. The men got together in the evening and talked the matter over. They could not understand it at all. Wasn't it just as much trouble to catch a fish regardless of whether his belly was white or black? Did the Danes suppose that a fisherman out in his boat could pick and choose among the fish down at the bottom of the sea? The final decision was not to submit to this foolishness.

Trouble started the next day, though it might have been avoided had the white men been cleverer. The boats came home from the sea, as always, and the process of weighing in the fish began. In accordance with the new ruling, the canning factory man refused some of the fish. The Eskimos protested.

If the white man would not buy *all* their fish, then they would not sell *any* of them.

"What will you do with your fish, then, if you don't sell them?" inquired the purchasing agent.

The natives had not stopped to figure that out, and for a time they were stumped. Then one of the most intelligent declared that he was going to show the Dane that the wisest solution would be for the factory to buy all the fish, after all. The manager inquired how he was going to prove that?

"This way," replied the Eskimo, and, seizing the white man by the shoulders, banged his head against the fence several times with great emphasis.

In a way he made his point, for the Eskimos were ultimately allowed to deliver all their fish at the factory, and they were then paid in accordance with the proportion of usable, white-bellied halibut to their total catch.

As an illustration of the proper way to work out problems with the natives, this episode was as bad as possible. It would not have been difficult to explain to those fishermen about the standards necessary to make the factory operate successfully, and secure their co-operation in providing the required kind of fish. Eskimos are quite capable of understanding such a matter. But in Holsteinsborg the relations between the natives and the Danes were not ideal, anyway.

And yet, the post manager, Mr. Rasmussen, was one of the finest men of his kind in Greenland.

He was not popular with the Eskimos, and they told many stories to illustrate his meanness, but he did manage to keep them working, and if a man could not get along as he was going, instead of making him an object of charity Mr. Rasmussen showed him another way of earning a living and started him out at it.

From the moment when she first set foot on Greenland Magdalene understood that she was welcome. Partly this was because she came with me, partly it was due to her own character, but undoubtedly some of her popularity came from the fact that she brought with her a box full of inexpensive jewelry from Berlin. The various pieces in that box were dealt out left and right to my old dancing partners and one-time lady friends. So Magdalene became a sort of myth in Greenland, an incomprehensible lady who preferred old women to young girls! Such a preference had never before been heard of.

From here on we were to travel in the customary Greenland way, by small boat. Its owner, Larsen, was a genuine salt-water fisherman from Denmark, kind and courageous. He was bound up to Godhavn to take some stuff to an official there, and we had arranged to go along with him. Our outfit surprised Magdalene, who up to this time was a complete amateur about travel in wilderness places. We had not been on Larsen's boat long when she was stupefied that I offered her a metal cup out of which to drink—I ought to have bought some china ones at the store! The pots did not look at all nice to her either, she declared, and she was going to do the cooking herself, but not till she had washed the utensils several times!

Meanwhile Larsen had started his motor, and for the first time in my career I was honored by having the flag of a Greenland colony hoisted for me.

Although he employed two natives as crew for his boat Larsen ran her almost singlehanded, and his manners were so attractive that he won Magdalene over to his side in no time. Our voyage started gaily, with the sun shining and a calm, bright sea. Holsteinsborg was soon hidden astern behind a steep point, and we began to run along with the open coast on our starboard side. Magdalene forgot her intention of washing the cups and pots, joined us merrily when we had coffee, and produced her cake, which had no long lifetime in that boat.

I could not take my eyes off the shapes and colors of the land as it went by us to starboard. Once more, after so long an absence, I was in my beloved Greenland, and I drank in the sight of every headland, cove, and rock.

When night came Magdalene went below and lay down on one of the two wooden benches in the small cabin, and after a while Larsen took the other one. As for me, I would not leave the deck, and lay down there for a while under the superb night sky and the stars.

In time we headed out into more open water in order to round a point and some islands, and the sea became rough. The powerboat was flung along from one wave top to the next, and time and again Magdalene was thrown from her sleeping bench. She made no complaint about that, but it was naturally impossible for her to sleep under the circumstances. Only a really experienced small-boat sailor could have done so. I was proud of the way she took these minor hardships.

When we got once more into the lee of the sheltering islands Larsen came on deck to navigate the boat into the harbor of Agto.

We were to spend Sunday at Agto before pushing off for our next long trip up the coast, and when we got into the port it was four o'clock in the morning. At that season, of course, it is light even at such an unchristian hour, but anyway you can never come to an Eskimo settlement without finding somebody awake.

A Danish-looking man came hurrying out in his underwear and hoisted the Danish flag to show that the trading post was awake and ready to receive whoever wanted to visit it.

It did not take us long to discover that the trader was a man named Stjernebo, and a special sort of host he turned out to be, as will appear later. Although I had never met him before, we soon struck up an acquaintance and learned that he had just married a beautiful young native girl. This was the first occasion upon which she had had to act as hostess to strangers, and she was somewhat embarrassed.

Stjernebo was a magician at heart; from childhood he had practiced making things disappear until he was shockingly proficient at it, and he could also conjure the most surprising things out of the noses, hats, or mouths of ordinary people. He demanded the most obvious reaction of astonishment from his wife each time that he performed his sleight-of-hand tricks, and after a while it grew hard for her to put on a convincing act in this respect.

Nowhere can a meal be more delicious than in one of the small homes of Greenland. The rooms are cozy and the people kind; the food is simple but the hospitality overflowing. However, our dinner at Stjernebo's house was hardly similar to others that I remembered. When the rest of us sat down our host remained standing. At first I thought he was going to say grace, but it developed that his idea was to attract our attention. As we all stared at him, wondering what was up, he lifted the cover from a bowl and from somewhere or other three live puppies, a book, and several pieces of paper materialized. But when he came to pour himself some beer he had to remove another puppy and two whole loaves of bread from his glass. When he worked the pepper mill a fortune in coins tumbled to his plate. Of course, we all dutifully applauded, as we were expected to do, but Larsen, our sailor friend, was a neighbor of Stjernebo's, living less than a hundred miles away, and from the way he greeted these tricks I suspected that he had seen them before.

At this moment a message came for me, saying that I was not to forget "my Sofie." Magdalene asked what it meant, and I had to tell her.

The story was soon told. Sofie was, in a way, a dependent of mine. She was neither young nor attractive, and the latter adjective never had applied to her. But she had once been married to a friend of mine, a Dane with whom I had been on an expedition years before. He had settled down in Greenland with a job as captain of a small coastwise schooner, and here he had married Sofie. I had visited at his home, known and liked him for years. He was one of those men who are all too rare in the world, who do not run away from obligations; who have the courage to marry the girl they love regardless of race or color. But taking a native wife had shut him out of the white society of the place where he lived. In spite of his experience and knowledge of life, so superior to theirs, the Danish families barely tolerated him. There was, of course, nothing new or surprising in such a story; it has happened in many times and places.

My friend finally died, and his widow, Sofie, was left with two children and a pension of only fifty crowns, or eleven dollars, a year. I heard about what had happened while I was away in

Thule and arranged to send her ten crowns a month, or a little more than two dollars.

That may sound like nothing at all in America, but in Greenland it amounts to considerable. Then one winter I traveled south and came to the colony where she was. Sofie came to me and complained that she was not getting the money I had allotted for her, and why was that when I had promised it to her?

I went to the leading people of the place and investigated. From them I learned that they had seen fit to stop her support because of her conduct, which had not been "orderly."

What had she done, I inquired?

"Oh, it's the kind of thing we can't discuss," they said.

Finally I forced them to admit that on the previous summer, when a ship had appeared, she had gone aboard. The next day she had showed up at the store with money obviously earned in a way not to be mentioned. When I heard that I lost my temper and asked them what *they* had done for poor Sofie? Had they made it possible for her to earn a decent living? I wound up my lecture by declaring that since I had found Sofie to be an industrious woman, from then on I would allow her twenty crowns a month so that she could see that she was not forgotten by all her friends.

After that, of course, they had to consent and pay her the money. Twenty crowns a month up there is quite a sum, and from that time on Sofie regained her lost social caste. In fact, she began once again to dispense hospitality herself, and coffee was served so frequently at her house that young men began to visit there again. A widow with an established income was worth thinking about, and several of the men in town did stop to think about her. One of them was an artist named Peter Olsen, a locally famous Greenland composer, a violinist, and more than that, both teacher and preacher in his community.

Neither his art nor his religion had managed to keep his feet off the ground. He was sufficiently down to earth, in fact, to marry Sofie, though she was, as I have said before, neither very young nor specially beautiful.

The first I knew of this development was when a letter arrived from Olsen telling me of his marriage to Sofie, assuring me that his love for her was great, and asking God to bless me for what I had done for her in the past. I replied by congratulating

him, and I really meant it. I also congratulated myself, for I saw
no reason to continue sending Sofie money any longer, now that
she was married to a well-to-do and salaried man. So my letter
expressed my pleasure and wished them all sorts of luck.

Later, I learned that Peter was not only disappointed by the
loss of Sofie's income but felt himself in a measure betrayed.
I hope he did not show it by his treatment of her. It had been a
long time since I had heard of either of them, and here was this
message for me to come to her house in Agto to take coffee with
her. After I had sketched out this story for her, Magdalene
seemed to accept my explanation for the truth it was, and I took
her along with me as a measure of protection.

Sofie had not added to her looks in the interim. She was as
thin as a rail, and I thought her husband exhibited all the symp-
toms of an advanced case of tuberculosis. Still, he was cordial and
played his violin for us while we had coffee.

The midwife at Agto was very much of a personage, a *grande
dame*. She dressed in parti-colored clothes and talked louder
than everyone else. We saw a good deal of her at Stjernebo's
house because her services were shortly to be in demand there.
Such a prospect always makes women of her profession popular
with young brides. Magdalene and this woman formed a fast
friendship, somewhat to my surprise.

The night before we sailed we had a wonderful evening at
Stjernebo's house. He was no common man. I have already described his feats as a conjurer, but I have not mentioned his
habit of practicing his art all the time, even when we were talking about serious matters, upon which he was often well informed. He had spent some time on the east coast as a trapper
and related interesting experiences he had had there. He went
on to explain his theory of how the whole country might be
colonized and made profitable by a system of sheep and fur
farms.

These were ideas worth talking about, but while he was
presenting them the listener would be taken aback by seeing a
deck of cards appear out of the air and fly into his sleeve, or
noticing the inexplicable disappearance of a box. Stjernebo also
told some good stories of the time when he had been a soldier,
but I could not appreciate them to the full because he was simultaneously causing six silver teaspoons to pass through his mouth
and out from his spine.

All the while he talked he made no reference whatever to this difficult and unusual way of handling spoons, but kept on telling me how he wanted Copenhagen fortified so that no German should ever get his foot inside the place.

Meanwhile, Magdalene was struggling along with the midwife and our hostess, but as they spoke not a word of Danish the conversation there was kept alive by Magdalene's showing them the things she had brought along as gifts. Her two friends got rather more of them than she had planned, much against her will. The pair of them were smarter at getting than Magdalene was at keeping.

We sailed next morning in a pouring rain. The sea was calm, and we simply sat and watched the flood come down while we chugged our way along between the innumerable islands on our route.

At Kangaitsiak we went ashore for a short time to see an old friend of mine who was trader at the settlement. The populace remembered me as a man who had once shot an eagle there. As it was my first eagle, custom decreed that I had to set the inhabitants up to coffee. Now here I was, back again with a white wife who had never before been in the place. The popular vote on that circumstance was that another round of coffee was called for, particularly since they were all so poor that there had been no *kaffeeklatsch* in town for a half year. We objected that we had to hurry on our way, but they said that would be all right if we simply left them the coffee and sugar.

Egedesminde is a large colony but not a pleasant one. The natives are far from industrious, there is an almost complete dearth of game, and the Danish inhabitants were quarreling among themselves so bitterly that they scarcely dared show their heads out of doors. We could not look for much hospitality, but I knew that the daughter of an old friend of mine, a Danish carpenter, was living here. Her name was Miss Wilhelmine Moller, and in the silent, if not dark, night, I went through the town and knocked at her door. She was a nurse in the district hospital, and it must have been a hard and thankless life. A young woman alone in Greenland does not have any too much fun. Although all Wilhelmine had in the way of a dwelling was one room in the attic of the hospital building, she made us very welcome and insisted on putting Magdalene into her bed for some additional rest.

Hers was a real hospitality of a kind not practiced by the other white people of that colony.

Our destination was Godhavn, which is situated across the width of Disko Bay and on Disko Island. Moreover, on this part of our run we were to have an extra passenger.

While we were still in Egedesminde this man had come to me to ask permission to go across the bay with us. His name was Peter S. Dalager, and his past reputation was such that most people thought the "S." stood for "scoundrel."

Oddly enough, his profession was painting: "an artist who missed his customers terribly," as he described himself to me. I could have mentioned scores of painters who had exactly the same feeling, but I realized that it was probably harder than usual for Peter S. to sell anything. Anyway, he had heard a rumor that the new *landsfoged,* or governor, at Godhavn was a connoisseur of art and a possible patron, so it occurred to him to go there at once and check up. No doubt this story of his was sincere as far as it went, but I knew the man of old, and was aware of his smartness.

In fact, I thought I saw through his scheme, which was peculiar to Greenland.

To grasp it you must understand that in comparison to the cost of other things, travel in Greenland is extremely expensive. If you hire a pilot, for instance, he is entitled to one crown for every four miles covered plus a daily salary, and you are under obligation to return him to his home and family. As long as he is away from them he is entitled to full pay, without regard to delays of wind or weather. Furthermore, it is worth bearing in mind that anyone whose advice and assistance is secured during a passage may claim to be a pilot *and collect pilot's wages for the entire trip.*

This situation was what I suspected Peter S. Dalager of having in the back of his mind. Indeed, he actually suggested that if we allowed him to join us, he could help with navigation and point out the best route to us, and so on. I promptly informed him that I knew the way across Disko Bay like the palm of my hand and that no advisory pilot was needed. With some misgivings, though, I did tell him he could ride along with us as a sheer passenger, and bring his canvasses with him.

Our boat's nose was headed out toward the open sea, and we gradually dropped Egedesminde astern. After a while our course brought us close to Hunde Island, where the trader was an old friend of mine, Nickolaj Rossing. We decided to put in for a few hours and visit with him.

Hunde Island is remarkable in a number of ways. The finest kayak hunters on the west coast of Greenland live there. The place is really not one island, but several, so small and low that when a storm blows up the wind-driven spray is carried clean over them and drenches the natives' houses and everything else. The result is that houses have to be built small and flat to avoid being blown away, and no real fresh water is to be found because the spindrift makes all the standing pools and ponds brackish. The native hunters are industrious and full of courage. They actually prefer to go out in their fragile skin kayaks when the waves are running high. Although at such times they require help at the moment of launching their craft, once out in open water it is far easier to capture seals, who are never as alert in a rough sea as they are in a calm.

It is by no means easy to handle a kayak in a rough sea. One danger is that if the paddler takes the crest of a wave sitting up-right he may have his spine broken, and to avoid this danger the hunter turns his kayak and himself bottom up. In that way the force of the breaking wave is taken on the keel, and after it has passed, he dexterously rights himself and his boat and paddles along until the trick has to be repeated.

As we rounded the point of the harbor, we saw that the natives had hurried to the crest of the hill to catch one last sight of us. They stood there, waving as long as they were in sight, and no one who has seen the Greenland people in their picturesque costumes standing and waving from a hill will ever forget the picture. The colors of their garments are those of nature herself, and they blend with the landscape so as to seem at once a part of it, and yet distinctly themselves.

Before we reached Godhavn we ran into the worst storm I have ever experienced. The way we and our gear were slung about would look comic in a film or sound amusing in a story, but I don't enjoy such moments. I merely try to act like a man who is in control of everything and remains unflustered no matter what happens.

In all my experience it seemed to me that I could not re-member a gale worse than this one, and what made it twice as bad was that I had Magdalene along with me. Since she had

never been in a storm like this she went along with me in the
trusting belief that I could manage such situations like no other
man in the world. When she found herself in the midst of such
a welter of wind and water as we were in that day, she merely
assumed that things were always like that in the Arctic.

Slowly, very slowly, we raised the mountains of Disko Island
and saw them grow up into the sky ahead of us. By the time we
reached the entrance to Godhavn Harbor we were both hungry
and tired, and how I did enjoy rounding that familiar point
and running into the lee of the peninsula!

It was all just as I remembered it.

3

THE COLONY ITSELF WAS ASLEEP BY THE TIME WE DROPPED ANCHOR,
but there were some children playing around the water front,
and they set up a shout when our boat appeared. No one had expected us to arrive at such an hour and with the weather what it
was, but soon many of the adults came down to meet us, and
even my old friend Thorsen, the local company manager,
derricked his huge body out of bed somehow and came to meet
us. How that man had expanded since I had last seen him!

His housekeeper turned out to be a woman with whom I
had danced when she was a girl. Now she had lost her teeth, and
with them, her looks. However, we had a thousand things to talk
over connected with the old days, and I must say that she took
wonderful care of both of us.

Mr. Bertelsen was at that time the governor of North Greenland, and I met him in Godhavn. He was a brilliant young man
who had been educated as a lawyer and appointed to the Greenland post for a sort of interim term while the regular governor
had a two-year sabbatical leave. It was a joy to me to sit and talk
to Mr. Bertelsen and listen to his intelligent conversation; all too
often there is an unexpressed hostility between those who come
up to the Arctic to visit and criticize everything they see and the
people who have lived in the North for many years. These
temporary visitors are known as "summermen," and no more
derogatory epithet can be applied to a man than that term.

Later I found the same sort of distinction drawn in Alaska, where the old-timers are proudly distinguished by the title of "sourdough."

Magdalene enjoyed her visits at the governor's house, and perhaps even more those we made at the home of Dr. Porsild. He was in charge of the scientific station maintained by the Danish government at Godhavn, and though he was away during the time of our visit Magdalene and Mrs. Porsild discussed the special problems of the Arctic housewife and never seemed to run out of material for conversation on that topic.

One particular change which had affected Greenland very deeply since I had lived there was the coming of the wireless. A powerful radio station had been erected, and Godhavn was the communications center, both radio and telegraph. The post was run by a Mr. Holten-Moller, and from him I had my first introduction into the whole field of radio and its potentialities. The natives looked on him as a sort of conjurer or wizard, and the white people admired him extravagantly. He was not only intelligent and kindly, but as a radioman he was in contact with the whole world and in consequence was rather more than ordinarily interested in international affairs and the outside world.

Another of Mr. Holten-Moller's interests was sport. He had introduced organized competition into the native community, and a real sports contest was scheduled while we were at Godhavn. I received a special invitation to the affair, and was even allowed to put up a few prizes.

One event on the program was kayak paddling, an art that ought not to be forgotten. Nowadays many of the younger boys have other things to do than learn this difficult skill, and likewise it is true that in some parts of Greenland skins for the boats are now hard to come by. But to encourage this traditional sport various prizes were offered at this Eskimo gymkhana for such special dexterities as turning around fast, paddling for speed, and the other stunts which are possible with these small and elegant vessels. The competitors in these events were not numerous, nor was their skill impressive, but they all got prizes.

Next came the running races. Eskimos are not built for running, but the contestants did what they could. The most amusing race here was the one for mothers carrying babies in their hoods. . . . The afternoon wagged along with equal pleasure for the contestants and the spectators until the shooting competition. Here the natives demonstrated that they could still be as childish as possible from the European point of view.

There were three prizes in the shooting competition: the first a pair of blue jeans from the store to fit the winner, the second two boxes of cartridges, and the third a cash award of two crowns. When the shooting was concluded the high man had scored a total of twenty points, and the blue jeans were clearly awardable to him. Next came two men who had tied at eighteen points each, and then a boy with a total of seventeen. In accordance with the preliminary regulation that in case of a tie the two deadlocked men should draw for the prize, the two men drew. One of them, of course, won, and so got the packages of cartridges.

But then the two-crown third prize was given to the boy with the score of seventeen!

The second-place man who had lost out on the draw for the prize felt that he had been betrayed. He had shot better than the boy who got the money, and he demanded that he receive the third prize. The case was put up to me for arbitration, and I decided that the second man with the score of eighteen was entitled to the prize money. This decision occasioned a roar from the crowd and a near riot.

The reactions of these innocent natives were worth observing. They talked and talked in such voices that you would have thought an invading army had landed on their beach. Some of them came to me and argued the matter. Even God was brought into it before long, for one of the amateur logicians declared the man who had drawn the shorter slip had been singled out by his Heavenly Father. He had shot a score of eighteen, all right, but obviously, "God did not want him to win the cartridges. If He had, the man would have drawn the longer slip." The fact that seventeen was the third score was what caused most of the confusion. If seventeen was the third-best score, by Eskimo logic the man who had shot it was entitled to the third prize.

I tried to counter this confusing suggestion by talking about shooting ability, urging that the three best shots were entitled to the three prizes, and attempted to explain that this settlement I had made was the way it was always handled in similar cases elsewhere.

"It may be all right to settle things that way among white men," was the answer, "but not here among *human beings!*"

One friend of mine at Godhavn whom I was careful to visit was Mathias Broberg, an old Eskimo who by this time had become blind and who was now almost wholly alone. Only his old friends remembered him, and never did Knud or I visit Godhavn but what we went to see him every day that we were there. He looked like an old hero resting and retired, happy in the honors which had been bestowed upon him, and if there were more justice in the world that would indeed have been his position.

When we chugged out of Godhavn we believed that we were well supplied with food, for Mr. Thorsen and his Mete had given us enough delicacies to last for an entire day and we did not expect the trip to take any longer than that. On this point we were uncomfortably mistaken.

We stopped briefly at Skansen and, later, at the settlement of Ujarassusuk.

The weather was not looking any too promising, and though the coal mine at Kutligssat was not far away we began to be afraid that the wind, which was freshening out of the west, might prevent us from landing. There is no harbor at all near the mine, and since the wind definitely turned against us as we chugged along, we decided that it would be wisest to find a sheltered anchorage rather than continue. The only possible place was behind a promontory a few miles short of the mine, and we finally agreed that Magdalene and I would land there and walk alongshore to the mine itself.

By this time we were definitely hungry. The trip had taken longer than we expected, and our provisions had been divided with our native crew, who had not figured into Mete's calculations back in Godhavn when she was supplying our food. It is sad but true that when you hire a crew in Greenland to take you somewhere or other, even if you warn them that they are to bring their own provisions and pay them to do so they will still expect you to feed them. If you do not, they carry on with empty stomachs, but the looks they cast on you when you cook and eat your own meals, and the way they gobble up the remainders, will always touch your heart.

The captain of our motorboat was a man named Karl Tygesen, a former traveling companion of mine and one with whom I had more fun than many another. After he first met Magdalene he had taken me aside and admitted that he had been afraid I would be spoiled and as snobbish as the rest of his white friends when they married white women. But no. "Your wife is just like the rest of us, and as good as she is beautiful."

No higher praise was in Karl Tygesen's power.

The time came for us to part from him and go ashore. Aboard the boat the last piece of bread had been eaten, but Karl said that they would all sleep and as soon as the weather calmed they could run on to Kutligssat, carrying our luggage, and stock up on provisions there for their return to Godhavn.

Magdalene and I were put ashore with difficulty because of the surf, but once we had the firm ground under our feet we felt safe and began to enjoy the world around us—the fine grass, the blooming flowers, and the sun. Magdalene told me how happy she felt to be along on this trip and we even sat down from time to time to listen to the songs of the snow buntings and other birds, whose voices were everywhere. By and by we came to a small creek which we forded but which made us look to our footing. But even that was fun, and so, too, was the next little stream. After that we came to one that amounted to a young river, with fast-running water and full of slippery stones. Magdalene did not like the look of it, and I got her across after I located a fordable spot only by assuring her that this was positively the last stream we should encounter.

In a short while I was proved a liar, for we came upon still another which was even worse. These summer rivers were no joke. In a streaming freshet like each of those we encountered, with the water coming down from mountain heights and running at full speed, it is impossible for anyone to stand up if the water comes above the knees. The pressure simply bowls you over.

This particular river looked bad. Under the surface there was nothing but round and rolling stones which offered no footing. The stream was broad, and we had to wade and wade, looking for a fordable place. Magdalene had to be careful, and I was having none too easy a time managing myself and trying to help her. Suddenly she exclaimed that she was dizzy, and, being sure that was due to staring at the racing water, I told her to look away from it and up into the sky. She did so, mistook her footing and would have been swept away if I had not caught her.

In this unpleasant fix I could not help comparing her with Navarana. She and Magdalene were two of a kind; they never blamed me, but kept fighting ahead for all they were worth.

It took us a long time and a weary amount of effort to get back to the bank of the river from which we had started. The moment we reached firm ground Magdalene sat down and rested; she was practically at the end of her resources. And we had seven rivers yet to cross for the second time if we headed back to the boat. It looked like a hopeless prospect. All this time, ironically, we could see the powerboat far out on the water, and it looked like the most desirable craft in the world to us. Aboard her were bunks where we could sleep and be warm. Cold, wet, and hungry, we sat and simply stared at her for a while, and then took up the trail back. Every river we had crossed had to be reforded, and they were running deeper by this time. Magdalene, who was wet through, had the worst of it; each new trip into that numbing glacier water felt colder to her than the one before, and to make matters worse a wind sprang up and cut right through our clothes.

Magdalene was brave and managed to keep going, but the river crossings were almost too much for her. Even when we returned to the landing place our path was far from smooth. The swell had augmented and the surf was so high that though the men aboard the launch could see us, they were unable to come ashore and pick us up. There were now two craft lying off shore, for while we had been walking the boat of the doctor at Jacobshavn had come up. Like our own, it had been bound for Kutligssat, and, recognizing the impossibility of landing there, it had taken shelter under the lee of the same promontory. Karl Tygesen and one of his men first tried to come in to us in the dinghy from his boat, but it was promptly swamped, and he had all he could do to save himself and his man. Then he took the skiff from the doctor's boat and tried again, but there was clearly no possibility of landing, and he had to turn around and go back.

We watched these attempts to reach us with anxiety and impatience, standing on the beach in the cold wind and wishing we had something to eat. When the second attempt to land a boat had failed we resigned ourselves to a long wait. There was nothing to do but lie down and try to keep as warm and quiet as possible. I gathered some grass, and we bunked up against each other to keep warm.

So ended my first whole day alone with Magdalene in the country where she believed I had mastered everything.

About twenty-four hours after we had eaten our last bite of food we suddenly became aware that a man was standing close to us. We must have been dozing for a while. At any rate, it was Karl Tygesen, who had finally landed but wrecked his dinghy in doing so. He had no food with him, and the only news he brought was that the doctor's crew had told him that it was no use trying to walk along the coast toward the mine because the rivers at this season were unfordable.

Six more hours went by, and then the sea had calmed enough for the crew of the doctor's boat to land and pick us up. They proved to be not overstocked with food themselves, but they did have some dreadful coffee, which tasted like hot nectar to us, and some flinty store biscuits which Magdalene could scarcely chew but which she declared were delicious. We went below for some sleep, and when we waked the weather was calm enough to start the motors and go on to the mine. There we received a hospitable reception, a wonderful meal, and warm beds. The luxury of all this was indescribably agreeable, and in a short time we were ourselves again.

While Magdalene was talking with the manager's wife I went out to visit some of the workers at the mine.

The miners at Kutligssat were far from a miserable lot. They looked happy and lived in fine small houses. Most of them had dogs and hunting gear which they used on Sundays. There was a store in the settlement, with good merchandise at fair prices on its shelves. All in all, I was impressed with their condition.

Next day Knud Rasmussen arrived with his daughter, Inge. It had been three years since I had traveled with him or since we had been any place together, really, except Denmark. Our reunion was exuberant. We were both in the mood to go off at once and renew our youth. Any sort of trip together appealed to us, but the first opportunity to present itself was a rather melancholy one.

Knud informed me he had word that an aunt of his who lived at the head of a nearby fjord was sick, and he proposed that we should start together at once to see her. It would be like the old days, when we had the world by the tail, to travel together. As the first step he commandeered the governor's motorboat and ordered Karl Tygesen to take us to Qeqertaq, where his aunt lived.

When I heard him start off in this highhanded way I held

up a warning finger and told him that this was not cricket. The governor was too fine a man for us to snitch his boat in this fashion, and besides, hadn't we both grown older? We could not behave as we used to in the old days. Knud demolished these arguments with his special brand of logic. If the governor was as fine a man as I claimed he would be glad to lend us his boat and so reunite a sick aunt with her beloved nephew. Then, suddenly a kayakman arrived and announced that Knud's aunt was dead.

Knud promptly decided that the funeral would take place immediately instead of after four days. "Since I could not get to my aunt in time to see her alive," he said, "I at least want to stand beside her grave."

He told all the natives to come along at once, for his time was limited. We loaded our boat with as many as possible, told the rest to hurry along in their skin boats, and set out.

Mikkel, Knud's nephew by adoption, received us in proper fashion. He told us about the old lady's last hours, and he, too, said that the funeral had been set for four days hence. Knud protested that decision, said that we were able to be present only this one day, and that the ceremony would have to take place at once. He hired a group of men to dig a grave immediately, and quite a job it was in frozen soil. He put three carpenters to work making a coffin.

That was the sort of man Knud was; he could do anything and everything. And he did not forget a single detail; he ordered food from the settlement across the fjord and saw to it that everyone had a real meal. The coffee was to be served after we left because we had to make haste, and coffee drinking is a ceremony of some duration in Greenland.

As the time for the funeral approached the population filed past the dead woman lying in her coffin, with her strong, thin face looking as if she were asleep. Silent tears were shed in many an instance. Knud Rasmussen delivered a eulogy and funeral oration before the coffin was lowered into the earth. He spoke about the time he had come here to visit his uncle; he reminded his hearers of the great catches of seals and white whales which his uncle, and later his aunt, had organized. He paid full tribute to the past, and then, as the natives sang a slow hymn, the grave was filled in.

We had to leave at once, so Knud arranged the customary

kaffeeklatsch in a special way. He bought the coffee himself, as there was no use in allowing the trader to profiteer on it, and had two large pots placed over heaped-up fires. Then the entire amount of coffee was cooked in those pots. (Thus no one was tempted to hold out some of the beans for his or her personal use later.) While the fires were crackling and the coffee boiling in the caldrons Knud gave a farewell address.

The whole village went along after us, and we thought they were merely accompanying us to say good-by. But just as we were about to let go the bow and stern lines some of them asked us where they were to go to get paid? We inquired what payment they meant. Then it developed that they had all regarded themselves as hired attendants at the funeral, the proof of which was that Knud himself had asked them to join the group, had brought some of them here in his own boat, and had told the rest to hurry up.

There was a crowd of about a hundred people claiming this pay, and it was a large group for this part of the world. The money to buy them all off would run high.

Suddenly Knud jumped ashore and began his third speech of the occasion. The words came from his lips in a steady stream, and though he rarely lost his temper this was one of the times when he did, and to good effect. He began by advising them to go back up the bank and get their coffee, because this coffee party was the last he would ever give at this place. He hoped that sometime they would realize the loss they had sustained by his aunt's death and come to regret this behavior of theirs. They hadn't the faintest hope of any payment from him, but they had succeeded in making him angry and erasing all the good memories he had of Qeqertaq.

At once a torrent of voices broke out, all protesting that he should not vent his anger at them. They did not want any money—that was merely something foolish their tongues had said. If Knud felt unhappy about the matter nothing could persuade them to accept a thing from him. They must have expressed themselves in the wrong fashion; what they had meant was that if Knud had by any chance intended to give them something by way of recompense for missing a day's hunting they were willing to accept it.

After this face-saving answer to Knud's tirade they streamed

up the hill again to the coffee caldrons, and we cast off our lines
and headed away from the dock.

The best friend Knud and I had in all Greenland, a native
named "Little Jonas," lived at Proeven. He was a small man, as
his name suggests, but an important figure in his community for
all of that. In the old days he had been a great hunter and a fine
provider, though we always thought that his industriousness was
largely due to his wife, Agathe, who was a strong lady of high
character, endowed with little charm but a notably speedy
tongue. She had only one tooth left in her mouth, but it showed
every time she spoke, and she was always speaking.

Jonas and Agathe had no children of their own, but their
home was always filled with relatives and protégés. (It was, by
the way, the only house in the entire settlement with a proper
roof.) In it Jonas now received Knud and myself as if we were
kings, while Magdalene and Inge were instantly accepted as if
they were his own daughters. Cakes and coffee were promptly
forthcoming, and even a bottle of liquor—a substance that made
Jonas smile with pleasure even when he was only thinking about
it. However, he touched not a drop himself—not as long as there
was a ship in the harbor.

Jonas had an important duty to fulfill, one that required a
clear head. He was the self-appointed port watchman for the
nights when vessels were berthed at Proeven.

"When the king sends us up ships," said Jonas once, to explain
his unrequired services, "with food and guns and clothes, it
would be bad if something went wrong here in our harbor. So
long as I am awake nothing serious can happen!"

Sometimes his motive in hanging around the ships was mis-
construed. Young mates who did not know him would think he
was just another man who wanted a job; they did not understand
that he was on duty merely out of a sense of pride and responsibility. Once while he was standing his self-imposed watch a cook
on one boat had ordered him to clean a mess of fish. Of course
Jonas had cleaned fish when he was a boy, but since that remote
time he had always had somebody to do things like that for him,
and the cook's order was, from Jonas' point of view, an insult.
Still, he felt that the man could not know who he was, and he
cleaned the fish as a sort of joke.

Next morning when the mate discovered that he had done
it on top of one of the hatches, inevitably dirtying one of the tar-
paulins in the process, Jonas received a powerfully worded repri-
mand in the best nautical manner.

Silently Little Jonas listened to the tirade. When it was over
he answered in his own tongue, "Well, I perceive that you are
mad! Well, well, I can let it pass this time, because you are perhaps kinder on other mornings." Nothing could disturb the little
man in his cheerful philosophy and sense of importance.

When the time came for Knud and me to go on to Upernivik,
Little Jonas insisted upon accompanying us.

There were some changes at Upernivik since my day; a new
church, many fine modern houses, and even a graded road from
the colony down to the harbor. But the people were the same as
ever, poor and too lazy to hunt, but eager and industrious at begging and thinking up hard-luck stories. I knew every one of the
inhabitants, and all their stories.

The manager of the post there, Mr. Lemche-Otto, and his
wife were beyond all competition the finest hosts in Greenland.
We arrived late at night, when everyone was in bed, but nothing
could prevent Mrs. Lemche-Otto from getting up, hustling her
cook and maids out of their beds, and preparing a dinner with
all the trimmings—many courses, wines, and every delicacy
possible.

Next morning I took Magdalene with me to see the grave
of Navarana. It was situated high on top of the hill overlooking
the colony, and its beautiful tombstone marked it out from
the other graves.

From Upernivik we continued toward Thule on a small vessel,
the *Doris*. My old friend Captain Pedersen was aboard, and so
was Axel Ahlman, the Swedish author. He was an old friend of
Knud's, too, and had written and lectured about him and his
exploits for years. Now for the first time he had come to look
at this part of the Arctic, about which he had written and studied
for so many years.

That cabin was far from commodious; it was a problem to
know how to stow ourselves in it. On the way across the Atlantic,
Axel Ahlman had slept in the bunk there, and Captain Pedersen, whose status this summer was that of pilot, had occupied
the mate's cabin. The mate, suitably recompensed for the discomfort and loss of dignity, had been berthed with the crew. In

the end he was fortunate, for he had at least a bed of his own, and the same could not be said for any of the rest of us.

There were fourteen passengers aboard and just one small bunk to divide among the lot. Such a situation called forth all the organizing genius of Knud Rasmussen. He marshaled us around with laughter and a joke for every inconvenience, and finally we settled down after a fashion. Magdalene and Inge slept together in the captain's berth, while Miss Jacobsen, a young nurse who was going up to the hospital at Thule, drew the captain's sofa. Knud and an Eskimo selected the floor of the cabin for their beds, and the tiny room was stuffed to the limit. The air in there was so thick you could have cut it with a knife, but Knud lent a courtly atmosphere to the whole proceeding by serving tea, of a morning, to the ladies in their beds, and we were all too lighthearted to object to minor discomforts.

Anyhow, there was no trouble about getting to sleep the first night, not after the strenuous hospitality of the Lemche-Ottos. Everyone slept twelve solid hours.

I myself chose to sleep in the open air out on deck. Most of the time it was glorious out there, and whenever it became rainy or cold I could crawl under a tarpaulin. I shared my quarters underneath it with an Eskimo who was on his way north to visit some relatives. It was hard for me to sleep, though, for we were bound up to Melville Bay and Thule, the country which meant more to me than any other.

Captain Pedersen sat beside me on deck, and we talked of how many contrasting aspects Melville Bay can have under different weather conditions and seasons of the year.

It is a treacherous piece of water; it is known as "the whaler's graveyard," though on this trip we did not see a single piece of floating ice outside the inevitable bergs. The motor tramped us steadily along, and we made our northing with no hindrance whatever.

After a while fog set in, and fog is the worst conceivable thing to encounter in northern seas, because navigation has to rely so much on the eyes of the pilot. One can never be sure of precise directions, and then there is the hazard of the icebergs. The only way of avoiding them is to call to them, that is, blow the ship's siren. If a berg is lying nearby it throws the sound back from the direction in which it is situated, and it is astonishing how distinctly you can "hear" icebergs in this way.

We sailed ahead very slowly; the fog, formed of incalculable billions of minute ice crystals in the air, pressed close around us and produced a sort of white rainbow which made vision doubly difficult. Once in a while, as we approached some huge berg, the mist would brighten into a white glow of warning, and we would sheer off cautiously. In this way we proceeded for hours, Captain Pedersen and I talking and looking out into the fog. At last I fell asleep.

Ice and fog should not alarm a man whose business it is to navigate through them, but I did not like the fact that we were unable to tell precisely where we were. Suddenly, as Pedersen and I were chatting, up forward, a glow of light seemed to come up around the ship and I realized that we had begun to run into floe ice. I went to the skylight and called down into the cabin that we had run into ice. Those below seemed to think it was a good joke. They hurried up on deck, though—Magdalene, Inge, and Miss Jacobsen in nightdresses and fur coats—and took a look. After a moment or two they remarked that it was a poor show and went below once more. We heard them singing and laughing down there.

Good show or not, the masses of ice around us were growing larger. We might have backed out easily enough when we first entered the field, but as we turned and twisted to escape we only encountered more and more floes. Evidently there was a movement in the pack itself, and we knew that pack ice could move faster than a vessel caught in it. Bump and punch and sneak and push as we could, we were caught fast, and it was no pleasant situation.

Almost without warning a gigantic iceberg came towering straight up against us. Crew and passengers were summoned on deck, and we stood watching its tremendous approach, closer and closer. At last it was almost within arm's length; a fragment of ice from its cliff-steep flank fell onto our foredeck and crushed some of the gear there.

Then, as if it had meant only to give us a warning, it abruptly changed its course and drifted off to port.

This last-minute reprieve caused us all to draw several deep breaths. As a matter of fact, the incident was a great stroke of luck, for there was a considerable patch of clear water in the wake of the berg, and without hesitation we picked up speed and entered it. We deduced that the pack ice in which we had been

trapped was not a general condition but rather a field of floes
rounded up by the action of several great bergs moving in the
same general direction, and this did indeed prove to be the case.
After several hours we came upon comparatively spread ice and
were able to proceed at reduced speed but in safety. Soon the fog
began to lift and we made out the familiar shape of Cape York
far out on our horizon.

For the last night and day of the trip we sailed steadily along
a well-known coast where Knud and I had hunted and trapped
during the many winters of our life at Thule. When Saunders
Island hove in sight I called for all the party to come on deck;
we were due to raise Thule Mountain in half an hour. They
came up from below and we stood together for the last hour of
the voyage.

4

MAGDALENE WAS KEEPING A KEEN LOOKOUT FOR MEQUSAQ, AND
finally a native boat came out to our ship. The Eskimos were
dressed in their finest—white anoraks, white bearskin pants, and
white sealskin kamiks, and there among them was Mequsaq,
sitting aft beside the man at the tiller. He was the great man of
this occasion, of course; his parents were coming to see him.

But when Mequsaq came on deck he just looked at us and
then ran forward to join the rest of the children in the party,
which had come aboard en masse. Magdalene was disappointed
by his manners, and perhaps hurt; she could not realize that this
was his Eskimo way of prolonging the happy feeling inside him.

I understood how he felt, and for a time we let him go, but
then the more prominent of the natives were invited aft to take
coffee with us, and I went to get him.

"My future hunting companion," I addressed him, "somebody here wants to see you!"

Without turning his head he replied, "Why? Are not any
present older and wiser? Don't talk to the young ones!"

In spite of this modest speech I dragged him along with me,
and he was happy to be compelled to go down into the cabin and
sit with us.

But it was the same story later on, after we had gone ashore.

I took Magdalene into my old home, and between the interruptions of everyone in the settlement who crowded in to talk to me, I showed her the place where I had lived so long. Then it was time to go visiting, take a look at the children who had been born since I was last there, and listen to stories of success and the inevitable complaints. The first house to which we went was that of Enok and Palika, with whom Mequsaq lived.

Even in so familiar a place as his own home Mequsaq's shyness kept him from joining us. He played outside the house and was not to be persuaded into coming in with us.

His foster parents told us that when the news we were coming came in the day before, via radio, Mequsaq could not stop talking and singing, and he did not sleep that night. When his elders told him to keep quiet he replied that it was impossible because his father and mother were coming to see him. Yet, after such intense anticipation, he ran away from us and hid himself!

It was a typical example of Eskimo psychology.

It was only after the day was ended, though of course it was light up there even at night. Mequsaq entered the room where Magdalene and I were sleeping. We did not hear him come in because he walked on tiptoe, but we knew that he had come because he placed himself on the bed right between us and on top of the blankets. The entire night long I felt his little hand in mine while we lay there.

I had told Magdalene that on no account was any of our visitors to be allowed to depart without having had something to eat or drink. She had only a primus stove on which to cook, and her civilized notions of sanitation made hospitality quite a chore. She insisted on washing a cup each time it was used, although to serve every visitor with a clean cup was an innovation in Thule and something generally regarded as impossible. The women sat round and marveled at her, but she stuck to it, washing each cup or plate before it was used again. They pointed out to newcomers what a peculiarly fine woman they were visiting—she had her singular habits of course, notably the curious one of washing everything before it was used!

I tried to explain to her how much unnecessary work she was making for herself, but she was not to be dissuaded, and there she sat, brewing tea, baking pancakes, and serving them to my old friends hour after hour. She seemed to enjoy it, and certainly she made a great impression on all of them, especially on my onetime traveling partner Inukitsork. He was staying at Thule for the time being and was quite captivated by Magdalene. At every meal we had he felt it his duty to assist by eating as much as he could and by bringing in as many people to introduce to us as he could find. He never grew weary of recommending Magdalene's food, and above all, her quaint way of serving it.

In fact, he told us both that he had fallen in love with her.

"If it happens," he said, "that you, Peterssuaq, feel somewhat tired of her for a while, I should be more than happy if you felt like staying with my miserable wife Tukumerk. I will take care of Magdalene as long as you like!"

Of course Magdalene was flattered by this Eskimo compliment. However, we had to tell him that while he was welcome in our house, and while we liked him, there was a certain limit that had to be drawn. Inukitsork was not the man to take even so mild a rebuff without protecting his personal pride.

"Well," he observed finally, "anyway, I hope you both understand that this is the most forceful way I have to express my appreciation of Magdalene!"

That evening he went out in his kayak and was gone for hours. He returned late the following morning with a real Eskimo delicacy, a supply of year-old *mattak*, or white-whale skin, by this time in a thoroughly ripe condition, as may be imagined. With this *mattak* as the *pièce de résistance*, he invited the whole settlement to a party in Magdalene's honor.

During the two days that the rest of them were out at Saunders Island, Mequsaq and I went up to the head of the inlet to pick up some meat which had been cached there early in the spring. Some of my friends went with us, and we spent the night shooting geese and eating seals, and life offers no more agreeable way of passing the time.

I had hoped we should get a narwhal on this trip, for I very much wanted Magdalene to taste one while the meat was still fresh. Luck was not with us there, but it was in another respect, for while we were paddling along too close under the lee of the glacier wall a huge block of ice fell off it and missed us by an eyelash. Had it landed on our boat there would have been no trace of us left, and as it was the splash raised a wave that half swamped the craft. In the excitement the two young fellows who were doing the rowing dropped their oars and they floated away from us. Now being in a boat without oars is bad enough at any time, but doubly so when you are drifting under the overhang of a glacier that may shed an iceberg on your head at any second.

In this emergency we tried paddling with our hands, but that did not produce much in the way of speed, and it occurred to me that it would be a good idea to break up two of the bottom boards of our boat and use them for paddles. Nobody had anything to say against this suggestion for they all considered that I was the proper person to make decisions. Was not I a man who had been to far countries and knew more than they ever should?

So I wrenched up one of the bottom boards with my bare hands. Unfortunately, I discovered that in this boat the bottom boards had been nailed directly onto the planking of the outer hull by large nails. Furthermore, the planks of the hull had been worn to paper thinness by repeated scraping against the ice. So when I wrenched up the board for a paddle, I instantly made a large hole in the outer skin of the boat, through which gushed a torrent of icy water.

There were seven of us in the craft, and at the rate the water was coming in we should have sunk in a hurry, had not Boatsman, with real presence of mind, seized one of the small boys in the party and jammed him stern first into the hole in the bottom of the boat. His shape fitted the opening nicely, and this variation on the story of the Dutch boy who held his thumb in the hole in the dike worked well. However, Boatsman had to sit on the small boy to keep him in place, for the water in the neighborhood of that glacier was painfully cold.

With my single board, secured at such a drastic cost, I paddled away for all I was worth, and managed to get the boat within reaching distance of one of the lost oars. With that we were able to get out of range of the falling ice and eventually, after some hours, to shore.

It was on Mequsaq's account that I decided not to go on the trip up to the icecap which Knud Rasmussen had arranged during our visit. Our days in Thule were few enough without leaving Mequsaq for several of them. Magdalene went, however, and it was a real adventure for her. I saw the party off; her sled had a boy named Miteng for driver, and the loads were so light that she was able to ride all the time except when the going was over rock or loose stones. Even when there was no snow it was possible for them to ride as long as there was grass under the runners.

Wisely enough, Knud had cut the equipment down to an absolute minimum. Their sleeping bags were only of blankets, and thin ones at that. Magdalene told me later that during the first night's halt she got up, put on all her skin clothes again, and never undressed for the rest of the trip. Another thing that surprised them not too pleasantly was the rigor of Knud's discipline on this trip. He forbade them to use more than a single lump of sugar in their tea, limited the amount of bread they were allowed, and rationed the supplies in careful earnest.

They began to see that the easiest sort of expedition life is sitting at home reading about it. Conditions on the icecap were very different from the comparatively warm valley where they had started. After traversing glaciers and glacier streams they found themselves in a world where everything was freezing and, summer though it was, snow was drifting. They finally returned full of their new experiences and knowledge, and proud of having traveled to the Greenland icecap.

We who had stayed behind hurried up the hill to meet them as they came back, and that evening a party was organized to celebrate their return. Axel Ahlman made a speech in Swedish, and the rest of us in Eskimo, and things were going strong. There is no telling how long the affair might have lasted, had not a gale suddenly sprung up from the southwest.

From that quarter of the compass it can come on to blow so hard that no one can stand against it, and in less than an hour at that. So we all hurried off in diverse directions to make what preparations we could against what was coming.

Magdalene and I had the best of it—we were living in my old house, which had weathered so many gales in the past. We stood inside and watched the force of the storm; right while we did so we saw Knud's tent lifted away from over him; he was sitting inside it drinking coffee with a few friends. The moment his tent blew away, all his blankets, books, papers, and utensils went streaming after it, and even the coffeepot was blown bumping along over the stones. Knud was able to save nothing except himself; he did manage to make his way into a house nearby. A little later a beached boat was lifted into the air like a balloon, and though it was built of heavy planks it was slung from rock to rock by the storm and smashed to pieces.

So there we sat in my house, and Mequsaq with us. Each time a powerful gust shook the building he would grab my hands and laugh with joy. Because his parents were there he felt that he was perfectly safe.

Inukitsork declared that this was the first summer gale of the year. Just after the ice had gone out that spring they had had a minor blow, nothing like this, which had almost given them all cause to mourn. Mequsaq was the reason for their alarm.

When Hans Nielsen, the trader, received a radio message saying that Magdalene and I had started for Greenland, he told the rest of the settlement at once, and there was, Inukitsork said, a good deal of happiness, and most of all on the part of Mequsaq. He laughed and chattered and kept asking when our ship would be visible round the cape out to the west. Probably none of them there really knew, and in any case they did not explain things to him. Whether his yearning got the better of him or he actually believed that we were coming any hour I don't know, but while the rest of them were sitting around talking about me and what kind of wife I had got for myself, Mequsaq quietly disappeared.

When the tents began to flap at the approach of this spring blow they looked around for the boy and he was not there. It was discovered quickly that he had taken a kayak; Tine, his adopted sister, spotted him far out in the water, paddling away. How he got the boat into the water is a mystery, but somehow he had managed it. These northern Eskimos do not have covered or decked kayaks of the sort commonly associated with Eskimos. Their boats are open and of course with a very low freeboard, so that it is impossible to use them in the slightest sea. And now, there was Mequsaq, far out from shore in a strong wind. Nobody dared go after him. Since he was down wind, it might have been possible to reach him, but how could they get back against the wind, and how tow his craft?

There was nothing for it but to hurry over to the other side of the peninsula, where the trading post had its boat on the beach. They all did so at once, and several men went out in her after the boy. By the time they reached the place where he was last seen he had gone much farther. Inukitsork said that it took them as long as it takes the sun "to go from a man's nose to his ear" to reach him. All the way out the men had talked of how angry they were with the boy, and of how to punish him, but when they caught up with him they could not retain their anger.

He was so little, and yet he was not tired, but paddling strongly along, and when the boat came up to him he merely shouted:

"One is trying to meet his relatives!"

It was clear, Inukitsork observed, that his longing for our ship was greater than his fear of the wind.

While I was still talking about this escape of Mequsaq's a man came in the door of our house. It must have been a difficult thing for him to have crossed the peninsula from the native encampment in the teeth of that wind, but his face showed that something had happened. He told us what it was; old Asivak had gone. The wind had taken her and blown her over the edge of a cliff into the sea, and now she was dead and even her body was lost.

The man, whose name was Kraviak, said that the poor old woman had gone out into the storm to try to save some meat which she had been drying. To keep it away from the dogs she had put it right on the edge of the cliff, but as the wind blew harder and harder she began to worry about its being lost. In spite of the warnings of everyone, she crawled out on her hands and knees to attend to it; that meat may well have been the only thing she had in the world.

They saw her reach the place where it was, and bend over. Then the wind seemed to lift her into the air and she disappeared over the edge of the cliff. The rest of them hurried out to try to help her, and the first to arrive on the scene saw her body below them, lying on the rocks. Then it was swept away by the current.

"Alas!" they said, "nobody will ever get her again, no grave receive her old bones and give her a rest in her great sleep."

Poor old Asivak! I remembered her well. She and I used to have plenty of fun together in the old days. She had been a sort of local fortuneteller and diviner of future events, but since my last time in these parts the radio had been invented, and her importance in the community had consequently declined.

Her great-grandchildren were her only joy in life, and she had been consoling herself also with the thought that when Peter came he would give her a new woolen shirt. (That used to be her standard fee for forecasting the summer ships.) She also told the little great-grandchildren that her tent would be full of sugar and tea and biscuits, hoping to bribe them to sleep with her instead of with their mother. She promised them that if they would only open their mouths while they were asleep she would stay awake and put sugar lumps between their lips, and when they felt those they would realize that their great-grandmother was a friend of a white man.

Luckily I did just happen to have a woolen shirt for her, and she got two boxes of sugar and some small biscuits into the bargain. So the children really came to her and slept in her tent, and their mother was pleased, too, for when she wanted to visit us or walk down to look at the ship she could leave them safely with the old woman.

The meat which old Asivak dried was the only thing that was really her own, and which she could give as a personal gift. In trying to save it she had lost her life, and in her perished one of the last Eskimos familiar with the ancient traditions of her nation. Her life had been a long, hard fight against nature, and in the end, nature had conquered. She must have been attractive as a young girl; at any rate, men had desired her, both white whalers and native hunters. She had given birth to sons and daughters and had worked hard all her life, only to see her children die before she did. Her last surviving close relatives were her young granddaughter and grandson.

Magdalene and I felt that on the whole Mequsaq was in good hands. The man with whom he lived, Enok, was a missionary from down south. He was no educated man, but a simple hunter from Jacobshavn who believed earnestly in God and wanted to spread the seeds of his simple faith farther north. So he had come to Jens Olsen's bailiwick at Thule. As often happens, he had begun to relax the intensity of his fervor and was becoming rather more like other men as time went by. He and his wife Palika were devoted to Mequsaq.

On this visit Mequsaq had showed himself specially fond of Magdalene, much more so than he had before when he was in Denmark with us. While she was away on the trip to the icecap he kept saying that now she would not be back until the next year, only to have us assure him to the contrary. He refused to eat because she was not there, and fasted for a whole day.

It was difficult to know what was best for him. I knew that nowhere in the world were people as happy as here in Greenland, so why take him home to Denmark, educate him, and expose him to all the evils from which we ourselves suffered?

Before our departure there was to be a real feast to celebrate the official opening of the new hospital and the raising of the Danish flag over it. For many of the guests, who had come from afar, a real meal was served. It was the staple of the time and place, walrus meat, cut up into big chunks and boiled in large pots. Four women acted as cooks and kept the fires going by stoking them with chunks of blubber and peat, and every time one of their pots came to a boil they yelled out the glad tidings. The condition of the meat was judged by stabbing it with a fork, or simply with the fingers.

Those who did not like their meat too well boiled could have it *abasok*—which meant practically raw. The rest waited only a little longer. As soon as any pot was ready the chunks of meat were forked up and placed on big stones beside the fires to keep warm, and cups of the thick, fat-covered blood soup were dipped out of the pots and handed round. Each man sipped as much as he wanted and handed the cup along to his neighbor. Though it may not sound so, this soup is actually delicious and tastes something like chocolate.

What a happy people these were, who could eat the same thing every day and yet enjoy it enormously on occasions like this because it is eaten under novel surroundings!

At eleven o'clock of the day following the start of the festivities, and while things were still going strong, Captain Pedersen warned us that the ice condition was favorable and that the *Doris* would start in two hours. We had to pack our things in a hurry and get aboard as soon as possible; all of us scrambled about, making last-minute preparations.

While Magdalene and I were throwing our things together little Mequsaq sat on the edge of the bed and watched us. It was only at this eleventh hour that he realized he actually was going to be left behind and that Magdalene and I would be gone very soon. For two hours he sat watching us.

"Father go, Mother go, Mequsaq no go," he kept saying over and over, hoping against hope that we would contradict him.

When we piled all our gifts for him on a sled, so that they could be taken to Bibiat's house, he became somewhat consoled. There was a canvas tent for him, boxes of cookies and candies, fine cakes of soap, and everything we could think of. As the load piled up the natives began to gather round, and Mequsaq, in the old and generous Eskimo way, began to divide what he had with them. Magdalene came out just in time to prevent him from handing out his canned goods and glasses of jam. We told the natives not to let him part with anything; he was to give the entire load to Bibiat so that she could dole the things out to him during the winter.

I had told him that I was coming back next year, and the promise had helped ease his grief, but it was plain that he was heartbroken at being left behind. I could see him, from the deck of the *Doris,* standing stiffly on the beach, not waving at us and scarcely looking at the boat except for occasional glances out of the corners of his eyes to see if we were really going. If the vessel had not got swiftly under way at that very moment I might have called to him to come aboard with us and go home to Denmark.

Yet it was best for him to remain there.

His tragedy was in being too much of an Eskimo to be happy in Denmark, and too much of a Dane to be wholly satisfied in Greenland.

5

SO IT WAS THAT WE LEFT THULE, MY GREENLAND HOME. THE *Doris* slid along, out through the fjord I knew better than any other in the world.

All the arrangements for a film expedition I was to head the following year had been made in satisfactory style. Boatsman was to be my right-hand man, and he was to provide for an adequate number of native-style dwellings at Neqé, where I had decided to establish the camp. He himself would be on hand the next year with the necessary equipment, dogs, sleds, and all the rest. Everything would be ready for us when we came back and I felt satisfied that things would be in shape for the movie people, comforting myself in my feeling of loneliness with the thought of that expedition to come.

The sun shone steadily as we chugged into Upernivik harbor. Fat Sofie had pancakes waiting for us, and in spite of knowing that I was soon to sit down to a full meal, I did not dare refuse her. Along with the pancakes we had a running recital of her troubles, and this time one of them was serious. It centered in my adopted son, Peter, the son of an old friend of mine who had died.

It appeared that she had expected Peter to marry her daughter Susa, and she did have some reason to expect him to obey her wishes, since she had kept house for his father for years and felt herself entitled to Peter's respect and obedience. Peter had been led astray and had married a girl named Maria at Proeven. Maria's father, Augustinus, who had once been a great family friend, was the devil—according to Sofie—who had brought all this trouble upon her.

Things would not have been so bad, even then, if Susa had not bragged about her approaching marriage far and wide. The news that her prospective bridegroom had already taken another wife made her lose caste, and in a fit of pique she had gone off as a servant on a summer hunting trip with some of the employees of the trading post. She had a wonderful time on this trip, of course, and the evidence of that fact appeared the following spring in the form of twins. Unfortunately, neither of the two men whom she could identify as the probable father of her babies was eligible as a husband. One, a young Danish assistant manager, had already been discharged and sent home to Denmark. The other was a young carpenter, a good fellow whom she would have been glad to have, but he had gone and married another girl at Christmastime and was now out of the question. Poor Susa had nothing but trouble out of her situation, and to add to it, one of the twins died, and the young carpenter insisted that it was the one which he had sired, declaring that the other was the child of the absent Dane. I sent for young Peter to come and justify himself if he could.

His story was a sad one.

Upon arriving at Proeven he was ordered to repair a couple of boats there. All the people in Proeven, and especially those with marriageable daughters, invited him to stay with them. The most insistent of all was Peter's old friend, Augustinus. Finally Peter accepted the man's proffered hospitality and moved in.

Thereupon it developed that Augustinus' quarters were less generous than his invitation, and he had only two feather beds. However, no matter. His daughter Maria's bed was plenty wide enough for two. After a while Peter turned in with the girl, who was notably homely, and some time later Augustinus covered the windows to shut out the light. This had the effect of making soft-

brained Peter forget how unattractive Maria really was, and ultimately nature took her inevitable course. Immediately afterward
the disgraced girl and the insulted father set up a tremendous
row. Augustinus declared that Peter would have to marry his
daughter.

"So he looked very firm about it," Peter declared, "and he
insisted upon my marrying her before I left. He told me, too,
that perhaps our children would not look like their mother. Very
often that was the case, he said. But they all do!"

Well, nothing I could say to the unfortunate boy would mend
matters by this time, and we were in a hurry.

Once more we were headed south, and since a few of our
passengers had disembarked at Upernivik there was somewhat
more room aboard, though it was still crowded in the cabin
below.

Rockwell Kent and I took a little side trip from Egedesminde.
On the way we came across a camp of caribou hunters and decided to stay with them for a while.

A caribou camp is a pleasant place; the people are always
gay and merry, and they behave much as they used to in the old
days before missionaries came into the country. All the members
of a tribe or settlement, both young and old who are fit for some
weeks in the open, go out on these caribou trips. The men do the
hunting and carry into camp the animals they are able to kill.
Then they lie around and relax until time to go out on a fresh
foray.

When he goes out to hunt, each man selects a girl to follow
him and help carry home his game. After taking leave of the rest
of the hunt, what each couple does in the wilderness is strictly
their own affair. They tramp ahead until they locate an animal
and the hunter kills it. Then they cut the meat into pieces small
enough to carry, and when the hunter is lucky enough to kill
more than one caribou at a time they make camp for a few
days to dry the meat.

While they wait for the sun to cure the flesh it is customary
to build a low shelter of rocks, roof it with the freshly taken
skins anchored down with rocks against the wind, and spend
some idyllic days together. So they sleep and spend their hours
together in a happiness that is perfectly innocent because there is
no sense of sin or wrongdoing connected with it.

At the camp we visited there was an old woman named Malia

who was sick. We brought her coffee, though, and any Eskimo woman in the world who is not both dead and stone cold will sit up for coffee. As she sipped the hot drink she told us the story of how she came to be weak and ill, as we saw her, and as I listened to her account I thought once again of how unremittingly severe the life of these people can be.

Malia and a niece of hers had gone up into the hills to gather some *kvaner,* an edible plant which is a good deal like the European rhubarb.

"We went up and came to a high mountain," old Malia continued in a quavering voice. "I remembered it. I had several times been here before when I was still able to carry a burden of meat for the young men hunting. Across the mountain we forded a river, and it was difficult because of the severe current. We had to go in up to our waists, but I had my little pot along and some coffee to put in it, so when we got to the other side we started a fire, had a good, hot drink, and forgot our discomfort. Our journey lasted one more day, but when we reached the valley the *kvaner* stalks were so numerous and high that it was difficult to select the best ones. They were all alike, and my only regret was that we could not carry all of them back with us.

"After we had gathered a big load for each of us we decided to return to the camp through another valley, hoping to find an easier and shorter way into this place where the *kvaner* grew so large and good. After a while we ran into a lake and had to follow along the edge of the water. But in doing so we came to a big river which was running down into the lake. Thinking it possible to ford the stream, we waded out but soon found ourselves in dangerously deep water and still not past the middle. It could not be done.

"We returned to the bank from which we had started and we were both very cold and wet. The wind began to blow harder than before, and it came on to rain. I refused to let Kadara take my load, and neither was I willing to throw it away. Following along the river we came at last to a place where it was very broad, and we said to each other that such a broad stream could not be too fast-running or deep. Indeed, we were able to ford it there, but on the other side I was terribly tired. Two days' travel were still ahead of us, and the only food we had was our *kvaner,* which did not warm us nor give us much strength.

"The rain would not stop. Now I felt as cold as if it had been winter. Long before this my footgear had worn out, and I put grass under the soles of my feet, but it did not last long each time I did so. Our sopping clothes were glued to our bodies, and every gust of wind cut right through them. My niece Kadara could stand it better; she was young and fat. But I am an old hag, and what heat is there in us? My burden weighed me down so much that when we stopped to rest, and sat down, I could not straighten up again.

"Then I cried a little and told Kadara to go down to the camp and ask for help. She refused to leave me, and so I had to go on, crawling on my hands and knees with the bundle of *kvaner* still on my back. No matter what happened to me, I had determined to hang on to that.

"Once again I came to the end of my strength and fainted from exhaustion. When I recovered I told Kadara to go on, save herself, and leave me alone to die. I knew that I could not keep on, but still she refused to leave me, and every time I got angry and ordered her to go away she would turn her face toward me and walk backward on her heels around me.

"I came to the extreme limit of my endurance, but in front of us was a mountain which I recognized. In my young days, when everyone liked me, I used to go walking on it. I knew that if we could only climb that, the rest of the way would be downhill, but from where was I to collect the strength to go up? Again I told Kadara to go away, and her refusal made me so angry, and the silly way she walked around me and kept looking at me was so infuriating, that I almost forgot my weakness and managed to scramble upward with her.

"We reached the top before the next day. My, it was cold up there! The wind was sharp as a knife.

"It was not possible for either of us to go farther when we had climbed the mountain. So we tried to lie down together, get a little warm, and rest. That was a mistake. We could get no warmth or rest, and when I tried to rise again the strength had gone out of my legs entirely and my back felt like nothing but one unendurable pain. Still Kadara stayed stubborn and refused to go ahead for help; she said that if she went down into the camp she would not be able to walk up again, and in that case nobody would find me.

"After a while I neither felt nor thought anything more. Blackness overwhelmed me. The next thing I knew, several people were standing around me; they raised me in their arms and bore me away. Not realizing exactly what was happening, I was bitterly disappointed when I found myself back in camp with caribou skins over me and hot soup to drink. I had made up my mind at first that I was dead, and that it was the angels who were lifting me up. It was a wonderful feeling. Now I perceive that I still have several things to endure before that becomes really true.

"But," she said calmly, "I have tasted death, and it tasted so fine that I shall never be afraid of it again."

While we listened to this story I noticed that the old woman's fingers were as wrinkled as if she had been washing all day long, and indeed, her whole body was equally so. Once in a while she would be seized by a spasm of trembling, but she declared that her rheumatism was entirely gone, and that was something gained out of her ordeal. As for Kadara, when we asked for her, intending to give her the praise that was due for her courage and loyalty in saving her old aunt's life, we found that she was not in camp. The very day after the rescue of the old woman she had gone out with a young hunter, and the pair of them had not yet returned.

The *Disko* kept forging southward, but we had to put in at every colony, on account of the official party we had aboard. In due time we reached the capital of Greenland, Godthaab. More Danes live in this town than in any other colony, of course. For my part, I find those towns better in which only one white family is located. In Godthaab there was a rising pseudo-European culture of evening dresses and Danish footgear and formal manners—all the discomforts of civilization with few of its compensations. In this settlement the people lost the pleasures of the northern kind of life. All this, however, did not bother me much, for in South Greenland I was not too popular. My many newspaper articles back home did not endear me to officialdom, and I was not invited to many of the banquets and parties. Instead, Magdalene, Rockwell Kent, and I wandered around the place talking to the natives and looking at the terrible monuments of the capital city.

We amused ourselves sometimes by turning up at dances to which we had not been invited. When somebody was giving a dinner in so small a place the fact could not be hidden, and every dinner meant a dance afterward, as this was about the only way of amusing the guests in this country. When we appeared none of the embarrassed hosts had the nerve to throw us out again, however much my critical writing of Greenland affairs may have caused them to want to do so.

Julianehaab!

No one who has not been there can imagine what this name connotes in Greenland. In Julianehaab the manager of the post wears a Stetson hat and breeches; there are two doctors and three interns in the hospital. In the public square stands a fountain! This is the colony where meat is actually slaughtered for export, and where there is not only a shipyard but a public waterworks which supplies all the houses. And only five years before, the town had been merely a typical Greenland port in the process of development.

Julianehaab is the southernmost colony of Greenland. Eskimos live in it right enough, but if you did not notice that the girls wore sealskin pants and the men spoke Eskimo, you would be positive that you were in one of the lovely small towns of Norway.

"Today it is almost a European town," I thought as I walked its streets. "The people of Julianehaab have leaped two centuries of progress in half a decade. The post manager, Mr. Ibsen, is in fact a modern angekok, a wizard with power to alter the very forces of nature."

Looking around me, I had the feeling that I was observing a moving picture rather than reality, and when I came upon the municipal bathhouse, built out of a handsome sandstone from the mountains, and saw not only the towels, the soap, the showers and the tubs with hot and cold water, but Eskimos using the place, actually bathing, I felt sure that the evidence of my eyes was an illusion.

Another testimonial to the growth of Julianehaab enterprise was the restaurant in which I ate. The progressive lady who started it was named Miklara, and her methods differed somewhat from those of restaurateurs in other countries. Her establishment sold coffee, tea, and cookies at three ore each. The coffee cost twelve ore, or about two and a half cents. Rolls, at six ore each, were another of her offerings.

One does not simply walk into this restaurant of Miklara's. Oh, no. The day before one wishes to eat there it is necessary to go to the proprietress, decide what is wanted down to the last single roll or cookie, and pay in advance. Miklara feels that she cannot risk having anything left over. After all, the rolls have both sugar and cinnamon on them! Furthermore, the prospective diner-out must tell Miklara who will be in the party. If the host plans to entertain someone whom she does not like she closes her restaurant at once.

That is not so queer as it sounds, for Miklara still has the old attitude of private hospitality in which she has been brought up.

Our sight-seeing took us, on another occasion, to Narsak, where the girls are traditionally the prettiest in Greenland. We had another fine picnic there, but the ancient beauties must have died out. I was loath to give up this appealing story and feared that the real belles were being kept undercover somewhere away from us, so I went visiting from house to house. Nothing outstanding in the way of pulchritude was to be found. I did speak to one of the older ladies about the old legend. She agreed that the story was true—it could be read in several books, in fact.

"Well," I said, "where are they, then, these lovely girls?"

"Why," she replied, "it is us. I am one of them."

That was sweet.

I met a certain native called Christian, who was, in a grim and terrible way, the most interesting man in his part of the world. His story is a fearful one, and I advise any of my readers who are distressed by brutality and horror to skip the next few pages, for there is no way of telling this man's history which will make the facts palatable to most civilized tastes.

This fellow, Christian, had belonged to the pagan natives on the east coast and had emigrated from that region to be baptized. If any man was in need of the Divine Mercy, he was the one.

His name before his baptism had been Autdárutá, and he had been an angekok, a dangerous man. But since he was a real hunter, and able to afford it, he had taken a certain girl named Sakua to be his second wife. Sakua had had many terrible experiences before she married this man. She had been present when the famous murderer Katiaja had been loose in the far north and had shot her husband and left him bleeding in the snow. The girl loved her husband deeply, and the sight of his suffering was too much for her. Out of the pity in her heart she had lifted a great rock and smashed in her husband's head. . . . That ended his suffering.

Sakua was a good girl, and Autdárutá, or Christian, favored her greatly. Some of the time he would have nothing at all to do with his first wife because of his feeling for the second, but then moods would come upon him when he treated the girl brutally and threw her out of his house. These were generally the times when he was angry because Sakua bore him no children. In the course of one of these quarrels he leaped to his feet and struck her in the face. She screamed and ran out and into the mountains. Furious, her husband took up his gun and pounded after her. After a time she heard his steps behind her, turned, and faced him.

"What do you want?" she cried.

"You are a miserable woman," was his answer. "You cannot bear children." He spat in fury. "You do not deserve to live," he said, and shot her through the breast.

"Why are you doing this?" she exclaimed as she fell. But she did not die, at least not at once.

Autdárutá was furious. He smashed at her head with the butt of his rifle, but still she would not die. He yelled at a small boy who was playing near the spot with a bow and arrow, and the child came over and gave him his small bow and short arrow. Autdárutá drew the shaft back and buried it in Sakua's belly. Then at last she died.

Still in a blind fury of rage, the man cut all her joints to prevent her spirit from returning to haunt him. He cut out her heart and ate it. And before he left her, he cut out her eyes. Her body he threw down on the beach near the edge of the water, and then he went home. He was near to permanent madness as a result of his having eaten that human heart, and when he got to his house he put Sakua's eyes in the oil lamp of his first wife, to remind her, he said, that her husband was a man for any wife to look out for.

He next killed one of Sakua's brothers and added his eyes to those of Sakua. Even this apparently did not satisfy the blood lust of Autdárutá, who must by this time have been in the state of Malays when they run amok. He wanted more killing, and he decided that the little girl of the man he had just murdered must also die. So he took her by the hand and walked up into the mountains with the child. There he left her to die of cold and starvation.

The terrified people of the settlement could hear her crying and calling for her father. Her voice sounded more and more hoarse and finally ceased altogether, so her despairing relatives concluded that she had lost herself in the mountains during the night. Just at they were talking about that the door opened and there stood the little girl, shivering from fear and cold. Everybody in the house kept quiet, but Autdárutá came for her just the same.

Again he led her out of the house. A short distance from the door he paused.

"My mind is full of pity for this child," he said, and picked her up by the legs.

Then he smashed her head against a rock. Her brains spattered out and she died instantly.

After his madness cooled, this terrible man began to brood about what he had done. Ultimately he left his tribe and went south and around to the west coast, where he asked to be baptized. For some time he was given a period of preparation and instruction and then became a member of the holy congregation of Frederiksdal, taking the name of Christian.

After that happened his fellow converts and co-religionists began to insist that the human eyes in his wife's blubber lamp should be removed. As they put it, the spirit of Jesus would have a hard time to enter the house as long as those eyes were there. Christian had lost his strength of will and agreed to do something about the eyes at once.

He took them with him and went up into the hills; two days later, when he came back, he did not have them any longer.

"Something is done," he told the curious. Then he added, "It almost took my breath." For some days after this he coughed horribly.

On our visit we found him living in a minute house full of smoke and entirely devoid of furniture or bedclothes. Yet in one corner I observed the finest kind of summer coat, practically new and with an elegant lining of silk. After we had made the customary expressions of mutual esteem I asked him about the coat, and he declared that Knud Rasmussen had given it to him.

"Of course," I said to myself. "Who else would have sent such a thing as that garment?"

Christian explained that he had seen a picture of some Danish men wearing coats like this one and had immediately asked Knud for a garment like them. Knud had promised to get him one, and never, never had Knud Rasmussen promised an Eskimo something and forgotten it.

As time had passed Christian apparently had lost his skill or energy as a hunter. In spite of the fine coat he was nearly destitute, and we bribed him to tell of his earlier life and crimes by promising him plenty of tobacco, four cakes of soap, and two pounds of coffee. As he recounted the tale he sounded quite proud of it, and he only begged me not to tell the local schoolteacher, who had forbidden him to think of himself as a murderer.

"You see," Christian explained, "that poor man has never had a chance in the world to experience having people fear him!"

One native whom we were fortunate to see was Kvanerssuaq, who was a very old man indeed, almost dying, but famous all through that region. He had heard we were coming and sent for us to come see him at his house.

Kvanerssuaq was famous as a mighty murderer and a medicine man of unusual powers. Had he not once caused a house to catch fire, even though he was not in it but at a settlement far away? Since several people died in that fire it was clear that he was a person to be propitiated. As an angekok he used to travel to the moon to determine for pregnant women the sex of their unborn children. Since the mother of a son has many advantages over the mother of a daughter, all his clients were naturally hoping for a boy. He told me first of all how he traveled to the moon to find out whether it was going to be a boy or a girl:

Launching his kayak, he would paddle far to the east until he reached the point where the sea and the land meet, at the line of the horizon. There he would find a huge ice floe, and it was necessary to carry the kayak across it. After a while he would come to a big lake, and on the way across it he would have to catch a seal. When he came to the opposite shore of the lake he would leave his kayak and carry the seal with him. This was so that he could give the meat to the savage dogs of the moon man, who would tear him to pieces if he had nothing to give them.

Once he reached the house of the moon man, he was always treated with great friendship. In the house was a pail of water, and by gazing down into this water he would learn whether the baby would be born a boy or a girl. Coming back, Kvanerssuaq would have as many troubles as on the way to the moon, and the whole trip seemed a great deal of trouble to take simply to know in advance the sex of a baby.

We decided to call at a settlement named Tuarpat to see if the people there were all right. When no one came down to greet us and not a soul so much as peeked out of a doorway we began to think there might be trouble. After a time we saw an old woman come out of a house and totter down to the beach.

"We did not welcome you," she said, "because at this place no joy is to be found to give to visitors."

Her words had a tragic ring to them, delivered as they were in a trembling voice by a bent old woman standing in the sunshine. The stamp of sorrow was on her face, and after a time we were able to find out the story of the settlement's tragedy.

Two days before we arrived a small party of nine youngsters from this village had rowed over to the other side of the inlet, at low tide, to gather clams. They were the finest young people of the settlement. Clams were plentiful, and after eating all they could they went up the hills and gathered berries.

Homeward bound in the silent night, they were very gay as they rowed along, talking and laughing. Little by little they fell silent, except for one girl who seemed more talkative than usual. She kept laughing and chattering away, and they could not stop her until, without warning, she keeled over in her seat. They lifted her up and discovered that she was dead.

All of them were terrified at this tragedy and not knowing what else to do doubled their efforts at the oars in their haste to get across the fjord. They were too saddened to have much to say to each other, but finally one boy began to talk, as if to cheer them up. He even told several jokes, but then the rest of them noticed that he began to speak incoherently and without sense and they began to be alarmed. He, too, stopped talking almost in the middle of a word, and down he fell, as dead as the girl.

One of the surviving girls cried especially loud because the lad who died was her cousin. She declared between her sobs that she thought whatever it was that had killed them had something to do with the clams they had eaten at their last meal on the beach, because there had been an odd taste in her mouth when she ate them, a taste which she thought was like beer. She cried inconsolably and could not be comforted. The others turned to the oars again, in a hurry to reach Tuarpat and escape their boat with its cargo of silent bodies which a short time before had been their friends. The weeping girl fell silent at last, and shortly afterward she told them that she was all right again now.

She would show them how little she cared, and even began to sing. The rest of them, horrified, told her to stop; the devil would hear her if she sang anything but hymns on such an occasion. This admonition made her laugh very loudly.

Over and over the peals of her laughter echoed across the water, and then she, too, stopped both laughing and breathing. The six survivors were by this time mute with fear. They dared not open their mouths. Had not the three who died done so while talking and laughing?

The instant their bow grated on the beach the six remaining members of the boatload leaped ashore and dashed for their various houses. Once inside their own doors, they burst into tears. In their haste they had not remembered to moor their boat, and some older men who had noticed this fact yelled at them to come back and do their duty. But when the youngsters paid no attention to their shouts the men thought it best to do the job themselves. They went down to lift the boat ashore, and there, in her bottom, they saw the dead faces of three of their own children.

When we arrived the bodies had already been buried. Undoubtedly the young people had died of clam poisoning, but we could think of no consolation for the bereaved community.

On the voyage up I had written almost half of a new novel, *The Sea Tyrant*. Once in Greenland, there had been no opportunity to work on the story, but now I returned to it and wrote and wrote, hour after hour.

We had magnificent weather. On the sixteenth of October we passed Cape Farewell. There was a fair and following breeze; the voyage and my work went well, and on the nineteenth of the month I set down the final period of the last chapter of the book.

After a day of rest I began to read the novel to Magdalene. Poor woman! She had no luck with me at all. Either she must serve as my good or bad conscience, or she must be impressed into service as a critic of my writing. This time she approved of the book, and I felt a sense of relief that it was finished. All in all, it was a happy voyage.

The Atlantic was kind to us, too. On the twenty-fifth of October we raised the naked cliffs of Norway, and the day after, came into Danish waters at Skagen, on the northern tip of the Danish Peninsula. Here we ran out of our good weather and a stiff gale tore down upon us. Magdalene and I stood on the bridge and watched it during the night.

The wind and sea went down considerably the next day, and we were now sheltered by the proximity of the land. All of us prepared for shore. The ship herself was washed down; Magdalene, Axel, and I put on our going-ashore clothes; and the captain stayed sober. The harbor of Copenhagen opened out before us, and the long voyage was completed.

6

BACK I WENT TO FARMING, WRITING, AND LECTURING. THEN, IN THE summer of 1929, I started for Greenland once more.

Of course nothing makes me happier than to be headed toward that Arctic country, and this trip promised to be a new sort of experience into the bargain. The Prime Minister of Denmark, Mr. Stauning, was going to visit the colony for the first time and take a personal look at conditions up there. I was to join him on the boat and help him with translating and advice, and at the same time I had an assignment from my paper to cover the story of the natives' reception of the first high Socialist official to visit them.

The rest of our party comprised Director Daugaard-Jensen, a Danish economist named Professor Berlin (who was a strong opponent of the government's), and various others.

Ours was a regular excursion-boat crossing at first, calm and without incident. There was little to do aboard, and I dislike idleness thoroughly. After a time the millpond weather deserted us and we ran into enough of a storm to put most of the passengers into their bunks. That gave me an opportunity to get back to my writing, and I got a chapter of my new novel, *Ivaloo*, done each day. Much of the remaining time was spent talking to Daugaard-Jensen and Stauning, and I learned a great deal from these two men.

The days wore past without much incident, and we were abreast, and past, Cape Farewell almost before we knew it. The passengers recovered from their *mal de mer*.

Our vessel came finally to the bay outside Julianehaab, but

fog and ice prevented our going into the port for another two days. When we did finally get in we found that Mr. Ibsen, the post manager, had the whole place in spick-and-span order. I went with Mr. Stauning to look over the different local enterprises belonging to the colony—the sheep farm, the slaughterhouse, the fisheries buildings, and the hospital.

It was always disillusioning to watch the Greenland managers conducting an inspection party round their posts. They would try to give a good impression not so much of the institutions in their charge as of themselves. They liked to call attention to what they personally had done to keep things up and improve them. But Mr. Stauning was a wise enough man to see through all this and discount it.

There was a certain amount of agriculture in the vicinity of Julianehaab, and there were two agricultural experts stationed there, partly to experiment with what was possible in that region, and partly to teach the natives more scientific methods.

Conditions in Greenland were similar to those in Iceland. The pasturage was mostly not cultivated at all, with the result that the grass had formed up into small hillocks all over the fields. Since a smooth and level field will carry much more grass, and can be worked far more readily, these hillocks have to be ironed out. The ancient Icelandic method of doing this was to thump them level with wooden clubs. A tractor and plow, of course, is decidedly more effective. The Greenland pastures were trenched and drained. We saw sizable ditches taking the water out of formerly swampy areas and discharging it into the sea.

From Julianehaab we sailed north to the place where Eric the Red had lived.

The present inhabitants are a couple of families of Eskimo settlers. Their houses are good and well built, they have fenced in some of their fields, and they own cows, horses, and especially sheep. The patriarch of them all was Otto Fredericksen, whom I had seen the year before. He greeted our party with dignity, and I could not help thinking that old Eric the Red must have been a good deal like this man, with his great red whiskers, his strong, heavy body, and his wide, assured stance.

Otto Fredericksen and his people were in the midst of their haying when we arrived. None of the grass was being wasted. They had even brought in some from a small field up in the hills, carrying it down on horseback. These horses were their greatest pride, and so anxious were they to impress the Prime Minister with the animals that Otto arranged a sort of rodeo to display their horsemanship.

Frankly, I have seen more expert riders in my time than those Eskimos. The peak of their skill was that they could make the horse go in the direction they wanted. Some of the young people rode them away from us and then back; the most daring of the lot actually was able to sit on his horse backward and stay with the animal, but this feat was beyond the others.

Our applause was too much for their discretion. Some of them prodded their animals into a trot, and two of the riders promptly fell off. They explained to us that it was very, very difficult to sit on a horse's back when the animal was moving, and totally impossible if the creature was "jumping." But they will master even that art in time. This was the first year that Otto Fredericksen had owned any horses, and they had not had much practice.

Next we visited the town of Igaligo. The entire population here is serious in character and deeply religious. A couple of years before our visit this characteristic had resulted in a somewhat fantastic occurrence which is worth setting down. First it must be explained that at one time wild swans used to be well known in Greenland. There were so many of them that certain place names still bear witness to their presence, but for many years they had been extinct.

One day, however, a flock of forty of these beautiful creatures came winging out of the sky and settled on the waters of the lake near Igaligo. The pious inhabitants were not surprised at their appearance—what more natural than that the gracious Lord should send them a delegation of His angels? Had they not been in close touch with heaven all their lives? With no trepidation, then, a group of them went out to greet and confer with the heavenly visitants.

As they approached a curious thing happened. The angels showed less friendliness than the reverent committee of welcome had expected. In fact, they flew a short distance farther up the valley.

Now there was in Igaligo a fine young man named Josef Egede who was both the local teacher and the minister. As the most direct approach to the Almighty which the congregation had hitherto enjoyed, he did not care especially for this angelic manifestation, and whether because of his superior intelligence or a most understandable envy he became suspicious of the whole miracle. Nevertheless, there was no choice for him but to go out with the welcoming committee. But when the disappointed faithful came up to the spot where the angels had been resting before their last retreat, Josef noticed a very suspicious circumstance. There were a number of droppings on the ground, and, knowing his Bible by heart, he was aware that there was no authority in it for a belief that the blessed angels either possessed bowels or upon occasion moved them. He leaped to the conclusion that whatever the visitors were, they were mundane beings.

After a time he remembered hearing about swans and then recalled what he had read about them in books. A great light dawned, and he told the congregation that their angels were nothing but a lot of big birds. Righteous anger possessed them all as soon as they realized that Josef was correct, and they felt ashamed of their gullibility. Guns were immediately fetched from the houses, and in a short time every one of the forty swans had been shot.

It was a pleasure to travel in the company of the Prime Minister. He was no ordinary man. I noticed that as we sailed from one colony to the next he would stay up nights, reading all the data he could find about the place we were to visit next. He surprised and impressed everyone by knowing their names and recognizing buildings and landmarks in places where he had never been before. In his treatment of Professor Berlin he was equally skillful; nothing was kept from this worthy savant, and he was treated with the utmost kindness. If he wanted to examine into something by himself, that was all right too.

Although this course of treatment did not appear to convert the professor, it did serve to neutralize him as an irritant factor, and keep him quiet.

When we steamed into Godhavn the Prime Minister really had a lesson in the cultural level to which the natives have attained. Scores of kayaks paddled out to meet our ship, the *Disko,* and as the boatmen recognized me they began to shout and call out in the most urgent fashion. Mr. Stauning heard their voices and watched their gestures, but of course he did not understand a single word; with an expression of some anxiety he turned to me and asked what had happened? He felt sure that some great and perhaps disastrous event must have happened to the colony.

There was nothing for it but to tell him what the natives wanted. The settlement radio had been out of order on the evening before our arrival and they had not been able to learn the result of an important American heavyweight boxing match. Tunney or Jack Dempsey, or whoever it was, occupied their minds to such an extent that they could not wait for news until our ship had a chance to anchor. There was a graphic demonstration of how much these people have become linked with the rest of the world!

The boat from Thule, the *Soekongen,* was already in the harbor when we arrived, and my heart leaped when I saw her, for I had asked Captain Pedersen to bring my boy Mequsaq down with him. I learned at once that he had arrived safely and was waiting for me, but when I went ashore he did not present himself. When I inquired where he was I was told that, true to his innate shyness, he had hidden himself among the other children and gone down to the wharf with them to look for something.

I understood by that how unbearable the excitement had become for him, and walked down to where he was standing.

"Aipasak [my future hunting companion]," I told him, "here I am."

"It happened that one sailed down here," he responded with dignity.

"It is planned," I told him, "that you should move over onto the big boat where I am staying."

"Am I somebody who decides?" was his modest answer.

"Your clothes?" I questioned him. "Where are they?"

His first reply was that he did not know, but when I warned him that we had best get them quickly he admitted the possibility that he had some.

"If something exists at all," he said finally, "it must be on board the ship, if the sailors have not thrown it overboard."

By this reply I understood that the boy had a very good and complete outfit, and we went down to the *Soekongen* to collect it. Captain Pedersen told me that in getting dressed that day Mequsaq had changed anoraks several times before he was satisfied that he was making the best possible appearance with which to impress me.

We got his bag and went aboard the *Disko* with it. There I installed him in my cabin, and in a few hours he had all his customary confidence back. Although he had never been able to talk well because he stuttered so terribly, he made me understand how he had been longing for Magdalene and me.

In one respect Mr. Stauning was something of a disappointment to the natives. They sent a delegation to him protesting that he did not wear a uniform, and they told him flatly that they had expected something a little more like the king, who had been up in these waters some years before. They admitted that his whiskers did help to give him dignity, and my own personal experience confirms that judgment. Sometimes I suspect that without my whiskers I should have no dignity at all!

On this trip, when the people saw that so important a man as the Prime Minister carried a noble set of chin whiskers, my own beard proved to them that I was of more importance than they had customarily thought me. This opinion was neatly put by an old woman whom I knew. She came pressing toward me through the crowd and asked permission to shake my hand. Somewhat surprised, I naturally assented, though she had never formerly asked my leave. I spoke of that.

"Yes, Peterssuaq," she answered, "but now that we see you in company with grand men with beards, that means that you must be somebody, and not just the person we always supposed you to be!"

Of all the fifteen colonies which Mr. Stauning had visited, Upernivik certainly won the prize. I think the Prime Minister really enjoyed himself there; I took him round to my house, where Fat Sofie lived, and she served us her inevitable pancakes. We ate them with pleasure and talked over our trip, for we were to say good-by to each other here.

7

I BOARDED THE *Disko* ONCE MORE, AND MEQUSAQ AND I WERE NOW southbound to Umanak.

A motorboat was waiting for me at that place, but before I went aboard her I left my boy in the town with some friends.

I was to help my old friend Dr. Wegener with an expedition across the icecap, and there would be no place for Mequsaq with this expedition. He understood that I would return for him soon. The launch carried me as far as a place called Qamarujuk, where a huge glacier comes down into the fjord. The boat's engineer was my native friend Tobias, a veteran of the Denmark Expedition, and he, Dr. Loewe, and I made up the boat's party.

Times change. At Qamarujuk we would have to begin a difficult and dangerous climb to the base camp, and in case the weather should not prove immediately propitious I found that Dr. Wegener had cached a small library of books for us to read. The first thing was to have something to eat, and we sat down to a repast of oatmeal and German coffee. The latter was more well intentioned than palatable, but so great was my admiration for Dr. Loewe that I dared not hurt his feelings by offering to take a hand in the cooking.

He was a superb man, second in command of the expedition and endowed with an energy of multiple horsepower. His hobby was mountaineering, and he had been to the top of many mountains which had never previously been scaled. The year before this he was the first ever to attain the summit of Umanak Mountain, which the world-famous American climber, Whymper, had declared years before to be insurmountable.

Before starting for the camp we had one errand to perform, which was to pick up some dogs for the expedition. We rented some fifty dogs from the natives (along with the necessary drivers), and when we reached Qamarujuk, Dr. Wegener was down at the beach to meet us.

Never on the face of the earth have I seen such an expedition as that was, organized on system, courage, and technique. Though it would be a long journey before I had seen all their accomplishments, I had a taste of the style in which the work was done right at the start. We were given a drink of hot lemonade before we set out—a very agreeable potion and an admirable preparation for Arctic walking. Then each of us clamped on "creepers" or metal soles to our shoes, with sharp hobnails on them, and shouldered our packs. So we set out.

Wegener and Loewe walked ahead, and I followed. Each of them was toting a terrific load, and I conceived the proud notion that I wanted mine made at least somewhat larger than it was.

The glacier was so steep that it was barely possible to walk on it. Those Germans were wonderful men. Up this precipitous ice they had brought the impedimenta of a large and modern expedition, as well as themselves and twenty-two Iceland horses. All along the trail the route was clearly marked by the horse dung of the Iceland ponies. They must have been over it often, I thought.

Of course I had heard about using these sturdy little Iceland ponies before, but the reports that I had received never proved to me that the animals had made good on Arctic expedition work. Yet I must admit that in the case of the Wegener expedition they were most valuable, perhaps because they were so well handled. For bringing masses of material up a steep glacier and across rocky ground they were simply indispensable, and hauled up load after load.

The pack train went on with us from Grunau, and it was interesting to watch the ponies working. They were tied together in a long chain and walked nimbly and sturdily, but they had to be watched all the time. The moment the way became steep and tricky they would try to put on more speed and jump over obstacles. This resulted either in hauling the ones behind violently and dangerously upward, or in yanking the leaders backward, with consequent danger of falls and losses of animals and burdens.

Nothing untoward happened. We went steadily ahead, stopping once in a while to breathe the ponies. After we had climbed a thousand feet or so the going was bad, but there were no accidents.

Then we came upon an amazing thing, something almost incredible in the Arctic: a real road. It turned out to be twelve kilometers long, or nearly eight miles, and it was no mere footpath or trail. That road snaked its way upward across the sides of cliffs, along the edge of giant moraines, and across mountain rivulets. When it came to a precipice, its outer edge was built up of piled stone, and its inner blasted bodily out of the rock. Wegener had anticipated the problems that building this road would present, and he had taken along a chemist to make the necessary explosives for the required blasting. So now the road ran as he had designed it, with a gradient of one meter in five.

Fourteen Germans and twelve Eskimos had built that road in three weeks, and it was double the length of all the other roads in Greenland combined.

It took Germans to perform such a feat. Of course, Robert Peary once built a road in Greenland, when he carted away his meteorite, but it was neither as long nor as good as this one.

All along the way I marveled at the construction. In fifty places they had to blast away solid rock, and in many others I noticed they had laid rocks down as a sort of fender to keep the horses from rubbing up against the cliffs and scraping off their packs.

At an elevation of 780 meters we again found ourselves out on the ice. The weather was inconveniently warm, so that the moraine water was running under the foot of the ice and the surface was dangerously smooth and slippery from the melting. All of us had to wear creepers on our shoes again.

That night we came to a camp which had been dubbed "Scheideck," after a place in Switzerland. It was situated at the innermost corner of the mountain facing the east. Here I met the famous Icelander, Vigfus, who had been in Greenland before on an expedition with I. P. Koch.

At Scheideck, I felt much more comfortable. The temperature was constantly below freezing, so my sweaty clothes dried and I felt comfortable once again. The only hardship I had to endure here was the patent mattress which the expedition proudly offered me. This contraption was some sort of steel-spring affair, and a total failure. Every time I so much as moved—to say nothing of turning over—it cracked and thundered so loudly that I would wake and jump up in terror, imagining that the icecap was breaking under me or that war had been declared. But I did not dare crawl away and leave the thing to its own devices because Wegener was so proud of it, and after all, it had been a lot of trouble to hoist it nine hundred meters into the air and miles inland to the edge of the icecap.

We left Scheideck in dog sleds, and I was thoroughly happy. I love the motion of those conveyances and the sound of the runners on the snow. We made good speed in spite of the crevasses, which were dangerous because of the thin layer of snow over them. Some of our dogs fell into them at the start and were lost, but then I had the pleasure of showing the natives a way of preventing the beasts from sliding out of their harness, and that saved quite a number of them, I think.

At the end of a half day of driving on dog sleds we saw our goal ahead of us, the camp for the motor sleds. I was to have the experience of traveling in one of these contraptions, for the first time, and our destination was far in toward the center of

the icecap. Deep in its heart the expedition was to establish a
meteorological station to study conditions during the winter,
and two men would have to stay in that isolated place for
months.

To ride on one of those sleds proved a pleasanter adventure
than I had expected, and an eye opener in the matter of speed.
Knud Rasmussen and I still held the record for traversing the
icecap from west to east; we had done it with sleds and dogs in
nineteen days. But these sleds could cruise along under power
across the ice at speeds of eighty to one hundred kilometers an
hour. They had been built in Finland and were driven by
motors developing 120 horsepower. The propellers were mounted
aft, so that the blown snow was whirled away behind us.

The passengers on one of these sleds sat forward in a small
enclosed cabin that held two men comfortably and three with a
good deal of squeezing. The driver had the best time of it, for his
companion had to sit and keep pumping away at the air pressure
which forced the gasoline from the tank below up into the motor
above.

What a job it had been to get those two power-operated sleds
up onto the icecap! (Of course they will remain there forever—
they cannot be salvaged from such a location as that.) They
were dragged up the thousand meters of elevation above sea
level, which is the floor of the icecap, by winches, an inch at a
time. Fifteen bridges had to be built across crevasses too wide
for them to cross, and those bridges had to be paved with packed
snow for the runners.

Those sturdy little ponies which had played such a large part
in the expedition's success were not to come out from it. At the
start of the trip there had been twenty-five of them, but one had
fallen into a crevasse and two had got broken legs from being
kicked by their fellows. These two were killed and eaten while I
was there, and they tasted extremely good.

The other twenty-two were butchered when there was no
more need for them, and their meat frozen to provide fresh food
during the winter.

I had parted from Wegener and Loewe with a feeling of sad-
ness that eventually proved to be prophetic. For that great
scientist and brave man Alfred Wegener was destined never to
return from the icecap on which I had last seen him. The time
came when it was imperative to relieve the men in the meteoro-

logical post in the heart of cold. The temperature then was constantly fifty or more degrees below zero, and in such extremes of frost the motor sleds could not be used. First of all thirteen natives with dog sleds were sent toward the tiny hut and the two men in it. Two days later the nine who were still alive staggered back to camp. On the next attempt Wegener and Loewe set out with four Eskimos, but it, too, failed. Later a third attempt was made, and it was on this journey that Alfred Wegener lost his life.

I reached Umanak in time to catch the last boat for home, and found Mequsaq waiting for me. He had been having a good time at the settlement, but for all that he was relieved to see me and feel perfectly sure that he was going to go home to Denmark.

On this voyage home I wrote, as is my usual custom, and thanked Providence that I was endowed with the desire to do so. If I had not had my manuscript to labor at I should have been forced to resort to the company of the passengers, and they would have proved boring. Not that human beings bore me; far from it. But there is an unreality to a passenger voyage, and people who travel seem to partake of that unreality while they are aboard a ship. No, I was much happier with my book, which was full of the people of my imagination, modeled after Greenland natives for the most part.

I intended this novel, *Ivaloo,* to have an epic quality, and its central character was really a portrait of my dear Navarana. Now that I had her boy, our son, in the very cabin with me, she came so vividly before my memory that it was almost as if she were with me again. I enjoyed writing that book, not only because of my feeling about Navarana, but because all the Greenland people in it were real to me.

8

AS IT TURNED OUT, WE NEVER DID FILM *Eskimo* IN GREENLAND. The film rights to the story were bought by Metro-Goldwyn-Mayer, and one day I found myself in Hollywood.

Hunt Stromberg, who was in charge of the project, decided to do the film in Alaska, instead of Greenland or Hudson Bay, and I was told to read up on Alaska, study the geography, and look at the mass of Arctic films put at my disposal. As an assistant I got a young man called John Mahin who had never been outside the United States, but he was a good writer with a talent for detecting the taste of the public.

As soon as the news leaked out that M-G-M was going to make the film in Alaska we were deluged by people who wanted to take part in the adventure. The applicants claimed to be actors, handymen, guides, kayak builders, hunters. More than six hundred people besieged us with their applications.

We needed an expedition ship, and I was sent down to San Pedro to inspect a vessel which belonged to M-G-M. I took along a Norwegian, Captain John Hegness, who had lived for years in Alaska. He had been engaged by M-G-M as an adviser. He was a very able and useful man, and we went down to San Pedro in the car which I had bought secondhand.

In the end it turned out that the ship we had accepted was to be burned up in another film, so I was sent to Seattle to find a vessel there. I went up with Hegness and Frank Messenger, who was in charge of our budget. We settled on *Nanook,* a vessel needing only minor alterations for our purpose. With my keen sense of economy I went shopping in Seattle for our equipment, explaining to my two companions that we would need cooking utensils, tents, and many other things. Three men to a tent would be all right, I assured them naïvely, and each man would cook his own food.

When Messenger realized what I was up to he quickly got me out of the store and explained the situation. He was going with us to Alaska, and he was not going to do any cooking, nor would he take along tools, or sewing material, or any of the things I considered necessary. We were going to take a staff of carpenters, mechanics, cooks, and other specialists to do the manual labor.

The ship should be chartered for one year, I told him. We should take it over empty, get our own crew, and purchase all our own supplies, which would save a lot of money. Messenger did not protest, he probably thought it useless to explain the "facts of life" in Hollywood to such as I. When we returned I discovered that the ship had been purchased outright by M-G-M— supposedly on my recommendation!

The day of departure dawned at last, and we set off with all the fanfare the M-G-M press agents could provide. Mothers and wives and sweethearts were on hand to say good-by to the brave men going up to the Arctic wilderness. The newspapers pictured me as a Viking, an Arctic chieftain, sailor, anything they could think of. They did not mention, fortunately, that I did not go on with the group. They did not know it because I left the train at the first station after we had pulled out of Hollywood. The scenario was far from finished and I had to return to Hollywood with my assistant to complete it. But in the final version of the film not much of my original story was left.

9

MAGDA STAYED BEHIND IN HOLLYWOOD, AND I WENT ON TO SEATTLE where I caught the passenger liner *Aleutian,* which took me to Juneau in Alaska. From Juneau I went to Seaward where I caught the train for Anchorage. There I met a number of Russian exiles. They were the "old Russians," the czarists, who had settled down in Alaska to wait for the return of the czar in all his glory. They were all dressed in black—a quiet, silent group without curiosity or hope.

After waiting for two days I was finally told that my plane to Nome was ready. A Finnish pilot was taking me in his hydroplane across the tundra and the mountains. We set off in beautiful weather, but when we ran into a heavy storm were forced to make a long detour. We had to fly east of Mount McKinley, and I was deeply impressed by the wild splendor of the scenery.

We had to go down for refueling at Unalakleet at the bottom of Norton Bay. I was very happy to meet the local Eskimos and to discover that I could understand their language. I visited their schoolhouse and was amazed to see twelve typewriters on a table in a classroom. The teacher, an American who did not speak the Eskimo language, explained to me that he always had typewriters for his pupils.

We soon took to the air again, and at last I arrived in Nome in the legendary land of the gold prospectors. I was met by one of the film photographers who told me that a big party was under way, and I was rushed off to the famous clubhouse. I was sober when I arrived and I was the only one to stay sober through the night.

From Nome we set sail and made good speed north. Eighty per cent of the expedition was seasick, and the rest of us enjoyed the peace and the plentiful meals. We went first to Teller, where we got hold of some motorboats and continued up the Taksak River until we found a spot where the scenery seemed suitable. A few men were sent ashore with sketches and materials to build an Eskimo tent village, and we continued up the river. Our first job was the shooting of the hunting scenes.

Fortunately we found a great number of walrus—to the great excitement of the Hollywood crowd. When we had all the walrus pictures we needed, a bear hunt was next on the list, and a large, curious bear obliged at once by walking toward us across the ice. The skipper, who was a tough Norwegian, saw the bear first and alerted the film crew. The film cameras were carefully arranged in the strategic locations and the photographers were ready to "shoot" the bear from every possible angle, once it came within range. The bear came steadily closer, and Van Dyke and I stood behind the first cameraman, ready with our guns if the bear should become too aggressive.

The whole point of the scene was to get an Eskimo near enough to the bear to kill the animal in a close-up fight. Suddenly the bear hesitated and before he could change his mind, I jumped down and threw myself flat on the ice, pretending to be a seal. I acted my part as best I could, and soon the bear was within range of the cameras.

"Action!" Van Dyke called out, and the cameras began turning, but at the same moment we heard a great bang above us. The skipper had used his gun and killed the precious bear with his first shot.

"I could not stand the temptation," he shouted happily from the barrel high in the mast where he had been keeping watch. But I think that was his last happy moment on the whole trip. Van Dyke exploded in the vilest fit of temper I had ever experienced. The poor Norwegian tried in vain to protest, but his voice was lost in the storm of fury. The skipper had spent five years in the Arctic with Roald Amundsen, and it had never dawned on him that he was not supposed to shoot bears whenever he wanted to.

We never met another bear under such ideal conditions, however, and the film had to do without this particular scene.

After this intermezzo we continued to Kotzebue and Point Hope where I visited the white people and the local Eskimos. We went all the way to Little Diomede Island where we had to stay over for engine repair, and I took the opportunity to cross over in a motorboat to Great Diomede Island, which is situated in the middle of Bering Strait and is Russian territory. Since I did not plan any revolution or any anti-Soviet propaganda I did not expect any difficulty.

The moment I arrived a large number of Eskimos crowded around my boat and babbled excitedly. Right behind them came a tall severe-looking man dressed in some strange uniform. He asked me who I was and what I was doing on Russian soil. Since I had no papers and the island was forbidden territory he could not give me any landing permit. And if I did not leave at once he would be compelled to arrest me and transport me to Moscow. This alternative did not tempt me, and I promised to go voluntarily. The Russian guard asked me quickly how long I had planned to stay on the island, and I told him I had expected to spend the evening with the Eskimos, six hours at the most.

After a moment of deep thought he announced that I could stay on the condition that I spend at least two hours in his house. He turned out to be a wonderful host, stuffing me with food and soup, tea and candy.

Our next port of call was Teller, which had been chosen as our headquarters. The great Lomen Reindeer Company had a large empty slaughterhouse there, and we were going to use it for all our interior shots. But first we continued up the Taksak River to pick the site for our summer camp. We had no trouble finding an ideal place beside the beautiful stream, and two separate camps were quickly established. The film crowd had decided to make their own camp "at least four miles away from the Eskimos." They feared that the "smell" would otherwise annoy the sensitive noses of the Hollywood people.

Since I would much rather stay with the Eskimos than in the Hollywood camp, and since it was necessary, anyhow, to have someone guard all the precious cameras, light equipment, and what not, I set up my tent among the natives. I was given all the necessary supplies and cooked my own food. I was looked down upon by the elite, but I was very happy.

When the work began the Hollywood crowd came down from the exclusive camp by way of motorboats, and a short distance away from the Eskimo camp we had to put up some separate tents in which the actresses could rest and make up. We did quite a lot of work, but whenever it rained the film people stayed at home, and I enjoyed life with the Eskimos.

There was a great difference, however, between the Alaskan Eskimos and the Greenlanders. In Alaska they would never touch an oar. One of the first days in camp an Eskimo asked me if he might borrow an outboard motor in which to cross the river. They wanted to pick berries on the other side. But as gasoline was scarce and the trip would take only ten minutes with a rowboat I turned down the request. Later I learned that if they could not go by motorboat they never went at all. They had forgotten how to row!

There were other differences. The Eskimos staged wild drinking parties which rather annoyed me because of the noise from their revelries. One night I was disturbed by a girl who came running into my tent, asking me to protect her against an Eskimo. When the man rushed into the tent a moment later and demanded that I hand over the girl I was forced to throw him out on his neck. The next morning I asked him about his behavior, and he told me that he and his companions had been drinking the methyl alcohol we had brought along for functional use.

I was horrified and told him the liquid was poisonous. He might go blind or die from it, but he laughed and said it was dangerous only for foolish Americans who had no knowledge of practical chemistry. The Eskimos agreed, however, to abstain from the methyl alcohol in the future, if I would let them have a final fling that evening. I wanted to see what kind of practical chemistry could render the poison harmless.

The method was simple enough. The Eskimos collected all their coffee grounds and added the alcohol to half a cup of grounds. After stirring thoroughly they filtered the mixture through a handkerchief. What resulted was quite harmless, they said.

The Eskimos caused us less trouble, however, than the members of the film expedition, who were convinced they were performing heroic feats and were all martyrs for M-G-M. "I do it only for the sake of the company" was the constant refrain. But I could not help thinking of their letters begging to be taken to the Arctic. They had been humble and grateful then, now they felt that gratitude was due them from M-G-M.

They caused us a lot of trouble. In the cast we had one Chinese and two Japanese girls who were going to play the roles of Eskimos. When we began shooting their scenes one of the girls turned up with a heavy make-up and the most magnificent hairdo I had ever seen. I asked her to let down her hair as no Eskimo ever looked like that. But she was not interested in looking like an Eskimo, only in looking beautiful. No matter what I said she insisted on using too much make-up and her shiny Hollywood hairdo. It was my job, however, to make the film authentic, so I walked up to her and began pulling down her hair.

"Help!" she screamed. "Help! Freuchen is attacking me!"

In a moment we were surrounded by an excited crowd, and the hysterical girl insisted that I had tried to rape her and that she must leave at once. She could not remain with an expedition where no girl was safe.

Van Dyke managed to calm her and to effect a compromise. She could appear in full war paint half the time, if she would leave her hair uncombed the rest of the time. Afterward he explained to me that there would be no film in the camera when she was "photographed" in all her artificial splendor. In due time the girl had some success in other films, mainly because she had appeared so authentic in *Eskimo*.

The three actresses had a very sweet girl, a half-Eskimo, as their personal maid, but they were far from satisfied. They wanted to have their separate maids, and they wanted the hairdresser from Nome to serve them as long as they remained on location. I told them such extravagance was absolutely out of the question. There were already forty-two of us in Alaska, and, in addition, all the Eskimos and laborers. M-G-M had to dish out five thousand dollars a day to keep us there, and I refused to increase our personnel. But they could not possibly manage with the one girl, they insisted.

"All right," I told them, impatient at last, "if you cannot manage to pull on your own stockings I'll do it for you."

The next day, they refused to work, saying that I had made indecent suggestions to them. I had made coarse jokes about intimate details of their clothes, and I had promised personally to dress them when they rose from their virginal beds in the morning.

I was the author and the Arctic expert, but I had also agreed to play the part of a villain in the film and to write all the publicity. I made up fantastic stories that caused quite a sensation. According to one yarn I sent off we had struck gold in Alaska, and soon cables came pouring in from wives of the actors, urging them to go all out for gold prospecting.

The villainous part I was to play in the film required that I beat up some sailors, cheat the Eskimos, and assault some of their women. I put it over without any trouble—even without makeup. My bearded face sufficed.

In February we had light enough to begin filming out of doors, and now I was really put to work. I had been thoughtless enough to let the action take place in an Eskimo village consisting of nineteen snowhouses, thinking that the Eskimos could build the houses in no time, once I had shown them where to place them. But none of our Eskimos had ever seen a snowhouse, and I had to do the whole job myself. Building a snowhouse in Greenland usually took me two hours; now I had to slave three days before I had completed the village. Had I known conditions in advance, I would have been satisfied with one igloo.

The rest of the crowd enjoyed their three idle days which they mainly spent razzing me. When I was through it was their turn to work as we began shooting the scenes. However, I was not allowed to rest. The filming had barely begun when we had one of those fatally mild spells and all the snowhouses melted.

We had to cancel the work for the rest of the day, but first we noted the exact position of every member of the cast, expecting to resume the scene in a day or two. The next morning the entire site of my village was flooded, and the warm weather continued day after day. We reported conditions to Hollywood, but Hollywood refused to believe us. The entire world knew that Alaska was always cold in winter, they angrily cabled in reply.

When the cold finally set in there was no building material. And I had to wait still longer for enough snow to fall before I could reconstruct the village. I studied the sketches and photos in order to duplicate the previous scenes and thus save all the film already taken. Finally the set was completed, not to my satisfaction but accurately enough to deceive the public, and we resumed our work.

We shot scene after scene, retake after retake. The dog teams came galloping from the right side, they came from the left. We made a number of mistakes, but everything was filmed and sent right off. Every other day the finished reels were taken down to Hollywood by plane. We had no technical facilities in Alaska, all the films were developed in California.

Suddenly we got a frantic stop signal from Hollywood. A cable explained that all the scenes taken in the rebuilt village had to be thrown away, as the mountains in the background, which had been snow covered in the first scenes, were completely bare in the second setup.

Waiting for the snow to cover up the mountains again was useless. We had to find a new location, and I was sent by plane to find a suitable place. Up to Point Barrow where there was not enough snow. Down to Fork River where there was no open space. Across to St. Michael and finally back to Nome where I found the ideal place near a small town. There was space enough and plenty of snow; the only drawback was a large wooden house that stood in our way. This obstacle was taken care of by our buying the house from the owner for five hundred dollars. As soon as the deal was closed we had the structure moved carefully to Nome, where the man who had lived in it got it back free of charge.

The whole cast, the technical crew, and the Eskimos were all flown to Nome, and by the time they were all safely installed I had built my igloo village for the third time. Once we got going Van Dyke was an effectual slave driver. He rushed through scene after scene, and in two months the job was done and we were ready to leave Alaska.

The air-transport service back to Fairbanks, where we were to catch the train, went all right until it was my turn. I was in a plane with Emil, the chef who had come along to cook for the expedition, and two of the actresses. Our pilot, Jerry Jones, was good enough, but we were out of luck. We had to go down near Nulato where markers on the ice would guide the pilot to a safe landing. But some Indians had played us a trick and moved the markers far out on the ice. They had no intention of causing trouble, but the result was disastrous. I heard a terrible crash, and the next moment I was thrown out of my seat, breaking the safety belt and landing on the floor in the other end of the cabin. Through the floor I looked right down on the ice.

We had come down way out on the Yukon River where the ice had broken up and frozen again. Nobody was hurt, fortunately, but we were far from shore and the snow was very deep. As the tallest man I had to march ahead and make way for the others, and for the first time in my life I walked in snow up to my neck.

Nobody came to our assistance, and we made our way to the house of the local storekeeper, who received us with open arms. Emil and I took the mishap very calmly, as this unexpected interlude in our return to civilization gave us a chance to repay the two young ladies for some of the trouble they had caused us.

Emil and I went to bed in our room and fell asleep immediately, only to be awakened by one of the girls who complained they were hungry.

"Wonderful!" we told them. "Here are the supplies—coffee, bread and butter, and cans. Let us know when the food is ready."

The girl thought we had gone crazy and told Emil indignantly to knock on their door when the meal was prepared.

"I don't know what sort of cooks you are," he said, "but if you two don't do the cooking there won't be anything to eat." He did not intend to touch a pot or pan till he was back in Hollywood, he told them. They turned to me in despair, but I supported Emil fully. In the end the Hollywood "stars" had to come down to earth, they prepared our food, and I ordered them to do the dishes and clean up afterward.

In the morning I woke them before dawn. "We have to wash and shave," I shouted through the door. "Get the fire going and bring us hot water at once." As soon as they had served us breakfast Jerry managed to get radio contact with Nome and reported the accident. Nome asked if we were all right, and Jerry replied we were in no hurry. I was only too happy to stay a little longer at Nulato. I had made friends among the Indians, who told me marvelous stories about the Indian chieftain Larion. I made a great many notes, and the result was my novel *The Law of Larion.*

But the girls were hysterical. They could never forgive us that we told Nome to complete the whole transport to Fairbanks before they sent a plane for us. Twice a day we saw the planes roar above Nulato, and the girls had to work for us for many days before the rescue plane finally appeared.

We took to the air once more and miraculously managed to get to Fairbanks where I had something of a comeback.

During the whole expedition my colleagues had looked down

upon me, partly because I had lived in the Eskimo camp and partly because I did not drink alcohol. In Fairbanks every moment of my day was occupied. The university asked me to give a series of lectures which bored the film crowd to death but impressed the faculty. I spoke in the Rotary Club, in the high school, all over the place. I visited the reservation where the university kept thirty-two musk oxen. They had been captured in East Greenland and brought to Alaska by Norwegian sealers. Two students were guarding the animals day and night to keep away the bears. They shot a lot of them.

Even the three actresses made me into a hero. When we left Fairbanks to board the steamer in Seward they realized that their great adventure was drawing to a close. They thought that I had a future in Hollywood and that I would surely make a series of new adventure films. They flattered me in every possible way. The two girls who had endured our interlude at Nulato told everyone about the dangers we had lived through, the hardships we had suffered. They praised my wonderful spirit which had saved the situation.

In due time *Eskimo* was completed and shown at several sneak previews. The reaction was very favorable and M-G-M was enthusiastic.

10

THE YEARS THAT FOLLOWED WERE DARK BUT NOT WITHOUT EXCITEment. With the Nazis in my homeland I naturally joined the underground and did what I could. Magdalene, Pipaluk, and I finally escaped to Sweden and ultimately I landed in New York where I lectured and wrote.

Magdalene and I were not made for each other, after all. She had decided, during the many months she had been without me, that she could never return to our way of life. She no longer felt able to share the turbulent existence to which I had exposed her for so many years. She felt I was perhaps too much of a vagrant for her delicate nerves. And we agreed to a parting of our ways and to a divorce in due time.

Many months later I was invited for a Christmas dinner by a good friend. He informed me that he had also asked "a widow

by the name of Mueller" for Christmas and hoped I would have
no objection.

He gave me the impression that "the widow" was some poor
creature whom he wanted to treat at Christmastime. To my
amazement the widow turned out to be the most beautiful
woman I had ever seen. I could not help staring at her all evening; in fact, I have a hard time still not doing so because "the
widow Mueller" became my wife Dagmar.

The following year, at the end of the hectic summer, Dagmar
returned to New York, I went north to Greenland—to my great
delight in the company of Pipaluk, who left her husband and
small daughter Navarana in Sweden, to return with me to
Greenland after so many eventful years.

We visited all the familiar places along the coast—Sukkertoppen, Godthaab, Holsteinsborg. And I was received by all the
Danish officials as a prehistoric animal. I could have made a book
out of the fantastic stories they told about my early years in
Greenland. Most of their tales were about some incredible adventurer I could no longer recognize as myself. It was a strange feeling to meet myself as a character from the Greenland sagas.

Our return to Thule was a great experience for both of us—in
more ways than one. As we passed Cape Athol and approached
my old home the radio operator handed me a message from the
State Department through the American consul in Godthaab:
"Any landing on the American side of the new Thule Harbor
would be disapproved!" I did not protest although it seemed
strange that I, a Dane, should be refused entrance to any part
of Greenland, particularly to a settlement which I had founded,
and which did not even have a name until Knud Rasmussen and
I decided to call it Thule. But I stayed away and spent my time
visiting all my old friends in Thule.

I introduced Pipaluk to her uncle Oaviarsuaq, the brother
of Navarana, and he took her to call on her childhood friends and
showed her the places where she had played as a little girl. I saw
my old friends, Odark and his new wife, whose first husband
had frozen to death on my sled on Melville Bay many years
before. And my friends could not conceal their deep concern
about the future of Thule and their way of life.

When I finally returned to New York I felt as if I had come
back to another world, another century.

After some more typically American adventures in New York

and Hollywood—including a strenuous few days in the company of a beauty queen—I was to return for the last time to Thule. The American Air Force was extending the fantastic Arctic air base in Thule. There were thousands of American soldiers and construction workers in my old peaceful home. But they knew next to nothing about Greenland, as they were not permitted to move outside a very limited area. I was asked by the engineers corps to deliver some lectures in Thule on the country and the Eskimos. I readily agreed and, naturally, asked the military authorities to handle my transportation. My request seemed simple, but it ran into such obstacles that I felt as if I were running my head against a stone wall.

There were daily flights to Thule, but no arrangements had been made for lecturers, and the engineers corps advised me to contact the army. I asked my old friend Colonel Bernt Balchen to assist me. There was nothing he would rather do, he assured me, but he said something about instructions from the Pentagon.

I waited and waited. Weeks went by. In the end I was compelled to admit that the airplane was not yet the fastest means of transportation between Greenland and the United States. I cut through red tape by the simple process of boarding a freighter for Greenland in Philadelphia. But the mysterious ways of bureaucracy followed me to Greenland. Some Americans who were going by air to Godthaab, to catch live falcons, asked me to take along some pigeons. I was thoughtless enough to agree and arrived in Godthaab with forty pigeons, only to discover that I had violated some recent regulations. Importation of live animals to Greenland was not allowed.

More appeals to the authorities and more delay. My American friends had an official permission to capture falcons, I insisted, and falcons cannot be captured without live pigeons as bait. The wise men put their worried noses into many books and returned with a wise ruling. If I left the pigeons in their cages they had not technically arrived in Greenland and I could leave them behind in Godthaab.

I went on north to Tovqussaq, the fishing station which had been established by private interests in order to demonstrate the superiority of private enterprise over government operation. A group of Danes and Eskimos were in charge, but they did not have the necessary experience. I wanted to assist them in the building up of a modern fishery industry, and in return for my services I was put in charge of the general store in Tovqussaq which I was supposed to operate for my own profit. There was never a lack of customers, the trade was brisk, but the whole settlement treated the fishery experiment as a picnic—and my profit was imaginary.

My experience and my advice did not help much in Tovqussaq. The undertaking was poorly organized and the men in charge made a mess of it, no matter how hard they tried.

From Tovqussaq I went up the Egedesminde district where I tried to make the Eskimos change their fishing ways. I urged them to go out to the open sea where they could catch whitefish and catfish which were in great demand. But the Eskimos could get all the codfish they wanted outside their front door with less effort and practically no tackle. Ocean fishing gave them more profit but much more work. All my pleas were in vain. All the whitefish and catfish they ever caught were those they got by chance when they went cod fishing. I spent some delightful days with old friends to whom I put the case for ocean fishing, but it was a lost cause. I had made no progress when I finally left Egedesminde and ran into a terrible storm.

We made our way slowly through the dark night and the heavy seas, watching out for treacherous ice. Suddenly we sighted some strange object far ahead. It was not land, for it was moving. It was not ice—the color was wrong. We approached very carefully until we could finally make it out. Thirteen tiny Portuguese fishing dories! They had been tied together, eight of them had a single occupant each, and the other five were empty. Their occupants had been drowned during the storm. For two days and two nights the Portuguese had been fighting the elements in their tiny helpless craft. They had given up all hope, they had lost their fishing tackle, their sails and masts. They were convinced we were sent to them by the Holy Virgin to whom they had been praying day and night.

We returned the men and their dories to their ship. Other Greenland boats had rescued a few more, but many were lost.

During the winter the first commercial plane from the Scandinavian Airlines System made a stop in Thule on the way from the United States to Copenhagen. Later a similar SAS plane, carrying passengers across the North Pole from Norway to Tokyo, stopped in Thule. My old home is no longer a remote spot outside civilization; it is a stopover on the main air routes of the world. I cannot help remembering that I gave the place its name, as I think back on the happy days I spent there.

I built the first house in Thule. Now I drove in an American car on paved highways, I saw road signs, I heard explosions from the distance where construction workers were busy removing a mountain. And behind this American city I looked at the second highest structure in the world, an observation tower for the weather service, more than twelve hundred feet high.

A road was being built across the inland ice to the east coast. Once Knud Rasmussen and I had made the trip in nineteen days —a record that will never be beaten, not by dog sleds. Today the shining cars are rushing across the icecap—ten cars in a caravan, driving for twenty hours. The men eat in their luxurious trailers as they drive. They sleep in comfortable berths in the places where Knud and I risked our lives with our Eskimo friends. I thought of the poetry of progress, the splendor of men conquering a nature considered invincible.

I looked at an open flame in Thule. By the beach a bonfire has been burning for three years. Refuse of every sort was going up in flames, but what was being burned in Thule would probably be considered priceless treasures by the people living outside the American city. No man can say what is waste and what is economy. Some people starve for lack of fat; in Thule the Eskimos throw away the fat because there is too much.

I met all my old friends who were making ready to leave Thule, to move farther north while I was going south again. I left my old home once more, the place of my youth and my dreams. I went back to another world.

A fragment of a leaf tossed by the winds, tossed far and wide by stormy seas and wild winds. The words of Odark, the wise old man, the friend of my youth, resound in my ears and my mind bridges the years. Odark has peace in his old age, and throughout time he and his people have taught me patience and peace.

"I need my peace, Pita," he told me when I saw him last. He was weary of all the things that had happened to his land, he was planning to go still farther north. He had to put more distance between himself and the noise across the bay. "I need to sit quietly in my house and contemplate the old days when I went with the great Piuli to the Navel of the Earth. Our trip took

many, many weeks and it called for the strength and courage of
men. Today they fly in a machine to the Navel of the Earth and
it takes no courage!"

But Odark did not complain. "Life is easier today than when
you first came to Thule, Pita," he told me. "Do you remember
the time when this useless old woman had to kill her child?"

He pointed to his wife, Qinoruna, and in my mind I saw the
night when I was fighting for my life in Melville Bay. My sole
companion had been Qinoruna's first husband. I had saved
him from the icy water, but he had died the next day. And his
wife had borne the dead man's child, but she had not wanted it
to live without a father. And she had been greatly honored because she had loved her child enough to kill it and keep it from
growing up without a father.

"We do not need to kill children any more," Odark told me.
"We can let them live and grow up without parents today. They
are taken care of. The king gives them food. I am an old weak
man, but the king takes care of me, he sends me money. You
were the one who taught us the value of money, Pita, and we
honor you for it."

I thought of the man who died in Melville Bay and I thought
of Black Mountain which was always there to guide us in the
bay. How many times I had looked at this landmark, how many
times I had hated the dark hostile mountain which was always
so far away. When the snow was deep and the dogs were tired,
when the ice seemed impassable under a cold hard moon and
lack of food sapped all one's strength, Black Mountain was always there, always as far away as ever. Time and again I had
forced myself not to look up, not to watch the distant landmark
before I felt it must have moved closer. When hours had gone
by, after a whole day's painful march, the distant goal was as far
away as ever. But I had learned to ignore it, to keep going after
the distant goal, never to give up.

Odark and Qaviarssuk had seen me come to Thule as a young
man, had seen me marry, had seen my wife Navarana bear my
children. We had all been tossed by the winds of fate. Navarana,
my wife, had found her grave in Greenland, my children were
far away. They had grown up in Thule, there they had waited
while Navarana and I were gone—sometimes for days, sometimes
for months. But we always returned to Thule. That was my home
and it always will be—even if the people move.

The wind blows, the world moves on. It rolls over three hundred Eskimos, their tents and their igloos. They do not complain.

"We go farther north," said Odark. "New men have moved in. They know not the old ways. They have little peace or dignity. They have taken the land. But our land is great—we move on. And we know that you are a wise man, Pita. One day you will see that there is less happiness in the land of the white man. *Sainak*—we are happy because you came to us, Pita, and we are happy because one day you will come back."

Yes, life is a journey, as my wise friend Odark told me. "We are being punished because we have stayed too long in one place, Pita. Life is journey without end!"

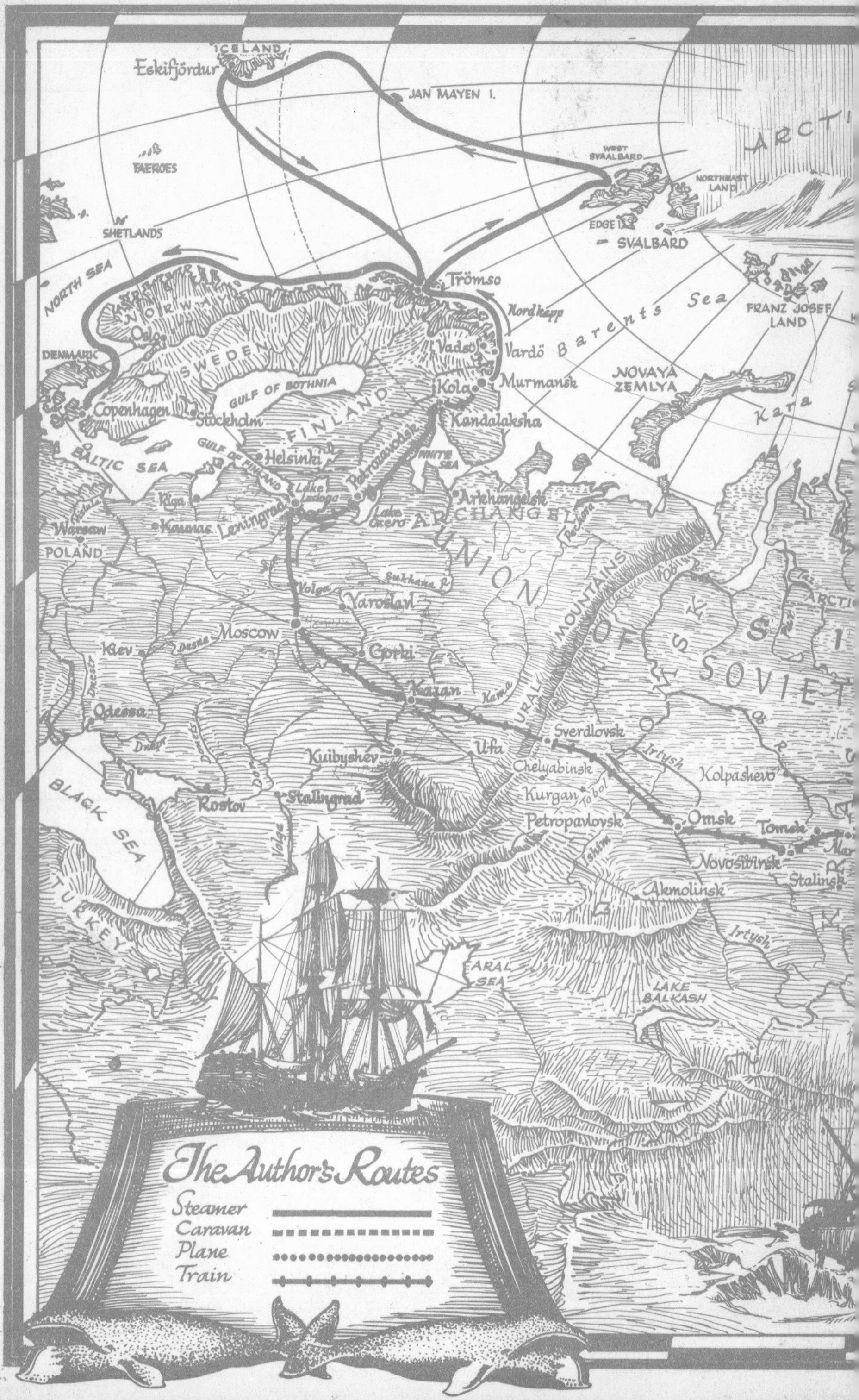
The Author's Routes
Steamer
Caravan
Plane
Train
ICELAND
Eskifjördur
JAN MAYEN I.
FAEROES
SHETLANDS
NORTH SEA
WEST SVALBARD
NORTHEAST LAND
EDGE I.
SVALBARD
Trömso
Nordkapp
Barents Sea
FRANZ JOSEF LAND
NORWAY
Oslo
DENMARK
SWEDEN
Vadsö
Vardö
Murmansk
Kola
Kandalaksha
NOVAYA ZEMLYA
Kara
GULF OF BOTHNIA
Copenhagen
Stockholm
FINLAND
Petrozavodsk
WHITE SEA
BALTIC SEA
GULF OF FINLAND
Helsinki
Lake Ladoga
Lake Onega
Archangelsk
ARCHANGEL
Riga
Kaunas
Leningrad
Warsaw
POLAND
UNION OF SOVIET
Volga
Sukhona R.
Yaroslavl
Moscow
Desna
Kiev
Gorki
URAL MOUNTAINS
Kazan
Kama
Odessa
Dnepr
Donets
Don
Sverdlovsk
Ufa
Kuibyshev
Chelyabinsk
Kurgan
Tobol
Irtysh
Kolpashevo
Ob R.
Rostov
Stalingrad
BLACK SEA
Volga
Petropavlovsk
Omsk
Tomsk
Novosibirsk
Stalinsk
Ishim
Akmolinsk
TURKEY
ARAL SEA
Irtysh
LAKE BALKASH
ARCTIC